THE MODERN LIBRARY

OF THE WORLD'S BEST BOOKS

Eighteenth-Century Plays

The publishers will be pleased to send, upon request, an illustrated folder setting forth the purpose and scope of THE MODERN LIBRARY, *and listing each volume in the series. Every reader of books will find titles he has been looking for, handsomely printed, in definitive editions, and at an unusually low price.*

Eighteenth-Century

Plays WITH AN INTRODUCTION BY

RICARDO QUINTANA

PROFESSOR OF ENGLISH, UNIVERSITY OF WISCONSIN

THE MODERN LIBRARY · NEW YORK

The texts of the plays in this volume are based upon the first editions, except *The London Merchant* (sixth edition, 1735), *She Stoops to Conquer* (fifth edition, 1773), and *The Rivals* (third edition, 1776) — these exceptions being made because the later editions show changes reliably believed to have been made by the authors.

A few emendations have been introduced on the authority of other early editions. For the sake of clarity, a moderate number of changes in spelling and punctuation have been made; for the same reason, a small number of imperative stage directions have been inserted.

CONTENTS

CONTENTS

INTRODUCTION

By Ricardo Quintana

1.

The literature of eighteenth-century England has definitely come into its own. There was a time when everyday criticism of the sort which determines the reaction of the average reader found it difficult to come to terms with the literary art of the Enlightenment. But that was because such criticism rested so largely in the romantic myth. Now that we have moved away from most of the attitudes and assumptions carried by that myth, we have been able to approach eighteenth-century literature in a more disengaged spirit. The results of a freer reading and of a more objective and incisive study of the literary works of this period are manifest in practically all present-day writing of a critical and scholarly nature concerned with the Age of the Enlightenment. At least two things have fixed themselves in our thoughts. At its best, eighteenth-century literary art—as in Swift, in Pope, in Fielding, in Johnson—is now seen as a sophisticated and calculated thing. Likewise, it is seen to embody and express a view of life which is deeper and more inclusive than was once realized. It is in such masterpieces as *Gulliver's Travels, Tom Jones,* and *Rasselas* that this art triumphs.

Unfortunately the English theater between 1700 and 1800 stands, as a whole, in unhappy contrast with most of what we now recognize as artistically valid in the work of this epoch. It was a matter of chance that so few playwrights of genuine talent and none of unmistakable genius flourished at this time, but the conditions governing everything connected with the eighteenth-century theater were such that it is difficult to believe that even genius could have overridden them. The drama of the Restoration had been called forth by a small, closed social group. What is best and most characteristic of this drama, in its comedy of manners and in its heroic tragedy, is a direct reflection of the tone and sentiments of this restricted circle of aristocratic patrons. But by Queen Anne's time (1702–1714) the social revolution which had been in progress throughout the seventeenth century was coming to the end of its first phase, and if English political life was about to be taken over by the great families of the time, English social life and in particular the London scene had already come under the influence of the new *bourgeoisie*. Many of the forms of eighteenth-century literature either profited by this advent of the new middle class to power, or —as in the case of periodical literature and the novel—virtually owed their existence to it. English drama, by exception, came perilously close to being ruined, and the degenerative process at work throughout the eighteenth century is seen to extend over much of the nineteenth. Today we date modern drama from its awakening in the 1880's and 1890's—an awakening which, significantly enough, was one of the consequences of that portentous revolt of the middle class against itself which marked the closing decades of the last century both in England and on the continent.

As we look back on the early years of the eighteenth century, we see clearly enough that certain new influences were already at work upon English drama when Dryden died in the spring of 1700. Two years previously, the attack on the stage as an institution had come to a head in the famous blast, *A Short View of the Immorality and Profaneness of the English Stage*, by Jeremy Collier, a non-juring clergyman. Collier was a thoroughgoing fanatic. If the English public seemed at the time to give him support, it was not that they desired—as Collier did—the total abolition of the theater, but rather that they had come to regard with increasing distaste the sort of dramatic fare, particularly in the way of comedy, which the patent theaters and the established dramatists had for years been offering them. Dryden himself had come to sense this change of taste:

> 'Tis well an old age is out,
> And time to begin a new.

This attack on the stage, the widely expressed feeling that the time had come for drama in the Restoration mode to purge itself, and the reform movement thus imposed on the playwrights—all of this was overdue. Coinciding with emergent Augustinism in letters—with its emphasis on stricter form —and with the newer views concerning propriety in social conduct, this reaction did not of itself commit English drama to its long period of decline. It was the convergence of a number of other forces at this particular moment which determined that course.

The substantial middle class, which had pretty generally avoided the theaters during the Restoration era, was now beginning to attend in increasing numbers. As the eighteenth-century audience became larger and increasingly diversified, there was an inevitable deterioration of taste; entertainment in the form of Italian opera, English opera, pantomime, and farce began to compete seriously with legitimate drama; and the playwrights were left confused and uncertain regarding the desires of the public. The standard repertoire as worked out by the established theaters reflected in its heterogeneous character the wide variety of tastes with which it was thought necessary to reckon. Heroic tragedies still held appeal for many of the older theatergoers; younger people, of Augustan rather than Restoration sensibilities, preferred the more decorous tragedy of Addison or the politely pathetic plays of Nicholas Rowe; and as the advance of the century saw a heightening of the humanitarian sense and of middle-class social consciousness, domestic tragedy came briefly into popularity. In comedy there was a similarly mixed array. Famous Restoration comedies of manners were still brought regularly to the boards, as were comedies of intrigue in the manner of Mrs. Behn and Mrs. Centlivre; and though what properly may be regarded as the chief episode in English drama of the eighteenth century was the establishment of sentimental comedy, the great popularity of this type by no means put an end to other forms of comedy. Without question the monopoly which the two patent theaters exercised during much of the period accounts to some extent for the notable lack of experimentalism in the drama of these years. An old play, successful season after season, or a new play written to a time-tested formula seemed the safer business venture. Sentimental comedy, domestic tragedy, and ballad opera are distinctive of eighteenth-century playwriting, but none of these was a strikingly new departure in the sense that Elizabethan tragedy, the heroic tragedy of Dryden, and the comedy of manners of Etherege, Wycherley, and Congreve had all been.

By the end of the century true tragedy and true comedy had both expired. The better writers knew nothing of the actual theater; when they employed dramatic form, they were mostly content to write closet dramas. Prose fiction, having established itself during the second half of the century, supplied much in the way of that realism and imaginative commentary which the drama was no longer able to give. As the theater succumbed completely to the demand of pure entertainment, comedy degenerated more and more to empty formula or to farce, and the place of tragedy was usurped by that bastardly imitation known as romantic melodrama.

But despite everything that is to be said in its disfavor, eighteenth-century drama still lays a compelling claim on our attention. The theater tells us a great deal about the society of an age, the pressures shaping its thought and behavior, and its imaginative patterns. If the sentimental comedy of this period strikes us as artistically deplorable, it can scarcely fail to interest us when considered from a sociological point of view. The decline of tragedy and the failure of domestic drama—the one form of eighteenth-century tragedy holding any promise of development—to gain a place for itself are likewise significant when seen in social terms. Not that all which still attracts us to this drama is of this strictly nonartistic order. Among the better-known plays of the eighteenth century there are a few which hold their own with the good plays of any period, while of the dramatists there are four at least—Gay, Fielding, Goldsmith, and Sheridan—who succeeded in translating the true eighteenth-century spirit, as we recognize it in the great non-dramatic works of prose and verse, into the forms and illusions of the theater. Finally, the lover of drama will surely see in such movements and trends as sentimental comedy, pathetic tragedy, ballad opera, political satire, and burlesque the fundamental vitality of the theater as an institution searching for expression, though often with indifferent results.

2.

Tragedy in certain of its eighteenth-century forms is represented in the present anthology by three plays, *Cato* (1713), *Jane Shore* (1714), and *The London Merchant* (1731). The standard repertoire of tragedies offered at Covent Garden and Drury Lane was, as already mentioned, a curiously hybrid affair, built up as it was of the most successful plays from the Restoration onwards. Place had been found, too, during the earlier part of the century, for a number of Elizabethan tragedies, but with the exception of Shakespeare's these had gradually been cut out. It is sometimes forgotten that it was in this eighteenth-century theater that Shakespearean tragedy

—sometimes "revised," to be sure, in most incredible ways—
first achieved preëminence. This fact should somewhat mitigate the contemptuous judgment often passed upon eighteenth-century taste in tragedy. It is only too apparent, however, that the spirit of the age did not encourage in its own
dramatists the search for genuine tragedy; and as the century
advanced, what with sentimentalism, the social prejudices of
the now dominant middle classes, and the preference for
melodrama, the true meaning of the tragic spectacle appears
to have been almost forgotten.

During the earlier part of the century there were, however,
a number of somewhat new departures and developments in
tragedy, and though any discussion of these today is probably bound to overemphasize distinctions and categories, the
dramatists in question were not wholly unconscious of minor
differences setting them apart from both predecessors and
contemporaries. It is sometimes said that eighteenth-century
tragedy is merely an extension of the heroic tragedy of the
Restoration. There is more than an element of truth in such a
view. Heroic tragedy—which to Dryden and his contemporaries seems to have meant tragedies in rhymed verse, but
which today is taken to include *All for Love* (1677) and the
host of subsequent plays likewise employing blank verse—
followed neither the Aristotelian pattern nor the Elizabethan.
It was rather a dramatic version of epic poetry and the prose
romance—a treatment of a heroic character by means of
panoramic scenes. Variety in theme and an infinite number
of plot complications were insured by the presence of a
heroine whose distressed love was both a complement and a
contrast to the superb strength and confidence of the hero.
Terror, in other words, here came to be replaced by admiration, pity by our sympathy for love in distress. It was not a
mode, this heroic tragedy, which led to a great literature. On
the other hand, it did most emphatically lead to something
appreciable, something distinctive in English drama. The
triumph, albeit the sole one, of this genre is Dryden's great
masterpiece, *All for Love*.

Nicholas Rowe (1674–1718) occupied an assured position
among the literary personalities of the Age of Queen Anne,
and by virtue of his three "she-tragedies"—*The Fair Penitent*
(1703), *The Tragedy of Jane Shore* (1714), and *The Tragedy of Lady Jane Gray* (1715)—won recognition as the leading dramatist of the time. Today we remember him not because of his moderate powers but because his plays reveal

so well how various elements in the older heroic tragedy
were passing directly over into the newer type of pathetic
tragedy. The Almahides of Dryden's period had all been
heroines in distress. In *Venice Preserved* (1682) and *The
Orphan* (1680) Otway had brought a heightened sensibility
to his studies of distressed womanhood, and Thomas Southerne had followed his lead in *The Fatal Marriage* (1694).
Two shifts in emphasis can be discerned. Whereas the older
heroic plays had dealt with heroes and heroines of royal line,
Otway and Southerne turned to women of lower estate. In
the second place, the emotional tone was changing. There is
much emotion *indicated* in heroic tragedy, but the emotions
expressed so volubly by the characters are not ours, which are
admiration for the hero, pleasurable pity for the heroine, and
a genuine exhilaration. By contrast, the famous heroines of
Otway—Monimia and Belvidera—arouse pity which can not
be described as pleasurable: it is sympathy, warm and deep.
The social and psychological prepossessions so well marked in
Restoration drama were in process of alteration, a middle-
class spirit fostering something approaching domestic tragedy,
and a softening in emotional attitude leading to manifestations of feeling unknown in the days of Charles II. The plays
of Rowe reflect both of these tendencies. Though *Jane Shore*
is not precisely bourgeois, its spirit is that of domestic tragedy,
and it leads into the work of George Lillo. At the same time
it is pathetic tragedy, and though the pathos is discreetly con-
trolled—much too discreetly, one feels—it bespeaks an emotionalism which by this time was in the air and which as
sentimentalism was already transforming English comedy.

There is little doubt that the most interesting of all eighteenth-century tragedies is *The London Merchant; or, The
History of George Barnwell*. George Lillo (1693–1739) was
a London dissenter, and besides writing a number of plays
seems to have followed in his father's footsteps as a jeweler.
He represents much the same social group as does Daniel
Defoe, and however widely the two men differed in tempera-
ment the same undertone runs through the work of both.
The London Merchant was written at the outset of Lillo's
career as a dramatist, having been preceded only by *Sylvia*,
produced some months earlier. As a domestic tragedy it has
its predecessors, as has frequently been pointed out, in such
Elizabethan or early Jacobean plays as *Arden of Feversham*,
Heywood's *A Woman Killed with Kindness*, and *A Yorkshire
Tragedy*—though it is doubtful whether Lillo was influenced

by them—and more immediately in Aaron Hill's *The Fatal Extravagance* (1721). What Lillo did, with that intuitive assurance which occasionally distinguishes an author's earliest work, was to fuse within the tragic mould social realism, the pathetic, and the moral ethos of middle-class England. Following his instinct for social realism, he used a story concerned with people of his own class—the merchant employer, the young apprentice, the employer's daughter, and the temptress, a woman of ruined virtue. The pathetic element, of which there is no suggestion in the first four acts, is preeminent in the closing scenes between the condemned hero, his friend Trueman, and the unfortunate Maria. But the central problem in tragedy of this naturalistic sort—though it is not suggested that Lillo saw it as a problem—is how to retain something of that thrill which the spectacle of ruin and death excites, while making it everywhere apparent that such disaster is common to the everyday walks of life and to be accounted for in everyday social terms. It is here that *The London Merchant* is in its way so curiously successful. Thorowgood's praise of merchants; his description of business as a science founded in reason and nature, and promoting the arts, industry, peace and plenty; Maria's pious sententiousness before her sufferings begin,—these we are justified in regarding as dramatic blemishes of the worst sort. Yet the air of self-satisfaction which is so apparent in all of this is, we must recognize, in close association with the kind of moral fear which Lillo has injected into the Barnwell-Millwood scenes, and with that fascinated horror in the presence of corrupting evil. There are those who maintain that the incursion of naturalism has made tragedy impossible, and that the drama of Lillo, of Ibsen, and of all such realists is an evasion of artistic principles and psychological truths proved in experience. They may be right, but even if they are most of us will still be willing to accept as another kind of tragedy the type of play of which *The London Merchant* is an early example.

But if the eighteenth century saw the first genuine efforts in the direction of a naturalistic tragedy, quite obviously it failed to sustain this type of drama. In the forties and fifties such plays as John Hewitt's *Fatal Falshood,* Thomas Cooke's *The Mournful Nuptials,* and Edward Moore's *The Gamester* kept domestic tragedy alive, but thereafter it dropped from sight, not to reappear until the last decades of the nineteenth century. Why this should have been so presents an interesting problem in analysis. Some light is thrown by what was happening in the field of comedy, where the sentimentalism which flourished so vigorously there defeated one of its purposes, which was a realistic treatment of everyday moral problems, by its refusal to deal with anything or anyone not properly "genteel." Middle-class drama was not adventurous, was not interested in characters and situations lying outside the realm of prosperity and comfort, and generally ended happily. It is not surprising that eventually the place of tragedy came to be usurped by melodrama.

Addison's *Cato* (1713) is the best-known example of the pseudo-classical tragedy of the age, a tragedy which reflects those pseudo-classical theories of dramatic propriety which had been emphasized in the critical writing of Addison himself, Steele, Dennis, Gildon, and others. *Cato* is certainly not a great play. It is not as bad a one, however, as most people who have not perused it are ready to assume. If there is nothing that truly stirs us, there is likewise little that offends, and while our verdict must go quite against Addison, we ought to acknowledge that his emphasis—Pope's *Prologue* should be noted—was right. In any case, the play which enjoyed such popularity in its own time has taken its place in dramatic history as the transitional point between the heroic tradition on the one hand and pseudo-classicism on the other. If there was any pattern to which the majority of tragedies written in the eighteenth century conform, it may be said to be the one given here by Addison.

3.

If the changes in form and emphasis which occurred in the case of tragedy are of decidedly minor importance from an artistic point of view, they are all reflections, in one way or another, of the transition from Restoration to Augustan society. Eighteenth-century comedy likewise reflects this cultural transition. It does so, however, with greater vividness, exhibiting at the same time a much more radical change in form, and on occasion rising to a level of excellence never attained by the tragedies of the period.

It was inevitable that the Restoration comedy of manners should undergo extensive change. For one thing, it had developed into an art form too demanding, too rigorous and exclusive, to maintain itself for very long. Again, as the limited society out of which it had sprung came to be enlarged by many new elements, the comic attitude which distinguishes it was bound to be modified by a softer and more charitable view of human folly. The earlier plays of Colley Cibber are clear enough evidence that the spirit of Restoration comedy, yet to achieve its finest expression in Congreve's *Way of the World* (1700), had nevertheless begun to yield to something essentially different. Cibber's *Love's Last Shift* (1696) has sometimes been called the first sentimental comedy; and here, as in his *Careless Husband* (1704), we hear of the tender emotions which assert themselves in crisis, and witness scenes of reconciliation or reform brought about by change of heart. As a result of much investigation and criticism, we have come to understand how complex a phenomenon this new sentimental comedy of the eighteenth century really was. Reference has already been made to the heightened emotionalism in the tragedies of Otway and Southerne. This emotionalism, centering in the theme of distressed womanhood, developed into the pathetic tragedy of Rowe, and in *Jane Shore* we find a complement to sentimental comedy. But this change in emotional tone is only one element. A consciousness of various social difficulties had begun to show itself in certain comedies by D'Urfey, Mrs. Behn, and others at the end of the seventeenth century. Shadwell is usually thought of as the foremost practitioner throughout the Restoration of the Jonsonian comedy of humors, but he had on at least one occasion—in *The Squire of Alsatia* (1688) —anticipated sentimental comedy by creating as one of his characters Sir Edward Belfond, "a man of great humanity and gentleness and compassion towards mankind." The growing awareness of the individual's social responsibilities was bound, sooner or later, to find expression not only in the drama but in most of the other literary forms of the eighteenth century. Thus the literature of sensibility is an extensive one, including much of the verse of the age and many of the best-known novels, and it naturally exhibits many varieties of artistic form, emotional quality, and informing social consciousness. Behind all of these manifestations in art and society are seen to lie two great movements, which between them largely determined the nature of English culture during the Enlightenment: the emergence of the middle class, and, correlated therewith, the establishment of a new point of view in ethics and everyday moral speculation. The world presented by sentimental comedy is not the aristocratic world of Restoration comedy but the comfortable society of eighteenth-century England, well-to-do, humane in outlook, addicted to the social virtues, increasingly self-satisfied. In depicting such a society, comedy underwent a change in its fundamental nature. Instead of showing folly and knavery, it showed error; instead of portraying the fool and knave as incorrigible and thus in a sense true to the laws of their own being, it portrayed the aberrant character as open to reformation once his better nature had been appealed to. But it is not enough to say that comedy was acquiring a social purpose; it was likewise taking over that theory of moral values and human behavior which, since the mid-decades of the seventeenth century, had been gradually displanting the more rigorous views of traditionalism. This softening of ethical theory can be discerned in many Anglican sermons preached as early as the 1680's, and can be traced in philosophical writing to a still earlier date. God, it was increasingly stressed, was a God of love as well as of vengeance; our beneficent emotions were pointed to as our closest approach to the Divine; men were urged to bear in mind the welfare of all, and by engaging in charity and good works to experience the greatest of all joys. The key phrases occurring in the ethical discourses of the time lead over directly into the novel and drama. The older view of man still prevailed in certain quarters—one thinks of Swift, of Samuel Johnson—but in sentimental comedy, whether of the acceptable variety which we have in Steele, or mawkish as it so often became, or humanitarian and reforming under the influence of the French Revolution, human nature was always seen as innately generous and quickly touched by the altruistic emotions.

Steele is rightly regarded as the true founder of sentimental comedy. In 1701, at the age of twenty-nine, he had published a reforming tract, *The Christian Hero,* which made benevolence, compassion, and a forgiving spirit the basis of conduct. Shortly thereafter was produced his first comedy, *The Funeral; or, Grief À-la-Mode,* which was followed by *The Lying Lover* (1703) and *The Tender Husband* (1705). Of these early plays *The Lying Lover* bears the clearest marks of sentimentality. As the *Preface* tells us, the hero Bookwit "makes false love, gets drunk, and kills his man; but in the fifth Act awakens from his debauch, with compunction and remorse . . ." His anguish and the mutual sorrows between an only child and a tender father are perhaps, Steele proceeds, "an injury to the rules of comedy, but I am sure they are a justice to those of morality." *The Conscious Lovers* is a much later play (1722), and although it serves to illustrate admirably the characteristics of early sentimental comedy, it is not Steele's best dramatic work. Again, the *Preface* is a most interesting statement, with its assertion that "anything that has its foundation in happiness and success must be allowed to be the object of comedy."

The history of sentimental comedy after Steele is not readily summed up. It established itself gradually, and by the end of the century had displaced the older forms; but it was forced to fight its way against the comedy of wit and laughter, it underwent certain changes as it passed into France and returned to England with a new emphasis on humanitarian reform, and in many instances it became merely stylized drama written to formula. Among the best remembered of its later practitioners are Hugh Kelly, Richard Cumberland, Edward Moore, and Thomas Holcroft. From the point of view of dramatic art, sentimental comedy suffered a check similar to that noted in the case of domestic tragedy. If bourgeois drama —in both comic and tragic mode—was realistic at the outset, it was not encouraged to push this realism to a conclusion. Sentimental comedy had originally undertaken to replace the characters and situations of Restoration comedy, which had come to seem fantastic, with figures and scenes recognizable by the average person. It had likewise substituted social purpose and the reform of manners for malicious wit. But its real world was allowed to degenerate into an ideal one where compassion meant gentility and from which "low" scenes and "low" characters were banished as unpleasant incursions into well-ordered society.

4.

The names of Goldsmith, Sheridan, Gay and Fielding suggest to the modern reader—or ought to—what is liveliest in eighteenth-century dramatic writing. As playwrights, all four men were moved not only by the comic muse but in various degrees and fashions by the satiric spirit as well. It is the satiric cast which gives to their plays a depth generally lacking elsewhere—an extended frame of reference for allusion and the multiple perceptions of wit to operate in.

Goldsmith and Sheridan we associate with sentimental comedy by reason of the ridicule which they both directed against it. From the days of Steele there had, indeed, been something of an anti-sentimental campaign under way, which we may still follow in various farces, satires, and critical essays—there are moments in *The Beggar's Opera* when the satire has sentiment chiefly in view. In the drama of Goldsmith and Sheridan this attack—which did not long delay the eventual triumph of sentimental comedy—reached its culmination. Goldsmith's first play, *The Good-Natured Man* (1768), was among other things an attack on the style of Kelly and Cumberland. In a subsequent essay—*Essay on the Theatre; or, A Comparison Between Laughing and Sentimental Comedy*—Goldsmith exposed the weakness of sentimental comedy with incisiveness and humor. Shortly thereafter came the triumphant production of *She Stoops to Conquer* (1773). Goldsmith's masterpiece is not all satire, to be sure. We generally read it as a comedy infused with good-natured humor and something like the free spirit of *Twelfth Night,* and as such it is presented in modern revivals. But as there is more humor in Swift than many have understood, so there is more satire in Goldsmith. How are we to take the *Vicar of Wakefield?* In *She Stoops to Conquer* we are not likely to miss the wonderful hit at "gentility" in the alehouse scene, nor the parody in the "sober, sentimental interview" between hero and heroine, but we may fail to recognize in Tony Lumpkin the complete reversal of the sentimental son.

Sheridan's spectacular career as a dramatist, which began with the production of *The Rivals* (1775) when he was twenty-three and ended four years later with *The Critic,* can blind us to the fact that his wit and his remarkable sense of theater are not balanced by the insight and intuition of drama at its greatest. *The School for Scandal* (1777) is undoubtedly his masterpiece, but the satirical elements in *The Rivals*—from *Prologue* to Bob Acres's sentimental swearing—give the earlier play a place beside *The Good-Natured Man* and *She Stoops to Conquer.*

We have come to recognize that sentiment and decorous neo-classicism do not fully account for the eighteenth-century spirit. There was always the indecorous, too, with its sense of the grotesque, its delight in exposing pretense, and its natural fondness for burlesque, parody, and other forms of ironic statement. If the energy which marked so many forms of life in eighteenth-century England sometimes seems to be missing from its polite letters, we have only to look to this other tradition to find it. Henry Fielding was a dramatist before he turned novelist, writing some twenty-six plays before Walpole's Licensing Act of 1737 caused him to turn to journalism,

the law, and finally to prose fiction. The best of his plays
came at the close of his dramatic career. They were, indeed,
one of the chief reasons for the new censorship of the theater,
for in both *Pasquin* (1736) and *The Historical Register for the
Year 1736* (1737) the anti-Walpole satire was of the broad-
est. *The Tragedy of Tragedies, or The Life and Death of
Tom Thumb the Great* (1731) is perhaps better fun in its
earliest and shorter form (*Tom Thumb, a Tragedy,* a two-act
burlesque of 1730), but only in the case of the longer play
did he venture, in printed edition, to follow Pope's *Dunciad
Variorum* in parodying criticism and scholarship by means of
preface and annotations. It is a burlesque of heroic tragedy—
it has been estimated that some forty-two plays are satirized
—and in this respect is akin to *The Rehearsal* of Restoration
days, but if we read it now it is because Fielding's energy and
love of nonsense have produced something which is more
than pastiche:

> Sure such a day as this was never seen!
> . . . .
> This day, O Mr. Doodle, is a day
> Indeed!—a day we never saw before.

There is, finally, the immortal *Beggar's Opera* (1728). Gay
was already a practiced dramatist when he took the play in
hand, and he had previously demonstrated in *The Shepherd's
Week* and *Trivia* that he understood the ironic art of burlesque. *The Beggar's Opera* is so many things all at the same
time that even the most matter-of-fact analysis—to say nothing of commentary like Mr. Empson's in *Some Versions of
Pastoral*—has a way of leaving the play itself behind. It is the
first ballad opera, making use of well-known airs for which
new words, appropriate to the dramatic context, had been
written. (Apparently the songs were originally intended to
be sung without musical accompaniment, but in the final re-
hearsals it was decided that a musician should write an overture and arrange the airs.) It is burlesque of Italian opera.
It is an ironic pastoral—a "Newgate allegory." It is a comedy
of manners. It satirizes sentimental comedy, heroic tragedy,
and the situations of romance. It was also part, as is sometimes
forgotten, of the great drive of the Tory satirists which was
devised during Swift's visits to England in 1726 and 1727.
Gulliver's Travels appeared in October 1726, and with the
success of *The Beggar's Opera* in January of 1728 the first

version of the *Dunciad* was held up until the following May. Yet despite the varied intentions which appear and the multiple perceptions constituting the wit, the most successful of all eighteenth-century plays is a comedy in its own right— the best comedy, there are some who would say, in the whole stretch of eighteenth-century drama.

SELECTED BIBLIOGRAPHY

Bateson, F. W., *English Comic Drama, 1700–1750*. Oxford, 1929.

Bernbaum, Ernest, *The Drama of Sensibility*. Boston, 1925.

Dobrée, Bonamy, *Restoration Comedy, 1660–1720*. Oxford, 1924.

Dobrée, Bonamy, *Restoration Tragedy, 1660–1720*. Oxford, 1929.

Fielding, Henry, *The Tragedy of Tragedies Or The Life and Death of Tom Thumb The Great With the Annotations of H. Scriblerus Secundus*. Edited by J. T. Hillhouse, New Haven, Conn., 1918.

Gagey, E. M., *Ballad Opera*. New York, 1937.

Green, C. C., *The Neo-Classic Theory of Tragedy in the Eighteenth Century*. Cambridge, Mass., 1934.

Krutch, J. W., *Comedy and Conscience after the Restoration*. New York, 1924.

Nettleton, G. H., *English Drama of the Restoration and Eighteenth Century (1642–1780)*. New York, 1914.

Nicoll, Alardyce, *The English Theatre. A Short History*. New York, 1936.

Nicoll, Alardyce, *A History of Early Eighteenth Century Drama, 1700–1750*. Cambridge, England, 1929.

Nicoll, Alardyce, *A History of Late Eighteenth Century Drama, 1750–1800*. Cambridge, England, 1929.

Schultz, W. E., *Gay's 'Beggar's Opera.'* New Haven, Conn., 1923.

Smith, D. F., *Plays about the Theatre in England*. London and New York, 1936.

Thorndike, A. H., *English Comedy*. New York, 1929.

Thorndike, A. H., *Tragedy*. Boston and New York, 1908.

Eighteenth Century
Plays

Cato

A Tragedy

BY JOSEPH ADDISON

Ecce spectaculum dignum, ad quod respiciat, intentus operi suo, Deus! Ecce par Deo dignum, vir fortis cum mala fortuna compositus! Non video, inquam, quid habeat in terris Jupiter pulchrius, si convertere animum velit, quam ut spectet Catonem, jam partibus non semel fractis, nihilominus inter ruinas publicas erectem. Seneca, de Divin. Prov. vi.[1]

PROLOGUE

BY MR. POPE

Spoken by JUBA

To wake the soul by tender strokes of art,
To raise the genius and to mend the heart,
To make mankind in conscious virtue bold,

[1] Here is a sight that God himself surveying his handiwork would find worthy to look upon. Here is a pair worthy of God's beholding: a brave man calm in the face of evil fortune. I repeat, I can envisage nothing that Jupiter, if he turned his gaze on earth, would behold there more beautiful than the spectacle of Cato standing stalwart amid the ruins of the state, though the cause to which he had allied himself had been crushed again and again.
—Seneca, *On Divine Providence*, **6**

Live o'er each scene and be what they behold:
For this the tragic Muse first trod the stage,
Commanding tears to stream through every age;
Tyrants no more their savage nature kept,
And foes to virtue wonder'd how they wept.
Our author shuns by vulgar springs to move
The hero's glory or the virgin's love;
In pitying love, we but our weakness show,
And wild ambition well deserves its woe.
Here tears shall flow from a more gen'rous cause,
Such tears as patriots shed for dying laws:
He bids your breasts with ancient ardor rise,
And calls forth Roman drops from British eyes.
Virtue confess'd in human shape he draws,
What Plato thought, and godlike Cato was:
No common object to your sight displays,
But what with pleasure heav'n itself surveys:
A brave man struggling in the storms of fate,
And greatly falling with a falling state!
While Cato gives his little senate laws,
What bosom beats not in his country's cause?
Who sees him act, but envies ev'ry deed?
Who hears him groan, and does not wish to bleed?
Ev'n when proud Cæsar, 'midst triumphal cars,
The spoils of nations, and the pomp of wars,
Ignobly vain and impotently great,
Show'd Rome her Cato's figure drawn in state;
As her dead father's rev'rend image past,
The pomp was darken'd and the day o'ercast,
The triumph ceas'd—tears gush'd from ev'ry eye;
The world's great victor past unheeded by;
Her last good man dejected Rome ador'd,
And honour'd Cæsar's less than Cato's sword.

Britons, attend: be worth like this approv'd,
And show you have the virtue to be mov'd.
With honest scorn the first fam'd Cato view'd
Rome learning arts from Greece, whom she subdu'd;
Our scene precariously subsists too long
On French translation and Italian song.
Dare to have sense yourselves; assert the stage,
Be justly warm'd with your own native rage.
Such plays alone should please a British ear,
As Cato's self had not disdain'd to hear.

DRAMATIS PERSONÆ

Men:

CATO
LUCIUS, *a Senator*
SEMPRONIUS, *a Senator*
JUBA, *Prince of Numidia*
SYPHAX, *General of the Numidians*
PORTIUS ⎫
MARCUS ⎭ *Sons of* CATO
DECIUS, *Ambassador from Cæsar*
Mutineers, Guards, etc.

Women:

MARCIA, *Daughter to* CATO
LUCIA, *Daughter to* LUCIUS

SCENE: *A Large Hall in the Governor's Palace of Utica*

DRAMATIS PERSONÆ

CATO

ACT I

PORTIUS, MARCUS

POR.   The dawn is overcast, the morning low'rs,
And heavily in clouds brings on the day,
The great, th' important day, big with the fate
Of Cato and of Rome. Our father's death
Would fill up all the guilt of civil war
And close the scene of blood. Already Cæsar
Has ravag'd more than half the globe, and sees
Mankind grown thin by his destructive sword:
Should he go further, numbers would be wanting
To form new battles and support his crimes.
Ye Gods, what havoc does ambition make
Among your works!
    MARC.   Thy steady temper, Portius,
Can look on guilt, rebellion, fraud, and Cæsar,
In the calm lights of mild philosophy;
I'm tortur'd, ev'n to madness, when I think
On the proud victor: ev'ry time he's nam'd
Pharsalia rises to my view—I see
Th' insulting tyrant prancing o'er the field
Strew'd with Rome's citizens, and drench'd in slaughter,
His horse's hoofs wet with patrician blood.
O Portius, is there not some chosen curse,
Some hidden thunder in the stores of heav'n,
Red with uncommon wrath, to blast the man
Who owes his greatness to his country's ruin?
    POR.   Believe me, Marcus, 'tis an impious greatness,
And mix'd with too much horror to be envy'd:
How does the lustre of our father's actions,
Through the dark cloud of ills that cover him,
Break out, and burn with more triumphant brightness!

7

His suff'rings shine, and spread a glory round him;
Greatly unfortunate, he fights the cause
Of honour, virtue, liberty, and Rome.
His sword ne'er fell but on the guilty head;
Oppression, tyranny, and power usurp'd,
Draw all the vengeance of his arm upon 'em.

MARC.   Who knows not this? But what can Cato do
Against a world, a base, degenerate world
That courts the yoke, and bows the neck to Cæsar?
Pent up in Utica he vainly forms
A poor epitome of Roman greatness,
And, cover'd with Numidian guards, directs
A feeble army and an empty senate,
Remnants of mighty battles fought in vain.
By heav'ns, such virtues, join'd with such success,
Distract my very soul: our father's fortune
Would almost tempt us to renounce his precepts.

POR.   Remember what our father oft has told us:
The ways of heav'n are dark and intricate,
Puzzled in mazes and perplext with errors;
Our understanding traces 'em in vain,
Lost and bewilder'd in the fruitless search;
Nor sees with how much art the windings run,
Nor where the regular confusion ends.

MARC.   These are suggestions of a mind at ease:
O Portius, didst thou taste but half the griefs
That wring my soul, thou couldst not talk thus calmly.
Passion unpity'd and successless love
Plant daggers in my heart, and aggravate
My other griefs. Were but my Lucia kind!——

POR.   (aside)   Thou seest not that thy brother is thy rival:
But I must hide it, for I know thy temper.
Now, Marcus, now, thy virtue's on the proof:
Put forth thy utmost strength, work ev'ry nerve,
And call up all thy father in thy soul:
To quell the tyrant love, and guard thy heart
On this weak side, where most our nature fails,
Would be a conquest worthy Cato's son.

MARC.   Portius, the counsel which I cannot take,
Instead of healing, but upbraids my weakness.
Bid me for honour plunge into a war
Of thickest foes, and rush on certain death,
Then shalt thou see that Marcus is not slow

To follow glory and confess his father.
Love is not to be reason'd down, or lost
In high ambition and a thirst of greatness;
'Tis second life, it grows into the soul,
Warms ev'ry vein, and beats in ev'ry pulse,
I feel it here: my resolution melts——

   POR.   Behold young Juba, the Numidian prince!
With how much care he forms himself to glory,
And breaks the fierceness of his native temper
To copy out our father's bright example.
He loves our sister Marcia, greatly loves her,
His eyes, his looks, his actions all betray it:
But still the smother'd fondness burns within him.
When most it swells and labours for a vent,
Then sense of honour and desire of fame
Drive the big passion back into his heart.
What! shall an African, shall Juba's heir
Reproach great Cato's son, and show the world
A virtue wanting in a Roman soul?

   MARC.   Portius, no more! your words leave stings behind
   'em.
Whene'er did Juba, or did Portius, show
A virtue that has cast me at a distance,
And thrown me out in the pursuits of honour?

   POR.   Marcus, I know thy generous temper well;
Fling but th' appearance of dishonour on it,
It straight takes fire, and mounts into a blaze.

   MARC.   A brother's suff'rings claim a brother's pity.

   POR.   Heav'n knows I pity thee: behold my eyes
Ev'n whilst I speak. Do they not swim in tears?
Were but my heart as naked to thy view,
Marcus would see it bleed in his behalf.

   MARC.   Why then dost treat me with rebukes, instead
Of kind condoling cares and friendly sorrow?

   POR.   O Marcus, did I know the way to ease
Thy troubled heart, and mitigate thy pains,
Marcus, believe me, I could die to do it.

   MARC.   Thou best of brothers, and thou best of friends!
Pardon a weak, distemper'd soul, that swells
With sudden gusts, and sinks as soon in calms,
The sport of passions—— but Sempronius comes:
He must not find this softness hanging on me.

                                 (*Exit*)

SCENE II

Enter SEMPRONIUS

SEMP. (*solus*) Conspiracies no sooner should be form'd
'Than executed. What means Portius here?
I like not that cold youth. I must dissemble,
And speak a language foreign to my heart.

SEMPRONIUS, PORTIUS

  Good morrow, Portius! let us once embrace,
Once more embrace, whilst yet we both are free.
To-morrow should we thus express our friendship,
Each might receive a slave into his arms:
This sun, perhaps, this morning sun's the last
That e'er shall rise on Roman liberty.
  POR. My father has this morning called together
To this poor hall his little Roman senate
(The leavings of Pharsalia) to consult
If yet he can oppose the mighty torrent
That bears down Rome, and all her Gods, before it,
Or must at length give up the world to Cæsar.
  SEMP. Not all the pomp and majesty of Rome
Can raise her senate more than Cato's presence.
His virtues render our assembly awful,
They strike with something like religious fear,
And make ev'n Cæsar tremble at the head
Of armies flush'd with conquest: O my Portius,
Could I but call that wondrous man my father,
Would but thy sister Marcia be propitious
To thy friend's vows, I might be bless'd indeed!
  POR. Alas! Sempronius, wouldst thou talk of love
To Marcia, whilst her father's life's in danger?
Thou might'st as well court the pale trembling vestal,
When she beholds the holy flame expiring.
  SEMP. The more I see the wonders of thy race,
The more I'm charm'd. Thou must take heed, my Portius!
The world has all its eyes on Cato's son.
Thy father's merit sets thee up to view,
And shows thee in the fairest point of light,
To make thy virtues or thy faults conspicuous.
  POR. Well dost thou seem to check my ling'ring here
On this important hour—— I'll straight away,
And while the fathers of the senate meet
In close debate to weigh th' events of war,

I'll animate the soldiers' drooping courage,
With love of freedom, and contempt of life.
I'll thunder in their ears their country's cause,
And try to rouse up all that's Roman in 'em.
'Tis not in mortals to command success,
But we'll do more, Sempronius; we'll deserve it.

(Exit)

SEMP. *(solus)* Curse on the stripling! how he apes his sire!
Ambitiously sententious!—— but I wonder
Old Syphax comes not; his Numidian genius
Is well dispos'd to mischief, were he prompt
And eager on it; but he must be spurr'd,
And every moment quicken'd to the course.
Cato has used me ill: he has refus'd
His daughter Marcia to my ardent vows.
Besides, his baffled arms and ruin'd cause
Are bars to my ambition. Cæsar's favour,
That show'rs down greatness on his friends, will raise me
To Rome's first honours. If I give up Cato,
I claim in my reward his captive daughter.
But Syphax comes!——

SCENE III

SYPHAX, SEMPRONIUS

SYPH.   Sempronius, all is ready;
I've sounded my Numidians, man by man,
And find 'em ripe for a revolt: they all
Complain aloud of Cato's discipline,
And wait but the command to change their master.
SEMP.   Believe me, Syphax, there's no time to waste;
Ev'n whilst we speak, our conqueror comes on,
And gathers ground upon us ev'ry moment.
Alas! thou know'st not Cæsar's active soul,
With what a dreadful course he rushes on
From war to war: in vain has nature form'd
Mountains and oceans to oppose his passage;
He bounds o'er all, victorious in his march,
The Alps and Pyreneans sink before him;
Through winds and waves and storms he works his way,
Impatient for the battle: one day more
Will set the victor thund'ring at our gates.
But tell me, hast thou yet drawn o'er young Juba?

That still would recommend thee more to Cæsar,
And challenge better terms.
    SYPH.   Alas! he's lost,
He's lost, Sempronius; all his thoughts are full
Of Cato's virtues——But I'll try once more
(For every instant I expect him here)
If yet I can subdue those stubborn principles
Of faith, of honour, and I know not what,
That have corrupted his Numidian temper,
And struck th' infection into all his soul.
    SEMP.   Be sure to press upon him ev'ry motive.
Juba's surrender, since his father's death,
Would give up Afric into Cæsar's hands,
And make him lord of half the burning zone.
    SYPH.   But is it true, Sempronius, that your senate
Is call'd together? Gods! thou must be cautious!
Cato has piercing eyes, and will discern
Our frauds, unless they're cover'd thick with art.
    SEMP.   Let me alone, good Syphax: I'll conceal
My thoughts in passion ('tis the surest way);
I'll bellow out for Rome and for my country,
And mouth at Cæsar till I shake the senate.
Your cold hypocrisy's a stale device,
A worn-out trick: wouldst thou be thought in earnest?
Clothe thy feign'd zeal in rage, in fire, in fury!
    SYPH.   In troth, thou'rt able to instruct grey hairs,
And teach the wily African deceit!
    SEMP.   Once more, be sure to try thy skill on Juba.
Meanwhile I'll hasten to my Roman soldiers,
Inflame the mutiny, and underhand
Blow up their discontents, till they break out
Unlook'd for, and discharge themselves on Cato.
Remember, Syphax, we must work in haste:
Oh, think what anxious moments pass between
The birth of plots and their last fatal periods.
Oh! 'tis a dreadful interval of time,
Fill'd up with horror all, and big with death!
Destruction hangs on ev'ry word we speak,
On ev'ry thought, till the concluding stroke
Determines all, and closes our design.   (*Exit*)
    SYPH. (*solus*)   I'll try if yet I can reduce to reason
This headstrong youth, and make him spurn at Cato.
The time is short, Cæsar comes rushing on us——
But hold! young Juba sees me, and approaches.

SCENE IV

JUBA, SYPHAX

JUBA.   Syphax, I joy to meet thee thus alone.
I have observ'd of late thy looks are fall'n,
O'ercast with gloomy cares and discontent;
Then tell me, Syphax, I conjure thee, tell me,
What are the thoughts that knit thy brow in frowns,
And turn thine eye thus coldly on thy prince?
    SYPH.   'Tis not my talent to conceal my thoughts,
Nor carry smiles and sunshine in my face,
When discontent sits heavy at my heart.
I have not yet so much the Roman in me.
    JUBA.   Why dost thou cast out such ungen'rous terms
Against the lords and sov'reigns of the world?
Dost thou not see mankind fall down before 'em,
And own the force of their superior virtue?
Is there a nation in the wilds of Afric,
Amidst our barren rocks and burning sands,
That does not tremble at the Roman name?
    SYPH.   Gods! where's the worth that sets this people up
Above your own Numidia's tawny sons!
Do they with tougher sinews bend the bow?
Or flies the javelin swifter to its mark,
Launch'd from the vigour of a Roman arm?
Who like our active African instructs
The fiery steed, and trains him to his hand?
Or guides in troops th' embattled elephant,
Loaden with war? These, these are arts, my prince,
In which your Zama does not stoop to Rome.
    JUBA.   These all are virtues of a meaner rank,
Perfections that are placed in bones and nerves.
A Roman soul is bent on higher views:
To civilize the rude, unpolish'd world,
And lay it under the restraint of laws;
To make man mild and sociable to man;
To cultivate the wild, licentious savage
With wisdom, discipline, and lib'ral arts,
Th' embellishments of life: virtues like these
Make human nature shine, reform the soul,
And break our fierce barbarians into men.
    SYPH.   Patience, kind heav'ns! Excuse an old man's
    warmth.

What are these wondrous civilizing arts,
This Roman polish, and this smooth behaviour,
That render man thus tractable and tame?
Are they not only to disguise our passions,
To set our looks at variance with our thoughts,
To check the starts and sallies of the soul,
And break off all its commerce with the tongue;
In short, to change us into other creatures
Than what our nature and the Gods design'd us?

    JUBA.   To strike thee dumb; turn up thy eyes to Cato!
There may'st thou see to what a godlike height
The Roman virtues lift up mortal man.
While good, and just, and anxious for his friends,
He's still severely bent against himself;
Renouncing sleep, and rest, and food, and ease,
He strives with thirst and hunger, toil and heat;
And when his fortune sets before him all
The pomps and pleasures that his soul can wish,
His rigid virtue will accept of none.

    SYPH.   Believe me, Prince, there's not an African
That traverses our vast Numidian deserts
In quest of prey, and lives upon his bow,
But better practises these boasted virtues.
Coarse are his meals, the fortune of the chase;
Amidst the running stream he slakes his thirst,
Toils all the day, and at th' approach of night
On the first friendly bank he throws him down,
Or rests his head upon a rock till morn:
Then rises fresh, pursues his wonted game,
And if the following day he chance to find
A new repast, or an untasted spring,
Blesses his stars, and thinks it luxury.

    JUBA.   Thy prejudices, Syphax, won't discern
What virtues grow from ignorance and choice,
Nor how the hero differs from the brute.
But grant that others could with equal glory
Look down on pleasures, and the baits of sense;
Where shall we find the man that bears affliction,
Great and majestic in his griefs, like Cato?
Heav'ns, with what strength, what steadiness of mind,
He triumphs in the midst of all his sufferings!
How does he rise against a load of woes,
And thank the Gods that throw the weight upon him!

    SYPH.   'Tis pride, rank pride, and haughtiness of soul:

I think the Romans call it stoicism.
Had not your royal father thought so highly
Of Roman virtue, and of Cato's cause,
He had not fall'n by a slave's hand inglorious;
Nor would his slaughter'd army now have lain
On Afric's sands, disfigur'd with their wounds,
To gorge the wolves and vultures of Numidia.
    JUBA.   Why dost thou call my sorrows up afresh?
My father's name brings tears into my eyes.
      SYPH.   Oh, that you'd profit by your father's ills!
      JUBA.   What wouldst thou have me do?
      SYPH.   Abandon Cato.
      JUBA.   Syphax, I should be more than twice an orphan
By such a loss.
      SYPH.   Ay, there's the tie that binds you!
You long to call him father. Marcia's charms
Work in your heart unseen, and plead for Cato.
No wonder you are deaf to all I say.
      JUBA.   Syphax, your zeal becomes importunate;
I've hitherto permitted it to rave,
And talk at large; but learn to keep it in,
Lest it should take more freedom than I'll give it.
      SYPH.   Sir, your great father never used me thus.
Alas, he's dead! But can you e'er forget
The tender sorrows, and the pangs of nature,
The fond embraces, and repeated blessings,
Which you drew from him in your last farewell?
Still must I cherish the dear, sad remembrance,
At once to torture and to please my soul.
The good old king, at parting, wrung my hand,
(His eyes brimful of tears) then sighing cried,
"Prithee, be careful of my son!"—his grief
Swell'd up so high, he could not utter more.
      JUBA.   Alas, thy story melts away my soul.
That best of fathers! how shall I discharge
The gratitude and duty which I owe him!
      SYPH.   By laying up his counsels in your heart.
      JUBA.   His counsels bade me yield to thy directions:
Then, Syphax, chide me in severest terms,
Vent all thy passion, and I'll stand its shock,
Calm and unruffled as a summer sea,
When not a breath of wind flies o'er its surface.
      SYPH   Alas, my Prince, I'd guide you to your safety.
      JUBA.   I do believe thou wouldst; but tell me how.

SYPH.   Fly from the fate that follows Cæsar's foes.

JUBA.   My father scorn'd to do 't.

SYPH.   And therefore died.

JUBA.   Better to die ten thousand thousand deaths,
Than wound my honour.

SYPH.   Rather say, your love.

JUBA.   Syphax, I've promis'd to preserve my temper.
Why wilt thou urge me to confess a flame
I long have stifled, and would fain conceal?

SYPH.   Believe me, Prince, 'tis hard to conquer love,
But easy to divert and break its force:
Absence might cure it, or a second mistress
Light up another flame, and put out this.
The glowing dames of Zama's royal court
Have faces flush'd with more exalted charms;
The sun, that rolls his chariot o'er their heads,
Works up more fire and colour in their cheeks:
Were you with these, my Prince, you'd soon forget
The pale, unripen'd beauties of the north.

JUBA.   'Tis not a set of features, or complexion,
The tincture of a skin, that I admire.
Beauty soon grows familiar to the lover,
Fades in his eye, and palls upon the sense.
The virtuous Marcia tow'rs above her sex:
True, she is fair (oh, how divinely fair!),
But still the lovely maid improves her charms
With inward greatness, unaffected wisdom,
And sanctity of manners. Cato's soul
Shines out in everything she acts or speaks,
While winning mildness and attractive smiles
Dwell in her looks, and with becoming grace
Soften the rigour of her father's virtues.

SYPH.   How does your tongue grow wanton in her praise!
But on my knees I beg you would consider——

Enter MARCIA *and* LUCIA

JUBA.   Hah! Syphax, is't not she! She moves this way:
And with her Lucia, Lucius's fair daughter.
My heart beats thick——I prithee, Syphax, leave me.

SYPH. (*aside*)   Ten thousand curses fasten on 'em both!
Now will this woman, with a single glance,
Undo what I've been lab'ring all this while.   (*Exit*)

JUBA.   Hail, charming maid! How does thy beauty smooth
The face of war, and make ev'n horror smile!

At sight of thee my heart shakes off its sorrows;
I feel a dawn of joy break in upon me,
And for a while forget th' approach of Cæsar.

    MARC.   I should be griev'd, young Prince, **to think my presence**
Unbent your thoughts, and slacken'd 'em to arms,
While, warm with slaughter, our victorious foe
Threatens aloud, and calls you to the field.

    JUBA.   O Marcia, let me hope thy kind concerns
And gentle wishes follow me to battle!
The thought will give new vigour to my arm,
Add strength and weight to my descending sword,
And drive it in a tempest on the foe.

    MARC.   My prayers and wishes always shall attend
The friends of Rome, the glorious cause of virtue,
And men approv'd of by the Gods and Cato.

    JUBA.   That Juba may deserve thy pious cares,
I'll gaze forever on thy godlike father,
Transplanting, one by one, into my life,
His bright perfections, till I shine like him.

    MARC.   My father never at a time like this
Would lay out his great soul in words, and waste
Such precious moments.

    JUBA.   Thy reproofs are just,
Thou virtuous maid; I'll hasten to my troops,
And fire their languid souls with Cato's virtue;
If e'er I lead them to the field, when all
The war shall stand rang'd in its just array
And dreadful pomp: then will I think on thee!
O lovely maid, then will I think on thee!
And, in the shock of charging hosts, remember
What glorious deeds should grace the man who hopes
For Marcia's love.   (*Exit*)

    LUC.   Marcia, you're too severe:
How could you chide the young good-natur'd prince,
And drive him from you with so stern an air,
A prince that loves and dotes on you to death?

    MARC.   'Tis therefore, Lucia, that I chide him from me.
His air, his voice, his looks, and honest soul
Speak all so movingly in his behalf,
I dare not trust myself to hear him talk.

    LUC.   Why will you fight against so sweet a passion,
And steel your heart to such a world of charms?

    MARC.   How, Lucia, wouldst thou have me sink away

In pleasing dreams, and lose myself in love,
When ev'ry moment Cato's life's at stake?
Cæsar comes arm'd with terror and revenge,
And aims his thunder at my father's head:
Should not the sad occasion swallow up
My other cares, and draw them all into it?

    LUC.   Why have not I this constancy of mind,
Who have so many griefs to try its force?
Sure, nature form'd me of her softest mould,
Enfeebled all my soul with tender passions,
And sunk me ev'n below my own weak sex:
Pity and love, by turns, oppress my heart.

    MARC.   Lucia, disburthen all thy care on me,
And let me share thy most retir'd distress;
Tell me who raises up this conflict in thee?

    LUC.   I need not blush to name them, when I tell thee
They're Marcia's brothers, and the sons of Cato.

    MARC.   They both behold thee with their sister's eyes,
And often have reveal'd their passion to me.
But tell me whose address thou favor'st most?
I long to know, and yet I dread to hear it.

    LUC.   Which is it Marcia wishes for?

    MARC.   For neither—
And yet for both. The youths have equal share
In Marcia's wishes, and divide their sister:
But tell me which of them is Lucia's choice?

    LUC.   Marcia, they both are high in my esteem,
But in my love——Why wilt thou make me name him?
Thou know'st it is a blind and foolish passion,
Pleas'd and disgusted with it knows not what.

    MARC.   O Lucia, I'm perplex'd; oh, tell me which
I must hereafter call my happy brother?

    LUC.   Suppose 'twere Portius, could you blame my choice?
O Portius, thou hast stol'n away my soul!
With what a graceful tenderness he loves!
And breathes the softest, the sincerest vows!
Complacency, and truth, and manly sweetness
Dwell ever on his tongue, and smooth his thoughts.
Marcus is overwarm: his fond complaints
Have so much earnestness and passion in them,
I hear him with a secret kind of dread,
And tremble at his vehemence of temper.

    MARC.   Alas, poor youth! how canst thou throw him from
        thee?

Lucia, thou know'st not half the love he bears thee;
Whene'er he speaks of thee, his heart's in flames,
He sends out all his soul in ev'ry word,
And thinks, and talks, and looks like one transported.
Unhappy youth! how will thy coldness raise
Tempests and storms in his afflicted bosom!
I dread the consequence.

  LUC.   You seem to plead
Against your brother Portius.

  MARC.   Heav'n forbid!
Had Portius been the unsuccessful lover,
The same compassion would have fall'n on him.

  LUC. Was ever virgin love distress'd like mine!
Portius himself oft falls in tears before me,
As if he mourn'd his rival's ill success,
Then bids me hide the motions of my heart,
Nor show which way it turns. So much he fears
The sad effects that it would have on Marcus.

  MARC. He knows too well how easily he's fir'd,
And would not plunge his brother in despair,
But waits for happier times, and kinder moments.

  LUC. Alas, too late I find myself involv'd
In endless griefs, and labyrinths of woe,
Born to afflict my Marcia's family,
And sow dissension in the hearts of brothers.
Tormenting thought! it cuts into my soul.

  MARC. Let us not, Lucia, aggravate our sorrows,
But to the Gods permit th' event of things.
Our lives, discolour'd with our present woes,
May still grow bright, and smile with happier hours.
 So the pure limpid stream, when foul with stains
Of rushing torrents and descending rains,
Works itself clear, and as it runs, refines;
Till, by degrees, the floating mirror shines,
Reflects each flow'r that on the border grows,
And a new heav'n in its fair bosom shows.   *(Exeunt)*

ACT II

SEMPRONIUS, LUCIUS

  SEMP. Rome still survives in this assembled senate!
Let us remember we are Cato's friends,
And act like men who claim that glorious title.

  LUC. Cato will soon be here, and open to us

Th' occasion of our meeting. Hark! he comes!

(*a sound of trumpets*)

May all the guardian Gods of Rome direct him!

Enter CATO

CATO.   Fathers, we once again are met in council.
Cæsar's approach has summon'd us together,
And Rome attends her fate from our resolves:
How shall we treat this bold, aspiring man?
Success still follows him and backs his crimes:
Pharsalia gave him Rome; Egypt has since
Receiv'd his yoke, and the whole Nile is Cæsar's.
Why should I mention Juba's overthrow,
And Scipio's death? Numidia's burning sands
Still smoke with blood. 'Tis time we should decree
What course to take. Our foe advances on us,
And envies us ev'n Libya's sultry deserts.
Fathers, pronounce your thoughts: are thy still fixt
To hold it out, and fight it to the last?
Or are your hearts subdu'd at length, and wrought
By time and ill success to a submission?
Sempronius, speak.

SEMP.   My voice is still for war.
Gods, can a Roman senate long debate
Which of the two to choose, slav'ry or death!
No, let us rise at once, gird on our swords,
And, at the head of our remaining troops,
Attack the foe, break through the thick array
Of his throng'd legions, and charge home upon him.
Perhaps some arm, more lucky than the rest,
May reach his heart, and free the world from bondage.
Rise, fathers, rise; 'tis Rome demands your help;
Rise, and revenge her slaughter'd citizens,
Or share their fate: the corps of half her senate
Manure the fields of Thessaly, while we
Sit here, delib'rating in cold debates,
If we should sacrifice our lives to honour,
Or wear them out in servitude and chains.
Rouse up, for shame! our brothers of Pharsalia
Point at their wounds, and cry aloud, "To battle!"
Great Pompey's shade complains that we are slow,
And Scipio's ghost walks unreveng'd amongst us.

CATO.   Let not a torrent of impetuous zeal
Transport thee thus beyond the bounds of reason:

True fortitude is seen in great exploits,
That justice warrants, and that wisdom guides;
All else is tow'ring frenzy and distraction.
Are not the lives of those who draw the sword
In Rome's defence entrusted to our care?
Should we thus lead them to a field of slaughter,
Might not th' impartial world with reason say
We lavish'd at our deaths the blood of thousands,
To grace our fall, and make our ruin glorious?
Lucius, we next would know what's your opinion.

    LUC.   My thoughts, I must confess, are turn'd on **peace.**
Already have our quarrels fill'd the world
With widows and with orphans: Scythia mourns
Our guilty wars, and earth's remotest regions
Lie half unpeopled by the feuds of Rome:
'Tis time to sheathe the sword, and spare mankind.
It is not Cæsar, but the Gods, my fathers,
The Gods declare against us, and repel
Our vain attempts. To urge the foe to battle,
(Prompted by blind revenge and wild despair)
Were to refuse th' awards of Providence,
And not to rest in heav'n's determination.
Already have we shown our love to Rome,
Now let us show submission to the Gods.
We took up arms, not to revenge ourselves,
But free the commonwealth; when this end fails,
Arms have no further use: our country's cause,
That drew our swords, now wrests 'em from our hands,
And bids us not delight in Roman blood,
Unprofitably shed; what men could do
Is done already: heav'n and earth will witness,
If Rome must fall, that we are innocent.

    SEMP. (*aside to* CATO)   This smooth discourse and **mild**
        behaviour oft
Conceal a traitor—— Something whispers me
All is not right—— Cato, beware of Lucius.

    CATO.   Let us appear nor rash nor diffident:
Immod'rate valour swells into a fault,
And fear, admitted into public councils,
Betrays like treason. Let us shun 'em both.
Fathers, I cannot see that our affairs
Are grown thus desp'rate. We have bulwarks round us:
Within our walls are troops enur'd to toil
In Afric's heats, and season'd to the sun;

Numidia's spacious kingdom lies behind us,
Ready to rise at its young prince's call.
While there is hope, do not distrust the Gods;
But wait at least till Cæsar's near approach
Force us to yield. 'Twill never be too late
To sue for chains and own a conqueror.
Why should Rome fall a moment ere her time?
No, let us draw her term of freedom out
In its full length, and spin it to the last.
So shall we gain still one day's liberty;
And let me perish, but in Cato's judgment,
A day, an hour, of virtuous liberty
Is worth a whole eternity in bondage.

Enter MARCUS

 MARC. Fathers, this moment, as I watch'd the gates,
Lodg'd on my post, a herald is arriv'd
From Cæsar's camp, and with him comes old Decius,
The Roman knight; he carries in his looks
Impatience, and demands to speak with Cato.
 CATO. By your permission, fathers, bid him enter.
          (*Exit* MARCUS)
Decius was once my friend, but other prospects
Have loos'd those ties, and bound him fast to Cæsar.
His message may determine our resolves.

Enter DECIUS

 DEC. Cæsar sends health to Cato.
 CATO.   Could he send it
To Cato's slaughter'd friends, it would be welcome.
Are not your orders to address the senate?
 DEC. My business is with Cato: Cæsar sees
The straits to which you're driv'n; and, as he knows
Cato's high worth, is anxious for his life.
 CATO. My life is grafted on the fate of Rome:
Would he save Cato? Bid him spare his country.
Tell your dictator this, and tell him Cato
Disdains a life which he has pow'r to offer.
 DEC. Rome and her senators submit to Cæsar;
Her gen'rals and her consuls are no more,
Who check'd his conquests, and deny'd his triumphs.
Why will not Cato be this Cæsar's friend?
 CATO. Those very reasons thou hast urg'd forbid it.
 DEC. Cato, I've orders to expostulate

And reason with you, as from friend to friend:
Think on the storm that gathers o'er your head,
And threatens ev'ry hour to burst upon it;
Still may you stand high in your country's honours,
Do but comply, and make your peace with Cæsar.
Rome will rejoice, and cast its eyes on Cato,
As on the second of mankind.

  CATO.   No more!
I must not think of life on such conditions.

  DEC. Cæsar is well acquainted with your virtues,
And therefore sets this value on your life:
Let him but know the price of Cato's friendship,
And name your terms.

  CATO.   Bid him disband his legions,
Restore the commonwealth to liberty,
Submit his actions to the public censure,
And stand the judgment of a Roman senate.
Bid him do this, and Cato is his friend.

  DEC. Cato, the world talks loudly of your wisdom——

  CATO. Nay more, though Cato's voice was ne'er employ'd
To clear the guilty, and to varnish crimes,
Myself will mount the rostrum in his favour,
And strive to gain his pardon from the people.

  DEC. A style like this becomes a conqueror.

  CATO. Decius, a style like this becomes a Roman.

  DEC. What is a Roman, that is Cæsar's foe?

  CATO. Greater than Cæsar, he's a friend to virtue.

  DEC. Consider, Cato, you're in Utica,
And at the head of your own little senate;
You don't now thunder in the Capitol,
With all the mouths of Rome to second you.

  CATO. Let him consider that who drives us hither:
'Tis Cæsar's sword has made Rome's senate little,
And thinn'd its ranks. Alas, thy dazzled eye
Beholds this man in a false glaring light,
Which conquest and success have thrown upon him;
Didst thou but view him right, thou'dst see him black
With murder, treason, sacrilege, and crimes
That strike my soul with horror but to name 'em.
I know thou look'st on me, as on a wretch
Beset with ills, and cover'd with misfortunes;
But, by the Gods I swear, millions of worlds
Should never buy me to be like that Cæsar.

  DEC. Does Cato send this answer back to Cæsar,

For all his gen'rous cares, and proffer'd friendship?

CATO. His cares for me are insolent and vain:
Presumptuous man! The Gods take care of Cato.
Would Cæsar show the greatness of his soul,
Bid him employ his care for these my friends,
And make good use of his ill-gotten pow'r,
By shelt'ring men much better than himself.

DEC. Your high unconquer'd heart makes you forget
That you're a man. You rush on your destruction.
But I have done. When I relate hereafter
The tale of this unhappy embassy,
All Rome will be in tears.   (*Exit* DECIUS)

SEMP.   Cato, we thank thee.
The mighty genius of immortal Rome
Speaks in thy voice, thy soul breathes liberty:
Cæsar will shrink to hear the words thou utter'st,
And shudder in the midst of all his conquests.

LUC. The senate owns its gratitude to Cato,
Who with so great a soul consults its safety,
And guards our lives, while he neglects his own.

SEMP. Sempronius gives no thanks on this account.
Lucius seems fond of life; but what is life?
'Tis not to stalk about, and draw fresh air
From time to time, or gaze upon the sun;
'Tis to be free. When liberty is gone,
Life grows insipid, and has lost its relish.
Oh, could my dying hand but lodge a sword
In Cæsar's bosom, and revenge my country,
By heav'ns, I could enjoy the pangs of death,
And smile in agony.

LUC.   Others perhaps
May serve their country with as warm a zeal,
Though 'tis not kindled into so much rage.

SEMP. This sober conduct is a mighty virtue
In lukewarm patriots.

CATO.   Come! no more, Sempronius.
All here are friends to Rome, and to each other.
Let us not weaken still the weaker side
By our divisions.

SEMP.   Cato, my resentments
Are sacrific'd to Rome——I stand reprov'd.

CATO. Fathers, 'tis time you come to a resolve.

LUC. Cato, we all go into your opinion,
Cæsar's behaviour has convinc'd the senate

We ought to hold it out till terms arrive.

SEMP. We ought to hold it out till death; but, Cato,
My private voice is drown'd amid the senate's.

CATO. Then let us rise, my friends, and strive to fill
This little interval, this pause of life,
(While yet our liberty and fates are doubtful)
With resolution, friendship, Roman brav'ry,
And all the virtues we can crowd into it;
That heav'n may say, it ought to be prolong'd.
Fathers, farewell! The young Numidian prince
Comes forward, and expects to know our counsels.

(*Exeunt* SENATORS)

Enter JUBA

CATO. Juba, the Roman senate has resolv'd,
Till time give better prospects, still to keep
The sword unsheath'd, and turn its edge on Cæsar.

JUBA. The resolution fits a Roman senate.
But, Cato, lend me for a while thy patience,
And condescend to hear a young man speak.
My father, when some days before his death
He order'd me to march for Utica
(Alas, I thought not then his death so near!)
Wept o'er me, press'd me in his aged arms,
And, as his griefs gave way, "My son," said he,
"Whatever fortune shall befall thy father,
Be Cato's friend; he'll train thee up to great
And virtuous deeds: do but observe him well,
Thou'lt shun misfortunes, or thou'lt learn to bear 'em."

CATO. Juba, thy father was a worthy prince,
And merited, alas! a better fate;
But heav'n thought otherwise.

JUBA.   My father's fate,
In spite of all the fortitude that shines
Before my face, in Cato's great example,
Subdues my soul, and fills my eyes with tears.

CATO. It is an honest sorrow, and becomes thee.

JUBA. My father drew respect from foreign climes:
The kings of Afric sought him for their friend;
Kings far remote, that rule, as fame reports,
Behind the hidden sources of the Nile,
In distant worlds, on t'other side the sun:
Oft have their black ambassadors appear'd,
Loaden with gifts, and fill'd the courts of Zama.

CATO.   I am no stranger to thy father's greatness.

JUBA.   I would not boast the greatness of my father,
But point out new alliances to Cato.
Had we not better leave this Utica,
To arm Numidia in our cause, and court
Th' assistance of my father's pow'rful friends?
Did they know Cato, our remotest kings
Would pour embattled multitudes about him;
Their swarthy hosts would darken all our plains,
Doubling the native horror of the war,
And making death more grim.

CATO.   And canst thou think
Cato will fly before the sword of Cæsar?
Reduc'd, like Hannibal, to seek relief
From court to court, and wander up and down,
A vagabond in Afric!

JUBA.   Cato, perhaps
I'm too officious, but my forward cares
Would fain preserve a life of so much value.
My heart is wounded, when I see such virtue
Afflicted by the weight of such misfortunes.

CATO.   Thy nobleness of soul obliges me.
But know, young Prince, that valour soars above
What the world calls misfortune and affliction.
These are not ills; else would they never fall
On heav'n's first fav'rites, and the best of men:
The Gods, in bounty, work up storms about us,
That give mankind occasion to exert
Their hidden strength, and throw out into practice
Virtues that shun the day, and lie conceal'd
In the smooth seasons and the calms of life.

JUBA.   I'm charm'd whene'er thou talk'st! I pant for virtue
And all my soul endeavours at perfection.

CATO.   Dost thou love watchings, abstinence, and toil,
Laborious virtues all? Learn them from Cato:
Success and fortune must thou learn from Cæsar.

JUBA.   The best good fortune that can fall on Juba,
The whole success at which my heart aspires,
Depends on Cato.

CATO.   What does Juba say?
Thy words confound me.

JUBA.   I would fain retract them,
Give 'em back again. They aim'd at nothing.

CATO.   Tell me thy wish, young Prince; make not my ear

A stranger to thy thoughts.

JUBA.   Oh, they're extravagant;
Still let me hide them.

CATO.   What can Juba ask
That Cato will refuse!

JUBA.   I fear to name it.
Marcia—inherits all her father's virtues.

CATO.   What wouldst thou say?

JUBA.   Cato, thou hast a daughter.

CATO.   Adieu, young Prince: I would not hear a word
Should lessen thee in my esteem: remember
The hand of fate is over us, and heav'n
Exacts severity from all our thoughts:
It is not now a time to talk of aught
But chains or conquest, liberty or death.   (*Exit*)

Enter SYPHAX

SYPH.   How's this, my Prince! What, cover'd with con-
        fusion?
You look as if yon stern philosopher
Had just now chid you.

JUBA.   Syphax, I'm undone!

SYPH.   I know it well.

JUBA.   Cato thinks meanly of me.

SYPH.   And so will all mankind.

JUBA.   I've open'd to him
The weakness of my soul, my love for Marcia.

SYPH.   Cato's a proper person to entrust
A love-tale with.

JUBA.   Oh, I could pierce my heart,
My foolish heart! Was ever wretch like Juba?

SYPH.   Alas, my Prince, how are you chang'd of late!
I've known young Juba rise before the sun,
To beat the thicket where the tiger slept,
Or seek the lion in his dreadful haunts:
How did the colour mount into your cheeks,
When first you rous'd him to the chase! I've seen you,
Ev'n in the Libyan dog-days, hunt him down,
Then charge him close, provoke him to the rage
Of fangs and claws, and stooping from your horse
Rivet the panting savage to the ground.

JUBA.   Prithee, no more!

SYPH.   How would the old king smile
To see you weigh the paws, when tipp'd with gold,

And throw the shaggy spoils about your shoulders!

JUBA.   Syphax, this old man's talk (though honey flow'd
In ev'ry word) would now lose all its sweetness.
Cato's displeas'd, and Marcia lost forever!

SYPH.   Young Prince, I yet could give you good advice.
Marcia might still be yours.

JUBA.   What say'st thou, Syphax?
By heav'ns, thou turn'st me all into attention.

SYPH.   Marcia might still be yours.

JUBA.   As how, dear Syphax?

SYPH.   Juba commands Numidia's hardy troops,
Mounted on steeds, unus'd to the restraint
Of curbs or bits, and fleeter than the winds:
Give but the word, we'll snatch this damsel up
And bear her off.

JUBA.   Can such dishonest thoughts
Rise up in man! wouldst thou seduce my youth
To do an act that would destroy my honour?

SYPH.   Gods, I could tear my beard to hear you talk!
Honour's a fine imaginary notion,
That draws in raw and unexperienc'd men
To real mischiefs, while they hunt a shadow.

JUBA.   Wouldst thou degrade thy prince into a ruffian?

SYPH.   The boasted ancestors of these great men,
Whose virtues you admire, were all such ruffians.
This dread of nations, this almighty Rome,
That comprehends in her wide empire's bounds
All under heav'n, was founded on a rape.
Your Scipios, Cæsars, Pompeys, and your Catos,
(These gods on earth) are all the spurious brood
Of violated maids, of ravish'd Sabines.

JUBA.   Syphax, I fear that hoary head of thine
Abounds too much in our Numidian wiles.

SYPH.   Indeed, my Prince, you want to know the world;
You have not read mankind; your youth admires
The throes and swellings of a Roman soul,
Cato's bold flights, th' extravagance of virtue.

JUBA.   If knowledge of the world makes man perfidious,
May Juba ever live in ignorance!

SYPH.   Go, go, you're young.

JUBA.   Gods, must I tamely bear
This arrogance unanswer'd! Thou'rt a traitor,
A false old traitor.

SYPH.   (aside) I have gone too far.

JUBA.   Cato shall know the baseness of thy soul.

SYPH. (*aside*)   I must appease this storm, or perish in it.

Young Prince, behold these locks that are grown white
Beneath a helmet in your father's battles.

JUBA.   Those locks shall ne'er protect thy insolence.

SYPH.   Must one rash word, th' infirmity of age,
Throw down the merit of my better years?
This the reward of a whole life of service!
(*aside*)   Curse on the boy! How steadily he hears me!

JUBA.   Is it because the throne of my forefathers
Still stands unfill'd, and that Numidia's crown
Hangs doubtful yet, whose head it shall enclose,
Thou thus presumest to treat thy prince with scorn?

SYPH.   Why will you rive my heart with such expressions?
Does not old Syphax follow you to war?
What are his aims? Why does he load with darts
His trembling hand, and crush beneath a casque
His wrinkled brows? What is it he aspires to?
Is it not this, to shed the slow remains,
His last poor ebb of blood, in your defense?

JUBA.   Syphax, no more! I would not hear you talk.

SYPH.   Not hear me talk! What, when my faith to Juba,
My royal master's son, is call'd in question?
My prince may strike me dead, and I'll be dumb:
But whilst I live, I must not hold my tongue,
And languish out old age in his displeasure.

JUBA.   Thou know'st the way too well into my heart,
I do believe thee loyal to thy prince.

SYPH.   What greater instance can I give? I've offer'd
To do an action which my soul abhors,
And gain you whom you love at any price.

JUBA.   Was this thy motive? I have been too hasty.

SYPH.   And 'tis for this my prince has call'd me traitor.

JUBA.   Sure thou mistakest; I did not call thee so.

SYPH.   You did indeed, my Prince, you call'd me traitor,
Nay, further, threaten'd you'd complain to Cato.
Of what, my Prince, would you complain to Cato?
That Syphax loves you, and would sacrifice
His life, nay more, his honour in your service.

JUBA.   Syphax, I know thou lov'st me, but indeed
Thy zeal for Juba carry'd thee too far.
Honour's a sacred tie, the law of kings,
The noble mind's distinguishing perfection,
That aids and strengthens virtue where it meets her,

And imitates her actions, where she is not:
It ought not to be sported with.

SYPH.   By heav'ns,
I'm ravish'd when you talk thus, though you chide me!
Alas, I've hitherto been us'd to think
A blind, officious zeal to serve my king
The ruling principle that ought to burn
And quench all others in a subject's heart.
Happy the people, who preserve their honour
By the same duties that oblige their prince!

JUBA.   Syphax, thou now begin'st to speak thyself.
Numidia's grown a scorn among the nations
For breach of public vows. Our Punic faith
Is infamous, and branded to a proverb.
Syphax, we'll join our cares, to purge away
Our country's crimes, and clear her reputation.

SYPH.   Believe me, Prince, you make old Syphax weep
To hear you talk—but 'tis with tears of joy.
If e'er your father's crown adorn your brows,
Numidia will be blest by Cato's lectures.

JUBA.   Syphax, thy hand! we'll mutually forget
The warmth of youth, and frowardness of age:
Thy prince esteems thy worth, and loves thy person.
If e'er the scepter comes into my hand,
Syphax shall stand the second in my kingdom.

SYPH.   Why will you overwhelm my age with kindness?
My joy grows burdensome, I shan't support it.

JUBA.   Syphax, farewell. I'll hence, and try to find
Some blest occasion that may set me right
In Cato's thoughts. I'd rather have that man
Approve my deeds, than worlds for my admirers.   (*Exit*)

SYPH. (*solus*)   Young men soon give, and soon forget
affronts;
Old age is slow in both—"A false old traitor!"
Those words, rash boy, may chance to cost thee dear:
My heart had still some foolish fondness for thee:
But hence! 'tis gone: I give it to the winds:
Cæsar, I'm wholly thine——

Enter SEMPRONIUS

SYPH.   All hail, Sempronius!
Well, Cato's senate is resolv'd to wait
The fury of a siege before it yields.

SEMP.   Syphax, we both were on the verge of fate:

Lucius declar'd for peace, and terms were offer'd
To Cato by a messenger from Cæsar.
Should they submit, ere our designs are ripe,
We both must perish in the common wreck,
Lost in a gen'ral, undistinguish'd ruin.

    SYPH.   But how stands Cato?

    SEMP.   Thou hast seen Mount Atlas:
While storms and tempests thunder on its brows,
And oceans break their billows at its feet,
It stands unmov'd, and glories in its height.
Such is that haughty man; his tow'ring soul,
'Midst all the shocks and injuries of fortune,
Rises superior, and looks down on Cæsar.

    SYPH.   But what's this messenger?

    SEMP.   I've practis'd with him,
And found a means to let the victor know
That Syphax and Sempronius are his friends.
But let me now examine in my turn:
Is Juba fixt?

    SYPH.   Yes, but it is to Cato.
I've try'd the force of every reason on him,
Sooth'd and caress'd, been angry, sooth'd again,
Laid safety, life, and int'rest in his sight,
But all are vain, he scorns them all for Cato.

    SEMP.   Come, 'tis no matter, we shall do without him.
He'll make a pretty figure in a triumph,
And serve to trip before the victor's chariot.
Syphax, I now may hope thou hast forsook
Thy Juba's cause, and wishest Marcia mine.

    SYPH.   May she be thine as fast as thou wouldst have her!

    SEMP.   Syphax, I love that woman; though I curse
Her and myself, yet, spite of me, I love her.

    SYPH.   Make Cato sure, and give up Utica,
Cæsar will ne'er refuse thee such a trifle.
But are thy troops prepar'd for a revolt?
Does the sedition catch from man to man,
And run among their ranks?

    SEMP.   All, all is ready.
The factious leaders are our friends, that spread
Murmurs and discontents among the soldiers.
They count their toilsome marches, long fatigues,
Unusual fastings, and will bear no more
This medley of philosophy and war.
Within an hour they'll storm the senate-house.

SYPH. Meanwhile I'll draw up my Numidian troops
Within the square, to exercise their arms,
And, as I see occasion, favour thee.
I laugh to think how your unshaken Cato
Will look aghast, while unforeseen destruction
Pours in upon him thus from every side.
So, where our wide Numidian wastes extend,
Sudden, th' impetuous hurricanes descend,
Wheel through the air, in circling eddies play,
Tear up the sands, and sweep whole plains away.
The helpless traveller, with wild surprise, ⎫
Sees the dry desert all around him rise,   ⎬
And smother'd in the dusty whirlwind dies. ⎭

(Exeunt)

ACT III

MARCUS *and* PORTIUS

MARC. Thanks to my stars, I have not rang'd about
The wilds of life, ere I could find a friend;
Nature first pointed out my Portius to me,
And early taught me, by her secret force,
To love thy person, ere I knew thy merit;
Till, what was instinct, grew up into friendship.
POR. Marcus, the friendships of the world are oft
Confed'racies in vice, or leagues of pleasure;
Ours has severest virtue for its basis,
And such a friendship ends not but with life.
MARC. Portius, thou know'st my soul in all its weakness;
Then prithee spare me on its tender side,
Indulge me but in love, my other passions
Shall rise and fall by virtue's nicest rules.
POR. When love's well tim'd 'tis not a fault to love.
The strong, the brave, the virtuous, and the wise
Sink in the soft captivity together.
I would not urge thee to dismiss thy passion,
(I know 'twere vain) but to suppress its force,
Till better times may make it look more graceful.
MARC. Alas! thou talk'st like one who never felt
Th' impatient throbs and longings of a soul
That pants and reaches after distant good.
A lover does not live by vulgar time:

Believe me, Portius, in my Lucia's absence
Life hangs upon me, and becomes a burden;
And yet, when I behold the charming maid,
I'm ten times more undone; while hope, and fear,
And grief, and rage, and love, rise up at once,
And with variety of pain distract me.

POR.   What can thy Portius do to give thee help?

MARC.   Portius, thou oft enjoy'st the fair one's presence:
Then undertake my cause, and plead it to her
With all the strength and heats of eloquence
Fraternal love and friendship can inspire.
Tell her thy brother languishes to death,
And fades away, and withers in his bloom;
That he forgets his sleep, and loathes his food,
That youth, and health, and war, are joyless to him:
Describe his anxious days and restless nights,
And all the torments that thou seest me suffer.

POR.   Marcus, I beg thee give me not an office
That suits with me so ill. Thou know'st my temper.

MARC.   Wilt thou behold me sinking in my woes?
And wilt thou not reach out a friendly arm,
To raise me from amidst this plunge of sorrows?

POR.   Marcus, thou canst not ask what I'd refuse.
But here, believe me, I've a thousand reasons——

MARC.   I know thou'lt say my passion's out of season,
That Cato's great example and misfortunes
Should both conspire to drive it from my thoughts.
But what's all this to one who loves like me!
Oh, Portius, Portius, from my soul I wish
Thou didst but know thyself what 'tis to love!
Then wouldst thou pity and assist thy brother.

POR. (aside)   What should I do! If I disclose my passion,
Our friendship's at an end: if I conceal it,
The world will call me false to a friend and brother.

MARC.   But see where Lucia, at her wonted hour,
Amid the cool of yon high marble arch,
Enjoys the noon-day breeze! Observe her, Portius!
That face, that shape, those eyes, that heav'n of beauty!
Observe her well, and blame me, if thou canst.

POR.   She sees us, and advances——

MARC.   I'll withdraw,
And leave you for a while. Remember, Portius,
Thy brother's life depends upon thy tongue.   (Exit)

Enter LUCIA

LUC.   Did not I see your brother Marcus here?
Why did he fly the place, and shun my presence?
   POR.   Oh, Lucia, language is too faint to show
His rage of love; it preys upon his life;
He pines, he sickens, he despairs, he dies:
His passions and his virtues lie confus'd,
And mixt together in so wild a tumult,
That the whole man is quite disfigur'd in him.
Heav'ns! would one think 'twere possible for love
To make such ravage in a noble soul!
Oh Lucia, I'm distrest! my heart bleeds for him;
Ev'n now, while thus I stand blest in thy presence,
A secret damp of grief comes o'er my thoughts,
And I'm unhappy, though thou smil'st upon me.
   LUC.   How wilt thou guard thy honour in the shock
Of love and friendship! think betimes, my Portius,
Think how the nuptial tie, that might ensure
Our mutual bliss, would raise to such a height
Thy brother's griefs, as might perhaps destroy him.
   POR.   Alas, poor youth! what dost thou think, my Lucia?
His gen'rous, open, undesigning heart
Has begg'd his rival to solicit for him.
Then do not strike him dead with a denial,
But hold him up in life, and cheer his soul
With the faint glimm'ring of a doubtful hope:
Perhaps, when we have pass'd these gloomy hours,
And weather'd out the storm that beats upon us——
   LUC.   No, Portius, no! I see thy sister's tears,
Thy father's anguish, and thy brother's death,
In the pursuit of our ill-fated loves.
And, Portius, here I swear, to heav'n I swear,
To heav'n, and all the pow'rs that judge mankind,
Never to mix my plighted hands with thine,
While such a cloud of mischiefs hangs about us,
But to forget our loves, and drive thee out
From all my thoughts, as far——as I am able.
   POR.   What hast thou said! I'm thunderstruck!——recall
Those hasty words, or I am lost forever.
   LUC.   Has not the vow already pass'd my lips?
The Gods have heard it, and 'tis seal'd in heav'n.
May all the vengeance that was ever poured
On perjur'd heads o'erwhelm me, if I break it!

POR. (*after a pause*)   Fixt in astonishment, I gaze upon
            thee;
Like one just blasted by a stroke from heav'n,
Who pants for breath, and stiffens, yet alive,
In dreadful looks: A monument of wrath!
    LUC.   At length I've acted my severest part,
I feel the woman breaking in upon me,
And melt about my heart! my tears will flow.
But oh, I'll think no more! the hand of fate
Has torn thee from me, and I must forget thee.
    POR.   Hard-hearted, cruel maid!
    LUC.   Oh, stop those sounds,
Those killing sounds! Why dost thou frown upon me?
My blood runs cold, my heart forgets to heave,
And life itself goes out at thy displeasure.
The Gods forbid us to indulge our loves,
But oh! I cannot bear thy hate and live!
    POR.   Talk not of love, thou never knew'st its force.
I've been deluded, led into a dream
Of fancied bliss. O Lucia, cruel maid!
Thy dreadful vow, loaden with death, still sounds
In my stunn'd ears. What shall I say or do?
Quick, let us part! Perdition's in thy presence,
And horror dwells about thee!—Hah, she faints!
Wretch that I am! what has my rashness done!
Lucia, thou injur'd innocence! thou best
And loveli'st of thy sex! awake, my Lucia,
Or Portius rushes on his sword to join thee.
——Her imprecations reach not to the tomb,
They shut not out society in death.——
But, hah, she moves! Life wanders up and down
Through all her face, and lights up ev'ry charm.
    LUC.   O Portius, was this well! to frown on her
That lives upon thy smiles! to call in doubt
The faith of one expiring at thy feet,
That loves thee more than ever woman loved!
——What do I say? My half-recover'd sense
Forgets the vow in which my soul is bound.
Destruction stands betwixt us! We must part.
    POR.   Name not the word, my frighted thoughts run back,
And startle into madness at the sound.
    LUC.   What wouldst thou have me do? Consider well
The train of ills our love would draw behind it.

Think, Portius, think, thou seest thy dying brother
Stabb'd at his heart, and all besmear'd with blood,
Storming at heav'n and thee! Thy awful sire
Sternly demands the cause, th' accursed cause,
That robs him of his son! poor Marcia trembles,
Then tears her hair, and frantic in her griefs
Calls out on Lucia! What could Lucia answer?
Or how stand up in such a scene of sorrow?

    POR.   To my confusion and eternal grief,
I must approve the sentence that destroys me.
The mist that hung about my mind clears up;
And now, athwart the terrors that thy vow
Has planted round thee, thou appear'st more fair,
More amiable, and risest in thy charms.
Loveli'st of women! Heav'n is in thy soul,
Beauty and virtue shine for ever round thee,
Bright'ning each other! Thou art all divine!

    LUC.   Portius, no more! thy words shoot through my heart,
Melt my resolves, and turn me all to love.
Why are those tears of fondness in thy eyes?
Why heaves thy heart? Why swells thy soul with sorrow?
It softens me too much—— Farewell, my Portius,
Farewell, though death is in the word, forever!

    POR.   Stay, Lucia, stay! What dost thou say? Forever?

    LUC.   Have I not sworn? If, Portius, thy success
Must throw thy brother on his fate, farewell—
Oh, how shall I repeat the word?—forever!

    POR.   Thus o'er the dying lamp th' unsteady flame
Hangs quiv'ring on a point, leaps off by fits,
And falls again, as loath to quit its hold.
Thou must not go, my soul still hovers o'er thee,
And can't get loose.

    LUC.   If the firm Portius shake
To hear of parting, think what Lucia suffers!

    POR.   'Tis true; unruffled and serene I've met
The common accidents of life, but here
Such an unlook'd-for storm of ills falls on me,
It beats down all my strength. I cannot bear it.
We must not part.

    LUC.   What dost thou say? Not part?
Hast thou forgot the vow that I have made?
Are there not heav'ns, and Gods, and thunder o'er us!
——But see, thy brother Marcus bends this way!
I sicken at the sight. Once more, farewell,

Farewell, and know thou wrong'st me, if thou think'st
Ever was love, or ever grief, like mine.   (*Exit*)

Enter MARCUS

MARC.   Portius, what hopes? How stands she? Am I
   doom'd
To life or death?

POR.   What wouldst thou have me say?

MARC.   What means this pensive posture? thou appear'st
Like one amaz'd and terrified.

POR.   I've reason.

MARC.   Thy downcast looks and thy disorder'd thoughts
Tell me my fate. I ask not the success
My cause has found.

POR.   I'm griev'd I undertook it.

MARC.   What! does the barb'rous maid insult my heart,
My aching heart! and triumph in my pains?
That I could cast her from my thoughts for ever!

POR.   Away! you're too suspicious in your griefs;
Lucia, though sworn never to think of love,
Compassionates your pains, and pities you!

MARC.   Compassionates my pains, and pities me!
What is compassion when 'tis void of love!
Fool that I was to choose so cold a friend
To urge my cause! Compassionates my pains!
Prithee what art, what rhet'ric didst thou use
To gain this mighty boon? She pities me!
To one that asks the warm returns of love,
Compassion's cruelty, 'tis scorn, 'tis death——

POR.   Marcus, no more! have I deserv'd this treatment?

MARC.   What have I said! O Portius, oh, forgive me!
A soul exasp'rated in ills falls out
With ev'rything, it's friend, its self—— But, hah!
What means that shout, big with the sounds of war?
What new alarm?

POR.   A second, louder yet,
Swells in the winds, and comes more full upon us.

MARC.   Oh, for some glorious cause to fall in battle!
Lucia, thou hast undone me! thy disdain
Has broke my heart: 'tis death must give me ease.

POR.   Quick, let us hence; who knows if Cato's life
Stand sure? O Marcus, I am warm'd; my heart
Leaps at the trumpet's voice, and burns for glory.

(*Exeunt*)

Enter SEMPRONIUS *with the Leaders of the mutiny*

SEMP.   At length the winds are rais'd, the storm blows
          high,
Be it your care, my friends, to keep it up
In its full fury, and direct it right,
Till it has spent itself on Cato's head.
Meanwhile I'll herd among his friends, and seem
One of the number, that whate'er arrive,
My friends and fellow soldiers may be safe.   (*Exit*)
    FIRST LEAD.   We all are safe, Sempronius is our friend,
Sempronius is as brave a man as Cato.
But hark! he enters. Bear up boldly to him;
Be sure you beat him down, and bind him fast:
This day will end our toils, and give us rest;
Fear nothing, for Sempronius is our friend.

Enter CATO, SEMPRONIUS, LUCIUS, PORTIUS, *and* MARCUS

    CATO.   Where are these bold, intrepid sons of war,
That greatly turn their backs upon the foe,
And to their general send a brave defiance?
    SEMP. (*aside*)   Curse on their dastard souls, they stand
          astonish'd!
    CATO.   Perfidious men! and will you thus dishonour
Your past exploits, and sully all your wars?
Do you confess 'twas not a zeal for Rome,
Nor love of liberty, nor thirst of honour,
Drew you thus far; but hopes to share the spoil
Of conquer'd towns and plunder'd provinces?
Fired with such motives you do well to join
With Cato's foes, and follow Cæsar's banners.
Why did I 'scape the invenom'd aspic's rage,
And all the fiery monsters of the desert,
To see this day? Why could not Cato fall
Without your guilt? Behold, ungrateful men,
Behold my bosom naked to your swords,
And let the man that's injur'd strike the blow.
Which of you all suspects that he is wrong'd,
Or thinks he suffers greater ills than Cato?
Am I distinguish'd from you but by toils,
Superior toils, and heavier weight of cares?
Painful pre-eminence!
    SEMP. (*aside*)   By heav'ns, they droop!
Confusion to the villains! All is lost.

CATO.   Have you forgotten Libya's burning waste,
Its barren rocks, parch'd earth, and hills of sand,
Its tainted air, and all its broods of poison?
Who was the first to explore th' untrodden path,
When life was hazarded in every step?
Or, fainting in the long, laborious march,
When on the banks of an unlook'd-for stream
You sunk the river with repeated draughts,
Who was the last in all your host that thirsted?

SEMP.   If some penurious source by chance appear'd,
Scanty of waters, when you scoop'd it dry,
And offer'd the full helmet up to Cato,
Did not he dash th' untasted moisture from him?
Did not he lead you through the mid-day sun,
And clouds of dust? Did not his temples glow
In the same sultry winds and scorching heats?

CATO.   Hence, worthless men! Hence! and complain to
    Cæsar
You could not undergo the toils of war,
Nor bear the hardships that your leader bore.

LUC.   See, Cato, see th' unhappy men! they weep!
Fear, and remorse, and sorrow for their crime,
Appear in ev'ry look, and plead for mercy.

CATO.   Learn to be honest men, give up your leaders,
And pardon shall descend on all the rest.

SEMP.   Cato, commit these wretches to my care.
First, let 'em each be broken on the rack,
Then, with what life remains, impal'd and left
To writhe at leisure round the bloody stake.
There let 'em hang, and taint the southern wind.
The partners of their crime will learn obedience,
When they look up and see their fellow-traitors
Stuck on a fork, and black'ning in the sun.

LUC.   Sempronius, why, why wilt thou urge the fate
Of wretched men?

SEMP.   How! wouldst thou clear rebellion?
Lucius (good man) pities the poor offenders,
That would imbrue their hands in Cato's blood.

CATO.   Forbear, Sempronius! See they suffer death,
But in their deaths remember they are men.
Strain not the laws to make their tortures grievous.
Lucius, the base, degenerate age requires
Severity, and justice in its rigour;
This awes an impious, bold, offending world,

Commands obedience, and gives force to laws.
When by just vengeance guilty mortals perish,
The Gods behold their punishment with pleasure,
And lay th' uplifted thunderbolt aside.

SEMP.　Cato, I execute thy will with pleasure.

CATO.　Meanwhile we'll sacrifice to liberty.
Remember, O my friends, the laws, the rights,
The gen'rous plan of pow'r deliver'd down,
From age to age, by your renown'd forefathers,
(So dearly bought, the price of so much blood)
Oh, let it never perish in your hands!
But piously transmit it to your children.
Do thou, great liberty, inspire our souls,
And make our lives in thy possession happy,
Or our deaths glorious in thy just defence.

(Exeunt CATO, *etc.)*

SEMPRONIUS *and the Leaders of the mutiny*

FIRST LEAD.　Sempronius, you have acted like yourself,
One would have thought you had been half in earnest.

SEMP.　Villain, stand off! base, grov'lling, worthless
　　　wretches,
Mongrels in faction, poor faint-hearted traitors!

SECOND LEAD.　Nay, now you carry it too far, Sempronius:
Throw off the mask, there are none here but friends.

SEMP.　Know, villains, when such paltry slaves presume
To mix in treason, if the plot succeeds,
They're thrown neglected by: but if it fails,
They're sure to die like dogs, as you shall do.
——Here, take these factious monsters, drag 'em forth
To sudden death.

Enter Guards

FIRST LEAD.　Nay, since it comes to this——

SEMP.　Dispatch 'em quick, but first pluck out their
　　　tongues,
Lest with their dying breath they sow sedition.

(Exeunt Guards with the Leaders)

Enter SYPHAX

SYPH.　Our first design, my friend, has prov'd abortive;
Still there remains an after-game to play:
My troops are mounted; their Numidian steeds
Snuff up the wind, and long to scour the desert:
Let but Sempronius head us in our flight,

We'll force the gate where Marcus keeps his guard,
And hew down all that would oppose our passage.
A day will bring us into Cæsar's camp.

SEMP.   Confusion! I have fail'd of half my purpose:
Marcia, the charming Marcia's left behind!

SYPH.   How! will Sempronius turn a woman's slave?

SEMP.   Think not thy friend can ever feel the soft
Unmanly warmth and tenderness of love.
Syphax, I long to clasp that haughty maid,
And bend her stubborn virtue to my passion:
When I have gone thus far, I'd cast her off.

SYPH.   Well said! that's spoken like thyself, Sempronius.
What hinders then, but that thou find her out,
And hurry her away by manly force?

SEMP.   But how to gain admission? for access
Is given to none but Juba and her brothers.

SYPH.   Thou shalt have Juba's dress and Juba's guards:
The doors will open, when Numidia's prince
Seems to appear before the slaves that watch them.

SEMP.   Heav'ns, what a thought is there! Marcia's my own!
How will my bosom swell with anxious joy,
When I behold her struggling in my arms,
With glowing beauty and disorder'd charms,
While fear and anger, with alternate grace,
Pant in her breast, and vary in her face!
So Pluto, seiz'd of Proserpine, convey'd
To hell's tremendous gloom th' affrighted maid,
There grimly smil'd, pleas'd with the beauteous prize,
Nor envy'd Jove his sunshine and his skies.

ACT IV

LUCIA *and* MARCIA

LUC.   Now tell me, Marcia, tell me from thy soul,
If thou believ'st it possible for woman
To suffer greater ills than Lucia suffers?

MAR.   O Lucia, Lucia, might my big-swoln heart
Vent all its griefs, and give a loose to sorrow:
Marcia could answer thee in sighs, keep pace
With all thy woes, and count out tear for tear.

LUC.   I know thou'rt doom'd, alike, to be belov'd
By Juba and thy father's friend, Sempronius;
But which of these has power to charm like Portius?

MAR.   Still must I beg thee not to name Sempronius?

Lucia, I like not that loud, boist'rous man;
Juba to all the brav'ry of a hero
Adds softest love, and more than female sweetness;
Juba might make the proudest of our sex,
Any of womankind, but Marcia, happy.

    LUC.   And why not Marcia? come, you strive in vain
To hide your thoughts from one who knows too well
The inward glowings of a heart in love.

    MAR.   While Cato lives, his daughter has no right
To love or hate, but as his choice directs.

    LUC.   But should this father give you to Sempronius?

    MAR.   I dare not think he will: but if he should—
Why wilt thou add to all the griefs I suffer
Imaginary ills, and fancy'd tortures?
I hear the sound of feet! they march this way!
Let us retire, and try if we can drown
Each softer thought in sense of present danger.
When love once pleads admission to our hearts,
(In spite of all the virtue we can boast)
The woman that deliberates is lost.   (*Exeunt*)

Enter SEMPRONIUS, *dressed like* JUBA, *with Numidian Guards*

    SEMP.   The deer is lodg'd. I've track'd her to her covert.
Be sure you mind the word, and when I give it,
Rush in at once, and seize upon your prey.
Let not her cries or tears have force to move you.
——How will the young Numidian rave, to see
His mistress lost! If aught could glad my soul,
Beyond th' enjoyment of so bright a prize,
'Twould be to torture that young gay barbarian.
——But hark, what noise! Death to my hopes! 'tis he,
'Tis Juba's self! there is but one way left:
He must be murder'd, and a passage cut
Through those his guards.—— Hah, dastards, do you tremble!
Or act like men, or by yon azure heav'n——

Enter JUBA

    JUBA.   What do I see? Who's this that dares usurp
The guards and habits of Numidia's prince?

    SEMP.   One that was born to scourge thy arrogance,
Presumptuous youth!

    JUBA.   What can this mean? Sempronius!

    SEMP.   My sword shall answer thee. Have at thy heart.

JUBA.   Nay, then beware thy own, proud, barb'rous man!

            (SEMPRONIUS *falls. His Guards surrender*)

SEMP.   Curse on my stars! Am I then doom'd to fall
By a boy's hand? disfigur'd in a vile
Numidian dress, and for a worthless woman?
Gods, I'm distracted! This my close of life!
Oh, for a peal of thunder that would make
Earth, sea, and air, and heav'n, and Cato tremble!   (*Dies*)

JUBA.   With what a spring his furious soul broke loose,
And left the limbs still quiv'ring on the ground!
Hence let us carry off those slaves to Cato,
That we may there at length unravel all
This dark design, this mystery of fate.

            (*Exit* JUBA, *with Prisoners, etc.*)

Enter LUCIA *and* MARCIA

LUC.   Sure 'twas the clash of swords; my troubled heart
Is so cast down, and sunk amidst its sorrows,
It throbs with fear and aches at every sound.
O Marcia, should thy brothers for my sake!——
I die away with horror at the thought.

MAR.   See, Lucia, see! here's blood! here's blood and murder!
Hah, a Numidian! Heav'ns preserve the prince:
The face lies muffled up within the garment.
But hah! death to my sight! a diadem,
And purple robes! O Gods! 'tis he, 'tis he,
Juba, the loveliest youth that ever warm'd
A virgin's heart, Juba lies dead before us!

LUC.   Now, Marcia, now call up to thy assistance
Thy wonted strength and constancy of mind;
Thou canst not put it to a greater trial.

MAR.   Lucia, look there, and wonder at my patience.
Have I not cause to rave, and beat my breast,
To rend my heart with grief, and run distracted?

LUC.   What can I think or say to give thee comfort?

MAR.   Talk not of comfort, 'tis for lighter ills:
Behold a sight that strikes all comfort dead.

Enter JUBA, *listening*

I will indulge my sorrows, and give way
To all the pangs and fury of despair:
That man, that best of men, deserv'd it from me.

JUBA.   What do I hear! and was the false Sempronius
That best of men? Oh, had I fall'n like him,
And could have thus been mourn'd, I had been happy!

     LUC.   Here will I stand, companion in thy woes,
And help thee with my tears! when I behold
A loss like thine, I half forget my own.

     MAR.   'Tis not in fate to ease my tortur'd breast.
This empty world, to me a joyless desert,
Has nothing left to make poor Marcia happy.

     JUBA.   I'm on the rack! Was he so near her heart?

     MAR.   Oh, he was all made up of love and charms,
Whatever maid could wish or man admire:
Delight of ev'ry eye! When he appear'd,
A secret pleasure gladden'd all that saw him;
But when he talk'd, the proudest Roman blush'd
To hear his virtues, and old age grew wise.

     JUBA.   I shall run mad——

     MAR.   O Juba! Juba! Juba!

     JUBA.   What means that voice? did she not call on Juba?

     MAR.   Why do I think on what he was! he's dead!
He's dead, and never knew how much I lov'd him.
Lucia, who knows but his poor bleeding heart,
Amidst its agonies, remember'd Marcia,
And the last words he utter'd called me cruel!
Alas, he knew not, hapless youth, he knew not
Marcia's whole soul was full of love and Juba!

     JUBA.   Where am I! do I live! or am indeed
What Marcia thinks! all is Elysium round me!

     MAR.   Ye dear remains of the most lov'd of men!
Nor modesty nor virtue here forbid
A last embrace, while thus——

     JUBA.   (*throwing himself before her*)   See, Marcia, see,
The happy Juba lives! he lives to catch
That dear embrace, and to return it too
With mutual warmth and eagerness of love.

     MAR.   With pleasure and amaze, I stand transported!
Sure, 'tis a dream! Dead and alive at once!
If thou art Juba, who lies there?

     JUBA.   A wretch,
Disguis'd like Juba, on a curst design.
The tale is long, nor have I heard it out;
Thy father knows it all. I could not bear
To leave thee in the neighbourhood of death,
But flew, in all the haste of love, to find thee.

I found thee weeping, and confess, this once
Am rapt with joy to see my Marcia's tears.

    MAR.   I've been surpris'd in an unguarded hour,
But must not now go back: the love, that lay
Half smother'd in my breast, has broke through all
Its weak restraints, and burns in its full lustre;
I cannot, if I would, conceal it from thee.

    JUBA.   I'm lost in ecstasy! and dost thou love,
Thou charming maid?

    MAR.   And dost thou live to ask it?

    JUBA.   This, this is life indeed! Life worth preserving!
Such life as Juba never felt till now!

    MAR.   Believe me, Prince, before I thought thee dead,
I did not know myself how much I lov'd thee.

    JUBA.   Oh fortunate mistake!

    MAR.   O happy Marcia!

    JUBA.   My joy! my best belov'd! my only wish!
How shall I speak the transport of my soul!

    MAR.   Lucia, thy arm! oh, let me rest upon it!
The vital blood, that had forsook my heart,
Returns again in such tumultuous tides,
It quite o'ercomes me. Lead to my apartment.
O Prince! I blush to think what I have said,
But fate has wrested the confession from me;
Go on, and prosper in the paths of honour,
Thy virtue will excuse my passion for thee,
And make the Gods propitious to our love.

                      (*Exeunt* MARCIA *and* LUCIA)

    JUBA.   I am so blest, I fear 'tis all a dream.
Fortune, thou now hast made amends for all
Thy past unkindness. I absolve my stars.
What though Numidia add her conquer'd towns
And provinces to swell the victor's triumph?
Juba will never at his fate repine;
Let Cæsar have the world, if Marcia's mine.   (*Exit*)

               (*A march at a distance*)

              Enter CATO *and* LUCIUS

    LUC.   I stand astonish'd! What, the bold Sempronius!
That still broke foremost through the crowd of patriots,
As with a hurricane of zeal transported,
And virtuous ev'n to madness——

    CATO.   Trust me, Lucius,

Our civil discords have produc'd such crimes,
Such monstrous crimes, I am surpris'd at nothing.
O Lucius! I am sick of this bad world!
The daylight and the sun grow painful to me.

Enter PORTIUS

But see where Portius comes! What means this haste?
Why are thy looks thus changed?

　　POR.　　　　　　　　　　　My heart is griev'd.
I bring such news as will afflict my father.

　　CATO.　　Has Cæsar shed more Roman blood?

　　POR.　　　　　　　　　　　　　　Not so.
The traitor Syphax, as within the square
He exercis'd his troops, the signal given,
Flew off at once with his Numidian horse
To the south gate, where Marcus holds the watch.
I saw, and call'd to stop him, but in vain,
He toss'd his arm aloft, and proudly told me
He would not stay and perish like Sempronius.

　　CATO.　　Perfidious men! But haste, my son, and see
Thy brother Marcus acts a Roman's part.

　　　　　　　　　　　　　　　　(*Exit* PORTIUS)

Lucius, the torrent bears too hard upon me:
Justice gives way to force: the conquer'd world
Is Cæsar's: Cato has no business in it.

　　LUC.　　While pride, oppression, and injustice reign,
The world will still demand her Cato's presence.
In pity to mankind, submit to Cæsar,
And reconcile thy mighty soul to life.

　　CATO.　　Would Lucius have me live to swell the number
Of Cæsar's slaves, or by a base submission
Give up the cause of Rome, and own a tyrant?

　　LUC.　　The victor never will impose on Cato
Ungen'rous terms. His enemies confess
The virtues of humanity are Cæsar's.

　　CATO.　　Curse on his virtues! They've undone his country.
Such popular humanity is treason——
But see young Juba! the good youth appears
Full of the guilt of his perfidious subjects.

　　LUC.　　Alas, poor prince! his fate deserves compassion.

Enter JUBA

　　JUBA.　　I blush and am confounded to appear
Before thy presence, Cato.

CATO.   What's thy crime?

JUBA.   I'm a Numidian.

CATO.   And a brave one too.
Thou hast a Roman soul.

JUBA.   Hast thou not heard
Of my false countrymen?

CATO.   Alas, young Prince,
Falsehood and fraud shoot up in every soil,
The product of all climes——Rome has its Cæsars.

JUBA.   'Tis generous thus to comfort the distress'd.

CATO.   'Tis just to give applause where 'tis deserv'd;
Thy virtue, Prince, has stood the test of fortune,
Like purest gold, that, tortur'd in the furnace,
Comes out more bright, and brings forth all its weight

JUBA.   What shall I answer thee? my ravish'd heart
O'erflows with secret joy: I'd rather gain
Thy praise, O Cato, than Numidia's empire.

Enter PORTIUS *hastily*

POR.   Misfortune on misfortune! Grief on grief!
My brother Marcus——

CATO.   Hah! what has he done?
Has he forsook his post? has he giv'n way?
Did he look tamely on, and let 'em pass?

POR.   Scarce had I left my father, but I met him
Borne on the shields of his surviving soldiers,
Breathless and pale, and cover'd o'er with wounds.
Long, at the head of his few faithful friends,
He stood the shock of a whole host of foes,
Till, obstinately brave, and bent on death,
Oppress'd with multitudes, he greatly fell.

CATO.   I'm satisfy'd.

POR.   Nor did he fall before
His sword had pierc'd through the false heart of Syphax:
Yonder he lies. I saw the hoary traitor
Grin in the pangs of death, and bite the ground.

CATO.   Thanks to the Gods! my boy has done his duty.
——Portius, when I am dead, be sure thou place
His urn near mine.

POR.   Long may they keep asunder!

LUC.   O Cato, arm thy soul with all its patience;
See where the corpse of thy dead son approaches!
The citizens and senators, alarm'd,
Have gather'd round it, and attend it weeping.

CATO. (*meeting the corpse*)   Welcome, my son! Here lay
   him down, my friends,
Full in my sight, that I may view at leisure
The bloody corse, and count those glorious wounds.
How beautiful is death, when earn'd by virtue!
Who would not be that youth? what pity is it
That we can die but once to serve our country!
Why sits this sadness on your brows, my friends?
I should have blush'd if Cato's house had stood
Secure, and flourish'd in a civil war.
——Portius, behold thy brother, and remember
Thy life is not thy own, when Rome demands it.
   JUBA. (*aside*)   Was ever man like this!
   CATO.   Alas, my friends!
Why mourn you thus? Let not a private loss
Afflict your hearts. 'Tis Rome requires our tears.
The mistress of the world, the seat of empire,
The nurse of heroes, the delight of gods,
That humbled the proud tyrants of the earth,
And set the nations free, Rome is no more.
O liberty! O virtue! O my country!
   JUBA. (*aside*)   Behold that upright man! Rome fills his eyes
With tears, that flow'd not o'er his own dead son.
   CATO.   Whate'er the Roman virtue has subdu'd,
The sun's whole course, the day and year, are Cæsar's.
For him the self-devoted Decii died,
The Fabii fell, and the great Scipios conquer'd;
Ev'n Pompey fought for Cæsar. Oh, my friends!
How is the toil of fate, the work of ages,
The Roman empire fall'n! O curst ambition!
Fall'n into Cæsar's hands! Our great forefathers
Had left him nought to conquer but his country.
   JUBA.   While Cato lives, Cæsar will blush to see
Mankind enslav'd, and be asham'd of empire.
   CATO.   Cæsar asham'd! has not he seen Pharsalia?
   LUC.   Cato, 'tis time thou save thyself and us.
   CATO.   Lose not a thought on me. I'm out of danger.
Heav'n will not leave me in the victor's hand.
Cæsar shall never say, "I've conquered Cato."
But, oh! my friends, your safety fills my heart
With anxious thoughts: a thousand secret terrors
Rise in my soul: how shall I save my friends!
'Tis now, O Cæsar, I begin to fear thee.
   LUC.   Cæsar has mercy, if we ask it of him.

CATO.   Then ask it, I conjure you! let him know
Whate'er was done against him, Cato did it.
Add, if you please, that I request it of him,
That I myself, with tears, request it of him,
The virtue of my friends may pass unpunish'd.
    Juba, my heart is troubled for thy sake.
Should I advise thee to regain Numidia,
Or seek the conqueror?——
    JUBA.   If I forsake thee
Whilst I have life, may heav'n abandon Juba!
    CATO.   Thy virtues, Prince, if I foresee aright,
Will one day make thee great; at Rome, hereafter,
'Twill be no crime to have been Cato's friend.
    Portius, draw near! My son, thou oft has seen
Thy sire engag'd in a corrupted state,
Wrestling with vice and faction: now thou seest me
Spent, overpow'r'd, despairing of success;
Let me advise thee to retreat betimes
To thy paternal seat, the Sabine field,
Where the Great Censor toil'd with his own hands,
And all our frugal ancestors were bless'd
In humble virtues and a rural life.
There live retir'd, pray for the peace of Rome,
Content thyself to be obscurely good.
When vice prevails, and impious men bear sway,
The post of honour is a private station.
    POR.   I hope my father does not recommend
A life to Portius that he scorns himself.
    CATO.   Farewell, my friends! if there be any of you
That dares not trust the victor's clemency,
Know, there are ships prepar'd by my command,
(Their sails already op'ning to the winds)
That shall convey you to the wished-for port.
Is there aught else, my friends, I can do for you?
The conqueror draws near. Once more farewell!
If e'er we meet hereafter, we shall meet
In happier climes, and on a safer shore,
Where Cæsar never shall approach us more.
                    (*pointing to the body of his dead son*)
There the brave youth, with love of virtue fired,
Who greatly in his country's cause expired,
Shall know he conquer'd. The firm patriot there
(Who made the welfare of mankind his care)

Though still by faction, vice, and fortune cross'd,
Shall find the gen'rous labour was not lost.

ACT V

CATO *solus, sitting in a thoughtful posture: in his hand Plato's*
    book on the immortality of the soul. A drawn sword on
    the table by him

    CATO.   It must be so——Plato, thou reason'st well!—
Else whence this pleasing hope, this fond desire,
This longing after immortality?
Or whence this secret dread, and inward horror,
Of falling into nought? Why shrinks the soul
Back on herself, and startles at destruction?
'Tis the divinity that stirs within us;
'Tis heav'n itself, that points out an hereafter,
And intimates eternity to man.
Eternity! thou pleasing, dreadful thought!
Through what variety of untried being,
Through what new scenes and changes must we pass!
The wide, th' unbounded prospect, lies before me;
But shadows, clouds, and darkness, rest upon it.
Here will I hold. If there's a pow'r above us,
(And that there is all Nature cries aloud
Through all her works) he must delight in virtue:
And that which he delights in must be happy.
But when! or where!—— This world was made for Cæsar.
I'm weary of conjectures—— This must end 'em.
                          (laying his hand on his sword)
    Thus am I doubly arm'd: my death and life,
My bane and antidote, are both before me:
This in a moment brings me to an end;
But this informs me I shall never die.
The soul, secur'd in her existence, smiles
At the drawn dagger, and defies its point.
The stars shall fade away, the sun himself
Grow dim with age, and nature sink in years;
But thou shalt flourish in immortal youth,
Unhurt amidst the war of elements,
The wrecks of matter, and the crush of worlds.
    What means this heaviness that hangs upon me?
This lethargy that creeps through all my senses?
Nature, oppress'd and harass'd out with care,
Sinks down to rest. This once I'll favour her,

That my awaken'd soul may take her flight,
Renew'd in all her strength, and fresh with life,
An off'ring fit for heav'n. Let guilt or fear
Disturb man's rest: Cato knows neither of 'em,
Indiff'rent in his choice to sleep or die.

Enter PORTIUS

But, hah! how's this, my son? Why this intrusion?
Were not my orders that I would be private?
Why am I disobey'd?
    POR.   Alas, my father!
What means this sword? this instrument of death?
Let me convey it hence!
    CATO.   Rash youth, forbear!
    POR.   Oh, let the pray'rs, th' entreaties of your friends,
Their tears, their common danger, wrest it from you.
    CATO.   Wouldst thou betray me? Wouldst thou give me up
A slave, a captive, into Cæsar's hands?
Retire, and learn obedience to a father,
Or know, young man!——
    POR.   O Sir, forgive your son,
Whose grief hangs heavy on him! O my father!
How am I sure it is not the last time
I e'er shall call you so! Be not displeas'd,
Oh, be not angry with me whilst I weep,
And, in the anguish of my heart beseech you
To quit the dreadful purpose of your soul.
    CATO.   Thou hast been ever good and dutiful.
                               (*embracing him*)
Weep not, my son. All will be well again.
The righteous Gods, whom I have sought to please,
Will succor Cato, and preserve his children.
    POR.   Your words give comfort to my drooping heart.
    CATO.   Portius, thou may'st rely upon my conduct.
Thy father will not act what misbecomes him.
But go, my son, and see if aught be wanting
Among thy father's friends; see them embark'd;
And tell me if the winds and seas befriend them.
My soul is quite weigh'd down with care, and asks
The soft refreshment of a moment's sleep.   (*Exit*)
    POR.   My thoughts are more at ease, my heart revives.

Enter MARCIA

O Marcia, O my sister, still there's hope!

Our father will not cast away a life
So needful to us all, and to his country.
He is retir'd to rest, and seems to cherish
Thoughts full of peace. He has dispatch'd me hence
With orders that bespeak a mind compos'd,
And studious for the safety of his friends.
Marcia, take care that none disturb his slumbers.   (*Exit*)

MAR.   O ye immortal pow'rs, that guard the good,
Watch round his couch, and soften his repose,
Banish his sorrows, and becalm his soul
With easy dreams; remember all his virtues!
And show mankind that goodness is your care.

Enter LUCIA

LUC.   Where is your father, Marcia, where is Cato?
MAR.   Lucia, speak low, he is retir'd to rest.
Lucia, I feel a gently-dawning hope
Rise in my soul. We shall be happy still.
LUC.   Alas, I tremble when I think on Cato,
In every view, in every thought I tremble!
Cato is stern, and awful as a God;
He knows not how to wink at human frailty,
Or pardon weakness that he never felt.
MAR.   Though stern and awful to the foes of Rome,
He is all goodness, Lucia, always mild,
Compassionate, and gentle to his friends.
Fill'd with domestic tenderness, the best,
The kindest father! I have ever found him
Easy, and good, and bounteous to my wishes.
LUC.   'Tis his consent alone can make us blest.
Marcia, we both are equally involv'd
In the same intricate, perplex'd distress.
The cruel hand of fate, that has destroy'd
Thy brother Marcus, whom we both lament——
MAR.   And ever shall lament, unhappy youth!
LUC.   Has set my soul at large, and now I stand
Loose of my vow. But who knows Cato's thoughts?
Who knows how yet he may dispose of Portius,
Or how he has determin'd of thyself?
MAR.   Let him but live! commit the rest to heav'n.

Enter LUCIUS

LUCIUS.   Sweet are the slumbers of the virtuous man!
O Marcia, I have seen thy godlike father:

Some pow'r invisible supports his soul,
And bears it up in all its wonted greatness.
A kind refreshing sleep is fall'n upon him:
I saw him stretch'd at ease, his fancy lost
In pleasing dreams: as I drew near his couch,
He smil'd, and cried, "Cæsar, thou canst not hurt me."

    MAR.   His mind still labours with some dreadful thought.

    LUCIUS.   Lucia, why all this grief, these floods of sorrow?
Dry up thy tears, my child, we all are safe
While Cato lives—his presence will protect us.

Enter JUBA

    JUBA.   Lucius, the horsemen are return'd from viewing
The number, strength, and posture of our foes,
Who now encamp within a short hour's march.
On the high point of yon bright western tower
We ken them from afar; the setting sun
Plays on their shining arms and burnish'd helmets,
And covers all the field with gleams of fire.

    LUCIUS.   Marcia, 'tis time we should awake thy father.
Cæsar is still dispos'd to give us terms,
And waits at distance till he hears from Cato.

Enter PORTIUS

Portius, thy looks speak somewhat of importance.
What tidings dost thou bring? methinks I see
Unusual gladness sparkling in thy eyes.

    POR.   As I was hasting to the port, where now
My father's friends, impatient for a passage,
Accuse the ling'ring winds, a sail arriv'd
From Pompey's son, who through the realms of Spain
Calls out for vengeance on his father's death,
And rouses the whole nation up to arms.
Were Cato at their head, once more might Rome
Assert her rights and claim her liberty.
But hark! What means that groan! Oh, give me way,
And let me fly into my father's presence.   (*Exit*)

    LUCIUS.   Cato, amidst his slumbers, thinks on Rome,
And in the wild disorder of his soul
Mourns o'er his country—— Hah! a second groan!
Heav'n guard us all——

    MAR.   Alas, 'tis not the voice
Of one who sleeps! 'tis agonizing pain,
'Tis death is in that sound——

Re-enter PORTIUS

POR.   Oh sight of woe!
O Marcia, what we fear'd is come to pass!
Cato is fall'n upon his sword——

LUCIUS.   O Portius,
Hide all the horrors of thy mournful tale,
And let us guess the rest.

POR.   I've rais'd him up,
And plac'd him in his chair, where, pale and faint,
He gasps for breath, and, as his life flows from him,
Demands to see his friends. His weeping servants,
Obsequious to his orders, bear him hither.

(*The back scene opens and discovers* CATO)

MAR.   O heav'n, assist me in this dreadful hour
To pay the last sad duties to my father.

JUBA.   These are thy triumphs, thy exploits, O Cæsar!

LUCIUS.   Now is Rome fall'n indeed!

(CATO *brought forward in his chair*)

CATO.   Here set me down——
Portius, come near me—— Are my friends embark'd?
Can anything be thought of for their service?
Whilst I yet live, let me not live in vain.
——O Lucius, art thou here? Thou are too good!
Let this our friendship live between our children;
Make Portius happy in thy daughter Lucia.
Alas, poor man, he weeps!—— Marcia, my daughter——
Oh, bend me forward!—— Juba loves thee, Marcia.
A senator of Rome, while Rome surviv'd,
Would not have match'd his daughter with a king,
But Cæsar's arms have thrown down all distinction;
Whoe'er is brave and virtuous, is a Roman.——
I'm sick to death—— Oh, when shall I get loose
From this vain world, th' abode of guilt and sorrow!
——And yet methinks a beam of light breaks in
On my departing soul. Alas, I fear
I've been too hasty. O ye pow'rs that search
The heart of man, and weigh his inmost thoughts,
If I have done amiss, impute it not!——
The best may err, but you are good, and——oh!

(*Dies*)

LUCIUS.   There fled the greatest soul that ever warm'd
A Roman breast. O Cato! O my friend!
Thy will shall be religiously observ'd.

But let us bear this awful corpse to Cæsar,
And lay it in his sight, that it may stand
A fence betwixt us and the victor's wrath;
Cato, though dead, shall still protect his friends.
    From hence, let fierce contending nations know
What dire effects from civil discord flow.
'Tis this that shakes our country with alarms,
And gives up Rome a prey to Roman arms,
Produces fraud, and cruelty, and strife,
And robs the guilty world of Cato's life.

                                        (*Exeunt omnes*)

EPILOGUE

BY DR. GARTH

Spoken by LUCIA

What odd fantastic things we women do!   ⎫
Who would not listen when young lovers woo?   ⎬
But die a maid, yet have the choice of two!   ⎭
Ladies are often cruel to their cost;
To give you pain, themselves they punish most.
Vows of virginity should well be weigh'd;
Too oft they're cancell'd, though in convents made.
Would you revenge such rash resolves—you may: ⎫
Be spiteful—and believe the thing we say;   ⎬
We hate you when you're easily said nay.   ⎭
How needless, if you knew us, were your fears!
Let love have eyes, and beauty will have ears.
Our hearts are form'd, as you yourselves would choose,
Too proud to ask, too humble to refuse:
We give to merit, and to wealth we sell;
He sighs with most success that settles well.
The woes of wedlock with the joys we mix;
'Tis best repenting in a coach and six.
    Blame not our conduct, since we but pursue
Those lively lessons we have learn'd from you:
Your breasts no more the fire of beauty warms,
But wicked wealth usurps the power of charms;
What pains to get the gaudy thing you hate,
To swell in show, and be a wretch in state!
At plays you ogle, at the Ring you bow;

Ev'n churches are no sanctuaries now.
There, golden idols all your vows receive;
She is no goddess that has nought to give.
Oh, may once more the happy age appear,
When words were artless, and the thoughts sincere;
When gold and grandeur were unenvy'd things,
And courts less coveted than groves and springs.
Love then shall only mourn when truth complains,
And constancy feel transport in its chains.
Sighs with success their own soft anguish tell,
And eyes shall utter what the lips conceal:
Virtue again to its bright station climb,
And beauty fear no enemy but time.
The fair shall listen to desert alone,
And every Lucia find a Cato's son.

The Tragedy
of Jane Shore

Written in Imitation of Shakespeare's Style

BY NICHOLAS ROWE

*Coniunx ubi pristinus illi
Respondet curis.*   Virg.[1]

PROLOGUE

To-night, if you have brought your good old taste,
We'll treat you with a downright English feast.
A tale which, told long since in homely wise,
Hath never fail'd of melting gentle eyes.
Let no nice sir despise our hapless dame
Because recording ballads chaunt her name;
Those venerable ancient song-enditers
Soar'd many a pitch above our modern writers:
They caterwaul'd in no romantic ditty,
Sighing for Phyllis's, or Chloe's pity.

1 Where her former husband responds to her woes.

Justly they drew the fair, and spoke her plain,
And sung her by her Christ'an name—'twas Jane.
Our numbers may be more refin'd than those,
But what we've gain'd in verse, we've lost in prose.
Their words no shuffling, double-meaning knew,
Their speech was homely, but their hearts were true.
In such an age, immortal Shakespeare wrote,
By no quaint rules nor hampering critics taught;
With rough, majestic force he mov'd the heart,
And strength and nature made amends for art.
Our humble author does his steps pursue,
He owns he had the mighty bard in view,
And in these scenes has made it more his care
To rouse the passions than to charm the ear.
Yet for those gentle beaux who love the chime,
The ends of acts still jingle into rhyme.
The ladies, too, he hopes, will not complain,
Here are some subjects for a softer strain,
A nymph forsaken, and a perjur'd swain.
What most he fears is, lest the dames should frown,
The dames of wit and pleasure about town,
To see our picture drawn unlike their own.
But lest that error should provoke to fury
The hospitable hundreds of Old Drury,
He bid me say, in our Jane Shore's defence,
She dol'd about the charitable pence,
Built hospitals, turn'd saint, and died long since.
For her example, whatsoe'er we make it,
They have their choice to let alone or take it.
Though few, as I conceive, will think it meet
To weep so sorely for a sin so sweet:
Or mourn and mortify the pleasant sense,
To rise in tragedy two ages hence.

DRAMATIS PERSONÆ

Men:

DUKE OF GLOSTER
LORD HASTINGS
WILLIAM CATESBY
SIR RICHARD RATCLIFFE
BELLMOUR
DUMONT
EARL OF DERBY

Women:

ALICIA
JANE SHORE

Several Lords of the Council, Guards, and Attendants

SCENE: *London*

THE TRAGEDY OF JANE SHORE

ACT I

SCENE I

SCENE: *The Tower*

Enter the DUKE OF GLOSTER, SIR RICHARD
RATCLIFFE, AND CATESBY

GLOST.   Thus far success attends upon our councils,
And each event has answer'd to my wish;
The queen and all her upstart race are quell'd;
Dorset is banish'd and her brother Rivers
Ere this lies shorter by the head at Pomfret.
The nobles have with joint concurrence nam'd me
Protector of the realm. My brother's children,
Young Edward and the little York, are lodg'd
Here, safe within the Tower. How say you, Sirs,
Does not this business wear a lucky face?
The scepter and the golden wreath of royalty
Seem hung within my reach.
RATCL.   Then take 'em to you
And wear them long and worthily; you are
The last remaining male of princely York:
(For Edward's boys, and the state esteems not of 'em)
And therefore on your sovereignty and rule
The commonweal does her dependence make,
And leans upon your Highness' able hand.
CAT.   And yet to-morrow does the council meet
To fix a day for Edward's coronation:
Who can expound this riddle?
GLOST.   That can I.
Those lords are each one my approv'd, good friends,
Of special trust and nearness to my bosom;
And howsoever busy they may seem,
And diligent to bustle in the state,
Their zeal goes on no farther than we lead,
And at our bidding stays.

CAT.   Yet there is one,
And he amongst the foremost in his power,
Of whom I wish your highness were assur'd:
For me, perhaps it is my nature's fault,
I own, I doubt of his inclining, much.

GLOST.   I guess the man at whom your words would point:
Hastings——

CAT.   The same.

GLOST.   He bears me great good will.

CAT.   'Tis true, to you, as to the Lord Protector
And Gloster's duke, he bows with lowly service:
But were he bid to cry, "God save King Richard,"
Then tell me in what terms he would reply.
Believe me, I have prov'd the man and found him:
I know he bears a most religious reverence
To his dead master Edward's royal memory,
And whither that may lead him is most plain;
Yet more—one of that stubborn sort he is
Who, if they once grow fond of an opinion,
They call it honour, honesty, and faith,
And sooner part with life than let it go.

GLOST.   And yet, this tough, impracticable heart
Is govern'd by a dainty-finger'd girl;
Such flaws are found in the most worthy natures;
A laughing, toying, wheedling, whimpering she
Shall make him amble on a gossip's message,
And take the distaff with a hand as patient
As e'er did Hercules.

RATCL.   The fair Alicia,
Of noble birth and exquisite of feature,
Has held him long a vassal to her beauty.

CAT.   I fear he fails in his allegiance there;
Or my intelligence is false, or else
The dame has been too lavish of her feast,
And fed him 'till he loathes.

GLOST.   No more, he comes.

Enter LORD HASTINGS

L. HAST. Health and the happiness of many days
Attend upon your grace.

GLOST.   My good Lord Chamberlain!
We're much beholden to your gentle friendship.

L. HAST.   My Lord, I come an humble suitor to you.

GLOST.   In right good time. Speak out your pleasure freely.

L. HAST.   I am to move your Highness in behalf
Of Shore's unhappy wife.

GLOST.   Say you? of Shore?

L. HAST.   Once a bright star that held her place on high:
The first and fairest of our English dames
While royal Edward held the sovereign rule.
Now sunk in grief, and pining with despair,
Her waning form no longer shall incite
Envy in woman, or desire in man.
She never sees the sun but through her tears,
And wakes to sigh the livelong night away.

GLOST.   Marry! the times are badly chang'd with her
From Edward's days to these. Then all was jollity,
Feasting and mirth, light wantonness and laughter,
Piping and playing, minstrelsy and masquing,
Till life fled from us like an idle dream,
A show of mommery without a meaning.
My brother, rest and pardon to his soul,
Is gone to his account; for this his minion.
The revel-rout is done.—— But you were speaking
Concerning her.—— I have been told that you
Are frequent in your visitation to her.

L. HAST.   No farther, my good Lord, than friendly pity
And tender-hearted charity allow.

GLOST.   Go to. I did not mean to chide you for it.
For, sooth to say, I hold it noble in you
To cherish the distressed.— On with your tale.

L. HAST.   Thus is it, gracious Sir, that certain officers,
Using the warrant of your mighty name,
With insolence unjust and lawless power
Have seiz'd upon the lands which late she held
By grant from her great master Edward's bounty.

GLOST.   Somewhat of this, but slightly, have I heard;
And though some counsellors of forward zeal,
Some of most ceremonious sanctity
And bearded wisdom, often have provok'd
The hand of justice to fall heavy on her,
Yet still in kind compassion of her weakness
And tender memory of Edward's love,
I have withheld the merciless, stern law
From doing outrage on her helpless beauty.

L. HAST.   Good heav'n, who renders mercy back for mercy,
With open-handed bounty shall repay you:
This gentle deed shall fairly be set foremost,

To screen the wild escapes of lawless passion
And the long train of frailties flesh is heir to.

GLOST.   Thus far, the voice of pity pleaded only;
Our farther and more full extent of grace
Is given to your request. Let her attend,
And to ourself deliver up her griefs.
She shall be heard with patience, and each wrong
At full redress'd. But I have other news
Which much import us both, for still my fortunes
Go hand in hand with yours; our common foes,
The queen's relations, our new-fangl'd gentry,
Have fall'n their haughty crests.— That for your privacy.

                                     (*Exeunt*)

SCENE II

SCENE: *An apartment in* JANE SHORE's *house*

Enter BELLMOUR *and* DUMONT

BELL.   How she has liv'd, you've heard my tale already;
The rest, your own attendance in her family,
Where I have found the means this day to place you,
And nearer observation best will tell you.
See! with what sad and sober cheer she comes.

Enter JANE SHORE

Sure, or I read her visage much amiss,
Or grief besets her hard. Save you, fair lady,
The blessings of the cheerful morn be on you,
And greet your beauty with its opening sweets.

J. SH.   My gentle neighbour! your good wishes still
Pursue my hapless fortunes. Ah! good Bellmour!
How few, like thee, enquire the wretched out,
And court the offices of soft humanity;
Like thee, reserve their raiment for the naked,
Reach out their bread to feed the crying orphan,
Or mix their pitying tears with those that weep:
Thy praise deserves a better tongue than mine
To speak and bless thy name. Is this the gentleman
Whose friendly service you commended to me?

BELL.   Madam! it is.

J. SH. (*aside*)   A venerable aspect!
Age sits with decent grace upon his visage,
And worthily becomes his silver locks;

He wears the marks of many years well spent,
Of virtue, truth well tried, and wise experience;
A friend like this would suit my sorrows well.
(*To* DUMONT) Fortune, I fear me, Sir, has meant you ill,
Who pays your merit with that scanty pittance
Which my poor hand and humble roof can give.
But to supply those golden vantages
Which elsewhere you might find, expect to meet
A just regard and value for your worth,
The welcome of a friend, and the free partnership
Of all that little good the world allows me.

  DUM. You overrate me much, and all my answer
Must be my future truth; let that speak for me
And make up my deserving.

  J. SH.   Are you of England?

  DUM. No, gracious lady, Flanders claims my birth;
At Antwerp has my constant biding been,
Where sometimes I have known more plenteous days
Than those which now my failing age affords.

  J. SH. Alas! at Antwerp! (*weeping*)—Oh, forgive my tears!
They fall for my offences—and must fall
Long, long ere they shall wash my stains away.
You knew perhaps—oh grief! oh shame!—my husband.

  DUM. I knew him well—but stay this flood of anguish;
The senseless grave feels not your pious sorrows:
Three years and more are past since I was bid,
With many of our common friends, to wait him
To his last peaceful mansion. I attended,
Sprinkled his clay-cold corse with holy drops,
According to our church's reverend rite,
And saw him laid, in hallow'd ground, to rest.

  J. SH. Oh! that my soul had known no joy but him;
That I had liv'd within his guiltless arms,
And dying slept in innocence beside him!
But now his honest dust abhors the fellowship,
And scorns to mix with mine.

Enter a Servant

  SERV.   The lady Alicia
Attends your leisure.

  J. SH.   Say I wish to see her.

               (*Exit Servant*)

Please, gentle Sir, one moment to retire,
I'll wait you on the instant, and inform you

Of each unhappy circumstance in which
Your friendly aid and counsel much may stead me.

(*Exeunt* BELLMOUR *and* DUMONT)

Enter ALICIA

ALIC.   Still, my fair friend, still shall I find you thus,
Still shall these sighs heave after one another,
These trickling drops chase one another still,
As if the posting messengers of grief
Could overtake the hours fled far away,
And make old time come back?

J. SH.   No, my Alicia,
Heaven and its saints be witness to my thoughts,
There is no hour of all my life o'erpast,
That I could wish should take its turn again.

ALIC.   And yet some of those days my friend has known,
Some of those years might pass for golden ones,
At least if womankind can judge of happiness.
What could we wish, we who delight in empire,
Whose beauty is our sovereign good, and gives us
Our reasons to rebel and power to reign,
What could we more than to behold a monarch,
Lovely, renown'd, a conqueror, and young,
Bound in our chains, and sighing at our feet?

J. SH.   'Tis true, the royal Edward was a wonder,
The goodly pride of all our English youth;
He was the very joy of all that saw him,
Form'd to delight, to love, and to persuade.
Impassive spirits and angelic natures
Might have been charm'd, like yielding human weakness,
Stoop'd from their heav'n and listen'd to his talking.
But what had I to do with kings and courts?
My humble lot had cast me far beneath him;
And that he was the first of all mankind,
The bravest and most lovely, was my curse.

ALIC.   Sure, something more than fortune join'd your
           loves;
Nor could his greatness, and his gracious form,
Be elsewhere match'd so well, as to the sweetness
And beauty of my friend.

J. SH.   Name him no more:
He was the bane and ruin of my peace.
This anguish and these tears, these are the legacies
His fatal love has left me. Thou wilt see me,

Believe me, my Alicia, thou wilt see me,
Ere yet a few short days pass o'er my head,
Abandon'd to the very utmost wretchedness.
The hand of pow'r has seiz'd almost the whole
Of what was left for needy life's support;
Shortly thou wilt behold me poor, and kneeling
Before thy charitable door for bread.

    ALIC. Joy of my life, my dearest Shore, forbear
To wound my heart with thy foreboding sorrows.
Raise thy sad soul to better hopes than these,
Lift up thy eyes and let 'em shine once more,
Bright as the morning sun above the mists.
Exert thy charms, seek out the stern Protector,
And soothe his savage temper with thy beauty:
Spite of his deadly, unrelenting nature,
He shall be mov'd to pity and redress thee.

    J. SH. My form, alas! has long forgot to please;
The scene of beauty and delight is changed,
No roses bloom upon my fading cheek,
Nor laughing graces wanton in my eyes;
But haggard grief, lean-looking, sallow care,
And pining discontent, a rueful train,
Dwell on my brow, all hideous and forlorn.
One only shadow of a hope is left me;
The noble-minded Hastings, of his goodness,
Has kindly underta'en to be my advocate,
And move my humble suit to angry Gloster.

    ALIC. Does Hastings undertake to plead your cause?
But wherefore should he not? Hastings has eyes;
The gentle lord has a right tender heart,
Melting and easy, yielding to impression,
And catching the soft flame from each new beauty.
But yours shall charm him long.

    J. SH.   Away, you flatterer!
Nor charge his generous meaning with a weakness
Which his great soul and virtue must disdain.
Too much of love thy hapless friend has prov'd,
Too many giddy, foolish hours are gone,
And in fantastic measures danc'd away:
May the remaining few know only friendship.
So thou, my dearest, truest, best Alicia,
Vouchsafe to lodge me in thy gentle heart
A partner there; I will give up mankind,
Forget the transports of encreasing passion,

And all the pangs we feel for its decay.

    ALIC. *(embracing)* Live! live and reign forever in my
      bosom,
Safe and unrivall'd there possess thy own;
And you, ye brightest of the stars above,
Ye saints that once were women here below,
Be witness of the truth, the holy friendship,
Which here to this my other self I vow.
If I not hold her nearer to my soul,
Than ev'ry other joy the world can give,
Let poverty, deformity and shame,
Distraction and despair seize me on earth,
Let not my faithless ghost have peace hereafter,
Nor taste the bliss of your celestial fellowship.

    J. SH.   Yes, thou art true, and only thou art true;
Therefore these jewels, once the lavish bounty
Of royal Edward's love, I trust to thee;   *(giving a casket)*
Receive this all that I can call my own,
And let it rest unknown and safe with thee:
That if the state's injustice should oppress me,
Strip me of all, and turn me out a wanderer,
My wretchedness may find relief from thee,
And shelter from the storm.

    ALIC.   My all is thine;
One common hazard shall attend us both,
And both be fortunate or both be wretched:
But let thy fearful, doubting heart be still,
The saints and angels have thee in their charge,
And all things shall be well. Think not, the good,
The gentle deeds of mercy thou hast done
Shall die forgotten all; the poor, the pris'ner,
The fatherless, the friendless, and the widow,
Who daily own the bounty of thy hand,
Shall cry to heav'n, and pull a blessing on thee;
Ev'n man, the merciless insulter, man,
Man, who rejoices in our sex's weakness,
Shall pity thee, and with unwonted goodness,
Forget thy failings and record thy praise.

    J. SH.   Why should I think that man will do for me
What yet he never did for wretches like me?
Mark by what partial justice we are judg'd;
Such is the fate unhappy women find,
And such the curse entail'd upon our kind,
That man, the lawless libertine, may rove

Free and unquestion'd through the wilds of love;
While woman, sense and nature's easy fool,
If poor, weak woman swerve from virtue's rule,
If, strongly charm'd, she leave the thorny way,
And in the softer paths of pleasure stray;
Ruin ensues, reproach and endless shame,
And one false step entirely damns her fame.
In vain with tears the loss she may deplore, ⎫
In vain look back to what she was before; ⎬
She sets, like stars that fall, to rise no more. ⎭

(Exeunt)

ACT II

Scene continues

Enter ALICIA

(Speaking to JANE SHORE as entering)

ALIC.   No farther, gentle friend; good angels guard you,
And spread their gracious wings about your slumbers.
  The drowsy night grows on the world, and now
The busy craftsman and o'er-labour'd hind
Forget the travail of the day in sleep:
Care only wakes, and moping Pensiveness;
With meagre, discontented looks they sit,
And watch the wasting of the midnight taper.
Such vigils must I keep, so wakes my soul,
Restless and self-tormented! O false Hastings!
Thou hast destroy'd my peace.   (knocking without)
                    What noise is that?
What visitor is this who with bold freedom
Breaks in upon the peaceful night and rest
With such a rude approach?

Enter a Servant

SERV.   One from the court,
Lord Hastings (as I think) demands my lady.
  ALIC.   Hastings! Be still my heart, and try to meet him
With his own arts: with falsehood.—— But he comes.

Enter LORD HASTINGS. Speaks to a Servant at entering

L. HAST.   Dismiss my train and wait alone without.
(aside)   Alicia here! Unfortunate encounter!
But be it as it may.

ALIC.   When humbly, thus,
The great descend to visit the afflicted,
When thus unmindful of their rest, they come
To soothe the sorrows of the midnight mourner;
Comfort comes with them, like the golden sun,
Dispels the sullen shades with her sweet influence,
And cheers the melchancholy house of care.

    L. HAST.   'Tis true, I would not overrate a courtesy,
Nor let the coldness of delay hang on it
To nip and blast its favour like a frost;
But rather chose, at this late hour, to come,
That your fair friend may know I have prevail'd:
The Lord Protector has receiv'd her suit,
And means to show her grace.

    ALIC.   My friend! my Lord!

    L. HAST.   Yes, lady, yours: none has a right more ample
To task my power than you.

    ALIC.   I want the words
To pay you back a compliment so courtly;
But my heart guesses at the friendly meaning,
And wo' not die your debtor.

    L. HAST.   'Tis well, madam.
But I would see your friend.

    ALIC.   O thou false lord!
I would be mistress of my heaving heart,
Stifle this rising rage, and learn from thee
To dress my face in easy, dull indifference:
But 'two'not be; my wrongs will tear their way,
And rush at once upon thee.

    L. HAST.   Are you wise!
Have you the use of reason? Do you wake?
What means this raving! this transporting passion?

    ALIC.   O thou cool traitor! thou insulting tyrant!
Dost thou behold my poor distracted heart,
Thus rent with agonizing love and rage,
And ask me what it means? Art thou not false?
Am I not scorn'd, forsaken, and abandon'd,
Left, like a common wretch, to shame and infamy;
Giv'n up to be the sport of villains' tongues,
Of laughing parasites, and lewd buffoons;
And all because my soul has doted on thee
With love, with truth, and tenderness unutterable?

    L. HAST.   Are these the proofs of tenderness and love?
These endless quarrels, discontents, and jealousies,

These never-ceasing wailings and complainings,
These furious starts, these whirlwinds of the soul,
Which every other moment rise to madness?

    ALIC.   What proof, alas! have I not given of love?
What have I not abandon'd to thy arms?
Have I not set at nought my noble birth,
A spotless fame and an unblemish'd race,
The peace of innocence and pride of virtue?
My prodigality has giv'n thee all,
And now I have nothing left me to bestow
You hate the wretched bankrupt you have made.

    L. HAST.   Why am I thus pursu'd from place to place,
Kept in the view, and cross'd at every turn?
In vain I fly, and like a hunted deer
Scud o'er the lawns and hasten to the covert;
Ere I can reach my safety, you o'ertake me
With the swift malice of some keen reproach,
And drive the winged shaft deep in my heart.

    ALIC.   Hither you fly, and here you seek repose;
Spite of the poor deceit, your arts are known,
Your pious, charitable, midnight visits.

    L. HAST.   If you are wise and prize your peace of mind,
Yet take the friendly counsel of my love;
Believe me true, nor listen to your jealousy;
Let not that devil which undoes your sex,
That cursed curiosity, seduce you
To hunt for needless secrets which, neglected,
Shall never hurt your quiet, but once known,
Shall sit upon your heart, pinch it with pain,
And banish the sweet sleep forever from you.
Go to!—— be yet advised,——

    ALIC.   Dost thou in scorn
Preach patience to my rage? and bid me tamely
Sit like a poor, contented idiot down,
Nor dare to think thou'st wrong'd me? Ruin seize thee,
And swift perdition overtake thy treachery!
Have I the least remaining cause to doubt?
Hast thou endeavour'd once to hide thy falsehood?
To hide it, might have spoke some little tenderness,
And shown thee half unwilling to undo me.
But thou disdain'st the weakness of humanity;
Thy words and all thy actions have confess'd it;
Ev'n now thy eyes avow it, now they speak,
And insolently own the glorious villainy.

L. HAST.   Well then, I own my heart has broke your chains.
Patient I bore the painful bondage long:
At length my generous love disdains your tyranny;
The bitterness and stings of taunting jealousy,
Vexatious days, and jarring joyless nights,
Have driv'n him forth to seek some safer shelter,
Where he may rest his weary wings in peace.

ALIC.   You triumph! do! And with gigantic pride
Defy impending vengeance. Heav'n shall wink;
No more his arm shall roll the dreadful thunder,
Nor send his light'nings forth. No more his justice
Shall visit the presuming sons of men,
But perjury, like thine, shall dwell in safety.

L. HAST.   Whate'er my fate decrees for me hereafter,
Be present to me now, my better angel!
Preserve me from the storm which threatens now,
And if I have beyond atonement sinn'd,
Let any other kind of plague o'ertake me,
So I escape the fury of that tongue.

ALIC.   Thy pray'r is heard—I go—but know, proud lord,
Howe'er thou scorn'st the weakness of my sex,
This feeble hand may find the means to reach thee,
Howe'er sublime in pow'r and greatness plac'd,
With royal favour guarded round and grac'd;
On eagle's wings my rage shall urge her flight,
And hurl thee headlong from thy topmost height;
Then like thy fate, superior will I sit,
And view thee fall'n and grov'ling at my feet;
See thy last breath with indignation go,
And tread thee sinking to the shades below.

(*Exit* ALICIA)

L. HAST.   How fierce a fiend is passion. With what wildness,
What tyranny untam'd, it reigns in woman.
Unhappy sex! whose easy, yielding temper
Gives way to every appetite alike;
Each gust of inclination, uncontroll'd,
Sweeps through their souls and sets 'em in an uproar;
Each motion of the heart rises to fury,
And love in their weak bosoms is a rage
As terrible as hate and as destructive.
So the wind roars o'er the wide fenceless ocean,
And heaves the billows of the boiling deep,
Alike from north, from south, from east, from west;
With equal force the tempest blows by turns

From every corner of the seaman's compass.
But soft ye now—for here comes one disclaims
Strife and her wrangling train. Of equal elements,
Without one jarring atom, was she form'd,
And gentleness and joy make up her being.

Enter JANE SHORE

Forgive me, fair one, if officious friendship
Intrudes on your repose, and comes thus late
To greet you with the tidings of success.
The princely Gloster has vouchsaf'd you hearing;
To-morrow he expects you at the court.
There plead your cause with never failing beauty,
Speak all your griefs and find a full redress.

J. SH. (*kneeling*)   Thus humbly let your lowly servant bend,
Thus let me bow my grateful knee to earth,
And bless your noble nature for this goodness.

L. HAST.   Rise, gentle dame; you wrong my meaning much;
Think me not guilty of a thought so vain,
To sell my courtesy for thanks like these.

J. SH.   'Tis true, your bounty is beyond my speaking;
But though my mouth be dumb, my heart shall thank you;
And when it melts before the throne of mercy,
Mourning and bleeding for my past offences,
My fervent soul shall breathe one prayer for you,
If prayers of such a wretch are heard on high,
That heav'n will pay you back when most you need
The grace and goodness you have shown to me.

L. HAST.   If there be aught of merit in my service,
Impute it there where most 'tis due, to love;
Be kind, my gentle mistress, to my wishes,
And satisfy my panting heart with beauty.

J. SH.   Alas! my Lord——

L. HAST.   Why bend thy eyes to earth?
Wherefore these looks of heaviness and sorrow?
Why breathes that sigh, my love? And wherefore falls
This trickling show'r of tears to stain thy sweetness?

J. SH.   If pity dwells within your noble breast
(As sure it does) oh speak not to me thus!

L. HAST.   Can I behold thee and not speak of love!
Ev'n now, thus sadly as thou stand'st before me,
Thus desolate, dejected, and forlorn,
Thy softness steals upon my yielding senses
Till my soul faints and sickens with desire;

How canst thou give this motion to my heart,
And bid my tongue be still?

    J. SH.   Cast round your eyes
Upon the highborn beauties of the court;
Behold, like opening roses, where they bloom,
Sweet to the sense, unsully'd all, and spotless;
There choose some worthy partner of your heart,
To fill your arms and bless your virtuous bed,
Nor turn your eyes this way, where sin and misery,
Like loathsome weeds, have overrun the soil,
And the destroyer shame has laid all waste.

    L. HAST.   What means this peevish, this fantastic change?
Where is thy wonted pleasantness of face?
Thy wonted graces, and thy dimpled smiles?
Where hast thou lost thy wit and sportive mirth,
That cheerful heart, which used to dance forever,
And cast a day of gladness all around thee?

    J. SH.   Yes, I will own I merit the reproach,
And for those foolish days of wanton pride
My soul is justly humbled to the dust:
All tongues, like yours, are licens'd to upbraid me,
Still to repeat my guilt, to urge my infamy,
And treat me like that abject thing I have been.
Yet let the saints be witness to this truth,
That now, though late, I look with horror back,
That I detest my wretched self, and curse
My past polluted life. All-judging heav'n,
Who knows my crimes, has seen my sorrow for them.

    L. HAST.   No more of this dull stuff. 'Tis time enough
To whine and mortify thyself with penance
When the decaying sense is pall'd with pleasure,
And weary nature tires in her last stage.
Then weep and tell thy beads, when alt'ring rheums
Have stain'd the lustre of thy starry eyes,
And failing palsies shake thy wither'd hand.
The present moments claim more generous use;
Thy beauty, night, and solitude reproach me
For having talk'd thus long.—— Come, let me press thee, (*laying hold on her*)
Pant on thy bosom, sink into thy arms,
And lose myself in the luxurious fold.

    J. SH.   Never! By those chaste lights above, I swear,
My soul shall never know pollution more!
(*kneeling*)   Forbear, my Lord! Here let me rather die;

Let quick destruction overtake me here,
And end my sorrows and my shame forever.

L. HAST. Away with this perverseness—— 'Tis too much.
(*striving*) Nay, if you strive—'tis monstrous affectation.

J. SH. Retire! I beg you, leave me——

L. HAST. Thus to coy it!——
With one who knows you, too.

J. SH. For mercy's sake——

L. HAST. Ungrateful woman! is it thus you pay
My services?

J. SH. Abandon me to ruin
Rather than urge me——

L. HAST. (*pulling her*) This way to your chamber;
There if you struggle——

J. SH. (*crying out*) Help! O gracious heaven!
Help! Save me! Help!

Enter DUMONT; *he interposes*

DUM. My Lord! for honour's sake——

L. HAST. Hah! What art thou? Begone!

DUM. My duty calls me
To my attendance on my mistress here.

J. SH. For pity let me go!

L. HAST. Avaunt! base groom——
At distance wait and know thy office better.

DUM. Forgo your hold, my Lord! 'tis most unmanly,
This violence——

L. HAST. Avoid the room this moment,
Or I will tread thy soul out.

DUM. No, my Lord——
The common ties of manhood call me now,
And bid me thus stand up in the defence
Of an oppress'd, unhappy, helpless woman.

L. HAST. And dost thou know me? Slave!

DUM. Yes, thou proud
lord!
I know thee well, know thee with each advantage
Which wealth, or power, or noble birth can give thee.
I know thee, too, for one who stains those honours,
And blots a long illustrious line of ancestry,
By poorly daring thus to wrong a woman.

L. HAST. 'Tis wondrous well! I see, my saint-like dame,
You stand provided of your braves and ruffians
To man your cause, and bluster in your brothel.

DUM.   Take back the foul reproach, unmanner'd railer,
Nor urge my rage too far, lest thou shouldst find
I have as daring spirits in my blood
As thou or any of thy race e'er boasted;
And though no gaudy titles grac'd my birth,
Titles, the servile courtier's lean reward,
Sometimes the pay of virtue, but more oft
The hire which greatness gives to slaves and sycophants,
Yet heav'n, that made me honest, made me more
Than ever king did when he made a lord.

    L. HAST.   Insolent villain! Henceforth let this teach thee
       (*draws and strikes him*)
The distance 'twixt a peasant and a prince.

    DUM.   Nay then, my Lord! (*drawing*) Learn you by this
       how well
An arm resolv'd can guard its master's life.

                       (*They fight*)

    J. SH.   Oh, my distracting fears! hold, for sweet heav'n!

    (*They fight*; DUMONT *disarms* LORD HASTINGS.)

    L. HAST.   Confusion! baffled by a base-born hind!

    DUM.   Now, haughty sir, where is our difference now?
Your life is in my hand, and did not honour,
The gentleness of blood, and inborn virtue
(Howe'er unworthy I may seem to you)
Plead in my bosom, I should take the forfeit.
But wear your sword again, and know, a lord
Oppos'd against a man is but a man.

    L. HAST.   Curse on my failing hand! Your better fortune
Has giv'n you vantage o'er me; but perhaps
Your triumph may be bought with dear repentance.

                       (*Exit*)

    J. SH.   Alas! What have you done! Know you the pow'r,
The mightiness that waits upon this lord?

    DUM.   Fear not, my worthiest mistress; 'tis a cause
In which heav'n's guard shall wait you. Oh, pursue,
Pursue the sacred counsels of your soul
Which urge you on to virtue; let not danger,
Nor the encumb'ring world, make faint your purpose!
Assisting angels shall conduct your steps,
Bring you to bliss, and crown your end with peace.

    J. SH.   Oh, that my head were laid, my sad eyes clos'd,
And my cold corse wound in my shroud to rest;
My painful heart will never cease to beat,

Will never know a moment's peace till then.

   DUM.   Would you be happy? Leave this fatal place,
Fly from the court's pernicious neighbourhood;
Where innocence is sham'd, and blushing modesty
Is made the scorner's jest; where hate, deceit,
And deadly ruin, wear the masks of beauty,
And draw deluded fools with shows of pleasure.

   J. SH.   Where should I fly, thus helpless and forlorn,
Of friends and all the means of life bereft?

   DUM.   Bellmour, whose friendly care still wakes to serve
     you,
Has found you out a little peaceful refuge.
Far from the court and the tumultuous city,
Within an ancient forest's ample verge,
There stands a lonely but a healthful dwelling,
Built for convenience and the use of life:
Around it fallows, meads, and pastures fair,
A little garden, and a limpid brook,
By nature's own contrivance, seem dispos'd;
No neighbours but a few poor simple clowns,
Honest and true, with a well-meaning priest.
No faction, or domestic fury's rage,
Did e'er disturb the quiet of that place
When the contending nobles shook the land
With York and Lancaster's disputed sway.
Your virtue, there, may find a safe retreat
From the insulting pow'rs of wicked greatness.

   J. SH.   Can there be so much happiness in store!
A cell like that is all my hopes aspire to.
Haste then, and thither let us wing our flight,
Ere the clouds gather and the wintry sky
Descends in storms to intercept our passage.

   DUM.   Will you then go? You glad my very soul.
Banish your fears, cast all your cares on me;
Plenty, and ease, and peace of mind shall wait you,
And make your latter days of life most happy.
O lady! But I must not, cannot tell you
How anxious I have been for all your dangers,
And how my heart rejoices at your safety.
So when the spring renews the flow'ry field,
And warns the pregnant nightingale to build,
She seeks the safest shelter of the wood,
Where she may trust her little tuneful brood,
Where no rude swains her shady cell may know,

No serpents climb, nor blasting winds may blow;
Fond of the chosen place, she views it o'er,
Sits there and wanders through the grove no more.
Warbling she charms it each returning night,
And loves it with a mother's dear delight.   (*Exeunt*)

ACT III

SCENE: *The Court*

Enter ALICIA *with a paper*

ALIC.   This paper to the great Protector's hand
With care and secrecy must be convey'd;
His bold ambition now avows its aim,
To pluck the crown from Edward's infant brow
And fix it on his own. I know he holds
My faithless Hastings adverse to his hopes
And much devoted to the orphan king;
On that I build. This paper meets his doubts,
And marks my hated rival as the cause
Of Hastings' zeal for his dead master's sons.
O jealousy! Thou bane of pleasing friendship,
Thou worst invader of our tender bosoms;
How does thy rancour poison all our softness,
And turn our gentle natures into bitterness!
     See where she comes! Once my heart's dearest blessing,
Now my chang'd eyes are blasted with her beauty,
Loathe that known face, and sicken to behold her.

Enter JANE SHORE

J. SH.   Now whither shall I fly to find relief?
What charitable hand will aid me now?
Will stay my failing steps, support my ruins,
And heal my wounded mind with balmy comfort?
Oh, my Alicia!
ALIC.   What new grief is this?
What unforeseen misfortune has surpris'd thee,
That racks thy tender heart thus?
J. SH.   Oh! Dumont!
ALIC.   Say! What of him?
J. SH.   That friendly, honest man,
Whom Bellmour brought of late to my assistance;
On whose kind cares, whose diligence and faith,

My surest trust was built, this very morn
Was seiz'd on by the cruel hand of pow'r,
Forc'd from my house, and borne away to prison.

    ALIC.   To prison, said you! Can you guess the cause?

    J. SH.   Too well, I fear. His bold defence of me
Has drawn the vengeance of Lord Hastings on him.

    ALIC.   Lord Hastings! Ha!

    J. SH.   Some fitter time must tell thee
The tale of my hard hap. Upon the present
Hang all my poor, my last remaining hopes.
Within this paper is my suit contain'd;
Here, as the princely Gloster passes forth,
I wait to give it on my humble knees,
And move him for redress.

           (*She gives the paper to* ALICIA, *who opens and seems
              to read it.*)

    ALIC. (*aside*)   Now for a wile
To sting my thoughtless rival to the heart,
To blast her fatal beauties, and divide her
Forever from my perjur'd Hastings' eyes.
The wanderer may then look back to me,
And turn to his forsaken home again.

                      (*pulling out the other paper*)
Their fashions are the same; it cannot fail.

    J. SH.   But see, the great Protector comes this way,
Attended by a train of waiting courtiers.
Give me the paper, friend.

    ALIC. (*aside*)   For love and vengeance!

                  (*She gives her the other paper*)

Enter the DUKE OF GLOSTER, SIR RICHARD RATCLIFFE, CATESBY,
    Courtiers, and other Attendants

    J. SH. (*kneeling*)   O noble Gloster, turn thy gracious eye,
Incline thy pitying ear to my complaint!
A poor, undone, forsaken, helpless woman
Intreats a little bread for charity,
To feed her wants and save her life from perishing.

    GLOST. (*receiving the paper, and raising her*) Arise, fair
        dame, and dry your watery eyes.
Beshrew me, but 'twere pity of his heart
That could refuse a boon to such a suitress.
Y'have got a noble friend to be your advocate;
A worthy and right gentle lord he is,
And to his trust most true. This present now

Some matters of the state detain our leisure;
Those once dispatch'd, we'll call for you anon
And give your griefs redress. Go to! be comforted.

J. SH. Good heav'ns repay Your Highness for this pity,
And show'r down blessings on your princely head.
Come, my Alicia, reach thy friendly arm,
And help me to support this feeble frame
That nodding totters with oppressive woe,
And sinks beneath its load.

(*Exeunt* JANE SHORE *and* ALICIA)

GLOST. Now, by my hollidame!
Heavy of heart she seems, and sore afflicted.
But thus it is when rude calamity
Lays its strong gripe upon these mincing minions;
The dainty gew-gaw forms dissolve at once,
And shiver at the shock. What says her paper?

(*seeming to read*)

Ha! What is this? Come nearer, Ratcliffe! Catesby!
Mark the contents, and then divine the meaning.

(*He reads*)

"Wonder not, princely Gloster, at the notice
This paper brings you from a friend unknown.
Lord Hastings is inclin'd to call you master,
And kneel to Richard, as to England's king;
But Shore's bewitching wife misleads his heart,
And draws his service to King Edward's sons.
Drive her away, you break the charm that holds him,
And he, and all his powers, attend on you."

RATCL. 'Tis wonderful!

CAT. The means by which it came
Yet stranger too!

GLOST. You saw it given but now.

RATCL. She could not know the purport.

GLOST. No, 'tis plain——
She knows it not; it levels at her life;
Should she presume to prate of such high matters,
The meddling harlot! Dear she should abide it.

CAT. What hand soe'er it comes from, be assur'd,
It means your Highness well——

GLOST. Upon the instant
Lord Hastings will be here. This morn I mean
To prove him to the quick; then if he flinch
No more but this, away with him at once;

He must be mine, or nothing.— But he comes!
Draw nearer this way and observe me well.

(They whisper)

Enter LORD HASTINGS

L. HAST.   This foolish woman hangs about my heart,
Lingers and wanders in my fancy still;
This coyness is put on, 'tis art and cunning,
And worn to urge desire— I must possess her;
The groom who lift his saucy hand against me,
Ere this is humbled and repents his daring.
Perhaps ev'n she may profit by th' example,
And teach her beauty not to scorn my pow'r.

GLOST.   This do, and wait me ere the council sits.

(Exeunt RATCLIFFE *and* CATESBY*)*
My Lord, y'are well encounter'd; here has been
A fair petitioner this morning with us;
Believe me, she has won me much to pity her.
Alas! her gentle nature was not made
To buffet with adversity. I told her
How worthily her cause you had befriended;
How much for your good sake we meant to do,
That you had spoke and all things should be well.

L. HAST.   Your Highness binds me ever to your service.

GLOST.   You know your friendship is most potent with us,
And shares our power. But of this enough,
For we have other matters for your ear.
The state is out of tune; distracting fears
And jealous doubts jar in our public councils;
Amidst the wealthy city murmurs rise,
Lewd railings and reproach on those that rule,
With open scorn of government; hence credit
And public trust 'twixt man and man are broke.
The golden streams of commerce are withheld,
Which fed the wants of needy hinds and artizans,
Who therefore curse the great and threat rebellion.

L. HAST.   The resty knaves are overrun with ease,
As plenty ever is the nurse of faction.
If in good days, like these, the headstrong herd
Grow madly wanton and repine, it is
Because the reins of power are held too slack,
And reverend authority of late
Has worn a face of mercy more than justice.

GLOST.   Beshrew my heart! but you have well divin'd

The source of these disorders. Who can wonder
If riot and misrule o'erturn the realm
When the crown sits upon a baby brow?
Plainly to speak, hence comes the general cry
And sum of all complaint: " 'Twill ne'er be well
With England" (thus they talk) "while children govern."

  L. HAST. 'Tis true the king is young; but what of that?
We feel no want of Edward's riper years
While Gloster's valour and most princely wisdom
So well supply our infant sovereign's place,
His youth's support, and guardian of his throne.

  GLOST. The council (much I'm bound to thank 'em for it)
Have placed a pageant scepter in my hand,
Barren of pow'r, and subject to control,
Scorn'd by my foes, and useless to my friends.
O worthy Lord! were mine the rule indeed,
I think I should not suffer rank offence
At large to lord it in the commonweal,
Nor would the realm be rent by discord thus,
Thus fear and doubt betwixt disputed titles.

  L. HAST. Of this I am to learn, as not supposing
A doubt like this——

  GLOST.   Ay, marry, but there is—
And that of much concern. Have you not heard
How, on a late occasion, Doctor Shaw
Has mov'd the people much about the lawfulness
Of Edward's issue? by right grave authority
Of learning and religion plainly proving
A bastard scion never should be grafted
Upon a royal stock; from thence, at full
Discoursing on my brother's former contract
To lady Elizabeth Lucy, long before
His jolly match with that same buxom widow,
The queen he left behind him.——

  L. HAST.   Ill befall
Such meddling priests, who kindle up confusion,
And vex the quiet world with their vain scruples!
By heav'n, 'tis done in perfect spite to peace,
As if they fear'd their trade were at an end
If laymen should agree. Did not the King,
Our royal master Edward, in concurrence
With his estates assembled, well determine
What course the sovereign rule should take henceforward?
When shall the deadly hate of faction cease,

When shall our long divided land have rest,
If every peevish, moody malcontent
Shall set the senseless rabble in an uproar,
Fright them with dangers, and perplex their brains
Each day with some fantastic, giddy change?

GLOST.   What if the same estates, the Lords and Commons,
Should alter——

L. HAST.   What?

GLOST.   The order of succession.

L. HAST.   Curse on the innovating hand attempts it!
Remember him, the villain, righteous heaven,
In thy great day of vengeance! Blast the traitor
And his pernicious counsels, who for wealth,
For pow'r, the pride of greatness or revenge,
Would plunge his native land in civil wars.

GLOST.   You go too far, my Lord.

L. HAST.   Your Highness' pardon——
Have we so soon forgot those days of ruin,
When York and Lancaster drew forth the battles;
When, like a matron butcher'd by her sons,
And cast beside some common way a spectacle
Of horror and affright to passers-by,
Our groaning country bled at every vein;
When murders, rapes, and massacres prevail'd;
When churches, palaces, and cities blaz'd;
When insolence and barbarism triumph'd,
And swept away distinction? Peasants trod
Upon the necks of nobles. Low were laid
The reverend crosier and the holy mitre,
And desolation cover'd all the land.
Who can remember this, and not, like me,
Here vow to sheath a dagger in his heart
Whose damn'd ambition would renew those horrors,
And set, once more, that scene of blood before us?

GLOST.   How now! So hot!

L. HAST.   So brave, and so resolv'd.

GLOST.   Is then our friendship of so little moment
That you could arm your hand against my life?

L. HAST.   I hope Your Highness does not think I meant it.
No, heaven forefend that e'er your princely person
Should come within the scope of my resentment.

GLOST.   O noble Hastings! nay, I must embrace you:
                                    (*embraces him*)
By holy Paul! y'are a right honest man;

The time is full of danger and distrust,
And warns us to be wary. Hold me not
Too apt for jealousy and light surmise
If, when I meant to lodge you next my heart,
I put your truth to trial. Keep your loyalty,
And live your king and country's best support:
For me, I ask no more than honour gives—
To think me yours, and rank me with your friends.

    L. HAST.   Accept what thanks a grateful heart should pay.
O princely Gloster! judge me not ungentle,
Of manners rude, and insolent of speech
If, when the public safety is in question,
My zeal flows warm and eager from my tongue.

    GLOST.   Enough of this; to deal in wordy compliment
Is much against the plainness of my nature.
I judge you by myself, a clear true spirit,
And as such once more join you to my bosom.
Farewell, and be my friend.   (*Exit* GLOSTER)

    L. HAST.   I am not read,
Not skill'd and practis'd in the arts of greatness,
To kindle thus, and give a scope to passion.
The Duke is surely noble; but he touch'd me
Ev'n on the tend'rest point, the master-string
That makes most harmony or discord to me.
I own the glorious subject fires my breast,
And my soul's darling passion stands confess'd.
Beyond or love's or friendship's sacred band,
Beyond myself I prize my native land:
On this foundation would I build my fame,
And emulate the Greek and Roman name;
Think England's peace bought cheaply with my blood,
And die with pleasure for my country's good.   (*Exit*)

ACT IV

Scene continues

Enter DUKE OF GLOSTER, RATCLIFFE, *and* CATESBY

    GLOST.   This was the sum of all, that he would brook
No alteration in the present state.
Marry! at last, the testy gentleman
Was almost mov'd to bid us bold defiance;
But there I dropp'd the argument, and changing

The first design and purpose of my speech,
I prais'd his good affection to young Edward,
And left him to believe my thoughts like his.
Proceed we then to this fore-mention'd matter
As nothing bound or trusting to his friendship.

RATCL.   Ill does it thus befall. I could have wish'd
This lord had stood with us. His friends are wealthy,
Thereto, his own possessions large and mighty;
The vassals and dependants on his power
Firm in adherence, ready, bold, and many;
His name had been of 'vantage to Your Highness,
And stood our present purpose much in stead.

GLOST.   This wayward and perverse declining from us
Has warranted at full the friendly notice
Which we this morn receiv'd. I hold it certain
This puling, whining harlot rules his reason,
And prompts his zeal for Edward's bastard brood.

CAT.   If she have such dominion o'er his heart,
And turn it at her will, you rule her fate
And should, by inference and apt deduction,
Be arbiter of his. Is not her bread,
The very means immediate to her being,
The bounty of your hand? Why does she live
If not to yield obedience to your pleasure,
To speak, to act, to think as you command?

RATCL.   Let her instruct her tongue to bear your message;
Teach every grace to smile in your behalf
And her deluding eyes to gloat for you;
His ductile reason will be wound about,
Be led and turn'd again, say and unsay,
Receive the yoke, and yield exact obedience.

GLOST.   Your counsel likes me well; it shall be follow'd.
She waits without, attending on her suit;
Go, call her in, and leave us here alone.

                              (*Exeunt* RATCLIFFE *and* CATESBY)

How poor a thing is he, how worthy scorn,
Who leaves the guidance of imperial manhood
To such a paltry piece of stuff as this is;
A moppet made of prettiness and pride,
That oft'ner does her giddy fancies change
Than glittering dew-drops in the sun do colours.——
Now shame upon it! Was our reason given
For such a use! to be thus puff'd about
Like a dry leaf, an idle straw, a feather,

The sport of every whiffling blast that blows?
Beshrew my heart, but it is wond'rous strange;
Sure, there is something more than witchcraft in them
That masters ev'n the wisest of us all.

Enter JANE SHORE

    Oh! you are come most fitly. We have ponder'd
On this your grievance: and though some there are—
Nay, and those great ones too—who would enforce
The rigour of our power to afflict you
And bear a heavy hand, yet fear not you:
We've ta'en you to our favour; our protection
Shall stand between, and shield you from mishap.

    J. SH.   The blessings of a heart with anguish broken
And rescu'd from despair attend Your Highness!
Alas! my gracious Lord! What have I done
To kindle such relentless wrath against me?
If in the days of all my past offences,
When most my heart was lifted with delight,
If I withheld my morsel from the hungry,
Forgot the widow's want, and orphan's cry;
If I have known a good I have not shar'd,
Nor call'd the poor to take his portion with me,
Let my worst enemies stand forth and now
Deny the succour which I gave not then.

    GLOST.   Marry, there are though I believe them not,
Who say you meddle in affairs of state:
That you presume to prattle, like a busybody,
Give your advice, and teach the lords o' th' council
What fits the order of the commonweal.

    J. SH.   Oh, that the busy world at least in this
Would take example from a wretch like me!
None then would waste their hours in foreign thoughts,
Forget themselves and what concerns their peace,
To tread the mazes of fantastic Falsehood,
To haunt her idle sounds and flying tales
Through all the giddy, noisy courts of rumour;
Malicious slander never would have leisure
To search with prying eyes for faults abroad,
If all, like me, consider'd their own hearts,
And wept the sorrows which they found at home.

    GLOST.   Go to! I know your power, and though I trust not
To every breath of fame, I'm not to learn
That Hastings is profess'd your loving vassal.

But fair befall your beauty: use it wisely,
And it may stand your fortunes much in stead,
Give back your forfeit land with large encrease,
And place you high in safety and in honour.
Nay, I could point a way, the which pursuing,
You shall not only bring yourself advantage,
But give the realm much worthy cause to thank you.

  J. SH. Oh! where or how—— Can my unworthy hand
Become an instrument of good to any?
Instruct your lowly slave, and let me fly
To yield obedience to your dread command.

  GLOST. Why, that's well said. Thus then—— Observe me
    well.
The state, for many high and potent reasons,
Deeming my brother Edward's sons unfit
For the imperial weight of England's crown——

  J. SH. (*aside*) Alas! for pity.

  GLOST.   Therefore have resolv'd
To set aside their unavailing infancy,
And vest the sovereign rule in abler hands.
This, though of great importance to the public,
Hastings, for very peevishness and spleen,
Does stubbornly oppose.

  J. SH.   Does he! Does Hastings!

  GLOST. Ay, Hastings.

  J. SH. Reward him for the noble deed, just heavens!
For this one action guard him and distinguish him
With signal mercies, and with great deliverance.
Save him from wrong, adversity and shame.
Let never-fading honours flourish round him,
And consecrate his name even to time's end:
Let him know nothing else but good on earth,
And everlasting blessedness hereafter.

  GLOST. How now!

  J. SH. The poor, forsaken, royal little ones!
Shall they be left a prey to savage power?
Can they lift up their harmless hands in vain,
Or cry to heaven for help and not be heard?
Impossible! O gallant, generous Hastings,
Go on, pursue! Assert the sacred cause:
Stand forth, thou proxy of all-ruling Providence,
And save the friendless infants from oppression.
The saints shall assist thee with prevailing prayers,
And warring angels combat on thy side.

GLOST.   You're passing rich in this same heavenly speech,
And spend it at your pleasure. Nay, but mark me!
My favour is not bought with words like these.
Go to!——you'll teach your tongue another tale.

J. SH.   No, though the royal Edward has undone me,
He was my king, my gracious master still;
He lov'd me too, though 'twas a guilty flame
And fatal to my peace, yet still he lov'd me;
With fondness, and with tenderness he doted,
Dwelt in my eyes, and liv'd but in my smiles.
And can I—oh, my heart abhors the thought—
Stand by and see his children robb'd of right?

GLOST.   Dare not, ev'n for thy soul, to thwart me further;
None of your arts, your feigning, and your foolery,
Your dainty, squeamish coying it, to me.
Go——to your lord, your paramour, begone!
Lisp in his ear, hang wanton on his neck,
And play your monkey gambols over to him.
You know my purpose; look that you pursue it,
And make him yield obedience to my will.
Do it——or woe upon thy harlot's head!

J. SH.   Oh, that my tongue had ev'ry grace of speech,
Great and commanding as the breath of kings,
Sweet as the poet's numbers, and prevailing
As soft persuasion to a love-sick maid;
That I had art and eloquence divine
To pay my duty to my master's ashes,
And plead till death the cause of injur'd innocence!

GLOST.   Ha! dost thou brave me, minion! Dost thou know
How vile, how very a wretch, my pow'r can make thee;
That I can let loose fear, distress, and famine,
To hunt thy heels like hell-hounds through the world;
That I can place thee in such abject state
As help shall never find thee; where repining
Thou shalt sit down and gnaw the earth for anguish,
Groan to the pitiless winds without return,
Howl like the midnight wolf amidst the desert,
And curse thy life in bitterness of misery?

J. SH.   Let me be branded for the public scorn,
Turn'd forth and driven to wander like a vagabond,
Be friendless and forsaken, seek my bread
Upon the barren, wild, and desolate waste,
Feed on my sighs, and drink my falling tears,

Ere I consent to teach my lips injustice,
Or wrong the orphan who has none to save him.
    GLOST.   'Tis well——we'll try the temper of your heart.
What ho! Who waits without?

Enter RATCLIFFE, CATESBY, *and Attendants*

    RATCL.   Your Highness' pleasure.
    GLOST. Go, some of you, and turn this strumpet forth!
Spurn her into the street; there let her perish
And rot upon a dunghill. Through the city
See it proclaim'd that none, on pain of death,
Presume to give her comfort, food, or harbour:
Who ministers the smallest comfort, dies.
Her house, her costly furniture and wealth,
The purchase of her loose, luxurious life,
We seize on, for the profit of the state.
Away! Begone!
    J. SH.   O thou most righteous judge—
Humbly, behold, I bow myself to thee,
And own thy justice in this hard decree:
No longer then my ripe offences spare,
But what I merit, let me learn to bear.
Yet since 'tis all my wretchedness can give,
For my past crimes my forfeit life receive;
No pity for my sufferings here I crave,
And only hope forgiveness in the grave.
          (*Exit* JANE SHORE *guarded by* CATESBY *and others*)
    GLOST. (*to* RATCLIFFE)   So much for this. Your project's at
      an end:
This idle toy, this hiding, scorns my power,
And sets us all at nought. See that a guard
Be ready at my call——
    RATCL.   The council waits
Upon Your Highness' leisure.
    GLOST.   Bid 'em enter.

Enter the DUKE OF BUCKINGHAM, EARL OF DERBY, BISHOP OF
ELY, LORD HASTINGS, *and others, as to the council. The*
DUKE OF GLOSTER *takes his place at the upper end; then
the rest sit*

    DER.   In happy time are we assembled here,
To point the day and fix the solemn pomp
For placing England's crown with all due rites

Upon our sovereign Edward's youthful brow.

L. HAST. Some busy, meddling knaves 'tis said there are,
As such will still be prating, who presume
To carp and cavil at his royal right;
Therefore I hold it fitting, with the soonest
T'appoint the order of the coronation;
So to approve our duty to the King,
And stay the babbling of such vain gainsayers.

DER. (to GLOSTER) We all attend to know Your Highness'
pleasure.

GLOST. My Lords! A set of worthy men you are,
Prudent and just, and careful for the state:
Therefore, to your most grave determination,
I yield myself in all things, and demand
What punishment your wisdom shall think meet
T'inflict upon those damnable contrivers
Who shall with potions, charms, and witching drugs,
Practise against our person and our life.

L. HAST. So much I hold the King Your Highness' debtor,
So precious are you to the commonweal,
That I presume, not only for myself,
But in behalf of these my noble brothers,
To say, whoe'er they be, they merit death.

GLOST. Then judge yourselves; convince your eyes of
truth. (pulling up his sleeve)
Behold my arm thus blasted, dry and wither'd,
Shrunk like a foul abortion, and decay'd,
Like some untimely product of the seasons,
Robb'd of its properties of strength and office.
This is the sorcery of Edward's wife,
Who in conjunction with that harlot Shore
And other like confederate midnight hags,
By force of potent spells, of bloody characters,
And conjurations horrible to hear,
Call fiends and spectres from the yawning deep,
And set the ministers of hell at work
To torture and despoil me of my life.

L. HAST. If they have done this deed——

GLOST. If they have done it!
Talk'st thou to me of if's, audacious traitor?
Thou art that strumpet witch's chief abettor,
The patron and complotter of her mischiefs,
And join'd in this contrivance for my death.
Nay, start not, Lords.—— What hoa! a guard there, Sirs!

Enter Guard

Lord Hastings, I arrest thee of high treason.
Seize him, and bear him instantly away;
He sha' not live an hour. By holy Paul!
I will not dine before his head be brought me!
Ratcliffe, stay you and see that it be done.
The rest that love me, rise and follow me.

       (*Exeunt* GLOSTER *and Lords following. Manent* LORD
               HASTINGS, RATCLIFFE, *and Guard*)

   L. HAST.   What! and no more but this—— how! to the scaf-
fold?
O gentle Ratcliffe! tell me, do I hold thee?
Or if I dream, what shall I do to wake,
To break, to struggle through this dread confusion?
For surely death itself is not so painful
As is this sudden horror and surprise.

   RATCL.   You heard; the Duke's commands to me were ab-
solute.
Therefore, my Lord, address you to your shrift
With all good speed you may. Summon your courage,
And be yourself; for you must die this instant.

   L. HAST.   Yes, Ratcliffe, I will take thy friendly counsel,
And die as a man should; 'tis somewhat hard
To call my scatter'd spirits home at once:
But since what must be, must be—let necessity
Supply the place of time and preparation,
And arm me for the blow. 'Tis but to die;
'Tis but to venture on that common hazard
Which many a time in battle I have run;
'Tis but to do what, at that very moment,
In many nations of the peopled earth,
A thousand and a thousand shall do with me;
'Tis but to close my eyes and shut out daylight,
To view no more the wicked ways of men,
No longer to behold the tyrant Gloster,
And be a weeping witness of the woes,
The desolation, slaughter, and calamities,
Which he shall bring on this unhappy land.

Enter ALICIA

   ALIC.   Stand off! and let me pass—— I will, I must
Catch him once more in these despairing arms,
And hold him to my heart.—— O Hastings, Hastings!

L. HAST.   Alas! Why com'st thou at this dreadful moment,
To fill me with new terrors, new distractions;
To turn me wild with thy distemper'd rage,
And shock the peace of my departing soul?
Away! I prithee, leave me!

ALIC.   Stop a minute—
Till my full griefs find passage.—— Oh, the tyrant!
Perdition fall on Gloster's head and mine.

L. HAST.   What means thy frantic grief?

ALIC.   I cannot speak—
But I have murder'd thee.— Oh, I could tell thee—!

L. HAST.   Speak, and give ease to thy conflicting passions:
Be quick, nor keep me longer in suspense;
Time presses, and a thousand crowding thoughts
Break in at once; this way and that they snatch,
They tear my hurry'd soul. All claim attention,
And yet not one is heard. Oh, speak and leave me,
For I have business would employ an age,
And but a minute's time to get it done in.

ALIC.   That, that's my grief—— 'Tis I that urge thee on,
Thus hunt thee to the toil, sweep thee from earth,
And drive thee down this precipice of fate.

L. HAST.   Thy reason is grown wild. Could thy weak hand
Bring on this mighty ruin? If it could,
What have I done so grievous to thy soul,
So deadly, so beyond the reach of pardon,
That nothing but my life can make atonement?

ALIC.   Thy cruel scorn had stung me to the heart,
And set my burning bosom all in flames.
Raving and mad I flew to my revenge,
And writ I know not what—told the Protector,
That Shore's detested wife by wiles had won thee
To plot against his greatness. He believ'd it
(Oh, dire event of my pernicious counsel),
And while I meant destruction on her head,
H' has turned it all on thine.

L. HAST.   Accursed jealousy!
O merciless, wild, and unforgiving fiend!
Blindfold it runs to undistinguish'd mischief,
And murders all it meets. Curst be its rage,
For there is none so deadly; doubly curst
Be all those easy fools who give it harbour,
Who turn a monster loose among mankind,

Fiercer than famine, war, or spotted pestilence,
Baneful as death and horrible as hell.

ALIC.   If thou wilt curse, curse rather thine own falsehood;
Curse the lewd maxims of thy perjur'd sex,
Which taught thee first to laugh at faith and justice,
To scorn the solemn sanctity of oaths,
And make a jest of a poor woman's ruin;
Curse thy proud heart, and thy insulting tongue
That rais'd this fatal fury in my soul
And urged my vengeance to undo us both.

L. HAST.   Oh, thou inhuman! turn thy eyes away,
And blast me not with their destructive beams:
Why should I curse thee with my dying breath?
Begone! and let me sigh it out in peace.

ALIC.   Canst thou, O cruel Hastings, leave me thus!
Hear me, I beg thee—I conjure thee, hear me!
While with an agonizing heart, I swear
By all the pangs I feel, by all the sorrows,
The terrors and despair thy loss shall give me,
My hate was on my rival bent alone.
Oh! had I once divin'd, false as thou art,
A danger to thy life, I would have died,
I would have met it for thee, and made bare
My ready, faithful breast to save thee from it.

L. HAST.   Now mark! and tremble at heaven's just award.
While thy insatiate wrath and fell revenge
Pursu'd the innocence which never wrong'd thee,
Behold! the mischief falls on thee and me;
Remorse and heaviness of heart shall wait thee,
And everlasting anguish be thy potion;
For me, the snares of death are wound about me,
And now, in one poor moment, I am gone.
Oh! if thou hast one tender thought remaining,
Fly to thy closet, fall upon thy knee,
And recommend my parting soul to mercy.

ALIC. (*kneeling*)   Oh! yet, before I go forever from thee,
Turn thee in gentleness and pity to me,
And in compassion of my strong affliction,
Say, is it possible you can forgive
The fatal rashness of ungovern'd love?
For oh! 'tis certain, if I had not lov'd thee
Beyond my peace, my reason, fame, and life,
Desir'd to death, and doted to distraction,

This day of horror never should have known us.

    L. HAST. (*raising her*) Oh, rise, and let me hush thy
        stormy sorrows!
Assuage thy tears, for I will chide no more,
No more upbraid thee, thou unhappy fair one.
I see the hand of heav'n is arm'd against me,
And, in mysterious providence, decrees
To punish me by thy mistaking hand.
Most righteous doom! for, oh! while I behold thee,
Thy wrongs rise up in terrible array,
And charge thy ruin on me; thy fair fame,
Thy spotless beauty, innocence, and youth,
Dishonour'd, blasted, and betray'd by me.

    ALIC. And does thy heart relent for my undoing?
Oh, that inhuman Gloster could be mov'd
But half so easily as I can pardon!

    L. HAST. Here, then, exchange we mutually forgiveness.
So may the guilt of all my broken vows,
My perjuries to thee, be all forgotten,
As here my soul acquits thee of my death,
As here I part without one angry thought,
As here I leave thee with the softest tenderness,
Mourning the chance of our disastrous loves,
And begging heav'n to bless and to support thee.

    RATCL. My Lord, dispatch; the Duke has sent to chide me
For loitering in my duty.

    L. HAST.   I obey.

    ALIC. Insatiate, savage, monster! Is a moment
So tedious to thy malice? Oh, repay him,
Thou great Avenger; give him blood for blood!
Guilt haunt him! Fiends pursue him! Lightnings blast him!
Some horrid, cursed kind of death o'ertake him,
Sudden, and in the fullness of his sins!
That he may know how terrible it is
To want that moment he denies thee now.

    L. HAST. 'Tis all in vain, this rage that tears thy bosom;
Like a poor bird that flutters in its cage,
Thou beat'st thyself to death. Retire, I beg thee;
To see thee thus, thou know'st not how it wounds me;
Thy agonies are added to my own,
And make the burden more than I can bear.
Farewell—— Good angels visit thy afflictions
And bring thee peace and comfort from above.

    ALIC. Oh, stab me to the heart, some pitying hand,

Now strike me dead!

  L. HAST.   One thing I had forgot——
I charge thee by our present common miseries,
By our past loves, if yet they have a name,
By all thy hopes of peace here and hereafter,
Let not the rancour of thy hate pursue
The innocence of thy unhappy friend.
Thou know'st who 'tis I mean; oh! shouldst thou wrong her,
Just heav'n shall double all thy woes upon thee,
And make 'em know no end. Remember this
As the last warning of a dying man:
Farewell forever! (*The Guards carry* HASTINGS *off*)

  ALIC.   Forever! Oh, forever!
Oh, who can bear to be a wretch forever!
My rival too! His last thoughts hung on her,
And, as he parted, left a blessing for her.
Shall she be blest, and I be curst, forever?
No! Since her fatal beauty was the cause
Of all my suff'rings, let her share my pains;
Let her, like me, of ev'ry joy forlorn,
Devote the hour when such a wretch was born:
Like me to deserts and to darkness run,
Abhor the day, and curse the golden sun;
Cast ev'ry good, and ev'ry hope behind;
Detest the works of nature, loathe mankind;
Like me, with cries distracted fill the air, ⎫
Tear her poor bosom, rend her frantic hair, ⎬
And prove the torments of the last despair. ⎭

              (*Exit*)

ACT V

SCENE: *The street*

Enter BELLMOUR *and* DUMONT, *or* SHORE

  SH. You saw her then?

  BELL.   I met her, as returning
In solemn penance from the public cross.
Before her, certain rascal officers,
Slaves in authority, the knaves of justice,
Proclaim'd the tyrant Gloster's cruel orders.
On either side her march'd an ill-look'd priest,
Who with severe, with horrid, haggard eyes,

Did ever and anon by turns upbraid her,
And thunder in her trembling ear damnation.
Around her, numberless the rabble flow'd,
Should'ring each other, crowding for a view,
Gaping and gazing, taunting and reviling;
Some pitying, but those, alas! how few!
The most, such iron hearts we are, and such
The base barbarity of human kind,
With insolence and lewd reproach pursu'd her,
Hooting and railing, and with villainous hands
Gathering the filth from out the common ways,
To hurl upon her head.

SH.   Inhuman dogs!
How did she bear it?

BELL.   With the gentlest patience.
Submissive, sad, and lowly was her look;
A burning taper in her hand she bore,
And on her shoulders, carelessly confus'd,
With loose neglect her lovely tresses hung;
Upon her cheek a faintish flush was spread;
Feeble she seem'd, and sorely smit with pain,
While barefoot as she trod the flinty pavement,
Her footsteps all along were mark'd with blood.
Yet silent still she pass'd and unrepining;
Her streaming eyes bent ever on the earth,
Except when in some bitter pang of sorrow
To heav'n she seemed in fervent zeal to raise,
And beg that mercy man deny'd her here.

SH.   When was this piteous sight?

BELL.   These last two days.
You know my care was wholly bent on you,
To find the happy means of your deliverance,
Which but for Hastings' death I had not gain'd.
During that time, although I have not seen her,
Yet divers trusty messengers I've sent,
To wait about and watch a fit convenience
To give her some relief; but all in vain.
A churlish guard attends upon her steps,
Who menace those with death that bring her comfort
And drive all succour from her.

SH.   Let 'em threaten.
Let proud oppression prove its fiercest malice;
So heav'n befriend my soul, as here I vow
To give her help and share one fortune with her.

BELL. Mean you to see her thus, in your own form?

SH. I do.

BELL. And have you thought upon the consequence?

SH. What is there I should fear?

BELL. Have you examin'd
Into your inmost heart, and tried at leisure
The several secret springs that move the passions?
Has Mercy fix'd her empire there so sure,
That Wrath and Vengeance never may return?
Can you resume a husband's name, and bid
That wakeful dragon, fierce resentment, sleep?

SH. Why dost thou search so deep, and urge my memory
To conjure up my wrongs to life again?
I have long labour'd to forget myself,
To think on all time, backward, like a space
Idle and void, where nothing e'er had being.
But thou hast peopled it again; Revenge
And Jealousy renew their horrid forms,
Shoot all their fires, and drive me to distraction.

BELL. Far be the thought from me! my care was only
To arm you for the meeting. Better were it
Never to see her than to let that name
Recall forgotten rage, and make the husband
Destroy the generous pity of Dumont.

SH. Oh! thou hast set my busy brain at work,
And now she musters up a train of images
Which to preserve my peace I had cast aside
And sunk in deep oblivion—— Oh, that form!
That angel-face on which my dotage hung!
How have I gaz'd upon her! till my soul
With very eagerness went forth towards her,
And issu'd at my eyes. Was there a gem
Which the sun ripens in the Indian mine,
Or the rich bosom of the ocean yields—
What was there art could make, or wealth could buy,
Which I have left unsought to deck her beauty?
What could her king do more?— And yet she fled.

BELL. Away with that sad fancy.

SH. Oh, that day!
The thought of it must live forever with me.
I met her, Bellmour, when the royal spoiler
Bore her in triumph from my widow'd home!
Within his chariot by his side she sate
And listen'd to his talk with downward looks;

Till sudden, as she chanc'd aside to glance,
Her eyes encounter'd mine.— Oh, then, my friend!
Oh, who can paint my grief and her amazement!
As at the stroke of death, twice turn'd she pale,
And twice a burning crimson blush'd all o'er her;
Then, with a shriek heart-wounding, loud she cried,
While down her cheeks two gushing torrents ran
Fast falling on her hands, which thus she wrung.
Mov'd at her grief, the tyrant ravisher,
With courteous action woo'd her oft to turn;
Earnest he seem'd to plead, but all in vain;
Ev'n to the last she bent her sight towards me,
And follow'd me—till I had lost myself.

    BELL.   Alas, for pity! Oh, those speaking tears!
Could they be false? Did she not suffer with you?
And though the King by force possess'd her person,
Her unconsenting heart dwelt still with you.
If all her former woes were not enough,
Look on her now; behold her where she wanders,
Hunted to death, distress'd on every side,
With no one hand to help; and tell me, then,
If ever misery were known like hers.

    SH.   And can she bear it? Can that delicate frame
Endure the beating of a storm so rude?
Can she, for whom the various seasons chang'd
To court her appetite and crown her board,
For whom the foreign vintages were press'd,
For whom the merchant spread his silken stores,
Can she—
Intreat for bread, and want the needful raiment
To wrap her shivering bosom from the weather?
When she was mine, no care came ever nigh her.
I thought the gentlest breeze that wakes the spring
Too rough to breathe upon her. Cheerfulness
Danc'd all the day before her, and at night
Soft slumbers waited on her downy pillow.
Now sad and shelterless, perhaps, she lies
Where piercing winds blow sharp, and the chill rain
Drops from some penthouse on her wretched head,
Drenches her locks, and kills her with the cold.
It is too much.—— Hence with her past offences;
They are aton'd at full.—— Why stay we then?
Oh! let us haste, my friend, and find her out.

    BELL.   Somewhere about this quarter of the town,

I hear the poor, abandon'd creature lingers.
Her guard, though set with strictest watch to keep
All food and friendship from her, yet permit her
To wander in the streets, there choose her bed,
And rest her head on what cold stone she pleases.
 SH. Here let us then divide, each in his round
To search her sorrows out; whose hap it is
First to behold her, this way let him lead
Her fainting steps, and meet we here together. *(Exeunt)*

Enter JANE SHORE, *her hair hanging loose on her
shoulders, and barefooted*

 J. SH. Yet, yet endure, nor murmur, O my soul!
For are not thy transgressions great and numberless?
Do they not cover thee, like rising floods,
And press thee like a weight of waters down?
Does not the hand of righteousness afflict thee;
And who shall plead against it? Who shall say
To pow'r almighty, "Thou hast done enough":
Or bid his dreadful rod of vengeance stay?
Wait then with patience till the circling hours
Shall bring the time of thy appointed rest
And lay thee down in death. The hireling thus
With labour drudges out the painful day,
And often looks with long expecting eyes
To see the shadows rise and be dismiss'd.
And hark! methinks the roar that late pursu'd me
Sinks like the murmurs of a falling wind,
And softens into silence. Does revenge
And malice then grow weary, and forsake me?
My guard, too, that observ'd me still so close,
Tire in the task of their inhuman office,
And loiter far behind. Alas! I faint,
My spirits fail at once.—— This is the door
Of my Alicia—bless'd opportunity!
I'll steal a little succour from her goodness
Now, while no eye observes me.

       (She knocks at the door)

Enter a Servant

       Is your lady,
My gentle friend, at home? Oh, bring me to her.

           (going in)

SERV. (*putting her back*)   Hold, mistress, whither **would**
      you?

J. SH.   Do you not know me?

SERV.   I know you well, and know my orders too.
You must not enter here.

J. SH.   Tell my Alicia,
'Tis I would see her.

SERV.   She is ill at ease
And will admit no visitor.

J. SH.   But tell her
'Tis I, her friend, the partner of her heart,
Wait at the door and beg——

SERV.   'Tis all in vain.
Go hence, and howl to those that will regard you.
                          (*Shuts the door, and exit*)

J. SH.   It was not always thus; the time has been
When this unfriendly door that bars my passage,
Flew wide, and almost leap'd from off its hinges
To give me entrance here; when this good house
Has pour'd forth all its dwellers to receive me;
When my approach has made a little holiday,
And ev'ry face was dress'd in smiles to meet me.
But now 'tis otherwise, and those who bless'd me
Now curse me to my face. Why should I wander,
Stray further on, for I can die ev'n here!
                          (*She sits down at the door*)

Enter ALICIA *in disorder, two Servants following*

ALIC.   What wretch art thou whose misery and baseness
Hangs on my door; whose hateful whine of woe
Breaks in upon my sorrows, and distracts
My jarring senses with thy beggar's cry?

J. SH.   A very beggar, and a wretch indeed;
One driv'n by strong calamity to seek
For succour here; one perishing for want,
Whose hunger has not tasted food these three days;
And humbly asks, for charity's dear sake,
A draught of water and a little bread.

ALIC.   And dost thou come to me, to me for bread?
I know thee not. Go, hunt for it abroad,
Where wanton hands upon the earth have scatter'd it,
Or cast it on the waters. Mark the eagle
And hungry vulture, where they wind the prey;
Watch where the ravens of the valley feed,

And seek thy food with them—— I know thee not.

J. SH.   And yet there was a time when my Alicia
Has thought unhappy Shore her dearest blessing,
And mourn'd that livelong day she pass'd without me;
When, pair'd like turtles, we were still together;
When often as we prattled arm in arm,
Inclining fondly to me, she has sworn
She lov'd me more than all the world beside.

ALIC.   Ha! say'st thou! Let me look upon thee well.
'Tis true—— I know thee now—— A mischief on thee!
Thou art that fatal fair, that cursed she,
That set my brain a-madding. Thou hast robb'd me;
Thou hast undone me—— Murder! Oh, my Hastings!
See, his pale, bloody head shoots glaring by me!
Give him me back again, thou soft deluder,
Thou beauteous witch——

J. SH.   Alas, I never wrong'd you!
Oh, then be good to me; have pity on me:
Thou never knew'st the bitterness of want,
And mayst thou never know it. Oh! bestow
Some poor remain, the voiding of thy table,
A morsel to support my famish'd soul.

ALIC.   Avaunt! and come not near me——

J. SH.   To thy hand
I trusted all, gave my whole store to thee:
Nor do I ask it back; allow me but
The smallest pittance, give me but to eat,
Lest I fall down and perish here before thee.

ALIC.   Nay, tell not me! Where is thy king, thy Edward,
And all the smiling, cringing train of courtiers
That bent the knee before thee?

J. SH.   Oh, for mercy!

ALIC.   Mercy? I know it not—for I am miserable.
I'll give thee Misery, for here she dwells.
This is her house, where the sun never dawns,
The bird of night sits screaming o'er the roof,
Grim spectres sweep along the horrid gloom,
And nought is heard but wailings and lamentings.
Hark! something cracks above! It shakes, it totters!
And see, the nodding ruin falls to crush me!
'Tis fall'n! 'tis here! I feel it on my brain!

1 SERV.   This sight disorders her.

2 SERV.   Retire, dear lady,
And leave this woman——

ALIC.   Let her take my counsel!
Why shouldst thou be a wretch? Stab, tear thy heart,
And rid thyself of this detested being;
I wo'not linger long behind thee here.
A waving flood of bluish fire swells o'er me;
And now 'tis out, and I am drown'd in blood.
Ha! what art thou, thou horrid headless trunk?
It is my Hastings! See, he wafts me on!
Away! I go! I fly! I follow thee.
But come not thou with mischief-making beauty
To interpose between us; look not on him;
Give thy fond arts and thy delusions o'er,
For thou shalt never, never part us more.

                    (*She runs off, her Servants following*)

J. SH.   Alas! She raves; her brain, I fear, is turn'd.
In mercy look upon her, gracious heaven,
Nor visit her for any wrong to me.
Sure, I am near upon my journey's end;
My head runs round, my eyes begin to fail,
And dancing shadows swim before my sight.
I can no more. (*Lies down*) Receive me, thou cold earth;
Thou common parent, take me to thy bosom,
And let me rest with thee.

                    Enter BELLMOUR

BELL.   Upon the ground!
Thy miseries can never lay thee lower.
Look up, thou poor afflicted one! thou mourner,
Whom none has comforted! Where are thy friends,
The dear companions of thy joyful days,
Whose hearts thy warm prosperity made glad,
Whose arms were taught to grow like ivy round thee,
And bind thee to their bosoms? "Thus with thee,
Thus let us live, and let us die," they said,
"For sure thou art the sister of our loves,
And nothing shall divide us."—Now where are they?

J. SH.   Ah! Bellmour, where indeed! They stand aloof,
And view my desolation from afar;
When they pass by, they shake their heads in scorn
And cry, "Behold the harlot and her end!"
And yet thy goodness turns aside to pity me!
Alas! there may be danger; get thee gone!
Let me not pull a ruin on thy head!
Leave me to die alone, for I am fall'n

Never to rise, and all relief is vain.

BELL.   Yet raise thy drooping head, for I am come
To chase away despair. Behold, where yonder
That honest man, that faithful, brave Dumont,
Is hasting to thy aid!

J. SH. (*raising herself and looking about*)   Dumont? Ha!
where?
Then heav'n has heard my pray'r; his very name
Renews the springs of life and cheers my soul.
Has he then 'scap'd the snare?

BELL.   He has: but see——
He comes, unlike to that Dumont you knew,
For now he wears your better angel's form,
And comes to visit you with peace and pardon.

Enter SHORE

J. SH.   Speak, tell me! Which is he? And oh! what would
This dreadful vision! See, it comes upon me——
It is my husband—— Ah!   (*She swoons*)

SH.   She faints! Support her!
Sustain her head while I infuse this cordial
Into her dying lips—from spicy drugs,
Rich herbs, and flow'rs the potent juice is drawn;
With wondrous force it strikes the lazy spirits,
Drives 'em around, and wakens life anew.

BELL.   Her weakness could not bear the strong surprise.
But see, she stirs! and the returning blood
Faintly begins to blush again, and kindle
Upon her ashy cheek——

SH. (*raising her up*)   So——gently raise her——

J. SH.   Ha! what art thou?——Bellmour!

BELL.   How fare you, lady?

J. SH.   My heart is thrill'd with horror——

BELL.   Be of courage——
Your husband lives! 'Tis he, my worthiest friend——

J. SH.   Still art thou there? Still dost thou hover round me?
Oh, save me, Bellmour, from his angry shade!

BELL.   'Tis he himself!——He lives!——Look up——

J. SH.   I dare not!
Oh, that my eyes could shut him out forever——

SH.   Am I so hateful then, so deadly to thee,
To blast thy eyes with horror? Since I'm grown
A burthen to the world, myself, and thee,
Would I had ne'er surviv'd to see thee more.

J. SH.   Oh, thou most injur'd! Dost thou live, indeed?
Fall then, ye mountains, on my guilty head;
Hide me, ye rocks, within your secret caverns;
Cast thy black veil upon my shame, O night,
And shield me with thy sable wing forever!

SH.   Why dost thou turn away?—Why tremble thus?
Why thus indulge thy fears, and in despair,
Abandon thy distracted soul to horror?
Cast every black and guilty thought behind thee,
And let 'em never vex thy quiet more.
My arms, my heart, are open to receive thee,
To bring thee back to thy forsaken home
With tender joy, with fond, forgiving love,
And all the longings of my first desires.

J. SH.   No, arm thy brow with vengeance, and appear
The minister of heav'n's enquiring justice;
Array thyself all terrible for judgment,
Wrath in thy eyes, and thunder in thy voice;
Pronounce my sentence, and if yet there be
A woe I have not felt, inflict it on me.

SH.   The measure of thy sorrows is complete,
And I am come to snatch thee from injustice.
The hand of pow'r no more shall crush thy weakness,
Nor proud oppression grind thy humble soul.

J. SH.   Art thou not risen by miracle from death?
Thy shroud is fall'n from off thee, and the grave
Was bid to give thee up, that thou might'st come
The messenger of grace and goodness to me,
To seal my peace and bless me ere I go.
Oh, let me then fall down beneath thy feet
And weep my gratitude forever there;
Give me your drops, ye soft-descending rains,
Give me your streams, ye never-ceasing springs,
That my sad eyes may still supply my duty,
And feed an everlasting flood of sorrow.

SH.   Waste not thy feeble spirits——I have long
Beheld, unknown, thy mourning and repentance;
Therefore my heart has set aside the past,
And holds thee white as unoffending innocence;
Therefore, in spite of cruel Gloster's rage,
Soon as my friend had broke my prison doors,
I flew to thy assistance. Let us haste
Now, while occasion seems to smile upon us,
Forsake this place of shame and find a shelter.

J. SH.   What shall I say to you? But I obey——

SH.   Lean on my arm——

J. SH.   Alas! I am wondrous faint:
But that's not strange; I have not eat these three days.

SH.   Oh, merciless! Look here, my love, I've brought thee
Some rich conserves.

J. SH.   How can you be so good?
But you were ever thus; I well remember
With what fond care, what diligence of love,
You lavish'd out your wealth to buy me pleasures,
Preventing every wish. Have you forgot
The costly string of pearl you brought me home
And tied about my neck? How could I leave you?

SH.   Taste some of this, or this——

J. SH.   You're strangely altered——
Say, gentle Bellmour, is he not? How pale
Your visage is become! Your eyes are hollow;
Nay, you are wrinkled too.——Alas the day!
My wretchedness has cost you many a tear
And many a bitter pang since last we parted.

SH.   No more of that—— Thou talk'st but dost not eat.

J. SH.   My feeble jaws forget their common office,
My tasteless tongue cleaves to the clammy roof,
And now a gen'ral loathing grows upon me.
Oh, I am sick at heart!

SH.   Thou murd'rous sorrow!
Wo't thou still drink her blood, pursue her still?
Must she then die? Oh, my poor penitent,
Speak peace to thy sad heart.—She hears me not;
Grief masters ev'ry sense. Help me to hold her——

Enter CATESBY, *with a Guard*

CAT.   Seize on 'em both, as traitors to the state.

BELL.   What means this violence?

                      (*Guard lay hold on* SHORE *and* BELLMOUR)

CAT.   Have we not found you,
In scorn of the Protector's strict command,
Assisting this base woman and abetting
Her infamy?

SH.   Infamy on thy head!
Thou tool of power, thou pander to authority!
I tell thee, knave, thou know'st of none so virtuous,
And she that bore thee was an Ethiop to her.

CAT.   You'll answer this at full.—— Away with 'em.

SH.   Is charity grown treason to your court?
What honest man would live beneath such rulers?
I am content that we shall die together.

CAT.   Convey the men to prison; but for her,
Leave her to hunt her fortune as she may.

J. SH.   I will not part with him!—— For me—for me!
Oh, must he die for me?
                    (*Following him as he is carried off. She falls*)
SH.   Inhuman villains!
                    (*Breaks from the Guard*)
Stand off! the agonies of death are on her——
She pulls, she gripes me hard with her cold hand.

J. SH.   Was this blow wanting to complete my ruin?
Oh, let him go, ye ministers of terror;
He shall offend no more, for I will die
And yield obedience to your cruel master.
Tarry a little, but a little longer,
And take my last breath with you.
SH.   O my love!——
Why have I liv'd to see this bitter moment,
This grief by far surpassing all my former!
Why dost thou fix thy dying eyes upon me
With such an earnest, such a piteous look,
As if thy heart were full of some sad meaning
Thou couldst not speak!

J. SH.   Forgive me!——but forgive me!
SH.   Be witness for me, ye celestial host,
Such mercy and such pardon as my soul
Accords to thee, and begs of heav'n to show thee,
May such befall me at my latest hour,
And make my portion blest or curst forever.

J. SH.   Then all is well, and I shall sleep in peace.
'Tis very dark, and I have lost you now.
Was there not something I would have bequeath'd you?
But I have nothing left me to bestow,
Nothing but one sad sigh. Oh, mercy, heav'n!   (*Dies*)
BELL.   There fled the soul,
And left her load of misery behind.

SH.   Oh, my heart's treasure! Is this pale, sad visage
All that remains of thee? Are these dead eyes
The light that cheer my soul? Oh, heavy hour!
But I will fix my trembling lips to thine
Till I am cold and senseless quite, as thou art.

What, must we part then?——

(To the Guards taking him away)
Will you?

(kissing her)
Fare thee well!

Now execute your tyrant's will, and lead me
To bonds or death; 'tis equally indifferent.

    BELL.   Let those who view this sad example know
What fate attends the broken marriage vow;
And teach their children in succeeding times,
No common vengeance waits upon these crimes,
When such severe repentance could not save,
From want, from shame, and an untimely grave.   (Exeunt)

EPILOGUE

Ye modest matrons all, ye virtuous wives,
Who lead with horrid husbands decent lives,
You who, for all you are in such a taking ⎫
To see your spouses drinking, gaming, raking, ⎬
Yet make a conscience still of cuckold-making, ⎭
What can we say your pardon to obtain?
This matter here was prov'd against poor Jane:
She never once deny'd it, but in short,
Whimper'd, and cried, "Sweet sir—I'm sorry for't."
'Twas well she met a kind, good-natur'd soul,
We are not all so easy to control:
I fancy one might find in this good town
Some would ha' told the gentleman his own;
Have answer'd smart, "To what do you pretend,
Blockhead!— As if I mustn't see a friend—
Tell me of hackney-coaches—jaunts to th' City—
Where should I buy my china—Faith, I'll fit ye—"
Our wife was of a milder, meeker spirit:
You!—lords and masters!—was not that some merit?
Don't you allow it to be virtuous bearing,
When we submit thus to your domineering?
Well, peace be with her; she did wrong most surely;
But so do many more who look demurely:
Nor should our mourning madam weep alone,
There are more ways of wickedness than one.
If the reforming stage should fall to shaming

Ill-nature, pride, hypocrisy, and gaming,
The poets frequently might move compassion,
And with she-tragedies o'errun the nation.
Then judge the fair offender, with good nature;
And let your fellow-feeling curb your satire.
What if our neighbours have some little failing,
Must we needs fall to damning and to railing?
For her excuse, too, be it understood, ⎫
That if the woman was not quite so good, ⎬
Her lover was a king, she flesh and blood. ⎭
And since she has dearly paid the sinful score,
Be kind at last, and pity poor Jane Shore.

The

Conscious Lovers

A Comedy

BY SIR RICHARD STEELE

Illud genus narrationis quod in personis positum est, debet habere sermonis festivitatem, animorum dissimilitudinem, gravitatem, lenitatem, spem, metum, suspicionem, desiderium, dissimulationem, misericordiam, rerum varietates, fortunæ commutationem, insperatum incommodum, subitam lætitiam, jucundum exitum rerum.

Cic. Rhetor ad Herenn. Lib. I.[1]

THE PREFACE

This comedy has been received with universal acceptance, for it was in every part excellently performed; and there needs no other applause of the actors but that they excelled according to the dignity and difficulty of the character they repre-

---

[1] The kind of story told on the stage should have gay speech, diversity of personages, seriousness, ease, hope, fear, suspicion, desire, make-believe, pity, variety of matter, change of fortune, unexpected trouble, sudden joy, and a happy outcome.

sented. But this great favour done to the work in acting renders the expectation still the greater from the author, to keep
up the spirit in the representation of the closet, or any other
circumstance of the reader, whether alone or in company: to
which I can only say that it must be remembered a play is to
be seen, and is made to be represented with the advantage of
action, nor can appear but with half the spirit without it; for
the greatest effect of a play in reading is to excite the reader
to go see it; and when he does so, it is then a play has the
effect of example and precept.

The chief design of this was to be an innocent performance,
and the audience have abundantly showed how ready they are
to support what is visibly intended that way; nor do I make
any difficulty to acknowledge that the whole was writ for the
sake of the scene of the fourth act, wherein Mr. Bevil evades
the quarrel with his friend, and hope it may have some effect
upon the Goths and Vandals that frequent the theatres, or a
more polite audience may supply their absence.

But this incident, and the case of the father and daughter,
are esteemed by some people no subjects of comedy; but I cannot be of their mind; for anything that has its foundation in
happiness and success must be allowed to be the object of
comedy, and sure it must be an improvement of it to introduce
a joy too exquisite for laughter, that can have no spring but in
delight, which is the case of this young lady. I must, therefore,
contend that the tears which were shed on that occasion
flowed from reason and good sense, and that men ought not to
be laughed at for weeping till we are come to a more clear notion of what is to be imputed to the hardness of the head and
the softness of the heart; and I think it was very politely said
of Mr. Wilks, to one who told him there was a general weeping for Indiana, "I'll warrant he'll fight ne'er the worse for
that." To be apt to give way to the impressions of humanity is
the excellence of a right disposition and the natural working of
a well-turned spirit. But as I have suffered by critics who are
got no farther than to enquire whether they ought to be
pleased or not, I would willingly find them properer matter for
their employment, and revive here a song which was omitted
for want of a performer, and designed for the entertainment
of Indiana; Sig. Carbonelli, instead of it, played on the fiddle,
and it is for want of a singer that such advantageous things are
said of an instrument which were designed for a voice. The
song is the distress of a love-sick maid, and may be a fit enter-

tainment for some small critics to examine whether the passion
is just or the distress male or female.

I.

From place to place forlorn I go,
With downcast eyes a silent shade;
Forbidden to declare my woe;
To speak, till spoken to, afraid.

II.

My inward pangs, my secret grief,
My soft consenting looks betray:
He loves, but gives me no relief:
Why speaks not he who may?

It remains to say a word concerning Terence, and I am extremely surprised to find what Mr. Cibber told me prove a
truth, that what I valued myself so much upon, the translation
of him, should be imputed to me as a reproach. Mr. Cibber's
zeal for the work, his care and application in instructing the
actors and altering the disposition of the scenes, when I was,
through sickness, unable to cultivate such things myself, has
been a very obliging favour and friendship to me. For this reason I was very hardly persuaded to throw away Terence's celebrated funeral, and take only the bare authority of the young
man's character; and how I have worked it into an Englishman, and made use of the same circumstances of discovering
a daughter when we least hoped for one, is humbly submitted
to the learned reader.

PROLOGUE

By MR. WELSTED

To win your hearts and to secure your praise,
The comic-writers strive by various ways:
By subtle stratagems they act their game,
And leave untry'd no avenue to fame.
One writes the spouse a beating from his wife,
And says each stroke was copy'd from the life.
Some fix all wit and humour in grimace,
And make a livelihood of Pinkey's face:

Here one gay show and costly habits tries,
Confiding to the judgment of your eyes:
Another smuts his scene (a cunning shaver),
Sure of the rakes' and of the wenches' favour.
Oft have these arts prevail'd; and, one may guess,
If practis'd o'er again, would find success.
But the bold sage, the poet of to-night,
By new and desp'rate rules resolv'd to write;
Fain would he give more just applauses rise,
And please by wit that scorns the aids of vice;
The praise he seeks from worthier motives springs,
Such praise as praise to those that give it brings.

    Your aid, most humbly sought, then, Britons, lend,
And lib'ral mirth like lib'ral men defend:
No more let ribaldry, with licence writ,
Usurp the name of eloquence or wit;
No more let lawless farce uncensur'd go,
The lewd dull gleanings of a Smithfield show.
'Tis yours with breeding to refine the age,
To chasten wit, and moralize the stage.

    Ye modest, wise and good, ye fair, ye brave,
To-night the champion of your virtues save;
Redeem from long contempt the comic name,
And judge politely for your country's fame.

DRAMATIS PERSONÆ

Men:

SIR JOHN BEVIL
MR. SEALAND
JOHN BEVIL JUNIOR, *in love with* INDIANA
CHARLES MYRTLE, *in love with* LUCINDA
CIMBERTON, *a coxcomb*
HUMPHREY, *an old servant to* SIR JOHN
TOM, *servant to* BEVIL JUNIOR
DANIEL, *a country boy, servant to* INDIANA

Women:

MRS. SEALAND, *second wife to* SEALAND
ISABELLA, *sister to* SEALAND
INDIANA, SEALAND'S *daughter by his first wife*
LUCINDA, SEALAND'S *daughter by his second wife*
PHILLIS, *maid to* LUCINDA

SCENE: *London*

THE CONSCIOUS LOVERS

ACT I

SCENE: SIR JOHN BEVIL'S *house*
Enter SIR JOHN BEVIL *and* HUMPHREY

SIR J. BEV. Have you ordered that I should not be interrupted while I am dressing?

HUMPH. Yes, Sir: I believed you had something of moment to say to me.

SIR J. BEV. Let me see, Humphrey; I think it is now full forty years since I first took thee to be about myself.

HUMPH. I thank you, Sir; it has been an easy forty years, and I have passed 'em without much sickness, care, or labour.

SIR J. BEV. Thou hast a brave constitution; you are a year or two older than I am, Sirrah.

HUMPH. You have ever been of that mind, Sir.

SIR J. BEV. You knave, you know it; I took thee for thy gravity and sobriety, in my wild years.

HUMPH. Ah, Sir! our manners were formed from our different fortunes, not our different age. Wealth gave a loose to your youth, and poverty put a restraint upon mine.

SIR J. BEV. Well, Humphrey, you know I have been a kind master to you; I have used you, for the ingenious nature I observed in you from the beginning, more like an humble friend than a servant.

HUMPH. I humbly beg you'll be so tender of me as to explain your commands, Sir, without any farther preparation.

SIR J. BEV. I'll tell thee, then. In the first place, this wedding of my son's, in all probability (shut the door) will never be at all.

HUMPH. How, Sir! not be at all? For what reason is it carried on in appearance?

SIR J. BEV. Honest Humphrey, have patience, and I'll tell thee all in order. I have myself, in some part of my life, lived, indeed, with freedom, but, I hope, without reproach. Now, I

115

thought liberty would be as little injurious to my son; therefore, as soon as he grew towards man, I indulged him in living
after his own manner: I knew not how, otherwise, to judge of
his inclination; for what can be concluded from a behaviour
under restraint and fear? But what charms me above all expression is that my son has never, in the least action, the most
distant hint or word, valued himself upon that great estate of
his mother's, which, according to our marriage settlement, he
has had ever since he came to age.

HUMPH.   No, Sir; on the contrary, he seems afraid of appearing to enjoy it before you or any belonging to you. He is
as dependent and resigned to your will as if he had not a
farthing but what must come from your immediate bounty.
You have ever acted like a good and generous father, and he
like an obedient and grateful son.

SIR J. BEV.   Nay, his carriage is so easy to all with whom he
converses, that he is never assuming, never prefers himself to
others, nor ever is guilty of that rough sincerity which a man
is not called to and certainly disobliges most of his acquaintance; to be short, Humphrey, his reputation was so fair in the
world, that old Sealand, the great India merchant, has offered
his only daughter and sole heiress to that vast estate of his, as
a wife for him. You may be sure I made no difficulties; the
match was agreed on, and this very day named for the wedding.

HUMPH.   What hinders the proceeding?

SIR J. BEV.   Don't interrupt me. You know I was last Thursday at the masquerade; my son, you may remember, soon
found us out. He knew his grandfather's habit, which I then
wore; and though it was the mode in the last age, yet the
maskers, you know, followed us as if we had been the most
monstrous figures in that whole assembly.

HUMPH.   I remember, indeed, a young man of quality, in
the habit of a clown, that was particularly troublesome.

SIR J. BEV.   Right; he was too much what he seemed to be.
You remember how impertinently he followed and teased us,
and would know who we were.

HUMPH.   (aside) I know he has a mind to come into that
particular.

SIR J. BEV.   Ay, he followed us till the gentleman who led
the lady in the Indian mantle presented that gay creature to
the rustic, and bid him (like Cymon in the fable) grow polite
by falling in love, and let that worthy old gentleman alone—
meaning me. The clown was not reformed, but rudely per-

sisted, and offered to force off my mask; with that the gentleman, throwing off his own, appeared to be my son, and, in his
concern for me, tore off that of the nobleman. At this they
seized each other; the company called the guards; and in the
surprise the lady swooned away; upon which my son quitted
his adversary, and had now no care but of the lady—when,
raising her in his arms, "Art thou gone," cried he, "forever?——
forbid it, heaven!" She revives at his known voice, and with
the most familiar, though modest, gesture, hangs in safety
over his shoulder weeping, but wept as in the arms of one
before whom she could give herself a loose, were she not under observation. While she hides her face in his neck, he carefully conveys her from the company.

HUMPH. I have observed this accident has dwelt upon
you very strongly.

SIR J. BEV. Her uncommon air, her noble modesty, the dignity of her person, and the occasion itself, drew the whole assembly together; and I soon heard it buzzed about, she was
the adopted daughter of a famous sea-officer who had served
in France. Now this unexpected and public discovery of my
son's so deep concern for her——

HUMPH. Was what, I suppose, alarmed Mr. Sealand, in
behalf of his daughter, to break off the match?

SIR J. BEV. You are right. He came to me yesterday and
said he thought himself disengaged from the bargain, being
credibly informed my son was already married, or worse, to
the lady at the masquerade. I palliated matters, and insisted
on our agreement; but we parted with little less than a direct
breach between us.

HUMPH. Well, Sir; and what notice have you taken of all
this to my young master?

SIR J. BEV. That's what I wanted to debate with you. I
have said nothing to him yet. But look you, Humphrey—— if
there is so much in this amour of his that he denies upon my
summons to marry, I have cause enough to be offended; and
then by my insisting upon his marrying to-day I shall know
how far he is engaged to this lady in masquerade, and from
thence only shall be able to take my measures. In the meantime I would have you find out how far that rogue, his man, is
let into his secret. He, I know, will play tricks as much to cross
me, as to serve his master.

HUMPH. Why do you think so of him, Sir? I believe he is
no worse than I was for you at your son's age.

SIR J. BEV. I see it in the rascal's looks. But I have dwelt on these things too long; I'll go to my son immediately, and while I'm gone, your part is to convince his rogue Tom that I am in earnest. I'll leave him to you.   (*Exit* SIR JOHN BEVIL)

HUMPH.   Well, though this father and son live as well together as possible, yet their fear of giving each other pain is attended with constant mutual uneasiness. I'm sure I have enough to do to be honest and yet keep well with them both. But they know I love 'em, and that makes the task less painful, however.—— Oh, here's the prince of poor coxcombs, the representative of all the better fed than taught.—— Ho! ho! Tom, whither so gay and so airy this morning?

Enter TOM, *singing*

TOM.   Sir, we servants of single gentlemen are another kind of people than you domestic ordinary drudges that do business; we are raised above you. The pleasures of board-wages, tavern dinners, and many a clear gain—vails, alas! you never heard or dreamt of.

HUMPH.   Thou hast follies and vices enough for a man of ten thousand a year, though 'tis but as t'other day that I sent for you to town to put you into Mr. Sealand's family, that you might learn a little before I put you to my young master, who is too gentle for training such a rude thing as you were into proper obedience. You then pulled off your hat to everyone you met in the street, like a bashful great awkward cub as you were. But your great oaken cudgel, when you were a booby, became you much better than that dangling stick at your button, now you are a fop. That's fit for nothing, except it hangs there to be ready for your master's hand when you are impertinent.

TOM.   Uncle Humphrey, you know my master scorns to strike his servants. You talk as if the world was now just as it was when my old master and you were in your youth—when you went to dinner because it was so much o'clock, when the great blow was given in the hall at the pantry door, and all the family came out of their holes in such strange dresses and formal faces as you see in the pictures in our long gallery in the country.

HUMPH.   Why, you wild rogue!

TOM.   You could not fall to your dinner till a formal fellow in a black gown said something over the meat, as if the cook had not made it ready enough.

HUMPH.   Sirrah, who do you prate after? Despising men of sacred characters! I hope you never heard my good young master talk so like a profligate.

TOM.   Sir, I say you put upon me, when I first came to town, about being orderly, and the doctrine of wearing shams to make linen last clean a fortnight, keeping my clothes fresh, and wearing a frock within doors.

HUMPH.   Sirrah, I gave you those lessons because I supposed at that time your master and you might have dined at home every day and cost you nothing; then you might have made a good family servant. But the gang you have frequented since at chocolate houses and taverns, in a continual round of noise and extravagance——

TOM.   I don't know what you heavy inmates call noise and extravagance; but we gentlemen, who are well fed and cut a figure, Sir, think it a fine life, and that we must be very pretty fellows who are kept only to be looked at.

HUMPH.   Very well, Sir! I hope the fashion of being lewd and extravagant, despising of decency and order, is almost at an end, since it is arrived at persons of your quality.

TOM.   Master Humphrey, ha! ha! you were an unhappy lad to be sent up to town in such queer days as you were. Why now, Sir, the lackeys are the men of pleasure of the age, the top gamesters; and many a laced coat about town have had their education in our parti-coloured regiment. We are false lovers; have a taste of music, poetry, billets-doux, dress, politics; ruin damsels; and when we are weary of this lewd town and have a mind to take up, whip into our masters' wigs and linen, and marry fortunes.

HUMPH.   Hey-day!

TOM.   Nay, Sir, our order is carried up to the highest dignities and distinctions; step but into the Painted Chamber, and by our titles you'd take us all for men of quality. Then, again, come down to the Court of Requests, and you see us all laying our broken heads together for the good of the nation; and though we never carry a question *nemine contradicente,* yet this I can say with a safe conscience (and I wish every gentleman of our cloth could lay his hand upon his heart and say the same), that I never took so much as a single mug of beer for my vote in all my life.

HUMPH.   Sirrah, there is no enduring your extravagance; I'll hear you prate no longer. I wanted to see you to enquire how things go with your master, as far as you understand them; I suppose he knows he is to be married to-day.

TOM. Ay, Sir, he knows it, and is dressed as gay as the sun; but, between you and I, my dear, he has a very heavy heart under all that gaiety. As soon as he was dressed I retired, but overheard him sigh in the most heavy manner. He walked thoughtfully to and fro in the room, then went into his closet; when he came out he gave me this for his mistress, whose maid, you know——

HUMPH. Is passionately fond of your fine person.

TOM. The poor fool is so tender, and loves to hear me talk of the world, and the plays, operas and ridottos for the winter, the parks and Belsize for our summer diversions; and "Lard!" says she, "you are so wild——but you have a world of humour."

HUMPH. Coxcomb! Well, but why don't you run with your master's letter to Mrs. Lucinda, as he ordered you?

TOM. Because Mrs. Lucinda is not so easily come at as you think for.

HUMPH. Not easily come at? Why, Sirrah, are not her father and my old master agreed that she and Mr. Bevil are to be one flesh before to-morrow morning?

TOM. It's no matter for that; her mother, it seems, Mrs. Sealand, has not agreed to it: and you must know, Mr. Humphrey, that in that family the grey mare is the better horse.

HUMPH. What dost thou mean?

TOM. In one word, Mrs. Sealand pretends to have a will of her own, and has provided a relation of hers, a stiff, starched philosopher and a wise fool, for her daughter; for which reason, for these ten days past, she has suffered no message nor letter from my master to come near her.

HUMPH. And where had you this intelligence?

TOM. From a foolish, fond soul that can keep nothing from me—one that will deliver this letter too, if she is rightly managed.

HUMPH. What! her pretty handmaid, Mrs. Phillis?

TOM. Even she, Sir; this is the very hour, you know, she usually comes hither, under a pretence of a visit to your housekeeper, forsooth, but in reality to have a glance at——

HUMPH. Your sweet face, I warrant you.

TOM. Nothing else in nature; you must know, I love to fret and play with the little wanton——

HUMPH. "Play with the little wanton!" What will this world come to!

TOM. I met her this morning in a new manteau and petticoat not a bit the worse for her lady's wearing, and she has always new thoughts and new airs with new clothes. Then, she never fails to steal some glance or gesture from every visitant at their house, and is, indeed, the whole town of coquettes at second hand.—— But here she comes; in one motion she speaks and describes herself better than all the words in the world can.

HUMPH.   Then I hope, dear Sir, when your own affair is over, you will be so good as to mind your master's with her.

TOM.   Dear Humphrey, you know my master is my friend, and those are people I never forget.

HUMPH.   Sauciness itself! but I'll leave you to do your best for him.   (*Exit*)

Enter PHILLIS

PHIL.   Oh, Mr. Thomas, is Mrs. Sugarkey at home? Lard! one is almost ashamed to pass along the streets. The town is quite empty, and nobody of fashion left in it; and the ordinary people do so stare to see anything dressed like a woman of condition, as it were, on the same floor with them, pass by. Alas! alas! it is a sad thing to walk. O Fortune! Fortune!

TOM.   What! a sad thing to walk? Why, Madam Phillis, do you wish yourself lame?

PHIL.   No, Mr. Tom, but I wish I were generally carried in a coach or chair, and of a fortune neither to stand nor go, but to totter, or slide, to be short-sighted, or stare, to fleer in the face, to look distant, to observe, to overlook, yet all become me; and if I was rich, I could twire and loll as well as the best of them. O Tom! Tom! is it not a pity that you should be so great a coxcomb, and I so great a coquette, and yet be such poor devils as we are?

TOM.   Mrs. Phillis, I am your humble servant for that——

PHIL.   Yes, Mr. Thomas, I know how much you are my humble servant, and know what you said to Mrs. Judy, upon seeing her in one of her lady's cast manteaus—that any one would have thought her the lady, and that she had ordered the other to wear it till it sat easy, for now only it was becoming—to my lady it was only a covering, to Mrs. Judy it was a habit. This you said, after somebody or other. O Tom! Tom! thou art as false and as base as the best gentleman of them all; but, you wretch, talk to me no more on the old odious subject. Don't, I say.

TOM (*in a submissive tone, retiring*)   I know not how to resist your commands, Madam.

PHIL.   Commands about parting are grown mighty easy to you of late.

TOM.   (*aside*) Oh, I have her; I have nettled and put her into the right temper to be wrought upon and set a-prating. —— Why, truly, to be plain with you, Mrs. Phillis, I can take little comfort of late in frequenting your house.

PHIL.   Pray, Mr. Thomas, what is it all of a sudden offends your nicety at our house?

TOM.   I don't care to speak particulars, but I dislike the whole.

PHIL.   I thank you, Sir, I am a part of that whole.

TOM.   Mistake me not, good Phillis.

PHIL.   Good Phillis! Saucy enough. But however——

TOM.   I say, it is that thou art a part which gives me pain for the disposition of the whole. You must know, Madam, to be serious, I am a man, at the bottom, of prodigious nice honour. You are too much exposed to company at your house. To be plain, I don't like so many, that would be your mistress's lovers, whispering to you.

PHIL.   Don't think to put that upon me. You say this because I wrung you to the heart when I touched your guilty conscience about Judy.

TOM.   Ah, Phillis! Phillis! if you but knew my heart!

PHIL.   I know too much on't.

TOM.   Nay, then, poor Crispo's fate and mine are one. Therefore give me leave to say, or sing at least, as he does upon the same occasion—   (*Sings*)

Se vedette, etc.

PHIL.   What, do you think I'm to be fobbed off with a song? I don't question but you have sung the same to Mrs. Judy too.

TOM.   Don't disparage your charms, good Phillis, with jealousy of so worthless an object; besides, she is a poor hussy, and if you doubt the sincerity of my love, you will allow me true to my interest. You are a fortune, Phillis——

PHIL.   What would the fop be at now? In good time, indeed, you shall be setting up for a fortune!

TOM.   Dear Mrs. Phillis, you have such a spirit that we shall never be dull in marriage when we come together. But I tell you, you are a fortune, and you have an estate in my hands.   (*He pulls out a purse; she eyes it*)

PHIL.   What pretence have I to what is in your hands, Mr. Tom?

TOM.   As thus: there are hours, you know, when a lady is neither pleased or displeased, neither sick or well; when she lolls or loiters; when she's without desires, from having more of everything than she knows what to do with.

PHIL.   Well, what then?

TOM.   When she has not life enough to keep her bright eyes quite open, to look at her own dear image in the glass.

PHIL.   Explain thyself, and don't be so fond of thy own prating.

TOM.   There are also prosperous and good-natured moments, as when a knot or a patch is happily fixed, when the complexion particularly flourishes.

PHIL.   Well, what then? I have not patience!

TOM.   Why, then—or on the like occasions—we servants who have skill to know how to time business see when such a pretty folded thing as this (*shows a letter*) may be presented, laid, or dropped, as best suits the present humour. And, Madam, because it is a long, wearisome journey to run through all the several stages of a lady's temper, my master, who is the most reasonable man in the world, presents you this to bear your charges on the road.   (*Gives her the purse*)

PHIL.   Now you think me a corrupt hussy.

TOM.   Oh, fie! I only think you'll take the letter.

PHIL.   Nay, I know you do, but I know my own innocence; I take it for my mistress's sake.

TOM.   I know it, my pretty one, I know it.

PHIL.   Yes, I say, I do it because I would not have my mistress deluded by one who gives no proof of his passion; but I'll talk more of this as you see me on my way home. No, Tom, I assure thee I take this trash of thy master's, not for the value of the thing, but as it convinces me he has a true respect for my mistress. I remember a verse to the purpose:

They may be false who languish and complain,
But they who part with money never feign.   (*Exeunt*)

SCENE II

SCENE: BEVIL JUNIOR's *lodgings*

BEVIL JUNIOR, *reading*

BEV. JUN.   These moral writers practise virtue after death. This charming Vision of Mirza! Such an author consulted in a morning sets the spirit for the vicissitudes of the day better than the glass does a man's person. But what a day have I to go through! to put on an easy look with an aching heart. If this lady my father urges me to marry should not refuse me, my dilemma is insupportable. But why should I fear it? is not she in equal distress with me? has not the letter I have sent her this morning confessed my inclination to another? Nay, have I not moral assurances of her engagements, too, to my friend Myrtle? It's impossible but she must give in to it: for sure, to be denied is a favour any man may pretend to. It must be so. Well, then, with the assurance of being rejected, I think I may confidently say to my father I am ready to marry her. Then let me resolve upon—what I am not very good at, though it is—an honest dissimulation.

Enter TOM

TOM.   Sir John Bevil, Sir, is in the next room.

BEV. JUN.   Dunce! Why did not you bring him in?

TOM.   I told him, Sir, you were in your closet.

BEV. JUN.   I thought you had known, Sir, it was my duty to see my father anywhere.

(*going himself to the door*)

TOM. (*aside*)   The devil's in my master! he has always more wit than I have.

BEV. JUN. (*introducing* SIR JOHN)   Sir, you are the most gallant, the most complaisant of all parents. Sure, 'tis not a compliment to say these lodgings are yours. Why would you not walk in, Sir?

SIR J. BEV.   I was loath to interrupt you unseasonably on your wedding-day.

BEV. JUN.   One to whom I am beholden for my birthday might have used less ceremony.

SIR J. BEV.   Well, Son, I have intelligence you have writ to your mistress this morning. It would please my curiosity to know the contents of a wedding-day letter, for courtship must then be over.

BEV. JUN.   I assure you, Sir, there was no insolence in it upon the prospect of such a vast fortune's being added to our family, but much acknowledgment of the lady's greater desert.

SIR J. BEV.   But, dear Jack, are you in earnest in all this? And will you really marry her?

BEV. JUN.   Did I ever disobey any command of yours, Sir? nay, any inclination that I saw you bent upon?

SIR J. BEV.   Why, I can't say you have, Son; but methinks in this whole business you have not been so warm as I could have wished you. You have visited her, it's true, but you have not been particular. Everyone knows you can say and do as handsome things as any man, but you have done nothing but lived in the general—been complaisant only.

BEV. JUN.   As I am ever prepared to marry if you bid me, so I am ready to let it alone if you will have me.

HUMPHREY *enters, unobserved*

SIR J. BEV.   Look you there now! Why, what am I to think of this so absolute and so indifferent a resignation?

BEV. JUN.   Think? that I am still your son, Sir. Sir, you have been married, and I have not. And you have, Sir, found the inconvenience there is when a man weds with too much love in his head. I have been told, Sir, that at the time you married, you made a mighty bustle on the occasion. There was challenging and fighting, scaling walls, locking up the lady, and the gallant under an arrest for fear of killing all his rivals. Now, Sir, I suppose you, having found the ill consequences of these strong passions and prejudices in preference of one woman to another, in case of a man's becoming a widower——

SIR J. BEV.   How is this!

BEV. JUN.   I say, Sir, experience has made you wiser in your care of me; for, Sir, since you lost my dear mother your time has been so heavy, so lonely, and so tasteless, that you are so good as to guard me against the like unhappiness, by marrying me prudentially by way of bargain and sale. For as you well judge, a woman that is espoused for a fortune is yet a better bargain if she dies; for then a man still enjoys what he did marry, the money, and is disencumbered of what he did not marry, the woman.

SIR J. BEV.   But pray, Sir, do you think Lucinda, then, a woman of such little merit?

BEV. JUN.   Pardon me, Sir, I don't carry it so far neither. I am rather afraid I shall like her too well; she has, for one of her fortune, a great many needless and superfluous good qualities.

SIR J. BEV.   I am afraid, Son, there's something I don't see yet, something that's smothered under all this raillery.

BEV. JUN.   Not in the least, Sir. If the lady is dressed and ready, you see I am. I suppose the lawyers are ready too.

HUMPH. (*aside*)   This may grow warm if I don't interpose.
—— Sir, Mr. Sealand is at the coffee-house, and has sent to speak with you.

SIR J. BEV.   Oh, that's well! Then I warrant the lawyers are ready. Son, you'll be in the way, you say——

BEV. JUN.   If you please, Sir, I'll take a chair, and go to Mr. Sealand's, where the young lady and I will wait your leisure.

SIR J. BEV.   By no means. The old fellow will be so vain if he sees——

BEV. JUN.   Ay; but the young lady, Sir, will think me so indifferent——

HUMPH.   (*aside to* BEVIL JUNIOR)   Ay, there you are right; press your readiness to go to the bride—he won't let you.

BEV. JUN.   (*aside to* HUMPHREY)   Are you sure of that?

HUMPH.   (*aside*)   How he likes being prevented!

SIR J. BEV.   (*looking on his watch*)   No, no. You are an hour or two too early.

BEV. JUN.   You'll allow me, Sir, to think it too late to visit a beautiful, virtuous young woman, in the pride and bloom of life, ready to give herself to my arms; and to place her happiness or misery, for the future, in being agreeable or displeasing to me, is a—— Call a chair!

SIR J. BEV.   No, no, no, dear Jack; this Sealand is a moody old fellow. There's no dealing with some people but by managing with indifference. We must leave to him the conduct of this day. It is the last of his commanding his daughter.

BEV. JUN.   Sir, he can't take it ill that I am impatient to be hers.

SIR J. BEV.   Pray, let me govern in this matter; you can't tell how humoursome old fellows are. There's no offering reason to some of 'em, especially when they are rich.—— (*aside*) If my son should see him before I've brought old Sealand into better temper, the match would be impracticable.

HUMPH.   Pray, Sir, let me beg you to let Mr. Bevil go.—— (*aside to* SIR JOHN)   See whether he will or not—— (*then to* BEVIL JUNIOR)   Pray, Sir, command yourself; since you see my master is positive, it is better you should not go.

BEV. JUN.   My father commands me as to the object of my affections, but I hope he will not as to the warmth and height of them.

SIR J. BEV.   (*aside*)   So! I must even leave things as I found them, and in the meantime, at least, keep old Sealand out of his sight.——Well, Son, I'll go myself and take orders in your affair. You'll be in the way, I suppose, if I send to you. I'll leave your old friend with you.—— Humphrey, don't let him stir, d'ye hear?—— Your servant, your servant!

(*Exit* SIR JOHN BEVIL)

HUMPH. I have a sad time on't, Sir, between you and my master. I see you are unwilling, and I know his violent inclinations for the match.—— I must betray neither and yet deceive you both, for your common good.—— Heaven grant a good end of this matter! But there is a lady, Sir, that gives your father much trouble and sorrow. You'll pardon me.

BEV. JUN. Humphrey, I know thou art a friend to both, and in that confidence I dare tell thee——that lady is a woman of honour and virtue. You may assure yourself I never will marry without my father's consent. But give me leave to say, too, this declaration does not come up to a promise that I will take whosoever he pleases.

HUMPH. Come, Sir, I wholly understand you. You would engage my services to free you from this woman whom my master intends you, to make way in time for the woman you have really a mind to.

BEV. JUN. Honest Humphrey, you have always been an useful friend to my father and myself; I beg you, continue your good offices, and don't let us come to the necessity of a dispute; for, if we should dispute, I must either part with more than life, or lose the best of fathers.

HUMPH. My dear master, were I but worthy to know this secret that so near concerns you, my life, my all should be engaged to serve you. This, Sir, I dare promise, that I am sure I will and can be secret. Your trust, at worst, but leaves you where you were; and if I cannot serve you, I will at once be plain and tell you so.

BEV. JUN. That's all I ask. Thou hast made it now my interest to trust thee. Be patient, then, and hear the story of my heart.

HUMPH. I am all attention, Sir.

BEV. JUN. You may remember, Humphrey, that in my last travels my father grew uneasy at my making so long a stay at Toulon.

HUMPH. I remember it; he was apprehensive some woman had laid hold of you.

BEV. JUN. His fears were just, for there I first saw this lady. She is of English birth: her father's name was Danvers, a younger brother of an ancient family, and originally an eminent merchant of Bristol, who, upon repeated misfortunes, was reduced to go privately to the Indies. In this retreat Providence again grew favourable to his industry, and in six years' time restored him to his former fortunes. On this he sent directions over that his wife and little family should follow him to the Indies. His wife, impatient to obey such welcome orders, would not wait the leisure of a convoy, but took the first occasion of a single ship, and, with her husband's sister only, and this daughter, then scarce seven years old, undertook the fatal voyage—for here, poor creature, she lost her liberty and life; she and her family, with all they had, were unfortunately taken by a privateer from Toulon. Being thus made a prisoner, though as such not ill-treated, yet the fright, the shock, and cruel disappointment seized with such violence upon her unhealthy frame, she sickened, pined, and died at sea.

HUMPH. Poor soul! Oh, the helpless infant!

BEV. JUN. Her sister yet survived, and had the care of her. The captain, too, proved to have humanity, and became a father to her; for having himself married an English woman, and being childless, he brought home into Toulon this her little country-woman, presenting her, with all her dead mother's movables of value, to his wife, to be educated as his own adopted daughter.

HUMPH. Fortune here seemed again to smile on her.

BEV. JUN. Only to make her frowns more terrible; for in his height of fortune this captain, too, her benefactor, unfortunately was killed at sea, and, dying intestate, his estate fell wholly to an advocate, his brother, who, coming soon to take possession, there found, among his other riches, this blooming virgin at his mercy.

HUMPH. He durst not, sure, abuse his power!

BEV. JUN. No wonder if his pampered blood was fired at the sight of her—in short, he loved. But when all arts and gentle means had failed to move, he offered, too, his menaces in vain, denouncing vengeance on her cruelty, demanding her to account for all her maintenance from her childhood, seized on her little fortune as his own inheritance, and was dragging her by violence to prison, when Providence at the instant interposed, and sent me, by miracle, to relieve her.

HUMPH. 'Twas Providence, indeed. But pray, Sir, after all this trouble how came this lady at last to England?

BEV. JUN. The disappointed advocate, finding she had so unexpected a support, on cooler thoughts descended to a composition, which I, without her knowledge, secretly discharged.

HUMPH. That generous concealment made the obligation double.

BEV. JUN. Having thus obtained her liberty, I prevailed, not without some difficulty, to see her safe to England, where no sooner arrived but my father, jealous of my being imprudently engaged, immediately proposed this other fatal match that hangs upon my quiet.

HUMPH.   I find, Sir, you are irrecoverably fixed upon this lady.

BEV. JUN.   As my vital life dwells in my heart; and yet you see what I do to please my father: walk in this pageantry of dress, this splendid covering of sorrow. But, Humphrey, you have your lesson.

HUMPH.   Now, Sir, I have but one material question——

BEV. JUN.   Ask it freely.

HUMPH.   Is it, then, your own passion for this secret lady, or hers for you, that gives you this aversion to the match your father has proposed you?

BEV. JUN.   I shall appear, Humphrey, more romantic in my answer than in all the rest of my story; for though I dote on her to death, and have no little reason to believe she has the same thoughts for me, yet in all my acquaintance and utmost privacies with her I never once directly told her that I loved.

HUMPH.   How was it possible to avoid it?

BEV. JUN.   My tender obligations to my father have laid so inviolable a restraint upon my conduct that till I have his consent to speak I am determined, on that subject, to be dumb forever.

HUMPH.   Well, Sir, to your praise be it spoken, you are certainly the most unfashionable lover in Great Britain.

Enter TOM

TOM.   Sir, Mr. Myrtle's at the next door, and, if you are at leisure, will be glad to wait on you.

BEV. JUN.   Whenever he pleases.—— Hold, Tom! did you receive no answer to my letter?

TOM.   Sir, I was desired to call again, for I was told her mother would not let her be out of her sight. But about an hour hence, Mrs. Lettice said, I should certainly have one.

BEV. JUN.   Very well.

HUMPH.   Sir, I will take another opportunity: in the meantime, I only think it proper to tell you that, from a secret I know, you may appear to your father as forward as you please to marry Lucinda, without the least hazard of its coming to a conclusion. Sir, your most obedient servant!

BEV. JUN.   Honest Humphrey, continue but my friend in this exigence and you shall always find me yours.

(*Exit* HUMPHREY)

I long to hear how my letter has succeeded with Lucinda——

but I think it cannot fail, for at worst, were it possible she could take it ill, her resentment of my indifference may as probably occasion a delay as her taking it right. Poor Myrtle, what terrors must he be in all this while? Since he knows she is offered to me and refused to him, there is no conversing or taking any measures with him for his own service. But I ought to bear with my friend, and use him as one in adversity:

All his disquiets by my own I prove;

The greatest grief's perplexity in love.   (*Exeunt*)

ACT II

SCENE I

Scene continues

Enter BEVIL JUNIOR *and* TOM

TOM.   Sir, Mr. Myrtle.

BEV. JUN.   Very well—do you step again, and wait for an answer to my letter.   (*Exit* TOM)

Enter MYRTLE

Well, Charles, why so much care in thy countenance? Is there anything in this world deserves it? You, who used to be so gay, so open, so vacant!

MYRT.   I think we have of late changed complexions. You, who used to be much the graver man, are now all air in your behaviour. But the cause of my concern may, for aught I know, be the same object that gives you all this satisfaction. In a word, I am told that you are this very day—and your dress confirms me in it—to be married to Lucinda.

BEV. JUN.   You are not misinformed. Nay, put not on the terrors of a rival till you hear me out. I shall disoblige the best of fathers if I don't seem ready to marry Lucinda; and you know I have ever told you you might make use of my secret resolution never to marry her, for your own service, as you please. But I am now driven to the extremity of immediately refusing or complying unless you help me to escape the match.

MYRT.   Escape? Sir, neither her merit or her fortune are below your acceptance. Escaping do you call it!

BEV. JUN.   Dear Sir, do you wish I should desire the match?

MYRT.   No, but such is my humourous and sickly state of mind since it has been able to relish nothing but Lucinda, that though I must owe my happiness to your aversion to this marriage, I can't bear to hear her spoken of with levity or unconcern.

BEV. JUN.   Pardon me, Sir; I shall transgress that way no more. She has understanding, beauty, shape, complexion, wit——

MYRT.   Nay, dear Bevil, don't speak of her as if you loved her, neither.

BEV. JUN.   Why, then, to give you ease at once, though I allow Lucinda to have good sense, wit, beauty, and virtue, I know another in whom these qualities appear to me more amiable than in her.

MYRT.   There you spoke like a reasonable and good-natured friend. When you acknowledge her merit and own your prepossession for another, at once you gratify my fondness and cure my jealousy.

BEV. JUN.   But all this while you take no notice, you have no apprehension, of another man that has twice the fortune of either of us.

MYRT.   Cimberton! Hang him, a formal, philosophical, pedantic coxcomb! for the sot, with all these crude notions of divers things, under the direction of great vanity and very little judgment, shows his strongest bias is avarice; which is so predominant in him that he will examine the limbs of his mistress with the caution of a jockey, and pays no more compliment to her personal charms than if she were a mere breeding animal.

BEV. JUN.   Are you sure that is not affected? I have known some women sooner set on fire by that sort of negligence than by——

MYRT.   No, no! hang him, the rogue has no art; it is pure, simple insolence and stupidity.

BEV. JUN.   Yet with all this, I don't take him for a fool.

MYRT.   I own the man is not a natural; he has a very quick sense, though very slow understanding. He says, indeed, many things that want only the circumstances of time and place to be very just and agreeable.

BEV. JUN.   Well, you may be sure of me if you can disappoint him; but my intelligence says the mother has actually sent for the conveyancer to draw articles for his marriage with Lucinda, though those for mine with her are, by her father's order, ready for signing. But it seems she has not thought fit to consult either him or his daughter in the matter.

MYRT.   Pshaw! a poor, troublesome woman. Neither Lucinda nor her father will ever be brought to comply with it; besides, I am sure Cimberton can make no settlement upon her without the concurrence of his great-uncle, Sir Geoffry, in the west.

BEV. JUN.   Well, Sir, and I can tell you that's the very point that is now laid before her counsel, to know whether a firm settlement can be made without this uncle's actual joining in it. Now pray consider, Sir, when my affair with Lucinda comes, as it soon must, to an open rupture, how are you sure that Cimberton's fortune may not then tempt her father, too, to hear his proposals?

MYRT.   There you are right, indeed; that must be provided against. Do you know who are her counsel?

BEV. JUN.   Yes, for your service I have found out that, too: they are Sergeant Bramble and old Target——by the way, they are neither of 'em known in the family. Now, I was thinking why you might not put a couple of false counsel upon her to delay and confound matters a little; besides, it may probably let you into the bottom of her whole design against you.

MYRT.   As how, pray?

BEV. JUN.   Why, can't you slip on a black wig and a gown, and be old Bramble yourself?

MYRT.   Ha! I don't dislike it. But what shall I do for a brother in the case?

BEV. JUN.   What think you of my fellow Tom? The rogue's intelligent, and is a good mimic. All his part will be but to stutter heartily, for that's old Target's case. Nay, it would be an immoral thing to mock him, were it not that his impertinence is the occasion of its breaking out to that degree. The conduct of the scene will chiefly lie upon you.

MYRT.   I like it of all things; if you'll send Tom to my chambers I will give him full instructions. This will certainly give me occasion to raise difficulties, to puzzle or confound her project for a while at least.

BEV. JUN.   I'll warrant you success: so far we are right, then. And now, Charles, your apprehension of my marrying her is all you have to get over.

MYRT.   Dear Bevil! though I know you are my friend, yet when I abstract myself from my own interest in the thing, I know no objection she can make to you or you to her, and therefore hope——

BEV. JUN.   Dear Myrtle, I am as much obliged to you for the cause of your suspicion as I am offended at the effect: but be assured, I am taking measures for your certain security, and that all things with regard to me will end in your entire satisfaction.

MYRT.   Well, I'll promise you to be as easy and as confident as I can, though I cannot but remember that I have more than life at stake on your fidelity.   (*going*)

BEV. JUN.   Then depend upon it, you have no chance against you.

MYRT.   Nay, no ceremony; you know I must be going.

(*Exit* MYRTLE)

BEV. JUN.   Well! this is another instance of the perplexities which arise, too, in faithful friendship. We must often in this life go on in our good offices even under the displeasure of those to whom we do them, in compassion to their weaknesses and mistakes. But all this while poor Indiana is tortured with the doubt of me! She has no support or comfort but in my fidelity, yet sees me daily pressed to marriage with another! How painful, in such a crisis, must be every hour she thinks on me! I'll let her see at least my conduct to her is not changed. I'll take this opportunity to visit her; for though the religious vow I have made to my father restrains me from ever marrying without his approbation, yet that confines me not from seeing a virtuous woman that is the pure delight of my eyes and the guiltless joy of my heart. But the best condition of human life is but a gentler misery.

To hope for perfect happiness is vain,
And love has ever its allays of pain.   (*Exit*)

SCENE II

Enter ISABELLA *and* INDIANA *in her own lodgings*

ISAB.   Yes, I say 'tis artifice, dear child: I say to thee again and again, 'tis all skill and management.

IND.   Will you persuade me there can be an ill design in supporting me in the condition of a woman of quality? attended, dressed, and lodged like one—in my appearance abroad and my furniture at home, every way in the most sumptuous manner—and he that does it has an artifice, a design in it?

ISAB.   Yes, yes.

IND.   And all this without so much as explaining to me that all about me comes from him!

ISAB.   Ay, ay, the more for that. That keeps the title to all you have the more in him.

IND.   The more in him! He scorns the thought——

ISAB.   Then he—— He—— He——

IND.   Well, be not so eager. If he is an ill man, let us look into his stratagems. Here is another of them. (*showing a letter*) Here's two hundred and fifty pound in bank notes, with these words: "To pay for the set of dressing-plate which will be brought home to-morrow." Why, dear Aunt, now here's another piece of skill for you, which I own I cannot comprehend, and it is with a bleeding heart I hear you say anything to the disadvantage of Mr. Bevil. When he is present I look upon him as one to whom I owe my life and the support of it —then, again, as the man who loves me with sincerity and honour. When his eyes are cast another way and I dare survey him, my heart is painfully divided between shame and love. Oh! could I tell you——

ISAB.   Ah! you need not: I imagine all this for you.

IND.   This is my state of mind in his presence, and when he is absent, you are ever dinning my ears with notions of the arts of men; that his hidden bounty, his respectful conduct, his careful provision for me, after his preserving me from utmost misery, are certain signs he means nothing but to make I know not what of me.

ISAB.   Oh! You have a sweet opinion of him, truly.

IND.   I have, when I am with him, ten thousand things, besides my sex's natural decency and shame, to suppress my heart, that yearns to thank, to praise, to say it loves him. I say, thus it is with me while I see him; and in his absence I am entertained with nothing but your endeavours to tear this amiable image from my heart and in its stead to place a base dissembler, an artful invader of my happiness, my innocence, my honour.

ISAB.   Ah, poor soul! has not his plot taken? don't you die for him? has not the way he has taken been the most proper with you? Oh! ho! He has sense, and has judged the thing right.

IND.   Go on, then, since nothing can answer you; say what you will of him. Heigh! ho!

ISAB.   Heigh! ho! indeed. It is better to say so, as you are now, than as many others are. There are, among the destroyers of women, the gentle, the generous, the mild, the affable, the humble, who all, soon after their success in their designs, turn to the contrary of those characters. I will own to you, Mr. Bevil carries his hypocrisy the best of any man living, but still he is a man, and therefore a hypocrite. They have usurped an exemption from shame for any baseness, any cruelty towards us. They embrace without love; they make vows without conscience of obligation; they are partners, nay, seducers to the crime wherein they pretend to be less guilty.

IND. (*aside*) That's truly observed.—— But what's all this to Bevil?

ISAB. This it is to Bevil and all mankind. Trust not those who will think the worse of you for your confidence in them—serpents who lie in wait for doves. Won't you be on your guard against those who would betray you? Won't you doubt those who would contemn you for believing 'em? Take it from me: fair and natural dealing is to invite injuries; 'tis bleating to escape wolves who would devour you! Such is the world—— (*aside*) and such (since the behaviour of one man to myself) have I believed all the rest of the sex.

IND. I will not doubt the truth of Bevil; I will not doubt it. He has not spoke it by an organ that is given to lying; his eyes are all that have ever told me that he was mine. I know his virtue, I know his filial piety, and ought to trust his management with a father to whom he has uncommon obligations. What have I to be concerned for? my lesson is very short. If he takes me forever, my purpose of life is only to please him. If he leaves me (which heaven avert), I know he'll do it nobly, and I shall have nothing to do but to learn to die, after worse than death has happened to me.

ISAB. Ay do, persist in your credulity! Flatter yourself that a man of his figure and fortune will make himself the jest of the town, and marry a handsome beggar for love.

IND. The town! I must tell you, Madam, the fools that laugh at Mr. Bevil will but make themselves more ridiculous; his actions are the result of thinking, and he has sense enough to make even virtue fashionable.

ISAB. O' my conscience, he has turned her head. Come, come; if he were the honest fool you take him for, why has he kept you here these three weeks without sending you to Bristol in search of your father, your family, and your relations?

IND. I am convinced he still designs it, and that nothing keeps him here but the necessity of not coming to a breach with his father in regard to the match he has proposed him. Beside, has he not writ to Bristol? and has not he advice that my father has not been heard of there almost these twenty years?

ISAB. All sham, mere evasion; he is afraid if he should

carry you hither, your honest relations may take you out of his hands and so blow up all his wicked hopes at once.

IND. Wicked hopes! did I ever give him any such?

ISAB. Has he ever given you any honest ones? Can you say, in your conscience, he has ever once offered to marry you?

IND. No! but by his behaviour I am convinced he will offer it the moment 'tis in his power, or consistent with his honour, to make such a promise good to me.

ISAB. His honour!

IND. I will rely upon it; therefore desire you will not make my life uneasy by these ungrateful jealousies of one to whom I am, and wish to be, obliged, for from his integrity alone I have resolved to hope for happiness.

ISAB. Nay, I have done my duty; if you won't see, at your peril be it.

IND. Let it be.—— This is his hour of visiting me.

ISAB. (*apart*) Oh! to be sure, keep up your form; don't see him in a bed-chamber. This is pure prudence, when she is liable, wherever he meets her, to be conveyed where'er he pleases.

IND. All the rest of my life is but waiting till he comes: I live only when I'm with him.   (*Exit*)

ISAB. Well, go thy ways, thou wilful innocent! I once had almost as much love for a man who poorly left me to marry an estate—and I am now, against my will, what they call an old maid: but I will not let the peevishness of that condition grow upon me; only keep up the suspicion of it, to prevent this creature's being any other than a virgin, except upon proper terms.   (*Exit*)

Re-enter INDIANA, *speaking to a Servant*

IND. Desire Mr. Bevil to walk in.—— Design! impossible! A base, designing mind could never think of what he hourly puts in practice. And yet, since the late rumour of his marriage, he seems more reserved than formerly; he sends in, too, before he sees me, to know if I am at leisure. Such new respect may cover coldness in the heart—it certainly makes me thoughtful. I'll know the worst at once; I'll lay such fair occasions in his way that it shall be impossible to avoid an explanation, for these doubts are insupportable.—— But see! he comes and clears them all.

Enter BEVIL JUNIOR

BEV. JUN. Madam, your most obedient! I am afraid I

broke in upon your rest last night—'twas very late before we parted, but 'twas your own fault: I never saw you in such agreeable humour.

IND. I am extremely glad we were both pleased, for I thought I never saw you better company.

BEV. JUN. Me, Madam! you rally; I said very little.

IND. But I am afraid you heard me say a great deal; and, when a woman is in the talking vein, the most agreeable thing a man can do, you know, is to have patience to hear her.

BEV. JUN. Then it's pity, Madam, you should ever be silent, that we might be always agreeable to one another.

IND. If I had your talent or power to make my actions speak for me, I might indeed be silent, and yet pretend to something more than the agreeable.

BEV. JUN. If I might be vain of anything in my power, Madam, 'tis that my understanding from all your sex has marked you out as the most deserving object of my esteem.

IND. Should I think I deserve this, 'twere enough to make my vanity forfeit the very esteem you offer me.

BEV. JUN. How so, Madam?

IND. Because esteem is the result of reason, and to deserve it from good sense, the height of human glory. Nay, I had rather a man of honour should pay me that, than all the homage of a sincere and humble love.

BEV. JUN. You certainly distinguish right, Madam; love often kindles from external merit only——

IND. But esteem arises from a higher source, the merit of the soul.

BEV. JUN. True, and great souls only can deserve it.

(*bowing respectfully*)

IND. Now I think they are greater still that can so charitably part with it.

BEV. JUN. Now, Madam, you make me vain, since the utmost pride and pleasure of my life is that I esteem you—as I ought.

IND. (*aside*) As he ought! Still more perplexing! He neither saves nor kills my hope.

BEV. JUN. But, Madam, we grow grave, methinks. Let's find some other subject. Pray, how did you like the opera last night?

IND. First give me leave to thank you for my tickets.

BEV. JUN. Oh, your servant, Madam! But pray tell me; you, now, who are never partial to the fashion, I fancy, must be the properest judge of a mighty dispute among the ladies,

that is, whether *Crispo* or *Griselda* is the more agreeable entertainment.

IND.   With submission, now, I cannot be a proper judge of
this question.

BEV. JUN.   How so, Madam?

IND.   Because I find I have a partiality for one of them.

BEV. JUN.   Pray, which is that?

IND.   I do not know—there's something in that rural cottage
of Griselda, her forlorn condition, her poverty, her solitude,
her resignation, her innocent slumbers, and that lulling *Dolce
sogno* that's sung over her; it had an effect upon me that—— in
short, I never was so well deceived at any of them.

BEV. JUN.   Oh! Now, then, I can account for the dispute:
Griselda, it seems, is the distress of an injured, innocent
woman; *Crispo,* that only of a man in the same condition;
therefore the men are mostly concerned for Crispo, and, by a
natural indulgence, both sexes for Griselda.

IND.   So that judgment, you think, ought to be for one,
though fancy and complaisance have got ground for the other.
Well! I believe you will never give me leave to dispute with
you on any subject, for I own *Crispo* has its charms for me too,
though in the main all the pleasure the best opera gives us is
but mere sensation. Methinks it's pity the mind can't have a
little more share in the entertainment. The music's certainly
fine, but, in my thoughts, there's none of your composers come
up to old Shakespeare and Otway.

BEV. JUN.   How, Madam! Why, if a woman of your sense
were to say this in the drawing-room——

Enter a Servant

SERV.   Sir, here's Signor Carbonelli says he waits your commands in the next room.

BEV. JUN.   A propos! You were saying yesterday, Madam,
you had a mind to hear him; will you give him leave to entertain you now?

IND.   By all means.—— Desire the gentleman to walk in.
                                        (*Exit Servant*)

BEV. JUN.   I fancy you will find something in this hand that
is uncommon.

IND.   You are always finding ways, Mr. Bevil, to make life
seem less tedious to me.

Enter Music Master

When the gentleman pleases.

(*After a sonata is played,* BEVIL *waits on the Master to the door, etc.*)

BEV. JUN. You smile, Madam, to see me so complaisant to one whom I pay for his visit. Now I own I think it is not enough barely to pay those whose talents are superior to our own (I mean such talents as would become our condition, if we had them). Methinks we ought to do something more than barely gratify them for what they do at our command only because their fortune is below us.

IND. You say I smile: I assure you it was a smile of approbation; for indeed, I cannot but think it the distinguishing part of a gentleman to make his superiority of fortune as easy to his inferiors as he can.—— (*aside*) Now once more to try him. —— I was saying just now, I believed you would never let me dispute with you, and I daresay it will always be so. However, I must have your opinion upon a subject which created a debate between my aunt and me just before you came hither. She would needs have it that no man every does any extraordinary kindness or service for a woman but for his own sake.

BEV. JUN. Well, Madam! Indeed, I can't but be of her mind.

IND. What, though he should maintain and support her, without demanding anything of her on her part?

BEV. JUN. Why, Madam, is making an expense in the service of a valuable woman (for such I must suppose her), though she should never do him any favour—nay, though she should never know who did her such service—such a mighty heroic business?

IND. Certainly! I should think he must be a man of an uncommon mould.

BEV. JUN. Dear Madam, why so? 'tis but, at best, a better taste in expense. To bestow upon one whom he may think one of the ornaments of the whole creation; to be conscious that from his superfluity an innocent, a virtuous spirit is supported above the temptations and sorrows of life! That he sees satisfaction, health, and gladness in her countenance, while he enjoys the happiness of seeing her (as that I will suppose too, or he must be too abstracted, too insensible)—— I say, if he is allowed to delight in that prospect, alas! what mighty matter is there in all this?

IND. No mighty matter in so disinterested a friendship!

BEV. JUN. Disinterested! I can't think him so. Your hero, Madam, is no more than what every gentleman ought to be and I believe very many are. He is only one who takes more delight in reflections than in sensations. He is more pleased with thinking than eating; that's the utmost you can say of him. Why, Madam, a greater expense than all this men lay out upon an unnecessary stable of horses.

IND.   Can you be sincere in what you say?

BEV. JUN.   You may depend upon it, if you know any such man, he does not love dogs inordinately.

IND.   No, that he does not.

BEV. JUN.   Nor cards, nor dice.

IND.   No.

BEV. JUN.   Nor bottle companions.

IND.   No.

BEV. JUN.   Nor loose women.

IND.   No, I'm sure he does not.

BEV. JUN.   Take my word, then, if your admired hero is not liable to any of these kind of demands, there's no such pre-eminence in this as you imagine. Nay, this way of expense you speak of is what exalts and raises him that has a taste for it; and, at the same time, his delight is incapable of satiety, disgust, or penitence.

IND.   But still I insist, his having no private interest in the action makes it prodigious, almost incredible.

BEV. JUN.   Dear Madam, I never knew you more mistaken. Why, who can be more a usurer than he who lays out his money in such valuable purchases? If pleasure be worth purchasing, how great a pleasure is it, to him who has a true taste of life, to ease an aching heart, to see the human countenance lighted up into smiles of joy, on the receipt of a bit of ore which is superfluous and otherwise useless in a man's own pocket? What could a man do better with his cash? This is the effect of a humane disposition where there is only a general tie of nature and common necessity. What then must it be when we serve an object of merit, of admiration!

IND.   Well! the more you argue against it, the more I shall admire the generosity.

BEV. JUN.   Nay, nay!——then, Madam, 'tis time to fly, after a declaration that my opinion strengthens my adversary's argument. I had best hasten to my appointment with Mr. Myrtle, and be gone while we are friends and—before things are brought to an extremity.   (*Exit carelessly*)

Enter ISABELLA

ISAB.   Well, Madam, what think you of him now, pray?

IND.   I protest, I begin to fear he is wholly disinterested in what he does for me. On my heart, he has no other view but the mere pleasure of doing it, and has neither good or bad designs upon me.

ISAB.   Oh! dear Niece! don't be in fear of both! I'll warrant you, you will know time enough that he is not indifferent.

IND.   You please me when you tell me so, for if he has any wishes towards me I know he will not pursue them but with honour.

ISAB.   I wish I were as confident of one as t'other. I saw the respectful downcast of his eye when you catched him gazing at you during the music. He, I warrant, was surprised, as if he had been taken stealing your watch. Oh, the undissembled, guilty look!

IND.   But did you observe any such thing, really? I thought he looked most charmingly graceful! How engaging is modesty in a man when one knows there is a great mind within. So tender a confusion! and yet, in other respects, so much himself, so collected, so dauntless, so determined!

ISAB.   Ah, Niece! there is a sort of bashfulness which is the best engine to carry on a shameless purpose: some men's modesty serves their wickedness, as hypocrisy gains the respect due to piety. But I will own to you, there is one hopeful symptom, if there could be such a thing as a distinterested lover. But it's all a perplexity, till—— till—— till——

IND.   Till what?

ISAB.   Till I know whether Mr. Myrtle and Mr. Bevil are really friends or foes. And that I will be convinced of before I sleep, for you shall not be deceived.

IND.   I'm sure I never shall if your fears can guard me. In the meantime I'll wrap myself up in the integrity of my own heart, nor dare to doubt of his.

As conscious honour all his actions steers,
So conscious innocence dispels my fears.   (*Exeunt*)

ACT III

SCENE: SEALAND'S *house*

Enter TOM, *meeting* PHILLIS

TOM.   Well, Phillis!—what, with a face as if you had never seen me before!—— (*aside*) What a work have I to do now? She has seen some new visitant at their house, whose airs she has catched, and is resolved to practise them upon me. Numberless are the changes she'll dance through before she'll answer this plain question, videlicet, "Have you delivered my master's letter to your lady?" Nay, I know her too well to ask an account of it in an ordinary way; I'll be in my airs as well as she.—— (*looking steadfastly at her*) Well, Madam, as unhappy as you are at present pleased to make me, I would not, in the general, be any other than what I am; I would not be a bit wiser, a bit richer, a bit taller, a bit shorter than I am at this instant.

PHIL.   Did ever anybody doubt, Master Thomas, but that you were extremely satisfied with your sweet self?

TOM.   I am, indeed. The thing I have least reason to be satisfied with is my fortune, and I am glad of my poverty. Perhaps if I were rich I should overlook the finest woman in the world, that wants nothing but riches to be thought so.

PHIL.   (*aside*) How prettily was that said! But I'll have a great deal more before I'll say one word.

TOM.   I should, perhaps, have been stupidly above her, had I not been her equal, and by not being her equal, never had opportunity of being her slave. I am my master's servant for hire; I am my mistress's from choice, would she but approve my passion.

PHIL.   I think it's the first time I ever heard you speak of it with any sense of the anguish, if you really do suffer any.

TOM.   Ah, Phillis! can you doubt, after what you have seen?

PHIL.   I know not what I have seen, nor what I have heard; but since I'm at leisure, you may tell me when you fell in love with me, how you fell in love with me, and what you have suffered or are ready to suffer for me.

TOM.   (*aside*) Oh, the unmerciful jade! when I'm in haste about my master's letter. But I must go through it.—— Ah! too well I remember when, and how, and on what occasion I wa first surprised. It was on the first of April, one thousand seven hundred and fifteen, I came into Mr. Sealand's service; I was then a hobbledehoy, and you a pretty little tight girl, a favourite handmaid of the housekeeper. At that time we neither of us knew what was in us. I remember I was ordered to get out the window, one pair of stairs, to rub the sashes clean; the person employed on the inner side was your charming self, whom I had never seen before.

PHIL.   I think I remember the silly accident. What made ye, you oaf, ready to fall down into the street?

TOM.   You know not, I warrant you. You could not guess

what surprised me. You took no delight when you immediately grew wanton in your conquest, and put your lips close
and breathed upon the glass, and when my lips approached,
a dirty cloth you rubbed against my face, and hid your beauteous form; when I again drew near, you spit, and rubbed,
and smiled at my undoing.

PHIL.   What silly thoughts you men have!

TOM.   We were Pyramus and Thisbe—but ten times harder
was my fate. Pyramus could peep only through a wall; I saw
her, saw my Thisbe in all her beauty, but as much kept from
her as if a hundred walls between, for there was more, there
was her will against me. Would she but yet relent! O Phillis!
Phillis! shorten my torment and declare you pity me.

PHIL.   I believe it's very sufferable; the pain is not so exquisite but that you may bear it a little longer.

TOM.   Oh, my charming Phillis! if all depended on my fair
one's will, I could with glory suffer. But, dearest creature, consider our miserable state.

PHIL.   How! Miserable!

TOM.   We are miserable to be in love and under the command of others than those we love—with that generous passion
in the heart, to be sent to and fro on errands, called, checked,
and rated for the meanest trifles. O Phillis! you don't know
how many china cups and glasses my passion for you has
made me break. You have broke my fortune as well as my
heart.

PHIL.   Well, Mr. Thomas, I cannot but own to you that I
believe your master writes and you speak the best of any men
in the world. Never was woman so well pleased with a letter
as my young lady was with his, and this is an answer to it.

                                        (*Gives him a letter*)

TOM.   This was well done, my dearest. Consider, we must
strike out some pretty livelihood for ourselves by closing their
affairs. It will be nothing for them to give us a little being of
our own, some small tenement, out of their large possessions:
whatever they give us, 'twill be more than what they keep for
themselves: one acre with Phillis would be worth a whole
county without her.

PHIL.   Oh, could I but believe you!

TOM.   If not the utterance, believe the touch of my lips.

                                              (*Kisses her*)

PHIL.   There's no contradicting you; how closely you
argue, Tom!

TOM.   And will closer, in due time. But I must hasten with this letter, to hasten towards the possession of you. Then, Phillis, consider how I must be revenged, look to it, of all your skittishness, shy looks, and at best but coy compliances.

PHIL.   O Tom! you grow wanton and sensual, as my lady calls it; I must not endure it. Oh! Foh! you are a man, an odious, filthy male creature; you should behave, if you had a right sense or were a man of sense, like Mr. Cimberton, with distance and indifference, or—let me see—some other becoming hard word, with seeming in-in-inadvertency, and not rush on one as if you were seizing a prey.—— But hush! the ladies are coming.—— Good Tom, don't kiss me above once, and be gone. Lard! we have been fooling and toying, and not considered the main business of our masters and mistresses.

TOM.   Why, their business is to be fooling and toying as soon as the parchments are ready.

PHIL.   Well remembered—— parchments! My lady, to my knowledge, is preparing writings between her coxcomb cousin, Cimberton, and my mistress, though my master has an eye to the parchments already prepared between your master, Mr. Bevil, and my mistress; and, I believe, my mistress herself has signed and sealed, in her heart, to Mr. Myrtle.—— Did I not bid you kiss me but once, and be gone? but I know you won't be satisfied.

TOM.   (*kissing her hand*)   No, you smooth creature, how should I!

PHIL.   Well, since you are so humble, or so cool, as to ravish my hand only, I'll take my leave of you like a great lady, and you a man of quality.   (*They salute formally*)

TOM.   Pox of all this state!

(*offers to kiss her more closely*)

PHIL.   No, prithee, Tom, mind your business! We must follow that interest which will take, but endeavour at that which will be most for us and we like most. Oh, here's my young mistress! (TOM *taps her neck behind, and kisses his fingers.*)   Go, ye liquorish fool!   (*Exit* TOM)

Enter LUCINDA

LUC.   Who was that you was hurrying away?

PHIL.   One that I had no mind to part with.

LUC.   Why did you turn him away then?

PHIL.   For your ladyship's service, to carry your ladyship's letter to his master. I could hardly get the rogue away.

LUC.   Why, has he so little love for his master?

PHIL.   No; but he has so much love for his mistress.

LUC. But I thought I heard him kiss you. Why do you suffer that?

PHIL. Why, Madam, we vulgar take it to be a sign of love. We servants, we poor people, that have nothing but our persons to bestow or treat for, are forced to deal and bargain by way of sample, and therefore, as we have no parchments or wax necessary in our agreements, we squeeze with our hands and seal with our lips to ratify vows and promises.

LUC. But can't you trust one another without such earnest down?

PHIL. We don't think it safe, any more than you gentry, to come together without deeds executed.

LUC. Thou art a pert, merry hussy.

PHIL. I wish, Madam, your lover and you were as happy as Tom and your servant are.

LUC. You grow impertinent.

PHIL. I have done, Madam; and I won't ask you what you intend to do with Mr. Myrtle, what your father will do with Mr. Bevil, nor what you all, especially my lady, mean by admitting Mr. Cimberton as particularly here as if he were married to you already; nay, you are married actually as far as people of quality are.

LUC. How's that?

PHIL. You have different beds in the same house.

LUC. Pshaw! I have a very great value for Mr. Bevil, but have absolutely put an end to his pretensions in the letter I gave you for him. But my father, in his heart, still has a mind to him, were it not for this woman they talk of; and I am apt to imagine he is married to her, or never designs to marry at all.

PHIL. Then Mr. Myrtle——

LUC. He had my parents' leave to apply to me, and by that has won me and my affections: who is to have this body of mine without 'em, it seems, is nothing to me. My mother says it's indecent for me to let my thoughts stray about the person of my husband; nay, she says a maid, rigidly virtuous, though she may have been where her lover was a thousand times, should not have made observations enough to know him from another man when she sees him in a third place.

PHIL. That is more than the severity of a nun, for not to see when one may is hardly possible; not to see when one can't is very easy. At this rate, Madam, there are a great many whom you have not seen who——

LUC. Mamma says the first time you see your husband

should be at that instant he is made so, when your father, with the help of the minister, gives you to him; then you are to see him, then you are to observe and take notice of him, because then you are to obey him.

PHIL.   But does not my lady remember you are to love as well as obey?

LUC.   To love is a passion, 'tis a desire, and we must have no desires. Oh! I cannot endure the reflection! With what insensibility on my part, with what more than patience, have I been exposed and offered to some awkward booby or other in every county of Great Britain!

PHIL.   Indeed, Madam, I wonder I never heard you speak of it before with this indignation.

LUC.   Every corner of the land has presented me with a wealthy coxcomb. As fast as one treaty has gone off, another has come on, till my name and person have been the tittle-tattle of the whole town. What is this world come to! No shame left! To be bartered for like the beasts of the fields, and that in such an instance as coming together to an entire familiarity and union of soul and body; oh! and this without being so much as well-wishers to each other, but for increase of fortune.

PHIL.   But Madam, all these vexations will end very soon in one for all. Mr. Cimberton is your mother's kinsman, and three hundred years an older gentleman than any lover you ever had; for which reason, with that of his prodigious large estate, she is resolved on him, and has sent to consult the lawyers accordingly—nay, has (whether you know it or no) been in treaty with Sir Geoffry, who, to join in the settlement, has accepted of a sum to do it, and is every moment expected in town for that purpose.

LUC.   How do you get all this intelligence?

PHIL.   By an art I have, I thank my stars, beyond all the waiting-maids in Great Britain; the art of listening, Madam, for your ladyship's service.

LUC.   I shall soon know as much as you do. Leave me, leave me, Phillis, begone! Here, here, I'll turn you out. My mother says I must not converse with my servants, though I must converse with no one else.   (*Exit* PHILLIS)
How unhappy are we who are born to great fortunes! No one looks at us with indifference, or acts towards us on the foot of plain dealing; yet by all I have been heretofore offered to or treated for I have been used with the most agreeable of all abuses, flattery. But now, by this phlegmatic fool I am used

as nothing, or a mere thing. He, forsooth! is too wise, too
learned, to have any regard to desires, and I know not what
the learned oaf calls sentiments of love and passion.—— Here
he comes with my mother. It's much if he looks at me; or if he
does, takes no more notice of me than of any other movable
in the room.

Enter MRS. SEALAND *and* MR. CIMBERTON

MRS. SEAL.   How do I admire this noble, this learned taste
of yours, and the worthy regard you have to our own ancient
and honourable house, in consulting a means to keep the
blood as pure and as regularly descended as may be.

CIMB.   Why, really, Madam, the young women of this age
are treated with discourses of such a tendency, and their im-
aginations so bewildered in flesh and blood, that a man of
reason can't talk to be understood. They have no ideas of happiness but what are more gross than the gratification of hunger
and thirst.

LUC.   (*aside*)   With how much reflection he is a coxcomb!

CIMB.   And in truth, Madam, I have considered it as a
most brutal custom that persons of the first character in the
world should go as ordinarily and with as little shame to bed
as to dinner with one another. They proceed to the propaga-
tion of the species as openly as to the preservation of the
individual.

LUC.   (*aside*)   She that willingly goes to bed to thee must
have no shame, I'm sure.

MRS. SEAL.   O Cousin Cimberton! Cousin Cimberton! how
abstracted, how refined is your sense of things! But indeed, it
is too true there is nothing so ordinary as to say, in the best
governed families, "My master and lady are gone to bed"; one
does not know but it might have been said of one's self.

(*hiding her face with her fan*)

CIMB.   Lycurgus, Madam, instituted otherwise; among the
Lacedæmonians the whole female world was pregnant, but
none but the mothers themselves knew by whom. Their meet-
ings were secret, and the amorous congress always by stealth,
and no such professed doings between the sexes as are toler-
ated among us under the audacious word "marriage."

MRS. SEAL.   Oh! had I lived in those days and been a
matron of Sparta, one might with less indecency have had ten
children, according to that modest institution, than one under
the confusion of our modern, barefaced manner.

LUC.   (*aside*)   And yet, poor woman, she has gone through the whole ceremony, and here I stand a melancholy proof of it.

MRS. SEAL. We will talk then of business. That girl walking about the room there is to be your wife. She has, I confess, no ideas, no sentiments, that speak her born of a thinking mother.

CIMB. I have observed her; her lively look, free air, and disengaged countenance speak her very——

LUC. Very what?

CIMB. If you please, Madam——to set her a little that way.

MRS. SEAL. Lucinda, say nothing to him; you are not a match for him. When you are married, you may speak to such a husband when you're spoken to. But I am disposing of you above yourself every way.

CIMB. Madam, you cannot but observe the inconveniences I expose myself to, in hopes that your ladyship will be the consort of my better part. As for the young woman, she is rather an impediment than a help to a man of letters and speculation. Madam, there is no reflection, no philosophy, can at all times subdue the sensitive life, but the animal shall sometimes carry away the man. Ha! ay, the vermilion of her lips——

LUC. Pray, don't talk of me thus.

CIMB. The pretty enough—— Pant of her bosom——

LUC. Sir!—— Madam, don't you hear him?

CIMB. Her forward chest——

LUC. Intolerable!

CIMB. High health——

LUC. The grave, easy impudence of him!

CIMB. Proud heart——

LUC. Stupid coxcomb!

CIMB. I say, Madam, her impatience while we are looking at her, throws out all attractions—her arms—her neck—what a spring in her step!

LUC. Don't you run me over thus, you strange unaccountable!

CIMB. What an elasticity in her veins and arteries!

LUC. I have no veins, no arteries.

MRS. SEAL. O child, hear him; he talks finely; he's a scholar; he knows what you have.

CIMB. The speaking invitation of her shape, the gathering of herself up, and the indignation you see in the pretty little thing. Now, I am considering her, on this occasion, but as one that is to be pregnant.

LUC. (aside) The familiar, learned, unseasonable puppy!

CIMB. And pregnant undoubtedly she will be yearly. I fear I shan't, for many years, have discretion enough to give her one fallow season.

LUC. Monster! there's no bearing it. The hideous sot! there's no enduring it, to be thus surveyed like a steed at sale.

CIMB. At sale! She's very illiterate—— But she's very well limbed too; turn her in; I see what she is.

(*Exit* LUCINDA, *in a rage*)

MRS. SEAL. Go, you creature, I am ashamed of you.

CIMB. No harm done.——You know, Madam, the better sort of people, as I observed to you, treat by their lawyers of weddings (*adjusting himself at the glass*) and the woman in the bargain, like the mansion-house in the sale of the estate, is thrown in, and what that is, whether good or bad, is not at all considered.

MRS. SEAL. I grant it, and therefore make no demand for her youth and beauty, and every other accomplishment, as the common world think 'em, because she is not polite.

CIMB. Madam, I know your exalted understanding, abstracted as it is from vulgar prejudices, will not be offended when I declare to you, I marry to have an heir to my estate, and not to beget a colony or a plantation. This young woman's beauty and constitution will demand provision for a tenth child at least.

MRS. SEAL. (*aside*) With all that wit and learning, how considerate! What an economist!—— Sir, I cannot make her any other than she is, or say she is much better than the other young women of this age, or fit for much besides being a mother; but I have given directions for the marriage settlements, and Sir Geoffry Cimberton's counsel is to meet ours here at this hour, concerning his joining in the deed which, when executed, makes you capable of settling what is due to Lucinda's fortune. Herself, as I told you, I say nothing of.

CIMB. No, no, no, indeed, Madam, it is not usual; and I must depend upon my own reflection and philosophy not to overstock my family.

MRS. SEAL. I cannot help her, Cousin Cimberton, but she is, for aught I see, as well as the daughter of anybody else.

CIMB. That is very true, Madam.

Enter a Servant, who whispers MRS. SEALAND

MRS. SEAL. The lawyers are come, and now we are to hear what they have resolved as to the point whether it's necessary that Sir Geoffry should join in the settlement, as being what

they call in the remainder. But, good Cousin, you must have
patience with 'em. These lawyers, I am told, are of a different
kind; one is what they call a chamber counsel, the other a
pleader. The conveyancer is slow, from an imperfection in his
speech, and therefore shunned the bar, but extremely passionate and impatient of contradiction. The other is as warm as he,
but has a tongue so voluble, and a head so conceited, he will
suffer nobody to speak but himself.

CIMB.   You mean old Sergeant Target and Counsellor
Bramble? I have heard of 'em.

MRS. SEAL.   The same.—— Show in the gentlemen.

(*Exit Servant*)

Re-enter Servant, introducing MYRTLE *and*
TOM *disguised as* BRAMBLE *and* TARGET

MRS. SEAL.   Gentlemen, this is the party concerned, Mr.
Cimberton; and I hope you have considered of the matter.

TAR.   Yes, Madam, we have agreed that it must be by in-
dent-dent-dent-dent——

BRAM.   Yes, Madam, Mr. Sergeant and myself have agreed,
as he is pleased to inform you, that it must be an indenture
tripartite, and tripartite let it be, for Sir Geoffry must needs
be a party; old Cimberton, in the year 1619, says, in that ancient roll in Mr. Sergeant's hands, as, recourse thereto being
had, will more at large appear——

TAR.   Yes, and by the deeds in your hands, it appears
that——

BRAM.   Mr. Sergeant, I beg of you to make no inferences
upon what is in our custody, but speak to the titles in your
own deeds. I shall not show that deed till my client is in town.

CIMB.   You know best your own methods.

MRS. SEAL.   The single question is whether the entail is
such that my cousin, Sir Geoffry, is necessary in this affair.

BRAM.   Yes, as to the lordship of Tretriplet, but not as to
the messuage of Grimgribber.

TAR.   I say that Gr-Gr- that Gr-Gr-Grimgribber, Grimgribber is in us; that is to say, the remainder thereof, as well as
that of Tr-Tr-triplet.

BRAM.   You go upon the deed of Sir Ralph, made in the
middle of the last century, precedent to that in which old
Cimberton made over the remainder, and made it pass to the
heirs general, by which your client comes in; and I question
whether the remainder even of Tretriplet is in him. But we are
willing to waive that, and give him a valuable consideration.

But we shall not purchase what is in us forever, as Grimgribber is, at the rate as we guard against the contingent of Mr.
Cimberton having no son. Then we know Sir Geoffry is the
first of the collateral male line in this family. Yet——

TAR.   Sir, Gr-Gr-ber is——

BRAM.   I apprehend you very well, and your argument
might be of force, and we would be inclined to hear that in all
its parts. But, Sir, I see very plain what you are going into. I
tell you, it is as probable a contingent that Sir Geoffry may die
before Mr. Cimberton, as that he may outlive him.

TAR.   Sir, we are not ripe for that yet, but I must say——

BRAM.   Sir, I allow you the whole extent of that argument;
but that will go no farther than as to the claimants under old
Cimberton. I am of opinion that, according to the instruction
of Sir Ralph, he could not dock the entail and then create a
new estate for the heirs general.

TAR.   Sir, I have not patience to be told that, when Gr-Gr-
ber——

BRAM.   I will allow it you, Mr. Sergeant; but there must
be the word "heirs for ever," to make such an estate as you
pretend.

CIMB.   I must be impartial, though you are counsel for my
side of the question. Were it not that you are so good as to
allow him what he has not said, I should think it very hard
you should answer him without hearing him. But, gentlemen,
I believe you have both considered this matter and are firm in
your different opinions. 'Twere better, therefore, you proceeded according to the particular sense of each of you and
gave your thoughts distinctly in writing. And do you see, Sirs,
pray let me have a copy of what you say, in English.

BRAM.   Why, what is all we have been saying? In English!
Oh! but I forgot myself; you're a wit. But, however, to please
you, Sir, you shall have it in as plain terms as the law will
admit of.

CIMB.   But I would have it, Sir, without delay.

BRAM.   That, Sir, the law will not admit of: the courts are
sitting at Westminster, and I am this moment obliged to be at
every one of them, and 'twould be wrong if I should not be in
the Hall to attend one of 'em at least; the rest would take it ill
else. Therefore I must leave what I have said to Mr. Sergeant's consideration, and I will digest his arguments on my
part, and you shall hear from me again, Sir.

(*Exit* BRAMBLE)

TAR.   Agreed, agreed.

CIMB. Mr. Bramble is very quick. He parted a little abruptly.

TAR. He could not bear my argument; I pinched him to the quick about that Gr-Gr-ber.

MRS. SEAL. I saw that, for he durst not so much as hear you. I shall send to you, Mr. Sergeant, as soon as Sir Geoffry comes to town, and then I hope all may be adjusted.

TAR. I shall be at my chambers at my usual hours.

(Exit)

CIMB. Madam, if you please, I'll now attend you to the tea table, where I shall hear from your ladyship reason and good sense, after all this law and gibberish.

MRS. SEAL. 'Tis a wonderful thing, Sir, that men of professions do not study to talk the substance of what they have to say in the language of the rest of the world. Sure, they'd find their account in it.

CIMB. They might, perhaps, Madam, with people of your good sense; but with the generality 'twould never do. The vulgar would have no respect for truth and knowledge if they were exposed to naked view.

Truth is too simple, of all art bereav'd:
Since the world will—why, let it be deceiv'd.   *(Exeunt)*

ACT IV

SCENE I

SCENE: BEVIL JUNIOR's *lodgings*

BEVIL JUNIOR, *with a letter in his hand, followed by* TOM

TOM. Upon my life, Sir, I know nothing of the matter. I never opened my lips to Mr. Myrtle about anything of your honour's letter to Madam Lucinda.

BEV. JUN. What's the fool in such a fright for? I don't suppose you did. What I would know is, whether Mr. Myrtle showed any suspicion, or asked you any questions, to lead you to say casually that you had carried any such letter for me this morning.

TOM. Why, Sir, if he did ask me any questions, how could I help it?

BEV. JUN. I don't say you could, oaf! I am not questioning you, but him. What did he say to you?

TOM. Why, Sir, when I came to his chambers, to be

dressed for the lawyer's part your honour was pleased to put
me upon, he asked me if I had been at Mr. Sealand's this
morning. So I told him, Sir, I often went thither—because, Sir,
if I had not said that, he might have thought there was something more in my going now than at another time.

BEV. JUN.   Very well!—— (*aside*) The fellow's caution, I
find, has given him this jealousy.—— Did he ask you no other
questions?

TOM.   Yes, Sir; now I remember as we came away in the
hackney coach from Mr. Sealand's, "Tom," says he, "as I came
in to your master this morning, he bade you go for an answer
to a letter he had sent. Pray, did you bring him any?" says he.
"Ah!" says I, "Sir, your honour is pleased to joke with me;
you have a mind to know whether I can keep a secret or no?"

BEV. JUN.   And so, by showing him you could, you told
him you had one?

TOM. (*confused*)   Sir——

BEV. JUN.   What mean actions does jealousy make a man
stoop to! How poorly has he used art with a servant to make
him betray his own master!—— Well, and when did he give
you this letter for me?

TOM.   Sir, he writ it before he pulled off his lawyer's gown,
at his own chambers.

BEV. JUN.   Very well; and what did he say when you
brought him my answer to it?

TOM.   He looked a little out of humour, Sir, and said it was
very well.

BEV. JUN.   I knew he would be grave upon't. Wait without.

TOM.   Humh! 'gad, I don't like this; I am afraid we are all
in the wrong box here.   (*Exit* TOM)

BEV. JUN.   I put on a serenity while my fellow was present; but I have never been more thoroughly disturbed. This
hot man! to write me a challenge, on supposed artificial dealing, when I professed myself his friend! I can live contented
without glory, but I cannot suffer shame. What's to be done?
But first let me consider Lucinda's letter again.   (*reads*)

"SIR,
"I hope it is consistent with the laws a woman ought to
impose upon herself, to acknowledge that your manner of
declining a treaty of marriage in our family, and desiring
the refusal may come from me, has something more engaging in it than the courtship of him who, I fear, will fall to
my lot, except your friend exerts himself for our common

safety and happiness. I have reasons for desiring Mr. Myrtle may not know of this letter till hereafter, and am your most obliged humble servant,

"Lucinda Sealand."

Well, but the postscript——   (*reads*)

"I won't, upon second thoughts, hide anything from you. But my reason for concealing this is that Mr. Myrtle has a jealousy in his temper which gives me some terrors; but my esteem for him inclines me to hope that only an ill effect which sometimes accompanies a tender love, and what may be cured by a careful and unblameable conduct."

Thus has this lady made me her friend and confidant, and put herself, in a kind, under my protection. I cannot tell him immediately the purport of her letter, except I could cure him of the violent and untractable passion of jealousy, and so serve him and her, by disobeying her in the article of secrecy, more than I should by complying with her directions. But then this duelling, which custom has imposed upon every man who would live with reputation and honour in the world——how must I preserve myself from imputations there? He'll, forsooth, call it or think it fear, if I explain without fighting. But his letter——I'll read it again——

"SIR,

"You have used me basely in corresponding and carrying on a treaty where you told me you were indifferent. I have changed my sword since I saw you, which advertisement I thought proper to send you against the next meeting between you and the injured

"Charles Myrtle."

Enter TOM

TOM.   Mr. Myrtle, Sir. Would your honour please to see him?

BEV. JUN.   Why, you stupid creature! Let Mr. Myrtle wait at my lodgings? Show him up.   (*Exit* TOM)

Well! I am resolved upon my carriage to him. He is in love, and in every circumstance of life a little distrustful, which I must allow for—— but here he is.

Enter TOM, *introducing* MYRTLE

Sir, I am extremely obliged to you for this honour.—— But, Sir, you, with your very discerning face, leave the room.

(*Exit* TOM)

Well, Mr. Myrtle, your commands with me?

MYRT. The time, the place, our long acquaintance, and many other circumstances which affect me on this occasion, oblige me, without farther ceremony or conference, to desire you would not only, as you already have, acknowledge the receipt of my letter, but also comply with the request in it. I must have farther notice taken of my message than these half lines—— "I have yours—I shall be at home."

BEV. JUN. Sir, I own I have received a letter from you in a very unusual style; but as I design everything in this matter shall be your own action, your own seeking, I shall understand nothing but what you are pleased to confirm face to face, and I have already forgot the contents of your epistle.

MYRT. This cool manner is very agreeable to the abuse you have already made of my simplicity and frankness, and I see your moderation tends to your own advantage and not mine; to your own safety, not consideration of your friend.

BEV. JUN. My own safety, Mr. Myrtle?

MYRT. Your own safety, Mr. Bevil.

BEV. JUN. Look you, Mr. Myrtle, there's no disguising that I understand what you would be at; but, Sir, you know I have often dared to disapprove of the decisions a tryant custom has introduced, to the breach of all laws, both divine and human.

MYRT. Mr. Bevii, Mr. Bevil, it would be a good first principle in those who have so tender a conscience that way, to have as much abhorrence of doing injuries as——

BEV. JUN. As what?

MYRT. As fear of answering for 'em.

BEV. JUN. As fear of answering for 'em! But that apprehension is just or blameable according to the object of that fear. I have often told you, in confidence of heart, I abhorred the daring to offend the Author of life, and rushing into His presence—I say, by the very same act, to commit the crime against Him, and immediately to urge on to His tribunal.

MYRT. Mr. Bevil, I must tell you, this coolness, this gravity, this show of conscience, shall never cheat me of my mistress. You have, indeed, the best excuse for life—the hopes of possessing Lucinda. But consider, Sir, I have as much reason to be weary of it, if I am to lose her; and my first attempt to recover her shall be to let her see the dauntless man who is to be her guardian and protector.

BEV. JUN. Sir, show me but the least glimpse of argument that I am authorized by my own hand to vindicate any lawless insult of this nature, and I will show thee, to chastise thee hardly deserves the name of courage—slight, inconsiderate man! There is, Mr. Myrtle, no such terror in quick anger; and you shall, you know not why, be cool, as you have, you know not why, been warm.

MYRT. Is the woman one loves so little an occasion of anger? You, perhaps, who know not what it is to love, who have your ready, your commodious, your foreign trinket for your loose hours, and from your fortune, your specious out-ward carriage, and other lucky circumstances, as easy a way to the possession of a woman of honour—you know nothing of what it is to be alarmed, to be distracted with anxiety and terror of losing more than life. Your marriage, happy man! goes on like common business, and in the interim you have your rambling captive, your Indian princess, for your soft mo-ments of dalliance—your convenient, your ready Indiana.

BEV. JUN. You have touched me beyond the patience of a man, and I'm excusable, in the guard of innocence (or from the infirmity of human nature, which can bear no more), to accept your invitation and observe your letter. Sir, I'll attend you.

Enter TOM

TOM. Did you call, Sir? I thought you did: I heard you speak aloud.

BEV. JUN. Yes; go call a coach.

TOM. Sir—master—Mr. Myrtle—friends—gentleman—what d'ye mean? I am but a servant, or——

BEV. JUN. Call a coach!   (*Exit* TOM)
                 (*a long pause, walking sullenly by each other*)
(*aside*) Shall I (though provoked to the uttermost) recover myself at the entrance of a third person, and that my servant, too, and not have respect enough to all I have ever been re-ceiving from infancy, the obligation to the best of fathers, to an unhappy virgin too, whose life depends on mine? (*shutting the door—— to* MYRTLE) I have, thank heaven, had time to recollect myself, and shall not, for fear of what such a rash man as you think of me, keep longer unexplained the false appearances under which your infirmity of temper makes you suffer, when perhaps too much regard to a false point of honour makes me prolong that suffering.

MYRT. I am sure Mr. Bevil cannot doubt but I had rather have satisfaction from his innocence than his sword.

BEV. JUN. Why, then, would you ask it first that way?

MYRT.   Consider, you kept your temper yourself no longer than till I spoke to the disadvantage of her you loved.

BEV. JUN.   True; but let me tell you, I have saved you from the most exquisite distress, even though you had succeeded in the dispute. I know you so well that I am sure to have found this letter about a man you had killed would have been worse than death to yourself. Read it.—(*aside*) When he is thoroughly mortified and shame has got the better of jealousy, when he has seen himself throughly, he will deserve to be assisted towards obtaining Lucinda.

MYRT.   (*aside*)   With what a superiority has he turned the injury on me, as the aggressor! I begin to fear I have been too far transported. "A treaty in our family" is not that saying too much? I shall relapse. But I find (on the postscript) "something like jealousy." With what face can I see my benefactor, my advocate, whom I have treated like a betrayer?—— Oh! Bevil, with what words shall I——

BEV. JUN.   There needs none; to convince is much more than to conquer.

MYRT.   But can you——

BEV. JUN.   You have o'erpaid the inquietude you gave me, in the change I see in you towards me. Alas! what machines are we! Thy face is altered to that of another man—to that of my companion, my friend.

MYRT.   That I could be such a precipitant wretch!

BEV. JUN.   Pray, no more!

MYRT.   Let me reflect how many friends have died by the hands of friends, for want of temper; and you must give me leave to say again and again how much I am beholden to that superior spirit you have subdued me with. What had become of one of us, or perhaps both, had you been as weak as I was, and as incapable of reason?

BEV. JUN.   I congratulate to us both the escape from ourselves, and hope the memory of it will make us dearer friends than ever.

MYRT.   Dear Bevil, your friendly conduct has convinced me that there is nothing manly but what is conducted by reason and agreeable to the practice of virtue and justice. And yet how many have been sacrificed to that idol, the unreasonable opinion of men! Nay, they are so ridiculous, in it, that they often use their swords against each other with dissembled anger and real fear.

Betray'd by honour and compell'd by shame,
They hazard being to preserve a name:

Nor dare enquire into the dread mistake,
Till plung'd in sad eternity they wake.   (*Exeunt*)

SCENE II

SCENE: *St. James's Park*

Enter SIR JOHN BEVIL *and* MR. SEALAND

SIR J. BEV.   Give me leave, however, Mr. Sealand, as we are upon a treaty for uniting our families, to mention only the business of an ancient house. Genealogy and descent are to be of some consideration in an affair of this sort.

MR. SEAL.   Genealogy and descent! Sir, there has been in our family a very large one. There was Galfrid the father of Edward, the father of Ptolemy, the father of Crassus, the father of Earl Richard, the father of Henry the Marquis, the father of Duke John——

SIR J. BEV.   What, do you rave, Mr. Sealand?—— all these great names in your family?

MR. SEAL.   These? Yes, Sir. I have heard my father name 'em all, and more.

SIR J. BEV.   Ay, Sir? and did he say they were all in your family?

MR. SEAL.   Yes, Sir, he kept 'em all. He was the greatest cocker in England. He said Duke John won him many battles, and never lost one.

SIR J. BEV.   Oh, Sir, your servant! you are laughing at my laying any stress upon descent; but I must tell you, Sir, I never knew anyone but he that wanted that advantage turn it into ridicule.

MR. SEAL.   And I never knew anyone who had many better advantages put that into his account. But, Sir John, value yourself as you please upon your ancient house, I am to talk freely of everything you are pleased to put into your bill of rates on this occasion. Yet, Sir, I have made no objections to your son's family. 'Tis his morals that I doubt.

SIR J. BEV.   Sir, I can't help saying that what might injure a citizen's credit may be no stain to a gentleman's honour.

MR. SEAL.   Sir John, the honour of a gentleman is liable to be tainted by as small a matter as the credit of a trader. We are talking of a marriage, and in such a case the father of a young woman will not think it an addition to the honour or credit of her lover that he is a keeper——

SIR J. BEV.   Mr. Sealand, don't take upon you to spoil my son's marriage with any woman else.

MR. SEAL.   Sir John, let him apply to any woman else, and have as many mistresses as he pleases.

SIR J. BEV.   My son, Sir, is a discreet and sober gentleman.

MR. SEAL.   Sir, I never saw a man that wenched soberly and discreetly that ever left it off; the decency observed in the practice hides, even from the sinner, the iniquity of it. They pursue it, not that their appetites hurry 'em away, but, I warrant you, because 'tis their opinion they may do it.

SIR J. BEV.   Were what you suspect a truth—— do you design to keep your daughter a virgin till you find a man unblemished that way?

MR. SEAL.   Sir, as much a cit as you take me for, I know the town and the world—and give me leave to say that we merchants are a species of gentry that have grown into the world this last century, and are as honourable, and almost as useful, as you landed folks that have always thought yourselves so much above us; for your trading, forsooth! is extended no farther than a load of hay or a fat ox. You are pleasant people, indeed, because you are generally bred up to be lazy; therefore, I warrant you, industry is dishonourable.

SIR J. BEV.   Be not offended, Sir; let us go back to our point.

MR. SEAL.   Oh, not at all offended! but I don't love to leave any part of the account unclosed; look you, Sir John, comparisons are odious, and more particularly so on occasions of this kind, when we are projecting races that are to be made out of both sides of the comparisons.

SIR J. BEV.   But my son, Sir, is, in the eye of the world, a gentleman of merit.

MR. SEAL.   I own to you, I think him so. But, Sir John, I am a man exercised and experienced in chances and disasters. I lost, in my earlier years, a very fine wife, and with her a poor little infant; this makes me, perhaps, overcautious to preserve the second bounty of Providence to me, and be as careful as I can of this child. You'll pardon me; my poor girl, Sir, is as valuable to me as your boasted son to you.

SIR J. BEV.   Why, that's one very good reason, Mr. Sealand, why I wish my son had her.

MR. SEAL.   There is nothing but this strange lady here, this *incognita,* that can be objected to him. Here and there a man falls in love with an artful creature, and gives up all the motives of life to that one passion.

SIR J. BEV. A man of my son's understanding cannot be supposed to be one of them.

MR. SEAL. Very wise men have been so enslaved, and when a man marries with one of them upon his hands, whether moved from the demand of the world or slighter reasons, such a husband soils with his wife for a month perhaps—then "Good b'w'ye, Madam!"—the show's over. Ah! John Dryden points out such a husband to a hair, where he says,

> And while abroad so prodigal the dolt is,
> Poor spouse at home as ragged as a colt is.

Now, in plain terms, Sir, I shall not care to have my poor girl turned a-grazing, and that must be the case when——

SIR J. BEV. But pray consider, Sir, my son——

MR. SEAL. Look you, Sir, I'll make the matter short. This unknown lady, as I told you, is all the objection I have to him; but, one way or other, he is, or has been, certainly engaged to her. I am therefore resolved this very afternoon to visit her. Now, from her behaviour or appearance I shall soon be let into what I may fear or hope for.

SIR J. BEV. Sir, I am very confident there can be nothing enquired into, relating to my son, that will not, upon being understood, turn to his advantage.

MR. SEAL. I hope that as sincerely as you believe it. Sir John Bevil, when I am satisfied in this great point, if your son's conduct answers the character you give him, I shall wish your alliance more than that of any gentleman in Great Britain—and so, your servant!   (*Exit*)

SIR J. BEV. He is gone in a way but barely civil; but his great wealth, and the merit of his only child, the heiress of it, are not to be lost for a little peevishness.

Enter HUMPHREY

Oh, Humphrey! you are come in a seasonable minute. I want to talk to thee, and to tell thee that my head and heart are on the rack about my son.

HUMPH. Sir, you may trust his discretion; I am sure you may.

SIR J. BEV. Why, I do believe I may, and yet I'm in a thousand fears when I lay this vast wealth before me. When I consider his prepossessions, either generous to a folly in an honourable love, or abandoned past redemption in a vicious one; and, from the one or the other, his insensibility to the fairest prospect towards doubling our estate: a father who knows how useful wealth is, and how necessary, even to those who despise it—I say a father, Humphrey, a father cannot bear it.

HUMPH.   Be not transported, Sir; you will grow incapable of taking any resolution in your perplexity.

SIR J. BEV.   Yet, as angry as I am with him, I would not have him surprised in anything. This mercantile rough man may go grossly into the examination of this matter, and talk to the gentlewoman so as to——

HUMPH.   No, I hope, not in an abrupt manner.

SIR J. BEV.   No, I hope not! Why, dost thou know anything of her, or of him, or of anything of it, or all of it?

HUMPH.   My dear master, I know so much that I told him this very day you had reason to be secretly out of humour about her.

SIR J. BEV.   Did you go so far? Well, what said he to that?

HUMPH.   His words were, looking upon me steadfastly: "Humphrey," says he, "that woman is a woman of honour."

SIR J. BEV.   How! Do you think he is married to her, or designs to marry her?

HUMPH.   I can say nothing to the latter, but he says he can marry no one without your consent while you are living.

SIR J. BEV.   If he said so much, I know he scorns to break his word with me.

HUMPH.   I am sure of that.

SIR J. BEV.   You are sure of that. Well! that's some comfort. Then I have nothing to do but to see the bottom of this matter during this present ruffle.—O Humphrey——

HUMPH.   You are not ill, I hope, Sir.

SIR J. BEV.   Yes, a man is very ill that's in a very ill humour. To be a father is to be in care for one whom you oftener disoblige than please by that very care. Oh, that sons could know the duty to a father before they themselves are fathers! But perhaps you'll say now that I am one of the happiest fathers in the world; but I assure you, that of the very happiest is not a condition to be envied.

HUMPH.   Sir, your pain arises, not from the thing itself, but your particular sense of it. You are overfond—nay, give me leave to say you are unjustly apprehensive from your fondness. My master Bevil never disobliged you, and he will —I know he will—do everything you ought to expect.

SIR J. BEV.   He won't take all this money with this girl. For aught I know, he will, forsooth, have so much moderation as to think he ought not to force his liking for any consideration.

HUMPH.   He is to marry her, not you; he is to live with her, not you, Sir.

SIR J. BEV.   I know not what to think. But I know nothing can be more miserable than to be in this doubt. Follow me; I must come to some resolution.   (*Exeunt*)

SCENE III

SCENE: BEVIL JUNIOR's *lodgings*

Enter TOM *and* PHILLIS

TOM.   Well, Madam, if you must speak with Mr. Myrtle, you shall; he is now with my master in the library.

PHIL.   But you must leave me alone with him, for he can't make me a present, nor I so handsomely take anything from him, before you: it would not be decent.

TOM.   It will be very decent, indeed, for me to retire and leave my mistress with another man.

PHIL.   He is a gentleman and will treat one properly.

TOM.   I believe so; but, however, I won't be far off, and therefore will venture to trust you. I'll call him to you.
          (*Exit* TOM)

PHIL.   What a deal of pother and sputter here is between my mistress and Mr. Myrtle from mere punctilio! I could, any hour of the day, get her to her lover, and would do it—but she, forsooth, will allow no plot to get him; but, if he can come to her, I know she would be glad of it. I must, therefore, do her an acceptable violence and surprise her into his arms. I am sure I go by the best rule imaginable. If she were my maid, I should think her the best servant in the world for doing so by me.

Enter MYRTLE *and* TOM

Oh, Sir! You and Mr. Bevil are fine gentlemen to let a lady remain under such difficulties as my poor mistress, and no attempt to set her at liberty or release her from the danger of being instantly married to Cimberton.

MYRT.   Tom has been telling—— but what is to be done?

PHIL.   What is to be done—when a man can't come at his mistress! Why, can't you fire our house, or the next house to us, to make us run out, and you take us?

MYRT.   How, Mrs. Phillis!

PHIL. Ay; let me see that rogue deny to fire a house, make a riot, or any other little thing, when there were no other way to come at me.

TOM. I am obliged to you, Madam.

PHIL. Why, don't we hear every day of people's hanging themselves for love, and won't they venture the hazard of being hanged for love? Oh! were I a man——

MYRT. What manly thing would you have me undertake, according to your ladyship's notion of a man?

PHIL. Only be at once what, one time or other, you may be, and wish to be, or must be.

MYRT. Dear girl, talk plainly to me, and consider I, in my condition, can't be in very good humour. You say, to be at once what I must be.

PHIL. Ay, ay—I mean no more than to be an old man; I saw you do it very well at the masquerade. In a word, old Sir Geoffry Cimberton is every hour expected in town to join in the deeds and settlements for marrying Mr. Cimberton. He is half blind, half lame, half deaf, half dumb; though as to his passions and desires he is as warm and ridiculous as when in the heat of youth.

TOM. Come to the business, and don't keep the gentleman in suspense for the pleasure of being courted, as you serve me.

PHIL. I saw you at the masquerade act such a one to perfection. Go and put on that very habit, and come to our house as Sir Geoffry. There is not one there but myself knows his person; I was born in the parish where he is lord of the manor. I have seen him often and often at church in the country. Do not hesitate, but come thither; they will think you bring a certain security against Mr. Myrtle, and you bring Mr. Myrtle! Leave the rest to me. I leave this with you, and expect—— They don't, I told you, know you; they think you out of town, which you had as good be for ever if you lose this opportunity. I must be gone; I know I am wanted at home.

MYRT. My dear Phillis!

(catches and kisses her, and gives her money)

PHIL. O fie! my kisses are not my own; you have committed violence; but I'll carry 'em to the right owner. (TOM *kisses her—To* TOM) Come, see me downstairs, and leave the lover to think of his last game for the prize.

(Exeunt TOM *and* PHILLIS)

MYRT. I think I will instantly attempt this wild expedient.

The extravagance of it will make me less suspected, and it
will give me opportunity to assert my own right to Lucinda,
without whom I cannot live. But I am so mortified at this
conduct of mine towards poor Bevil. He must think meanly
of me. I know not how to reassume myself and be in spirit
enough for such an adventure as this. Yet I must attempt it,
if it be only to be near Lucinda under her present perplexities; and sure—

The next delight to transport with the fair,
Is to relieve her in her hours of care.   (*Exit*)

ACT V

SCENE I

SCENE: SEALAND'S *house*

Enter PHILLIS, *with lights, before* MYRTLE, *disguised like old*
SIR GEOFFRY, *supported by* MRS. SEALAND, LUCINDA, *and*
CIMBERTON

MRS. SEAL.   Now I have seen you thus far, Sir Geoffry,
will you excuse me a moment while I give my necessary
orders for your accommodation?   (*Exit* MRS. SEALAND)

MYRT.   I have not seen you, Cousin Cimberton, since you
were ten years old; and as it is incumbent on you to keep
up our name and family, I shall, upon very reasonable terms,
join with you in a settlement to that purpose. Though I must
tell you, Cousin, this is the first merchant that has married
into our house.

LUC. (*aside*)   Deuce on 'em! am I a merchant because my
father is?

MYRT.   But is he directly a trader at this time?

CIMB.   There's no hiding the disgrace, Sir; he trades to
all parts of the world.

MYRT.   We never had one of our family before who descended from persons that did anything.

CIMB.   Sir, since it is a girl that they have, I am, for the
honour of my family, willing to take it in again, and to sink
her into our name, and no harm done.

MYRT.   'Tis prudently and generously resolved. Is this the
young thing?

CIMB.   Yes, Sir.

PHIL. (*to* LUCINDA)   Good Madam, don't be out of humour, but let them run to the utmost of their extravagance. Hear them out.

MYRT. Can't I see her nearer? My eyes are but weak.

PHIL. (*to* LUCINDA) Beside, I am sure the uncle has something worth your notice. I'll take care to get off the young one, and leave you to observe what may be wrought out of the old one for your good. (*Exit*)

CIMB. Madam, this old gentleman, your great-uncle, desires to be introduced to you and to see you nearer—— Approach, Sir.

MYRT. By your leave, young lady. (*puts on spectacles*) ——Cousin Cimberton! She has exactly that sort of neck and bosom for which my sister Gertrude was so much admired in the year sixty-one, before the French dresses first discovered anything in women below the chin.

LUC. (*aside*) What a very odd situation am I in!—though I cannot but be diverted at the extravagance of their humours, equally unsuitable to their age.—— Chin, quotha! I don't believe my passionate lover there knows whether I have one or not. Ha! ha!

MYRT. Madam, I would not willingly offend, but I have a better glass—— (*pulls out a large one*)

Enter PHILLIS *to* CIMBERTON

PHIL. Sir, my lady desires to show the apartment to you that she intends for Sir Geoffry.

CIMB. Well, Sir, by that time you have sufficiently gazed and sunned yourself in the beauties of my spouse there, I will wait on you again. (*Exeunt* CIMBERTON *and* PHYLLIS)

MYRT. Were it not, Madam, that I might be troublesome, there is something of importance, though we are alone, which I would say more safe from being heard.

LUC. There is something in this old fellow, methinks, that raises my curiosity.

MYRT. To be free, Madam, I as heartily contemn this kinsman of mine as you do, and am sorry to see so much beauty and merit devoted by your parents to so insensible a possessor.

LUC. Surprising!——I hope, then, Sir, you will not contribute to the wrong you are so generous as to pity, whatever may be the interest of your family.

MYRT. This hand of mine shall never be employed to sign anything against your good and happiness.

LUC.   I am sorry, Sir, it is not in my power to make you proper acknowledgments, but there is a gentleman in the world whose gratitude will, I am sure, be worthy of the favour.

MYRT.   All the thanks I desire, Madam, are in your power to give.

LUC.   Name them, and command them.

MYRT.   Only, Madam, that the first time you are alone with your lover you will with open arms receive him.

LUC.   As willingly as his heart could wish it.

MYRT.   Thus, then, he claims your promise.—— O Lucinda!

LUC.   Oh! a cheat! a cheat! a cheat!

MYRT.   Hush! 'tis I, 'tis I, your lover, Myrtle himself, Madam.

LUC.   Oh, bless me! what a rashness and folly to surprise me so—— But hush—— my mother.

Enter MRS. SEALAND, CIMBERTON, *and* PHILLIS

MRS. SEAL.   How now! what's the matter?

LUC.   O Madam! as soon as you left the room my uncle fell into a sudden fit, and—and—so I cried out for help to support him and conduct him to his chamber.

MRS. SEAL.   That was kindly done. Alas, Sir! how do you find yourself?

MYRT.   Never was taken in so odd a way in my life—pray, lead me! Oh! I was talking here—pray carry me—to my Cousin Cimberton's young lady——

MRS. SEAL.   (*aside*) My Cousin Cimberton's young lady! How zealous he is, even in his extremity, for the match! a right Cimberton.

(CIMBERTON *and* LUCINDA *lead him as one in pain, etc.*)

CIMB.   Pox! Uncle, you will pull my ear off.

LUC.   Pray, Uncle! you will squeeze me to death.

MRS. SEAL.   No matter, no matter—he knows not what he does. Come, Sir, shall I help you out?

MYRT.   By no means! I'll trouble nobody but my young cousins here.   (*They lead him off*)

PHIL.   But pray, Madam, does your ladyship intend that Mr. Cimberton shall really marry my young mistress at last? I don't think he likes her.

MRS. SEAL.   That's not material! Men of his speculation are above desires. But be it as it may, now I have given old

Sir Geoffry the trouble of coming up to sign and seal, with what countenance can I be off?

PHIL.   As well as with twenty others, Madam. It is the glory and honour of a great fortune to live in continual treaties, and still to break off: it looks great, Madam.

MRS. SEAL.   True, Phillis—yet to return our blood again into the Cimbertons' is an honour not to be rejected. But were not you saying that Sir John Bevil's creature, Humphrey, has been with Mr. Sealand?

PHIL.   Yes, Madam; I overheard them agree that Mr. Sealand should go himself and visit this unknown lady that Mr. Bevil is so great with; and if he found nothing there to fright him, that Mr. Bevil should still marry my young mistress.

MRS. SEAL.   How! nay, then, he shall find she is my daughter as well as his. I'll follow him this instant and take the whole family along with me. The disputed power of disposing of my own daughter shall be at an end this very night. I'll live no longer in anxiety for a little hussy that hurts my appearance wherever I carry her, and for whose sake I seem to be not at all regarded, and that in the best of my days.

PHIL.   Indeed, Madam, if she were married, your ladyship might very well be taken for Mr. Sealand's daughter.

MRS. SEAL.   Nay, when the chit has not been with me, I have heard the men say as much. I'll no longer cut off the greatest pleasure of a woman's life—the shining in assemblies —by her forward anticipation of the respect that's due to her superior. She shall down to Cimberton Hall—she shall—she shall!

PHIL.   I hope, Madam, I shall stay with your ladyship.

MRS. SEAL.   Thou shalt, Phillis, and I'll place thee then more about me. But order chairs immediately—I'll be gone this minute.   (*Exeunt*)

SCENE II

SCENE: *Charing Cross*

Enter MR. SEALAND *and* HUMPHREY

MR. SEAL.   I am very glad, Mr. Humphrey, that you agree with me that it is for our common good I should look thoroughly into this matter.

HUMPH.   I am, indeed, of that opinion; for there is no

artifice, nothing concealed, in our family, which ought in justice to be known. I need not desire you, Sir, to treat the lady with care and respect.

MR. SEAL. Master Humphrey, I shall not be rude, though I design to be a little abrupt and come into the matter at once, to see how she will bear upon a surprise.

HUMPH. That's the door, Sir; I wish you success.—(*While* HUMPHREY *speaks* SEALAND *consults his table book.*) I am less concerned what happens there because I hear Mr. Myrtle is well lodged as old Sir Geoffry; so I am willing to let this gentleman employ himself here, to give them time at home: for I am sure 'tis necessary for the quiet of our family Lucinda were disposed of out of it, since Mr. Bevil's inclination is so much otherwise engaged. (*Exit*)

MR. SEAL. I think this is the door. (*knocks*) I'll carry this matter with an air of authority, to enquire, though I make an errand to begin discourse. (*knocks again, and enter a Foot-boy*) So, young man! is your lady within?

BOY. Alack, Sir! I am but a country boy—I dan't know whether she is or noa; but an you'll stay a bit, I'll goa and ask the gentlewoman that's with her.

MR. SEAL. Why, Sirrah, though you are a country boy, you can see, can't you? you know whether she is at home, when you see her, don't you?

BOY. Nay, nay, I'm not such a country lad neither, master, to think she's at home because I see her. I have been in town but a month, and I lost one place already for believing my own eyes.

MR. SEAL. Why, Sirrah! have you learnt to lie already?

BOY. Ah, master! things that are lies in the country are not lies at London—I begin to know my business a little better than so. But an you please to walk in, I'll call a gentlewoman to you that can tell you for certain—she can make bold to ask my lady herself.

MR. SEAL. Oh! then she is within, I find, though you dare not say so.

BOY. Nay, nay! that's neither here nor there: what's matter whether she is within or no, if she has not a mind to see anybody?

MR. SEAL. I can't tell, Sirrah, whether you are arch or simple; but, however, get me a direct answer, and here's a shilling for you.

BOY. Will you please to walk in; I'll see what I can do for you.

MR. SEAL.   I see you will be fit for your business in time, child. But I expect to meet with nothing but extraordinaries in such a house.

BOY.   Such a house! Sir, you han't seen it yet. Pray walk in.

MR. SEAL.   Sir, I'll wait upon you.   (*Exeunt*)

SCENE III

SCENE: INDIANA'S *house*

Enter ISABELLA

ISAB.   What anxiety do I feel for this poor creature! What will be the end of her? Such a languishing, unreserved passion for a man that at last must certainly leave or ruin her— and perhaps both! Then the aggravation of the distress is, that she does not believe he will—not but, I must own, if they are both what they would seem, they are made for one another as much as Adam and Eve were, for there is no other of their kind but themselves.

Enter Boy

So, Daniel! what news with you?

BOY.   Madam, there's a gentleman below would speak with my lady.

ISAB.   Sirrah! don't you know Mr. Bevil yet?

BOY.   Madam, 'tis not the gentleman who comes every day, and asks for you, and won't go in till he knows whether you are with her or no.

ISAB.   Ha! that's a particular I did not know before.—— Well, be it who it will, let him come up to me.

(*Exit Boy, and re-enters with* MR. SEALAND; ISABELLA *looks amazed*)

MR. SEAL.   Madam, I can't blame your being a little surprised to see a perfect stranger make a visit, and——

ISAB.   I am indeed surprised!—— (*aside*) I see he does not know me.

MR. SEAL.   You are very prettily lodged here, Madam; in troth, you seem to have everything in plenty.—— (*aside, and looking about*) A thousand a year, I warrant you, upon this pretty nest of rooms and the dainty one within them.

ISAB.   (*apart*) Twenty years, it seems, have less effect in the alteration of a man of thirty than of a girl of fourteen— he's almost still the same. But alas! I find by other men, as well as himself, I am not what I was. As soon as he spoke I was convinced 'twas he. How shall I contain my surprise and satisfaction! he must not know me yet.

MR. SEAL. Madam, I hope I don't give you any disturbance, but there is a young lady here with whom I have a particular business to discourse, and I hope she will admit me to that favour.

ISAB. Why, Sir, have you had any notice concerning her? I wonder who could give it you.

MR. SEAL. That, Madam, is fit only to be communicated to herself.

ISAB. Well, Sir! you shall see her.—— (*aside*) I find he knows nothing yet, nor shall from me. I am resolved I will observe this interlude, this sport of nature and of fortune.—— You shall see her presently, Sir, for now I am as a mother, and will trust her with you. (*Exit*)

MR. SEAL. As a mother! right; that's the old phrase for one of those commode ladies, who lend out beauty for hire to young gentlemen that have pressing occasions. But here comes the precious lady herself. In troth, a very sightly woman!

Enter INDIANA

IND. I am told, Sir, you have some affair that requires your speaking with me.

MR. SEAL. Yes, Madam: there came to my hands a bill drawn by Mr. Bevil, which is payable to-morrow, and he, in the intercourse of business, sent it to me, who have cash of his, and desired me to send a servant with it; but I have made bold to bring you the money myself.

IND. Sir! was that necessary?

MR. SEAL. No, Madam; but, to be free with you, the fame of your beauty and the regard which Mr. Bevil is a little too well known to have for you, excited my curiosity.

IND. Too well known to have for me! Your sober appearance, Sir, which my friend described, made me expect no rudeness, or absurdity, at least.—— Who's there?—— Sir, if you pay the money to a servant 'twill be as well.

MR. SEAL. Pray, Madam, be not offended. I came hither on an innocent, nay, a virtuous design; and if you will have patience to hear me it may be as useful to you, as you are in a friendship with Mr. Bevil, as to my only daughter, whom I was this day disposing of.

IND. You make me hope, Sir, I have mistaken you. I am

composed again; be free, say on—— (*aside*) what I am afraid to hear.

MR. SEAL.   I feared, indeed, an unwarranted passion here, but I did not think it was in abuse of so worthy an object, so accomplished a lady as your sense and mien bespeak. But the youth of our age care not what merit and virtue they bring to shame, so they gratify——

IND.   Sir, you are going into very great errors; but as you are pleased to say you see something in me that has changed at least the colour of your suspicions, so has your appearance altered mine, and made me earnestly attentive to what has any way concerned you to enquire into my affairs and character.

MR. SEAL.   (*aside*) How sensibly, with what an air she talks!

IND.   Good Sir, be seated, and tell me tenderly—keep all your suspicions concerning me alive, that you may in a proper and prepared way acquaint me why the care of your daughter obliges a person of your seeming worth and fortune to be thus inquisitive about a wretched, helpless, friendless—— (*weeping*). But I beg your pardon: though I am an orphan, your child is not; and your concern for her, it seems, has brought you hither. I'll be composed; pray go on, Sir.

MR. SEAL.   How could Mr. Bevil be such a monster, to injure such a woman?

IND.   No, Sir, you wrong him; he has not injured me; my support is from his bounty.

MR. SEAL.   Bounty! when gluttons give high prices for delicates, they are prodigious bountiful!

IND.   Still, still you will persist in that error. But my own fears tell me all. You are the gentleman, I suppose, for whose happy daughter he is designed a husband by his good father, and he has, perhaps, consented to the overture. He was here this morning, dressed beyond his usual plainness—nay, most sumptuously—and he is to be, perhaps, this night a bridegroom.

MR. SEAL.   I own he was intended such; but, Madam, on your account, I have determined to defer my daughter's marriage till I am satisfied from your own mouth of what nature are the obligations you are under to him.

IND.   His actions, Sir, his eyes, have only made me think he designed to make me the partner of his heart. The goodness and gentleness of his demeanour made me misinterpret all. 'Twas my own hope, my own passion, that deluded me;

he never made one amorous advance to me. His large heart
and bestowing hand have only helped the miserable. Nor
know I why, but from his mere delight in virtue, that I have
been his care, the object on which to indulge and please
himself with pouring favours.

MR. SEAL.   Madam, I know not why it is, but I, as well as
you, am methinks afraid of entering into the matter I came
about; but 'tis the same thing as if we had talked never so
distinctly: he ne'er shall have a daughter of mine.

IND.   If you say this from what you think of me, you
wrong yourself and him. Let not me, miserable though I may
be, do injury to my benefactor. No, Sir, my treatment ought
rather to reconcile you to his virtues. If to bestow without a
prospect of return; if to delight in supporting what might,
perhaps, be thought an object of desire, with no other view
than to be her guard against those who would not be so disinterested—if these actions, Sir, can in a careful parent's eye
commend him to a daughter, give yours, Sir, give her to my
honest, generous Bevil. What have I to do but sigh and weep,
to rave, run wild, a lunatic in chains, or, hid in darkness,
mutter in distracted starts and broken accents my strange,
strange story!

MR. SEAL.   Take comfort, Madam.

IND.   All my comfort must be to expostulate in madness,
to relieve with frenzy my despair, and shrieking to demand
of fate, "Why—why was I born to such variety of sorrows?"

MR. SEAL.   If I have been the least occasion——

IND.   No, 'twas heaven's high will I should be such—to be
plundered in my cradle! tossed on the seas! and even there
an infant captive! to lose my mother, hear but of my father!
to be adopted! lose my adopter! then plunged again in worse
calamities!

MR. SEAL.   An infant captive!

IND.   Yet then to find the most charming of mankind, once
more to set me free from what I thought the last distress; to
load me with his services, his bounties and his favours; to
support my very life in a way that stole, at the same time,
my very soul itself from me!

MR. SEAL.   And has young Bevil been this worthy man?

IND.   Yet then, again, this very man to take another! without leaving me the right, the pretence, of easing my fond
heart with tears! For, oh! I can't reproach him, though the
same hand that raised me to this height now throws me down
the precipice.

MR. SEAL. Dear lady! Oh, yet one moment's patience: my heart grows full with your affliction. But yet there's something in your story that——

IND. My portion here is bitterness and sorrow.

MR. SEAL. Do not think so. Pray answer me: does Bevil know your name and family?

IND. Alas, too well! Oh, could I be any other thing than what I am! I'll tear away all traces of my former self, my little ornaments, the remains of my first state, the hints of what I ought to have been——

(*In her disorder she throws away a bracelet, which* SEALAND *takes up, and looks earnestly on it.*)

MR. SEAL. Ha! what's this? My eyes are not deceived? It is, it is the same! the very bracelet which I bequeathed my wife at our last mournful parting!

IND. What said you, Sir! Your wife! Whither does my fancy carry me? What means this unfelt motion at my heart? And yet again my fortune but deludes me; for if I err not, Sir, your name is Sealand, but my lost father's name was——

MR. SEAL. Danvers! was it not?

IND. What new amazement! That is, indeed, my family.

MR. SEAL. Know, then, when my misfortunes drove me to the Indies, for reasons too tedious now to mention, I changed my name of Danvers into Sealand.

Enter ISABELLA

ISAB. If yet there wants an explanation of your wonder, examine well this face: yours, Sir, I well remember. Gaze on, and read in me your sister, Isabella.

MR. SEAL. My sister!

ISAB. But here's a claim more tender yet—your Indiana, Sir, your long-lost daughter.

MR. SEAL. O my child! my child!

IND. All-gracious heaven! is it possible! do I embrace my father!

MR. SEAL. And do I hold thee? These passions are too strong for utterance. Rise, rise, my child, and give my tears their way.—O my Sister!   (*embracing her*)

ISAB. Now, dearest Niece, my groundless fears, my painful cares no more shall vex thee. If I have wronged thy noble lover with too hard suspicions, my just concern for thee, I hope, will plead my pardon.

MR. SEAL. Oh! make him, then, the full amends, and be yourself the messenger of joy. Fly this instant! tell him all these wondrous turns of Providence in his favour! Tell him I have now a daughter to bestow which he no longer will decline; that this day he still shall be a bridegroom; nor shall a fortune, the merit which his father seeks, be wanting; tell him the reward of all his virtues waits on his acceptance.

(*Exit* ISABELLA)

My dearest Indiana! (*turns and embraces her*)

IND.   Have I then, at last, a father's sanction on my love? his bounteous hand to give, and make my heart a present worthy of Bevil's generosity?

MR. SEAL.   O my child! how are our sorrows past o'erpaid by such a meeting! Though I have lost so many years of soft paternal dalliance with thee, yet, in one day to find thee thus, and thus bestow thee in such perfect happiness, is ample, ample reparation! And yet again, the merit of thy lover——

IND.   Oh, had I spirits left to tell you of his actions! how strongly filial duty has suppressed his love, and how conceal-ment still has doubled all his obligations; the pride, the joy of his alliance, Sir, would warm your heart, as he has con-quered mine.

MR. SEAL.   How laudable is love when born of virtue! I burn to embrace him——

IND.   See, Sir, my aunt already has succeeded, and brought him to your wishes.

Enter ISABELLA, *with* SIR JOHN BEVIL, BEVIL JUNIOR, MRS. SEALAND, CIMBERTON, MYRTLE *and* LUCINDA

SIR J. BEV. (*entering*)   Where, where's this scene of won-der? Mr. Sealand, I congratulate, on this occasion, our mutual happiness. Your good sister, Sir, has, with the story of your daughter's fortune, filled us with surprise and joy. Now all exceptions are removed; my son has now avowed his love, and turned all former jealousies and doubts to approbation; and, I am told, your goodness has consented to reward him.

MR. SEAL.   If, Sir, a fortune equal to his father's hopes can make this object worthy his acceptance.

BEV. JUN.   I hear your mention, Sir, of fortune, with pleas-ure only as it may prove the means to reconcile the best of fathers to my love. Let him be provident, but let me be happy. — (*embracing* INDIANA) My ever-destined, my ac-knowledged wife!

IND.   Wife! Oh, my ever loved! my lord! my master!

SIR J. BEV.   I congratulate myself, as well as you, that I

had a son who could, under such disadvantages, discover your great merit.

MR. SEAL. O Sir John! how vain, how weak is human prudence! What care, what foresight, what imagination could contrive such blest events to make our children happy as Providence in one short hour has laid before us?

CIMB. (*to* MRS. SEALAND) I am afraid, Madam, Mr. Sealand is a little too busy for our affair: if you please, we'll take another opportunity.

MRS. SEAL. Let us have patience, Sir.

CIMB. But we make Sir Geoffry wait, Madam.

MYRT. O Sir! I am not in haste.

(*During this* BEVIL JUNIOR *presents* LUCINDA *to* IN-DIANA.)

MR. SEAL. But here—here's our general benefactor! Excellent young man, that could be at once a lover to her beauty and a parent to her virtue.

BEV. JUN. If you think that an obligation, Sir, give me leave to overpay myself, in the only instance that can now add to my felicity, by begging you to bestow this lady on Mr. Myrtle.

MR. SEAL. She is his without reserve; I beg he may be sent for.—— Mr. Cimberton, notwithstanding you never had my consent, yet there is, since I last saw you, another objection to your marriage with my daughter.

CIMB. I hope, Sir, your lady has concealed nothing from me?

MR. SEAL. Troth, Sir! nothing but what was concealed from myself—another daughter, who has an undoubted title to half my estate.

CIMB. How, Mr. Sealand! Why then, if half Mrs. Lucinda's fortune is gone, you can't say that any of my estate is settled upon her. I was in treaty for the whole, but if that is not to be come at, to be sure there can be no bargain. Sir, I have nothing to do but to take my leave of your good lady, my cousin, and beg pardon for the trouble I have given this old gentleman.

MYRT. That you have, Mr. Cimberton, with all my heart.

(*discovers himself*)

OMN. Mr. Myrtle!

MYRT. And I beg pardon of the whole company that I assumed the person of Sir Geoffry, only to be present at the danger of this lady's being disposed of, and in her utmost exigence to assert my right to her; which, if her parents will ratify, as they once favoured my pretensions, no abatement of fortune shall lessen her value to me.

LUC.   Generous man!

MR. SEAL.   If, Sir, you can overlook the injury of being in treaty with one who as meanly left her as you have generously asserted your right in her, she is yours.

LUC.   Mr. Myrtle, though you have ever had my heart, yet now I find I love you more because I bring you less.

MYRT.   We have much more than we want, and I am glad any event has contributed to the discovery of our real inclinations to each other.

MRS. SEAL.   (*aside*) Well! However, I'm glad the girl's disposed of, anyway.

BEV. JUN.   Myrtle, no longer rivals now, but brothers!

MYRT.   Dear Bevil, you are born to triumph over me. But now our competition ceases; I rejoice in the pre-eminence of your virtue, and your alliance adds charms to Lucinda.

SIR J. BEV.   Now, ladies and gentlemen, you have set the world a fair example. Your happiness is owing to your constancy and merit, and the several difficulties you have struggled with evidently show

     Whate'er the generous mind itself denies,
     The secret care of Providence supplies.   (*Exeunt*)

EPILOGUE

By MR. WELSTED

INTENDED TO BE SPOKEN BY INDIANA

Our author, whom intreaties cannot move,
Spite of the dear coquetry that you love,
Swears he'll not frustrate (so he plainly means),
By a loose epilogue, his decent scenes.
Is it not, Sirs, hard fate I meet to-day,
To keep me rigid still beyond the play?
And yet I'm sav'd a world of pains that way.
I now can look, I now can move at ease,
Nor need I torture these poor limbs to please,
Nor with the hand or foot attempt surprise,
Nor wrest my features, nor fatigue my eyes.
Bless me! what freakish gambols have I play'd!
What motions tried, and wanton looks betray'd!

Out of pure kindness all, to overrule
The threaten'd hiss, and screen some scribbling fool.
With more respect I'm entertain'd to-night:
Our author thinks I can with ease delight.
My artless looks while modest graces arm,
He says I need but to appear and charm.
A wife so form'd, by these examples bred,
Pours joy and gladness round the marriage bed;
Soft source of comfort, kind relief from care,
And 'tis her least perfection to be fair.
The nymph with Indiana's worth who vies,
A nation will behold with Bevil's eyes.

The
Beggar's Opera

BY JOHN GAY

Nos hæc novimus esse nihil.[1]   Martial

---

[1] We know these things to be nothing at all.

DRAMATIS PERSONÆ

Men:

PEACHUM
LOCKIT
MACHEATH
FILCH
JEMMY TWITCHER
CROOK-FINGERED JACK
WAT DREARY
ROBIN OF BAGSHOT ⎫ MACHEATH'S *Gang*
NIMMING NED ⎬
HARRY PADINGTON
MATT OF THE MINT
BEN BUDGE ⎭
BEGGAR
PLAYER
Constables, Drawer, Turnkey, etc.

Women:

MRS. PEACHUM
POLLY PEACHUM
LUCY LOCKIT
DIANA TRAPES
MRS. COAXER ⎫
DOLLY TRULL ⎬
MRS. VIXEN
BETTY DOXY
JENNY DIVER ⎬ *Women of the Town*
MRS. SLAMMEKIN
SUKY TAWDRY
MOLLY BRAZEN ⎭

INTRODUCTION

BEGGAR, PLAYER

BEGGAR. If poverty be a title to poetry, I am sure nobody can dispute mine. I own myself of the company of beggars; and I make one at their weekly festivals at St. Giles's. I have a small yearly salary for my catches, and am welcome to a dinner there whenever I please, which is more than most poets can say.

PLAYER. As we live by the Muses, 'tis but gratitude in us to encourage poetical merit wherever we find it. The Muses, contrary to all other ladies, pay no distinction to dress, and never partially mistake the pertness of embroidery for wit, nor the modesty of want for dulness. Be the author who he will, we push his play as far as it will go. So (though you are in want) I wish you success heartily.

BEGGAR. This piece I own was originally writ for the celebrating the marriage of James Chanter and Moll Lay, two most excellent ballad-singers. I have introduced the similes that are in all your celebrated operas: the swallow, the moth, the bee, the ship, the flower, etc. Besides, I have a prison scene, which the ladies always reckon charmingly pathetic. As to the parts, I have observed such a nice impartiality to our two ladies, that it is impossible for either of them to take offence. I hope I may be forgiven, that I have not made my opera throughout unnatural, like those in vogue; for I have no recitative; excepting this, as I have consented to have neither prologue nor epilogue, it must be allowed an opera in all its forms. The piece indeed hath been heretofore frequently represented by ourselves in our great room at St. Giles's, so that I cannot too often acknowledge your charity in bringing it now on the stage.

PLAYER. But I see 'tis time for us to withdraw; the actors are preparing to begin.—— Play away the overture.

(Exeunt)

THE BEGGAR'S OPERA

ACT I

SCENE I

SCENE: *Peachum's house*

PEACHUM *sitting at a table with a large book of accounts before him*

AIR I. *An old woman clothed in grey*

Through all the employments of life,
    Each neighbour abuses his brother;
Whore and rogue they call husband and wife:
    All professions be-rogue one another.
The priest calls the lawyer a cheat,
    The lawyer be-knaves the divine;
And the statesman, because he's so great,
    Thinks his trade as honest as mine.

A lawyer is an honest employment; so is mine. Like me, too, he acts in a double capacity, both against rogues and for 'em; for 'tis but fitting that we should protect and encourage cheats, since we live by 'em.

SCENE II

PEACHUM, FILCH

FILCH. Sir, Black Moll hath sent word her trial comes on in the afternoon, and she hopes you will order matters so as to bring her off.

PEACH. Why, she may plead her belly at worst; to my knowledge she hath taken care of that security. But as the wench is very active and industrious, you may satisfy her that I'll soften the evidence.

FILCH. Tom Gagg, Sir, is found guilty.

PEACH. A lazy dog! When I took him the time before, I told him what he would come to if he did not mend his hand.

This is death without reprieve. I may venture to book him.

(writes)

"For Tom Gagg, forty pounds." Let Betty Sly know that I'll save her from transportation, for I can get more by her staying in England.

FILCH.   Betty hath brought more goods into our lock to-year, than any five of the gang; and in truth, 'tis a pity to lose so good a customer.

PEACH.   If none of the gang take her off, she may, in the common course of business, live a twelve-month longer. I love to let women scape. A good sportsman always lets the hen partridges fly, because the breed of the game depends upon them. Besides, here the law allows us no reward; there is nothing to be got by the death of women—except our wives.

FILCH.   Without dispute, she is a fine woman! 'Twas to her I was obliged for my education, and (to say a bold word) she hath trained up more young fellows to the business than the gaming-table.

PEACH.   Truly, Filch, thy observation is right. We and the surgeons are more beholden to women than all the professions besides.

AIR II. *The bonny grey-eyed morn*

FILCH.   'Tis woman that seduces all mankind,
> By her we first were taught the wheedling arts:
Her very eyes can cheat; when most she's kind,
> She tricks us of our money with our hearts.
For her, like wolves by night we roam for prey,
> And practise ev'ry fraud to bribe her charms;
For suits of love, like law, are won by pay,
> And beauty must be fee'd into our arms.

PEACH.   But make haste to Newgate, boy, and let my friends know what I intend; for I love to make them easy one way or other.

FILCH.   When a gentleman is long kept in suspense, penitence may break his spirit ever after. Besides, certainty gives a man a good air upon his trial, and makes him risk another without fear or scruple. But I'll away, for 'tis a pleasure to be the messenger of comfort to friends in affliction.

SCENE III

PEACHUM

But 'tis now high time to look about me for a decent execution against next sessions. I hate a lazy rogue, by whom one can get nothing till he is hanged. (*reading*) "A register of the gang. Crook-fingered Jack." A year and a half in the service. Let me see how much the stock owes to his industry; one, two, three, four, five gold watches, and seven silver ones. A mighty clean-handed fellow! Sixteen snuff-boxes, five of them of true gold. Six dozen of handkerchiefs, four silver-hilted swords, half a dozen of shirts, three tie-periwigs, and a piece of broadcloth. Considering these are only the fruits of his leisure hours, I don't know a prettier fellow, for no man alive hath a more engaging presence of mind upon the road. "Wat Dreary, alias Brown Will," an irregular dog, who hath an underhand way of disposing of his goods. I'll try him only for a sessions or two longer upon his good behaviour. "Harry Padington," a poor petty-larceny rascal, without the least genius; that fellow, though he were to live these six months, will never come to the gallows with any credit. "Slippery Sam"; he goes off the next sessions, for the villain hath the impudence to have views of following his trade as a tailor, which he calls an honest employment. "Matt of the Mint," listed not above a month ago, a promising sturdy fellow, and diligent in his way; somewhat too bold and hasty, and may raise good contributions on the public, if he does not cut himself short by murder. "Tom Tipple," a guzzling soaking sot, who is always too drunk to stand himself, or to make others stand. A cart is absolutely necessary for him. "Robin of Bagshot, alias Gorgon, alias Bluff Bob, alias Carbuncle, alias Bob Booty—"

SCENE IV

PEACHUM, MRS. PEACHUM

MRS. PEACH. What of Bob Booty, husband? I hope nothing bad hath betided him. You know, my dear, he's a favourite customer of mine. 'Twas he made me a present of this ring.

PEACH. I have set his name down in the black-list, that's all, my dear; he spends his life among women, and as soon as his money is gone, one or other of the ladies will hang him for the reward, and there's forty pound lost to us forever.

MRS. PEACH. You know, my dear, I never meddle in matters of death; I always leave those affairs to you. Women indeed are bitter bad judges in these cases, for they are so partial to the brave, that they think every man handsome who is going to the camp or the gallows.

AIR III. *Cold and raw*

If any wench Venus's girdle wear,
   Though she be never so ugly;
Lilies and roses will quickly appear,
   And her face look wond'rous smugly.
Beneath the left ear so fit but a cord,
   (A rope so charming a zone is!)
The youth in his cart hath the air of a lord,
   And we cry, "There dies an Adonis!"

But really, husband, you should not be too hard-hearted, for
you never had a finer, braver set of men than at present. We
have not had a murder among them all, these seven months.
And truly, my dear, that is a great blessing.

PEACH.   What a dickens is the woman always a-whimper-
ing about murder for? No gentleman is ever looked upon the
worse for killing a man in his own defence; and if business
cannot be carried on without it, what would you have a gentleman do?

MRS. PEACH.   If I am in the wrong, my dear, you must excuse me, for nobody can help the frailty of an overscrupulous
conscience.

PEACH.   Murder is as fashionable a crime as a man can be
guilty of. How many fine gentlemen have we in Newgate
every year, purely upon that article! If they have wherewithal
to persuade the jury to bring it in manslaughter, what are
they the worse for it? So, my dear, have done upon this subject. Was Captain Macheath here this morning, for the bank-
notes he left with you last week?

MRS. PEACH.   Yes, my dear; and though the bank had
stopped payment, he was so cheerful and so agreeable! Sure
there is not a finer gentleman upon the road than the captain!
If he comes from Bagshot at any reasonable hour he hath
promised to make one this evening with Polly and me, and
Bob Booty, at a party of quadrille. Pray, my dear, is the captain rich?

PEACH.   The captain keeps too good company ever to
grow rich. Marybone and the chocolate-houses are his undoing. The man that proposes to get money by play should
have the education of a fine gentleman, and be trained up to
it from his youth.

MRS. PEACH.   Really, I am sorry upon Polly's account the
captain hath not more discretion. What business hath he to

keep company with lords and gentlemen? he should leave
them to prey upon one another.

PEACH.   "Upon Polly's account!" What a plague does the
woman mean?—"Upon Polly's account!"

MRS. PEACH.   Captain Macheath is very fond of the girl.

PEACH.   And what then?

MRS. PEACH.   If I have any skill in the ways of women, I
am sure Polly thinks him a very pretty man.

PEACH.   And what then? You would not be so mad to have
the wench marry him! Gamesters and highwaymen are generally very good to their whores, but they are very devils to
their wives.

MRS. PEACH.   But if Polly should be in love, how should
we help her, or how can she help herself? Poor girl, I am in
the utmost concern about her.

AIR IV. *Why is your faithful slave disdain'd?*

> If love the virgin's heart invade,
> How, like a moth, the simple maid
>   Still plays about the flame!
> If soon she be not made a wife,
> Her honour's sing'd, and then for life
>   She's—what I dare not name.

PEACH.   Look ye, wife. A handsome wench in our way of
business is as profitable as at the bar of a Temple coffee-
house, who looks upon it as her livelihood to grant every
liberty but one. You see I would indulge the girl as far as prudently we can. In anything but marriage! After that, my dear,
how shall we be safe? Are we not then in her husband's
power? For a husband hath the absolute power over all a
wife's secrets but her own. If the girl had the discretion of a
court lady, who can have a dozen young fellows at her ear
without complying with one, I should not matter it; but Polly
is tinder, and a spark will at once set her on a flame. Married! If the wench does not know her own profit, sure she
knows her own pleasure better than to make herself a property! My daughter to me should be, like a court lady to a
minister of state, a key to the whole gang. Married! If the
affair is not already done, I'll terrify her from it, by the example of our neighbours.

MRS. PEACH.   Mayhap, my dear, you may injure the girl.
She loves to imitate the fine ladies, and she may only allow
the captain liberties in the view of interest.

PEACH. But 'tis your duty, my dear, to warn the girl against her ruin, and to instruct her how to make the most of her beauty. I'll go to her this moment, and sift her. In the meantime, wife, rip out the coronets and marks of these dozen of cambric handkerchiefs, for I can dispose of them this afternoon to a chap in the City.

SCENE V

MRS. PEACHUM

Never was a man more out of the way in an argument than my husband! Why must our Polly, forsooth, differ from her sex, and love only her husband? And why must Polly's marriage, contrary to all observation, make her the less followed by other men? All men are thieves in love, and like a woman the better for being another's property.

AIR V. *Of all the simple things we do*

A maid is like the golden ore,
    Which hath guineas intrinsical in't
Whose worth is never known, before
    It is tried and impress'd in the mint.
A wife's like a guinea in gold,
    Stamp'd with the name of her spouse;
Now here, now there; is bought, or is sold;
    And is current in every house.

SCENE VI

MRS. PEACHUM, FILCH

MRS. PEACH. Come hither, Filch— (*aside*) I am as fond of this child as though my mind misgave me he were my own. He hath as fine a hand at picking a pocket as a woman, and is as nimble-fingered as a juggler.— If an unlucky session does not cut the rope of thy life, I pronounce, boy, thou wilt be a great man in history. Where was your post last night, my boy?

FILCH. I plied at the opera, Madam; and considering 'twas neither dark nor rainy, so that there was no great hurry in getting chairs and coaches, made a tolerable hand on't. These seven handkerchiefs, Madam.

MRS. PEACH. Coloured ones, I see. They are of sure sale from our warehouse at Redriff among the seamen.

FILCH. And this snuff-box.

MRS. PEACH. Set in gold! A pretty encouragement this to
a young beginner.

FILCH. I had a fair tug at a charming gold watch. Pox
take the tailors for making the fobs so deep and narrow! It
stuck by the way, and I was forced to make my escape under
a coach. Really, Madam, I fear I shall be cut off in the flower
of my youth, so that every now and then (since I was
pumped) I have thoughts of taking up and going to sea.

MRS. PEACH. You should go to Hockley in the Hole and to
Marybone, child, to learn valour. These are the schools that
have bred so many brave men. I thought, boy, by this time
thou hadst lost fear as well as shame. Poor lad! how little does
he know as yet of the Old Bailey! For the first fact I'll insure
thee from being hanged; and going to sea, Filch, will come
time enough upon a sentence of transportation. But now,
since you have nothing better to do, even go to your book, and
learn your catechism; for really a man makes but an ill figure
in the ordinary's paper, who cannot give a satisfactory answer
to his questions. But, hark you, my lad. Don't tell me a lie;
for you know I hate a liar. Do you know of anything that hath
passed between Captain Macheath and our Polly?

FILCH. I beg you, Madam, don't ask me; for I must either
tell a lie to you or to Miss Polly; for I promised her I would
not tell.

MRS. PEACH. But when the honour of our family is concerned——

FILCH. I shall lead a sad life with Miss Polly, if ever she
come to know that I told you. Besides, I would not willingly
forfeit my own honour by betraying anybody.

MRS. PEACH. Yonder comes my husband and Polly. Come,
Filch, you shall go with me into my own room, and tell me
the whole story. I'll give thee a most delicious glass of a
cordial that I keep for my own drinking.

SCENE VII

PEACHUM, POLLY

POLLY. I know as well as any of the fine ladies how to
make the most of myself and of my man too. A woman knows
how to be mercenary, though she hath never been in a court
or at an assembly. We have it in our natures, Papa. If I allow
Captain Macheath some trifling liberties, I have this watch

and other visible marks of his favour to show for it. A girl who
cannot grant some things, and refuse what is most material,
will make but a poor hand of her beauty, and soon be thrown
upon the common.

AIR VI. *What shall I do to show how much I love her?*

Virgins are like the fair flower in its lustre,
    Which in the garden enamels the ground;
Near it the bees in play flutter and cluster,
    And gaudy butterflies frolic around.
But, when once pluck'd, 'tis no longer alluring,
    To Covent Garden 'tis sent (as yet sweet),
There fades, and shrinks, and grows past all enduring,
    Rots, stinks, and dies, and is trod under feet.

PEACH.   You know, Polly, I am not against your toying and
trifling with a customer in the way of business, or to get out a
secret, or so. But if I find out that you have played the fool
and are married, you jade you, I'll cut your throat, hussy.
Now you know my mind.

SCENE VIII

PEACHUM, POLLY, MRS. PEACHUM

AIR VII. *Oh London is a fine town*

MRS. PEACHUM (*in a very great passion*)
Our Polly is a sad slut! nor heeds what we have taught her.
I wonder any man alive will ever rear a daughter!
For she must have both hoods and gowns, and hoops to swell
    her pride,
With scarfs and stays, and gloves and lace; and she will have
    men beside;
And when she's dress'd with care and cost, all-tempting, fine
    and gay,
As men should serve a cowcumber, she flings herself away.
    Our Polly is a sad slut, etc.

You baggage! you hussy! you inconsiderate jade! had you
been hanged, it would not have vexed me, for that might have
been your misfortune; but to do such a mad thing by choice!
The wench is married, husband.
    PEACH.   Married! The captain is a bold man, and will risk

anything for money; to be sure he believes her a fortune. Do you think your mother and I should have lived comfortably so long together, if ever we had been married? Baggage!

MRS. PEACH.   I knew she was always a proud slut; and now the wench hath played the fool and married, because forsooth she would do like the gentry. Can you support the expense of a husband, hussy, in gaming, drinking and whoring? have you money enough to carry on the daily quarrels of man and wife about who shall squander most? There are not many husbands and wives who can bear the charges of plaguing one another in a handsome way. If you must be married, could you introduce nobody into our family but a highwayman? Why, thou foolish jade, thou wilt be as ill used, and as much neglected, as if thou hadst married a lord!

PEACH.   Let not your anger, my dear, break through the rules of decency, for the captain looks upon himself in the military capacity, as a gentleman by his profession. Besides what he hath already, I know he is in a fair way of getting, or of dying; and both these ways, let me tell you, are most excellent chances for a wife.—— Tell me, hussy, are you ruined or no?

MRS. PEACH.   With Polly's fortune, she might very well have gone off to a person of distinction. Yes, that you might, you pouting slut!

PEACH.   What, is the wench dumb? Speak, or I'll make you plead by squeezing out an answer from you. Are you really bound wife to him, or are you only upon liking?

(pinches her)

POLLY. (*screaming*)   Oh!

MRS. PEACH.   How the mother is to be pitied who hath handsome daughters! Locks, bolts, bars, and lectures of morality are nothing to them: they break through them all. They have as much pleasure in cheating a father and mother as in cheating at cards.

PEACH.   Why, Polly, I shall soon know if you are married, by Macheath's keeping from our house.

AIR VIII. Grim king of the ghosts

POLLY.   Can love be controll'd by advice?
               Will Cupid our mothers obey?
           Though my heart were as frozen as ice,
               At his flame 'twould have melted away.
           When he kiss'd me so closely he press'd,

'Twas so sweet that I must have comply'd:
So I thought it both safest and best
To marry, for fear you should chide.

MRS. PEACH. Then all the hopes of our family are gone for ever and ever!

PEACH. And Macheath may hang his father and mother-in-law, in hope to get into their daughter's fortune.

POLLY. I did not marry him (as 'tis the fashion) coolly and deliberately for honour or money. But, I love him.

MRS. PEACH. Love him! worse and worse! I thought the girl had been better bred. O husband, husband! her folly makes me mad! my head swims! I'm distracted! I can't support myself——oh!   (*faints*)

PEACH. See, wench, to what a condition you have reduced your poor mother! a glass of cordial, this instant. How the poor woman takes it to heart! (POLLY *goes out and returns with it.*) Ah, hussy, now this is the only comfort your mother has left!

POLLY. Give her another glass, Sir; my mama drinks double the quantity whenever she is out of order.—This, you see, fetches her.

MRS. PEACH. The girl shows such a readiness, and so much concern, that I could almost find in my heart to forgive her.

AIR IX. *O Jenny, O Jenny, where hast thou been?*

O Polly, you might have toy'd and kiss'd.
By keeping men off, you keep them on.
POLLY.   But he so teas'd me,
And he so pleas'd me,
What I did, you must have done.

MRS. PEACH. Not with a highwayman.—You sorry slut!

PEACH. A word with you, wife. 'Tis no new thing for a wench to take man without consent of parents. You know 'tis the frailty of woman, my dear.

MRS. PEACH. Yes, indeed, the sex is frail. But the first time a woman is frail, she should be somewhat nice, methinks, for then or never is the time to make her fortune. After that, she hath nothing to do but to guard herself from being found out, and she may do what she pleases.

PEACH. Make yourself a little easy; I have a thought shall soon set all matters again to rights. Why so melancholy, Polly?

since what is done cannot be undone, we must all endeavour
to make the best of it.

MRS. PEACH.   Well, Polly; as far as one woman can forgive
another, I forgive thee.—— Your father is too fond of you,
hussy.

POLLY.   Then all my sorrows are at an end.

MRS. PEACH.   A mighty likely speech, in troth, for a wench
who is just married!

AIR X. *Thomas, I cannot*

POLLY.   I, like a ship in storms, was toss'd;
   Yet afraid to put in to land;
  For seiz'd in the port the vessel's lost,
   Whose treasure is contraband.
    The waves are laid,
    My duty's paid.
   Oh joy beyond expression!
    Thus, safe ashore,
    I ask no more,
   My all is in my possession.

PEACH.   I hear customers in t'other room. Go, talk with
'em, Polly; but come to us again, as soon as they are gone.—
But, hark ye, child, if 'tis the gentleman who was here yesterday about the repeating watch, say, you believe we can't get
intelligence of it till to-morrow. For I lent it to Suky Straddle,
to make a figure with it to-night at a tavern in Drury Lane. If
t'other gentleman calls for the silver-hilted sword, you know
Beetle-browed Jemmy hath it on, and he doth not come from
Tunbridge till Tuesday night, so that it cannot be had till
then.

SCENE IX

PEACHUM, MRS. PEACHUM

PEACH.   Dear wife, be a little pacified. Don't let your passion run away with your senses. Polly, I grant you, hath done
a rash thing.

MRS. PEACH.   If she had had only an intrigue with the fellow, why the very best families have excused and huddled up
a frailty of that sort. 'Tis marriage, husband, that makes it a
blemish.

PEACH.   But money, wife, is the true fuller's earth for reputations: there is not a spot or a stain but what it can take out. A rich rogue now-a-days is fit company for any gentleman; and the world, my dear, hath not such a contempt for roguery as you imagine. I tell you, wife, I can make this match turn to our advantage.

MRS. PEACH.   I am very sensible, husband, that Captain Macheath is worth money, but I am in doubt whether he hath not two or three wives already, and then if he should die in a session or two, Polly's dower would come into dispute.

PEACH.   That, indeed, is a point which ought to be considered.

AIR XI. *A soldier and a sailor*

A fox may steal your hens, Sir,
A whore your health and pence, Sir,
Your daughter rob your chest, Sir,
Your wife may steal your rest, Sir,
    A thief your goods and plate.
But this is all but picking;
With rest, pence, chest, and chicken,
It ever was decreed, Sir,
If lawyer's hand is fee'd, Sir,
    He steals your whole estate.

The lawyers are bitter enemies to those in our way. They don't care that anybody should get a clandestine livelihood but themselves.

SCENE X

MRS. PEACHUM, PEACHUM, POLLY

POLLY.   'Twas only Nimming Ned. He brought in a damask window-curtain, a hoop-petticoat, a pair of silver candlesticks, a periwig, and one silk stocking, from the fire that happened last night.

PEACH.   There is not a fellow that is cleverer in his way, and saves more goods out of the fire than Ned. But now, Polly, to your affair; for matters must not be left as they are. You are married then, it seems?

POLLY.   Yes, Sir.

PEACH.   And how do you propose to live, child?

POLLY.   Like other women, Sir, upon the industry of my husband.

MRS. PEACH.   What, is the wench turned fool? A highway-man's wife, like a soldier's, hath as little of his pay as of his company.

PEACH.   And had not you the common views of a gentle-woman in your marriage, Polly?

POLLY.   I don't know what you mean, Sir.

PEACH.   Of a jointure, and of being a widow.

POLLY.   But I love him, Sir: how then could I have thoughts of parting with him?

PEACH.   Parting with him! Why, that is the whole scheme and intention of all marriage articles. The comfortable estate of widowhood is the only hope that keeps up a wife's spirits. Where is the woman who would scruple to be a wife, if she had it in her power to be a widow whenever she pleased? If you have any views of this sort, Polly, I shall think the match not so very unreasonable.

POLLY.   How I dread to hear your advice! Yet I must beg you to explain yourself.

PEACH.   Secure what he hath got, have him peached the next sessions, and then at once you are made a rich widow.

POLLY.   What, murder the man I love! The blood runs cold at my heart with the very thought of it.

PEACH.   Fie, Polly! What hath murder to do in the affair? Since the thing sooner or later must happen, I dare say the captain himself would like that we should get the reward for his death sooner than a stranger. Why, Polly, the captain knows that as 'tis his employment to rob, so 'tis ours to take robbers; every man in his business. So that there is no malice in the case.

MRS. PEACH.   Ay, husband, now you have nicked the mat-ter. To have him peached is the only thing could ever make me forgive her.

AIR XII. *Now ponder well, ye parents dear*

POLLY.   Oh, ponder well! be not severe;
        So save a wretched wife!
    For on the rope that hangs my dear
        Depends poor Polly's life.

MRS. PEACH.   But your duty to your parents, hussy, obliges you to hang him. What would many a wife give for such an opportunity!

POLLY.   What is a jointure, what is widowhood to me? I know my heart. I cannot survive him.

AIR XIII. *Le printemps rappelle aux armes*

The turtle thus with plaintive crying,
   Her lover dying,
The turtle thus with plaintive crying,
   Laments her dove.
Down she drops, quite spent with sighing,
Pair'd in death, as pair'd in love.

Thus, Sir, it will happen to your poor Polly.

MRS. PEACH.   What, is the fool in love in earnest then? I hate thee for being particular. Why, wench, thou art a shame to thy very sex.

POLLY.   But hear, me Mother.—— If you ever loved——

MRS. PEACH.   Those cursed play-books she reads have been her ruin. One word more, hussy, and I shall knock your brains out, if you have any.

PEACH.   Keep out of the way, Polly, for fear of mischief, and consider of what is proposed to you.

MRS. PEACH.   Away, hussy. Hang your husband, and be dutiful.

SCENE XI

MRS. PEACHUM, PEACHUM

(POLLY *listening*)

MRS. PEACH.   The thing, husband, must and shall be done. For the sake of intelligence we must take other measures, and have him peached the next session without her consent. If she will not know her duty, we know ours.

PEACH.   But really, my dear, it grieves one's heart to take off a great man. When I consider his personal bravery, his fine stratagem, how much we have already got by him, and how much more we may get, methinks I can't find in my heart to have a hand in his death. I wish you could have made Polly undertake it.

MRS. PEACH.   But in a case of necessity—our own lives are in danger.

PEACH.   Then, indeed, we must comply with the customs of the world, and make gratitude give way to interest. He shall be taken off.

MRS. PEACH.   I'll undertake to manage Polly.

PEACH.   And I'll prepare matters for the Old Bailey.

SCENE XII

POLLY

Now I'm a wretch, indeed.—— Methinks I see him already in the cart, sweeter and more lovely than the nosegay in his hand!—I hear the crowd extolling his resolution and intrepidity!—— What volleys of sighs are sent from the windows of Holborn, that so comely a youth should be brought to disgrace!—— I see him at the tree! The whole circle are in tears! —even butchers weep!—— Jack Ketch himself hesitates to perform his duty, and would be glad to lose his fee by a reprieve. What then will become of Polly? As yet I may inform him of their design, and aid him in his escape.—— It shall be so.—— But then he flies, absents himself, and I bar myself from his dear, dear conversation! That too will distract me. If he keep out of the way, my papa and mama may in time relent, and we may be happy. If he stays, he is hanged, and then he is lost forever! He intended to lie concealed in my room, till the dusk of the evening. If they are abroad, I'll this instant let him out, lest some accident should prevent him.

(Exit, and returns)

SCENE XIII

POLLY, MACHEATH

AIR XIV. *Pretty Parrot, say*

MACH.   Pretty Polly, say,
           When I was away,
        Did your fancy never stray
           To some newer lover?
POLLY.   Without disguise,
           Heaving sighs,
           Doting eyes,
        My constant heart discover.
           Fondly let me loll!
MACH.   O pretty, pretty Poll.

POLLY.   And are *you* as fond as ever, my dear?
MACH.   Suspect my honour, my courage, suspect anything but my love. May my pistols miss fire, and my mare slip her shoulder while I am pursued, if I ever forsake thee!
POLLY.   Nay, my dear, I have no reason to doubt you, for

I find in the romance you lent me, none of the great heroes were ever false in love.

AIR XV.   *Pray, fair one, be kind*

MACH.   My heart was so free,
                    It rov'd like the bee,
              Till Polly my passion requited;
                    I sipp'd each flower,
                    I chang'd ev'ry hour,
              But here ev'ry flower is united.

POLLY.   Were you sentenced to transportation, sure, my dear you could not leave me behind you—could you?

MACH.   Is there any power, any force that could tear me from thee? You might sooner tear a pension out of the hands of a courtier, a fee from a lawyer, a pretty woman from a looking glass, or any woman from quadrille. But to tear me from thee is impossible!

AIR XVI.   *Over the hills and far away*

              Were I laid on Greenland's coast,
                    And in my arms embrac'd my lass:
              Warm amidst eternal frost,
                    Too soon the half year's night would pass.
POLLY.   Were I sold on Indian soil,
                    Soon as the burning day was clos'd,
              I could mock the sultry toil,
                    When on my charmer's breast repos'd.
MACH.   And I would love you all the day,
POLLY.   Every night would kiss and play,
MACH.   If with me you'd fondly stray
POLLY.   Over the hills and far away.

POLLY.   Yes, I would go with thee. But oh!—how shall I speak it? I must be torn from thee. We must part.

MACH.   How! Part!

POLLY.   We must, we must. My papa and mama are set against thy life. They now, even now are in search after thee. They are preparing evidence against thee. Thy life depends upon a moment.

AIR XVII.   *Gin thou wert mine own thing*

              Oh, what pain it is to part!
                    Can I leave thee, can I leave thee?
              Oh, what pain it is to part!

Can thy Polly ever leave thee?
But lest death my love should thwart,
And bring thee to the fatal cart,
Thus I tear thee from my bleeding heart!
Fly hence, and let me leave thee.

One kiss and then—one kiss—begone—farewell.

MACH.   My hand, my heart, my dear, is so riveted to thine, that I cannot unloose my hold.

POLLY.   But my papa may intercept thee, and then I should lose the very glimmering of hope. A few weeks, perhaps, may reconcile us all. Shall thy Polly hear from thee?

MACH.   Must I then go?

POLLY.   And will not absence change your love?

MACH.   If you doubt it, let me stay—and be hanged.

POLLY.   Oh, how I fear! how I tremble!—— Go—but when safety will give you leave, you will be sure to see me again; for till then Polly is wretched.

AIR XVIII. *O, the broom*

(*Parting, and looking back at each other with
fondness; he at one door, she at the other*)

MACH.   The miser thus a shilling sees,
Which he's oblig'd to pay,
With sighs resigns it by degrees,
And fears 'tis gone for aye.

POLLY.   The boy, thus, when his sparrow's flown,
The bird in silence eyes;
But soon as out of sight 'tis gone,
Whines, whimpers, sobs and cries.

ACT II

SCENE I

SCENE: *A tavern near Newgate*

JEMMY TWITCHER, CROOK-FINGERED JACK, WAT DREARY, ROBIN
OF BAGSHOT, NIMMING NED, HENRY PADINGTON, MATT OF
THE MINT, BEN BUDGE, *and the rest of the gang, at the
table, with wine, brandy and tobacco*

BEN.   But pr'ythee, Matt, what is become of thy brother Tom? I have not seen him since my return from transportation.

MATT.   Poor brother Tom had an accident this time twelve-month, and so clever a made fellow he was, that I could not save him from those flaying rascals the surgeons; and now, poor man, he is among the otamys at Surgeons' Hall.

BEN. So it seems, his time was come.

JEM. But the present time is ours, and nobody alive hath more. Why are the laws levelled at us? Are we more dishonest than the rest of mankind? What we win, gentlemen, is our own by the law of arms and the right of conquest.

CROOK. Where shall we find such another set of practical philosophers, who to a man are above the fear of death?

WAT. Sound men, and true!

ROBIN. Of tried courage, and indefatigable industry!

NED. Who is there here that would not die for his friend?

HARRY. Who is there here that would betray him for his interest?

MATT. Show me a gang of courtiers that can say as much.

BEN. We are for a just partition of the world, for every man hath a right to enjoy life.

MATT. We retrench the superfluities of mankind. The world is avaricious, and I hate avarice. A covetous fellow, like a jackdaw, steals what he was never made to enjoy, for the sake of hiding it. These are the robbers of mankind, for money was made for the free-hearted and generous, and where is the injury of taking from another what he hath not the heart to make use of?

JEM. Our several stations for the day are fix'd. Good luck attend us all. Fill the glasses.

AIR XIX. *Fill ev'ry glass*

MATT. Fill ev'ry glass, for wine inspires us,
        And fires us,
    With courage, love and joy.
    Women and wine should life employ.
    Is there aught else on earth desirous?

CHORUS. Fill ev'ry glass, etc.

SCENE II

To them enter MACHEATH

MACH. Gentlemen, well met. My heart hath been with you this hour; but an unexpected affair hath detained me. No ceremony, I beg you.

MATT. We were just breaking up to go upon duty. Am I to have the honour of taking the air with you, Sir, this evening upon the heath? I drink a dram now and then with the stage-coachmen in the way of friendship and intelligence, and I know that about this time there will be passengers upon the western road who are worth speaking with.

MACH.   I was to have been of that party—but——

MATT.   But what, Sir?

MACH.   Is there any man who suspects my courage?

MATT.   We have all been witnesses of it.

MACH.   My honour and truth to the gang?

MATT.   I'll be answerable for it.

MACH.   In the division of our booty, have I ever shown the least marks of avarice or injustice?

MATT.   By these questions something seems to have ruffled you. Are any of us suspected?

MACH.   I have a fixed confidence, gentlemen, in you all, as men of honour, and as such I value and respect you. Peachum is a man that is useful to us.

MATT.   Is he about to play us any foul play? I'll shoot him through the head.

MACH.   I beg you, gentlemen, act with conduct and discretion. A pistol is your last resort.

MATT.   He knows nothing of this meeting.

MACH.   Business cannot go on without him. He is a man who knows the world, and is a necessary agent to us. We have had a slight difference, and till it is accommodated I shall be obliged to keep out of his way. Any private dispute of mine shall be of no ill consequence to my friends. You must continue to act under his direction, for the moment we break loose from him, our gang is ruin'd.

MATT.   As a bawd to a whore, I grant you, he is to us of great convenience.

MACH.   Make him believe I have quitted the gang, which I can never do but with life. At our private quarters I will continue to meet you. A week or so will probably reconcile us.

MATT.   Your instructions shall be observed. 'Tis now high time for us to repair to our several duties; so till the evening at our quarters in Moorfields we bid you farewell.

MACH.   I shall wish myself with you. Success attend you.
                    (*sits down melancholy at the table*)

AIR xx. *March in Rinaldo, with drums and trumpets*

MATT.   Let us take the road.
            Hark! I hear the sound of coaches!
            The hour of attack approaches,

To your arms, brave boys, and load.
   See the ball I hold!
Let the chymists toil like asses,
  Our fire their fire surpasses,
   And turns all our lead to gold.

(*The gang, ranged in the front of the stage, load their pistols, and stick them under their girdles; then go off singing the first part in chorus.*)

SCENE III

MACHEATH, *Drawer*

MACH. What a fool is a fond wench! Polly is most confoundedly bit. I love the sex. And a man who loves money might as well be contented with one guinea, as I with one woman. The town perhaps hath been as much obliged to me, for recruiting it with free-hearted ladies, as to any recruiting officer in the army. If it were not for us and the other gentlemen of the sword, Drury Lane would be uninhabited.

AIR XXI. *Would you have a young virgin*

If the heart of a man is depress'd with cares,
The mist is dispell'd when a woman appears;
  Like the notes of a fiddle, she sweetly, sweetly
Raises the spirits, and charms our ears.
  Roses and lilies her cheeks disclose,
  But her ripe lips are more sweet than those.
      Press her,
      Caress her
      With blisses,
      Her kisses
Dissolve us in pleasure, and soft repose.

I must have women. There is nothing unbends the mind like them. Money is not so strong a cordial for the time.—— Drawer! (*Enter Drawer*) Is the porter gone for all the ladies, according to my directions?

DRAW. I expect him back every minute. But you know, Sir, you sent him as far as Hockley in the Hole for three of the ladies, for one in Vinegar Yard, and for the rest of them somewhere about Lewkner's Lane. Sure some of them are below, for I hear the bar bell. As they come I will show them up.—— Coming! coming!

SCENE IV

MACHEATH, MRS. COAXER, DOLLY TRULL, MRS. VIXEN, BETTY
    DOXY, JENNY DIVER, MRS. SLAMMEKIN, SUKY TAWDRY,
    and MOLLY BRAZEN

MACH. Dear Mrs. Coaxer, you are welcome. You look
charmingly today. I hope you don't want the repairs of quality, and lay on paint.—— Dolly Trull! kiss me, you slut; are
you as amorous as ever, hussy? You are always so taken up
with stealing hearts, that you don't allow yourself time to
steal anything else.—— Ah Dolly, thou wilt ever be a coquette.—— Mrs. Vixen, I'm yours; I always loved a woman of
wit and spirit; they make charming mistresses, but plaguy
wives.—— Betty Doxy! Come hither, hussy. Do you drink as
hard as ever? You had better stick to good wholesome beer;
for in troth, Betty, strong waters will in time ruin your constitution. You should leave those to your betters.—— What!
and my pretty Jenny Diver too! As prim and demure as ever!
There is not any prude, though ever so high bred, hath a
more sanctified look, with a more mischievous heart. Ah!
thou art a dear artful hypocrite.—— Mrs. Slammekin! as careless and genteel as ever! all you fine ladies, who know your
own beauty, affect an undress.—— But see, here's Suky Tawdry come to contradict what I was saying. Everything she
gets one way, she lays out upon her back. Why, Suky, you
must keep at least a dozen tally-men.—— Molly Brazen! (*She
kisses him.*) That's well done. I love a free-hearted wench.
Thou hast a most agreeable assurance, girl, and art as willing
as a turtle.—— But hark! I hear music. The harper is at the
door. "If music be the food of love, play on." Ere you seat
yourselves, ladies, what think you of a dance?—— Come in.
(*Enter Harper.*) Play the French tune, that Mrs. Slammekin
was so fond of.

      (*a dance* à la ronde *in the French manner; near the end
          of it this song and chorus*)

AIR XXII. *Cotillon*

> Youth's the season made for joys,
>   Love is then our duty;
> She alone who that employs,
>   Well deserves her beauty.
>   Let's be gay,
>   While we may,

Beauty's a flower, despis'd in decay.
Youth's the season, etc.

Let us drink and sport to-day,
Ours is not to-morrow.
Love with youth flies swift away,
Age is nought but sorrow.
Dance and sing,
Time's on the wing,
Life never knows the return of spring.
CHORUS.   Let us drink, etc.

MACH.   Now, pray ladies, take your places.—— Here, fellow. (*pays the Harper*) Bid the drawer bring us more wine. (*Exit Harper*) If any of the ladies choose gin, I hope they will be so free to call for it.

JENNY.   You look as if you meant me. Wine is strong enough for me. Indeed, Sir, I never drink strong waters, but when I have the colic.

MACH.   Just the excuse of the fine ladies! Why, a lady of quality is never without the colic.—— I hope, Mrs. Coaxer, you have had good success of late in your visits among the mercers.

COAX.   We have so many interlopers! Yet, with industry, one may still have a little picking. I carried a silver-flowered lutestring and a piece of black padesoy to Mr. Peachum's lock but last week.

VIX.   There's Molly Brazen hath the ogle of a rattlesnake. She riveted a linen-draper's eye so fast upon her, that he was nicked of three pieces of cambric before he could look off.

BRAZ.   O dear Madam! But sure nothing can come up to your handling of laces! And then you have such a sweet deluding tongue! To cheat a man is nothing; but the woman must have fine parts indeed who cheats a woman!

VIX.   Lace, Madam, lies in a small compass, and is of easy conveyance. But you are apt, Madam, to think too well of your friends.

COAX.   If any woman hath more art than another, to be sure, 'tis Jenny Diver. Though her fellow be never so agreeable, she can pick his pocket as coolly as if money were her only pleasure. Now that is a command of the passions uncommon in a woman!

JENNY.   I never go to the tavern with a man, but in the view of business. I have other hours, and other sort of men for my pleasure. But had I your address, Madam——

MACH. Have done with your compliments, ladies; and drink about.—— You are not so fond of me, Jenny, as you use to be.

JENNY. 'Tis not convenient, Sir, to show my fondness among so many rivals. 'Tis your own choice, and not the warmth of my inclination that will determine you.

AIR XXIII. *All in a misty morning*

> Before the barn-door crowing,
>   The cock by hens attended,
> His eyes around him throwing,
>   Stands for a while suspended.
> Then one he singles from the crew,
>   And cheers the happy hen;
> With how do you do, and how do you do,
>   And how do you do again.

MACH. Ah Jenny! thou art a dear slut.

TRULL. Pray, Madam, were you ever in keeping?

TAWD. I hope, Madam, I han't been so long upon the town, but I have met with some good fortune as well as my neighbours.

TRULL. Pardon me, Madam, I meant no harm by the question; 'twas only in the way of conversation.

TAWD. Indeed, Madam, if I had not been a fool, I might have lived very handsomely with my last friend. But upon his missing five guineas, he turned me off. Now I never suspected he had counted them.

SLAM. Who do you look upon, Madam, as your best sort of keepers?

TRULL. That, Madam, is thereafter as they be.

SLAM. I, Madam, was once kept by a Jew; and bating their religion, to women they are a good sort of people.

TAWD. Now for my part, I own I like an old fellow: for we always make them pay for what they can't do.

VIX. A spruce prentice, let me tell you, ladies, is no ill thing: they bleed freely. I have sent at least two or three dozen of them in my time to the plantations.

JENNY. But to be sure, Sir, with so much good fortune as you have had upon the road, you must be grown immensely rich.

MACH. The road, indeed, hath done me justice, but the gaming-table hath been my ruin.

AIR XXIV. *When once I lay with another man's wife*

JENNY.   The gamesters and lawyers are jugglers alike,
             If they meddle, your all is in danger.
          Like gypsies, if once they can finger a souse,
          Your pockets they pick, and they pilfer your
                    house,
          And give your estate to a stranger.

A man of courage should never put anything to the risk but
his life. (*She takes up his pistol*) These are the tools of a
man of honour. Cards and dice are only fit for cowardly
cheats, who prey upon their friends.

                              (TAWDRY *takes up the other*)

TAWD.   This, Sir, is fitter for your hand. Besides your loss
of money, 'tis a loss to the ladies. Gaming takes you off from
women. How fond could I be of you! but before company,
'tis ill-bred.

MACH.   Wanton hussies!

JENNY.   I must and will have a kiss to give my wine a zest.
     (*They take him about the neck, and make signs to*
     PEACHUM *and Constables, who rush in upon him*)

SCENE V

To them, PEACHUM *and Constables*

PEACH.   I seize you, Sir, as my prisoner.

MACH.   Was this well done, Jenny?—— Women are decoy
ducks; who can trust them! Beasts, jades, jilts, harpies, furies,
whores!

PEACH.   Your case, Mr. Macheath, is not particular. The
greatest heroes have been ruined by women. But, to do them
justice, I must own they are a pretty sort of creatures, if we
could trust them. You must now, Sir, take your leave of the
ladies, and if they have a mind to make you a visit, they will
be sure to find you at home. The gentleman, ladies, lodges in
Newgate. Constables, wait upon the captain to his lodgings.

AIR XXV. *When first I laid siege to my Chloris*

MACH.   At the tree I shall suffer with pleasure,
          At the tree I shall suffer with pleasure.
             Let me go where I will,
             In all kinds of ill,
          I shall find no such furies as these are.

PEACH.   Ladies, I'll take care the reckoning shall be discharged.

> (*Exit* MACHEATH, *guarded, with* PEACHUM *and Constables*)

SCENE VI

The Women remain

VIX.   Look ye, Mrs. Jenny, though Mr. Peachum may have made a private bargain with you and Suky Tawdry for betraying the captain, as we were all assisting, we ought all to share alike.

COAX.   I think Mr. Peachum, after so long an acquaintance, might have trusted me as well as Jenny Diver.

SLAM.   I am sure at least three men of his hanging, and in a year's time too (if he did me justice) should be set down to my account.

TRULL.   Mrs. Slammekin, that is not fair. For you know one of them was taken in bed with me.

JENNY.   As far as a bowl of punch or a treat, I believe Mrs. Suky will join with me. As for anything else, ladies, you cannot in conscience expect it.

SLAM.   Dear Madam——

TRULL.   I would not for the world——

SLAM.   'Tis impossible for me——

TRULL.   As I hope to be saved, Madam——

SLAM.   Nay, then I must stay here all night.

TRULL.   Since you command me.

> (*Exeunt with great ceremony*)

SCENE VII

SCENE: *Newgate*

LOCKIT, *Turnkeys,* MACHEATH, *Constables*

LOCK.   Noble Captain, you are welcome. You have not been a lodger of mine this year and half. You know the custom, Sir. Garnish, Captain, garnish. Hand me down those fetters there.

MACH.   Those, Mr. Lockit, seem to be the heaviest of the whole set. With your leave, I should like the further pair better.

LOCK. Look ye, Captain, we know what is fittest for our prisoners. When a gentleman uses me with civility, I always do the best I can to please him.—— Hand them down, I say.—— We have them of all prices, from one guinea to ten, and 'tis fitting every gentleman should please himself.

MACH. I understand you, Sir. (*gives money*) The fees here are so many, and so exorbitant, that few fortunes can bear the expense of getting off handsomely, or of dying like a gentleman.

LOCK. Those, I see, will fit the captain better.—— Take down the further pair.—— Do but examine them, Sir—never was better work. How genteelly they are made! They will fit as easy as a glove, and the nicest man in England might not be ashamed to wear them. (*He puts on the chains*) If I had the best gentleman in the land in my custody I could not equip him more handsomely. And so, Sir—I now leave you to your private meditations.

SCENE VIII

MACHEATH

AIR XXVI. *Courtiers, courtiers, think it no harm*

Man may escape from rope and gun;
　　Nay, some have out-liv'd the doctor's pill;
Who takes a woman must be undone,
　　That basilisk is sure to kill.
The fly that sips treacle is lost in the sweets,
　　So he that tastes woman, woman, woman,
He that tastes woman, ruin meets.

To what a woeful plight have I brought myself! Here must I (all day long, till I am hanged) be confined to hear the reproaches of a wench who lays her ruin at my door. I am in the custody of her father, and to be sure, if he knows of the matter I shall have a fine time on't betwixt this and my execution. But I promised the wench marriage. What signifies a promise to a woman? Does not man in marriage itself promise a hundred things that he never means to perform? Do all we can, women will believe us; for they look upon a promise as an excuse for following their own inclinations.—— But here comes Lucy, and I cannot get from her. Would I were deaf!

SCENE IX

MACHEATH, LUCY

LUCY.   You base man, you—how can you look me in the face after what hath passed between us? See here, perfidious wretch, how I am forced to bear about the load of infamy you have laid upon me. O Macheath! thou hast robbed me of my quiet—to see thee tortured would give me pleasure.

AIR XXVII. *A lovely lass to a friar came*

> Thus when a good huswife sees a rat
> In her trap in the morning taken,
> With pleasure her heart goes pit-a-pat
> In revenge for her loss of bacon.
>   Then she throws him
>   To the dog or cat,
> To be worried, crushed and shaken.

MACH.   Have you no bowels, no tenderness, my dear Lucy, to see a husband in these circumstances?

LUCY.   A husband!

MACH.   In every respect but the form, and that, my dear, may be said over us at any time. Friends should not insist upon ceremonies. From a man of honour, his word is as good as his bond.

LUCY.   'Tis the pleasure of all you fine men to insult the women you have ruined.

AIR XXVIII. *'Twas when the sea was roaring*

> How cruel are the traitors,
>   Who lie and swear in jest,
> To cheat unguarded creatures
>   Of virtue, fame, and rest!
> Whoever steals a shilling
>   Through shame the guilt conceals;
> In love the perjured villain
>   With boasts the theft reveals.

MACH.   The very first opportunity, my dear (have but patience) you shall be my wife in whatever manner you please.

LUCY.   Insinuating monster! And so you think I know nothing of the affair of Miss Polly Peachum.—— I could tear thy eyes out!

MACH. Sure, Lucy, you can't be such a fool as to be jealous of Polly!

LUCY. Are you not married to her, you brute, you?

MACH. Married! Very good. The wench gives it out only to vex thee, and to ruin me in thy good opinion. 'Tis true I go to the house; I chat with the girl, I kiss her, I say a thousand things to her (as all gentlemen do) that mean nothing, to divert myself; and now the silly jade hath set it about that I am married to her, to let me know what she would be at. Indeed, my dear Lucy, these violent passions may be of ill consequence to a woman in your condition.

LUCY. Come, come, Captain, for all your assurance, you know that Miss Polly hath put it out of your power to do me the justice you promised me.

MACH. A jealous woman believes everything her passion suggests. To convince you of my sincerity, if we can find the ordinary, I shall have no scruples of making you my wife; and I know the consequence of having two at a time.

LUCY. That you are only to be hanged, and so get rid of them both.

MACH. I am ready, my dear Lucy, to give you satisfaction—if you think there is any in marriage. What can a man of honour say more?

LUCY. So then it seems, you are not married to Miss Polly.

MACH. You know, Lucy, the girl is prodigiously conceited. No man can say a civil thing to her, but (like other fine ladies) her vanity makes her think he's her own for ever and ever.

AIR XXIX. *The sun had loos'd his weary teams*

The first time at the looking-glass
    The mother sets her daughter,
The image strikes the smiling lass
    With self-love ever after.
Each time she looks, she, fonder grown,
    Thinks ev'ry charm grows stronger.
But alas, vain maid, all eyes but your own
    Can see you are not younger.

When women consider their own beauties, they are all alike unreasonable in their demands; for they expect their lovers should like them as long as they like themselves.

LUCY. Yonder is my father—perhaps this way we may

light upon the ordinary, who shall try if you will be as good as your word. For I long to be made an honest woman.

SCENE X

PEACHUM, LOCKIT with an account-book

LOCK.   In this last affair, brother Peachum, we are agreed. You have consented to go halves in Macheath.

PEACH.   We shall never fall out about an execution. But as to that article, pray how stands our last year's account?

LOCK.   If you will run your eye over it, you'll find 'tis fair and clearly stated.

PEACH.   This long arrear of the government is very hard upon us! Can it be expected that we should hang our acquaintance for nothing, when our betters will hardly save theirs without being paid for it? Unless the people in employment pay better, I promise them for the future, I shall let other rogues live besides their own.

LOCK.   Perhaps, brother, they are afraid these matters may be carried too far. We are treated too by them with contempt, as if our profession were not reputable.

PEACH.   In one respect, indeed, our employment may be reckoned dishonest, because, like great statesmen, we encourage those who betray their friends.

LOCK.   Such language, brother, anywhere else might turn to your prejudice. Learn to be more guarded, I beg you.

AIR XXX. How happy are we

> When you censure the age,
> Be cautious and sage,
> Lest the courtiers offended should be:
> If you mention vice or bribe,
> 'Tis so pat to all the tribe;
> Each cries—"That was levell'd at me."

PEACH.   Here's poor Ned Clincher's name, I see. Sure, brother Lockit, there was a little unfair proceeding in Ned's case; for he told me in the condemned hold, that for value received, you had promised him a session or two longer without molestation.

LOCK.   Mr. Peachum, this is the first time my honour was ever called in question.

PEACH.   Business is at an end—if once we act dishonourably.

LOCK.   Who accuses me?

PEACH.   You are warm, brother.

LOCK.   He that attacks my honour, attacks my livelihood. And this usage, Sir, is not to be borne.

PEACH.   Since you provoke me to speak, I must tell you too, that Mrs. Coaxer charges you with defrauding her of her information-money, for the apprehending of Curl-pated Hugh. Indeed, indeed, brother, we must punctually pay our spies, or we shall have no information.

LOCK.   Is this language to me, Sirrah—who have saved you from the gallows, Sirrah?   (*collaring each other*)

PEACH.   If I am hanged, it shall be for ridding the world of an arrant rascal.

LOCK.   This hand shall do the office of the halter you deserve, and throttle you—you dog!

PEACH.   Brother, brother—we are both in the wrong—we shall be both losers in the dispute—for you know we have it in our power to hang each other. You should not be so passionate.

LOCK.   Nor you so provoking.

PEACH.   'Tis our mutual interest; 'tis for the interest of the world we should agree. If I said anything, brother, to the prejudice of your character, I ask pardon.

LOCK.   Brother Peachum—I can forgive as well as resent. Give me your hand. Suspicion does not become a friend.

PEACH.   I only meant to give you occasion to justify yourself. But I must now step home, for I expect the gentleman about this snuff-box, that Filch nimmed two nights ago in the park. I appointed him at this hour.

SCENE XI

LOCKIT, LUCY

LOCK.   Whence come you, hussy?

LUCY.   My tears might answer that question.

LOCK.   You have then been whimpering and fondling, like a spaniel, over the fellow that hath abused you.

LUCY.   One can't help love; one can't cure it. 'Tis not in my power to obey you, and hate him.

LOCK.   Learn to bear your husband's death like a reasonable woman. 'Tis not the fashion, now-a-days, so much as to affect sorrow upon these occasions. No woman would ever marry, if she had not the chance of mortality for a release. Act like a woman of spirit, hussy, and thank your father for what he is doing.

AIR XXXI. *Of a noble race was Shenkin*

LUCY.   Is then his fate decreed, Sir?
　　　　Such a man can I think of quitting?
　　　When first we met, so moves me yet,
　　　　Oh, see how my heart is splitting!

LOCK.   Look ye, Lucy—there is no saving him. So, I think,
you must even do like other widows—buy yourself weeds, and
be cheerful.

AIR XXXII

　　　You'll think, ere many days ensue,
　　　　This sentence not severe;
　　　I hang your husband, child, 'tis true,
　　　　But with him hang your care.
　　　　　Twang dang dillo dee.

Like a good wife, go moan over your dying husband. That,
child, is your duty. Consider, girl, you can't have the man and
the money too—so make yourself as easy as you can by getting
all you can from him.

SCENE XII

LUCY, MACHEATH

LUCY.   Though the ordinary was out of the way to-day, I
hope, my dear, you will, upon the first opportunity, quiet my
scruples. Oh, Sir!—my father's hard heart is not to be soft-
ened, and I am in the utmost despair.

MACH.   But if I could raise a small sum—— Would not
twenty guineas, think you, move him? Of all the arguments in
the way of business, the perquisite is the most prevailing.
Your father's perquisites for the escape of prisoners must
amount to a considerable sum in the year. Money well timed
and properly applied will do anything.

AIR XXXIII. *London ladies*

　　If you at an office solicit your due,
　　　And would not have matters neglected;
　　You must quicken the clerk with the perquisite too,
　　　To do what his duty directed.
　　Or would you the frowns of a lady prevent,

> She too has this palpable failing,
> The perquisite softens her into consent;
> That reason with all is prevailing.

LUCY.   What love or money can do shall be done: for all my comfort depends upon your safety.

SCENE XIII

LUCY, MACHEATH, POLLY

POLLY.   Where is my dear husband?—— Was a rope ever intended for this neck! Oh, let me throw my arms about it, and throttle thee with love! Why dost thou turn away from me? 'Tis thy Polly—'tis thy wife.

MACH.   Was ever such an unfortunate rascal as I am!

LUCY.   Was there ever such another villain!

POLLY.   O Macheath! was it for this we parted? Taken! imprisoned! tried! hanged!—cruel reflection! I'll stay with thee till death—no force shall tear thy dear wife from thee now. What means my love? Not one kind word! not one kind look! think what thy Polly suffers to see thee in this condition.

AIR XXXIV. *All in the Downs*

> Thus when the swallow, seeking prey,
>   Within the sash is closely pent,
> His consort, with bemoaning lay,
>   Without sits pining for th' event.
> Her chatt'ring lovers all around her skim;
> She heeds them not (poor bird!)—her soul's with him.

MACH.   (*aside*)   I must disown her.—— The wench is distracted.

LUCY.   Am I then bilked of my virtue? Can I have no reparation? Sure, men were born to lie, and women to believe them! O villain! villain!

POLLY.   Am I not thy wife? Thy neglect of me, thy aversion to me, too severely proves it. Look on me. Tell me, am I not thy wife?

LUCY.   Perfidious wretch!

POLLY.   Barbarous husband!

LUCY.   Hadst thou been hanged five months ago, I had been happy.

POLLY.   And I too. If you had been kind to me till death, it

would not have vexed me—and that's no very unreasonable request (though from a wife) to a man who hath not above
seven or eight days to live.

LUCY.   Art thou then married to another? Hast thou two
wives, monster?

MACH.   If women's tongues can cease for an answer—hear
me.

LUCY.   I won't. Flesh and blood can't bear my usage.

POLLY.   Shall I not claim my own? Justice bids me speak.

AIR XXXV. *Have you heard of a frolicsome ditty?*

MACH.   How happy could I be with either,
            Were t'other dear charmer away!
          But while you thus tease me together,
            To neither a word will I say;
            But tol de rol, etc.

POLLY.   Sure, my dear, there ought to be some preference
shown to a wife! At least she may claim the appearance of it.
He must be distracted with his misfortunes, or he could not
use me thus!

LUCY.   O villain, villain! thou hast deceived me—I could
even inform against thee with pleasure. Not a prude wishes
more heartily to have facts against her intimate acquaintance,
than I now wish to have facts against thee. I would have her
satisfaction, and they should all out.

AIR XXXVI. *Irish trot*

POLLY.   I'm bubbled.
LUCY.   ——I'm bubbled.
POLLY.   Oh, how I am troubled!
LUCY.   Bamboozled, and bit!
POLLY   ——My distresses are doubled.
LUCY.   When you come to the tree, should the hangman
                                    refuse,
          These fingers, with pleasure, could fasten the noose.
POLLY.   I'm bubbled, etc.

MACH.   Be pacified, my dear Lucy—this is all a fetch of
Polly's to make me desperate with you in case I get off. If I
am hanged, she would fain have the credit of being thought
my widow.—— Really, Polly, this is no time for a dispute of
this sort; for whenever you are talking of marriage, I am
thinking of hanging.

POLLY.   And hast thou the heart to persist in disowning me?

MACH.   And hast thou the heart to persist in persuading me that I am married? Why, Polly, dost thou seek to aggravate my misfortunes?

LUCY.   Really, Miss Peachum, you but expose yourself. Besides, 'tis barbarous in you to worry a gentleman in his circumstances.

AIR XXXVII

POLLY.   Cease your funning;
          Force or cunning
Never shall my heart trapan.
          All these sallies
          Are but malice
To seduce my constant man.
          'Tis most certain,
          By their flirting,
Women oft have envy shown;
          Pleas'd, to ruin
          Others' wooing;
Never happy in their own!

Decency, Madam, methinks. might teach you to behave yourself with some reserve with the husband, while his wife is present.

MACH.   But, seriously, Polly, this is carrying the joke a little too far.

LUCY.   If you are determined, Madam, to raise a disturbance in the prison, I shall be obliged to send for the turnkey to show you the door. I am sorry, Madam, you force me to be so ill-bred.

POLLY.   Give me leave to tell you, Madam, these forward airs don't become you in the least, Madam. And my duty, Madam, obliges me to stay with my husband, Madam.

AIR XXXVIII. *Good-morrow, gossip Joan*

LUCY.   Why, how now, Madam Flirt?
          If you thus must chatter;
And are for flinging dirt,
     Let's try who best can spatter;
          Madam Flirt!
POLLY.   Why, how now, saucy jade;
          Sure, the wench is tipsy!

(*to him*) How can you see me made
    The scoff of such a gypsy?
(*to her*) Saucy jade!

SCENE XIV

LUCY, MACHEATH, POLLY, PEACHUM

PEACH.   Where's my wench? Ah, hussy! hussy! Come you home, you slut; and when your fellow is hanged, hang yourself, to make your family some amends.

POLLY.   Dear, dear father, do not tear me from him—I must speak; I have more to say to him.—— Oh! twist thy fetters about me, that he may not haul me from thee!

PEACH.   Sure all women are alike! If ever they commit the folly, they are sure to commit another by exposing themselves. —— Away—not a word more—you are my prisoner now, hussy.

AIR XXXIX. *Irish howl*

POLLY.   No power on earth can e'er divide
    The knot that sacred love hath tied.
    When parents draw against our mind,
    The true-love's knot they faster bind.
        Ho ho ra in ambora,——*etc.*
            (*holding* MACHEATH, PEACHUM *pulling her*)

SCENE XV

LUCY, MACHEATH

MACH.   I am naturally compassionate, wife, so that I could not use the wench as she deserved; which made you at first suspect there was something in what she said.

LUCY.   Indeed, my dear, I was strangely puzzled.

MACH.   If that had been the case, her father would never have brought me into this circumstance. No, Lucy, I had rather die than be false to thee.

LUCY.   How happy am I if you say this from your heart! For I love thee so, that I could sooner bear to see thee hanged than in the arms of another.

MACH.   But couldst thou bear to see me hanged?

LUCY.   O Macheath, I can never live to see that day.

MACH.   You see, Lucy, in the account of love you are in my debt, and you must now be convinced that I rather choose to die than be another's. Make me, if possible, love thee more, and let me owe my life to thee. If you refuse to assist me.

Peachum and your father will immediately put me beyond all means of escape.

LUCY. My father, I know, hath been drinking hard with the prisoners, and I fancy he is now taking his nap in his own room. If I can procure the keys, shall I go off with thee, my dear?

MACH. If we are together, 'twill be impossible to lie concealed. As soon as the search begins to be a little cool, I will send to thee. Till then my heart is thy prisoner.

LUCY. Come then, my dear husband—owe thy life to me—and though you love me not, be grateful. But that Polly runs in my head strangely.

MACH. A moment of time may make us unhappy forever.

AIR XL. *The lass of Patie's mill*

LUCY.   I like the fox shall grieve,
            Whose mate hath left her side,
         Whom hounds, from morn to eve,
            Chase o'er the country wide.
         Where can my lover hide?
            Where cheat the wary pack?
         If love be not his guide,
            He never will come back!

ACT III

SCENE I

SCENE: *Newgate*

LOCKIT, LUCY

LOCK. To be sure, wench, you must have been aiding and abetting to help him to this escape.

LUCY. Sir, here hath been Peachum and his daughter Polly, and to be sure they know the ways of Newgate as well as if they had been born and bred in the place all their lives. Why must all your suspicion light upon me?

LOCK. Lucy, Lucy, I will have none of these shuffling answers.

LUCY. Well then—if I know anything of him I wish I may be burnt!

LOCK. Keep your temper, Lucy, or I shall pronounce you guilty.

LUCY. Keep yours, Sir. I do wish I may be burnt. I do!—and what can I say more to convince you?

LOCK. Did he tip handsomely? How much did he come down with? Come, hussy, don't cheat your father, and I shall not be angry with you. Perhaps you have made a better bargain with him than I could have done. How much, my good girl?

LUCY. You know, Sir, I am fond of him, and would have given money to have kept him with me.

LOCK. Ah, Lucy! thy education might have put thee more upon thy guard; for a girl in the bar of an ale-house is always besieged.

LUCY. Dear Sir, mention not my education—for 'twas to that I owe my ruin.

AIR XLI. *If love's a sweet passion*

When young at the bar you first taught me to score,
And bid me be free of my lips, and no more;
I was kiss'd by the parson, the squire, and the sot.
When the guest was departed, the kiss was forgot.
But his kiss was so sweet, and so closely he press'd,
That I langush'd and pin'd till I granted the rest.

If you can forgive me, Sir, I will make a fair confession, for to be sure, he hath been a most barbarous villain to me.

LOCK. And so you have let him escape, hussy—have you?

LUCY. When a woman loves, a kind look, a tender word can persuade her to anything—and I could ask no other bribe.

LOCK. Thou wilt always be a vulgar slut, Lucy. If you would not be looked upon as a fool, you should never do anything but upon the foot of interest. Those that act otherwise are their own bubbles.

LUCY. But love, Sir, is a misfortune that may happen to the most discreet woman, and in love we are all fools alike. Notwithstanding all he swore, I am now fully convinced that Polly Peachum is actually his wife. Did I let him escape (fool that I was!) to go to her? Polly will wheedle herself into his money, and then Peachum will hang him, and cheat us both.

LOCK. So I am to be ruined, because, forsooth, you must be in love!—a very pretty excuse!

LUCY. I could murder that impudent happy strumpet: I gave him his life, and that creature enjoys the sweets of it. Ungrateful Macheath!

AIR XLII. *South-Sea ballad*

My love is all madness and folly,
    Alone I lie,
    Toss, tumble, and cry,
What a happy creature is Polly!
    Was e'er such a wretch as I!
With rage I redden like scarlet,
That my dear inconstant varlet,
    Stark blind to my charms,
    Is lost in the arms
Of that jilt, that inveigling harlot!
    Stark blind to my charms,
    Is lost in the arms
Of that jilt, that inveigling harlot!
    This, this my resentment alarms.

LOCK.   And so, after all this mischief, I must stay here to
be entertained with your caterwauling, Mistress Puss! Out of
my sight, wanton strumpet! you shall fast and mortify yourself
into reason, with now and then a little handsome discipline to
bring you to your senses. Go!

SCENE II

LOCKIT

Peachum then intends to outwit me in this affair; but I'll
be even with him. The dog is leaky in his liquor, so I'll ply
him that way, get the secret from him, and turn this affair to
my own advantage. Lions, wolves, and vultures don't live together in herds, droves or flocks. Of all animals of prey, man
is the only sociable one. Every one of us preys upon his neighbour, and yet we herd together. Peachum is my companion,
my friend. According to the custom of the world, indeed, he
may quote thousands of precedents for cheating me—and
shall not I make use of the privilege of friendship to make him
a return?

AIR XLIII. *Packington's pound*

Thus gamesters united in friendship are found,
Though they know that their industry all is a cheat;
They flock to their prey at the dice-box's sound,
And join to promote one another's deceit.
    But if by mishap
    They fail of a chap,

To keep in their hands, they each other entrap.
Like pikes, lank with hunger, who miss of their ends,
They bite their companions, and prey on their friends.

Now, Peachum, you and I, like honest tradesmen, are to
have a fair trial which of us two can overreach the other.
Lucy! (*Enter* LUCY.) Are there any of Peachum's people
now in the house?

LUCY. Filch, Sir, is drinking a quartern of strong waters in
the next room with Black Moll.

LOCK. Bid him come to me.   (*Exit* LUCY)

SCENE III

LOCKIT, FILCH

LOCK. Why, boy, thou lookest as if thou wert half starved;
like a shotten herring.

FILCH. One had need have the constitution of a horse to
go thorough the business. Since the favourite child-getter was
disabled by a mishap, I have picked up a little money by
helping the ladies to a pregnancy against their being called
down to sentence. But if a man cannot get an honest livelihood any easier way, I am sure 'tis what I can't undertake for
another session.

LOCK. Truly, if that great man should tip off, 'twould be
an irreparable loss. The vigour and prowess of a knight errant
never saved half the ladies in distress that he hath done. But,
boy, canst thou tell me where thy master is to be found?

FILCH. At his lock, Sir, at the Crooked Billet.

LOCK. Very well. I have nothing more with you. (*Exit*
FILCH) I'll go to him there, for I have many important affairs
to settle with him; and in the way of those transactions I'll
artfully get into his secret. So that Macheath shall not remain
a day longer out of my clutches.   (*Exit*)

SCENE IV

SCENE: *A Gaming-House*

MACHEATH *in a fine tarnished coat*, BEN BUDGE,
MATT OF THE MINT

MACH. I am sorry, gentlemen, the road was so barren of
money. When my friends are in difficulties, I am always glad
that my fortune can be serviceable to them. (*gives them*

money) You see, gentlemen, 1 am not a mere court friend, who professes everything and will do nothing.

AIR XLIV. *Lillibullero*

The modes of the court so common are grown
    That a true friend can hardly be met;
Friendship for interest is but a loan,
    Which they let out for what they can get.
      'Tis true, you find
      Some friends so kind,
Who will give you good counsel themselves to defend.
      In sorrowful ditty,
      They promise, they pity,
But shift you, for money, from friend to friend.

But we, gentlemen, have still honour enough to break through the corruptions of the world. And while I can serve you, you may command me.

BEN. It grieves my heart that so generous a man should be involved in such difficulties as oblige him to live with such ill company, and herd with gamesters.

MATT. See the partiality of mankind! One man may steal a horse, better than another look over a hedge. Of all mechanics, of all servile handicraftsmen, a gamester is the vilest. But yet, as many of the quality are of the profession, he is admitted amongst the politest company. I wonder we are not more respected.

MACH. There will be deep play to-night at Marybone and consequently money may be picked up upon the road. Meet me there, and I'll give you the hint who is worth setting.

MATT. The fellow with a brown coat with a narrow gold binding, I am told, is never without money.

MACH. What do you mean, Matt? Sure you will not think of meddling with him! He's a good honest kind of a fellow, and one of us.

BEN. To be sure, Sir, we will put ourselves under your direction.

MACH. Have an eye upon the money-lenders. A rouleau or two would prove a pretty sort of an expedition. I hate extortion.

MATT. Those rouleaus are very pretty things. I hate your bank bills—there is such a hazard in putting them off.

MACH. There is a certain man of distinction who in his time hath nicked me out of a great deal of the ready. He is in

my cash, Ben; I'll point him out to you this evening, and you
shall draw upon him for the debt.——The company are met; I
hear the dice-box in the other room. So, gentlemen, your servant! You'll meet me at Marybone.   (*Exeunt*)

SCENE V

SCENE: PEACHUM'S *lock*

A *table with wine, brandy, pipes and tobacco*

PEACHUM, LOCKIT

LOCK.   The coronation account, brother Peachum, is of so
intricate a nature that I believe it will never be settled.

PEACH.   It consists, indeed, of a great variety of articles. It
was worth to our people, in fees, of different kinds, above ten
instalments. This is part of the account, brother, that lies open
before us.

LOCK.   A lady's tail of rich brocade—that, I see, is disposed
of.

PEACH.   To Mrs. Diana Trapes, the tally-woman, and she
will make a good hand on't in shoes and slippers, to trick out
young ladies, upon their going into keeping.

LOCK.   But I don't see any article of the jewels.

PEACH.   Those are so well known that they must be sent
abroad. You'll find them entered under the article of exporta-
tion. As for the snuff-boxes, watches, swords, etc., I thought it
best to enter them under their several heads.

LOCK.   Seven and twenty women's pockets complete, with
the several things therein contained; all sealed, numbered,
and entered.

PEACH.   But, brother, it is impossible for us now to enter
upon this affair. We should have the whole day before us. Besides, the account of the last half-year's plate is in a book by
itself, which lies at the other office.

LOCK.   Bring us then more liquor. To-day shall be for
pleasure—to-morrow for business.——Ah brother, those daughters of ours are two slippery hussies. Keep a watchful eye
upon Polly, and Macheath in a day or two shall be our own
again.

AIR XLV. *Down in the North Country*

LOCK.   What gudgeons are we men!
            Ev'ry woman's easy prey.

Though we have felt the hook, again
We bite and they betray.

The bird that hath been trapp'd,
When he hears his calling mate,
To her he flies, again he's clapp'd
Within the wiry grate.

PEACH. But what signifies catching the bird, if your daughter Lucy will set open the door of the cage?

LOCK. If men were answerable for the follies and frailties of their wives and daughters, no friends could keep a good correspondence together for two days. This is unkind of you, brother; for among good friends, what they say or do goes for nothing.

Enter a Servant

SERV. Sir, here's Mrs. Diana Trapes wants to speak with you.

PEACH. Shall we admit her, brother Lockit?

LOCK. By all means—she's a good customer, and a fine-spoken woman, and a woman who drinks and talks so freely will enliven the conversation.

PEACH. Desire her to walk in. (*Exit Servant*)

SCENE VI

PEACHUM, LOCKIT, MRS. TRAPES

PEACH. Dear Mrs. Dye, your servant!—one may know by your kiss that your gin is excellent.

TRAPES. I was always very curious in my liquors.

LOCK. There is no perfumed breath like it. I have been long acquainted with the flavour of those lips—han't I, Mrs. Dye?

TRAPES. Fill it up. I take as large draughts of liquor as I did of love. I hate a flincher in either.

AIR XLVI. *A shepherd kept sheep*

In the days of my youth I could bill like a dove, fa, la, la, etc.
Like a sparrow at all times was ready for love, fa, la, la, etc.
The life of all mortals in kissing should pass
Lip to lip while we're young—then the lip to the glass, fa, la, etc.

But now, Mr. Peachum, to our business. If you have blacks

of any kind, brought in of late: manteaus—velvet scarfs—petti-coats—let it be what it will—I am your chap—for all my ladies are very fond of mourning.

PEACH.   Why, look ye, Mrs. Dye—you deal so hard with us, that we can afford to give the gentlemen, who venture their lives for the goods, little or nothing.

TRAPES.   The hard times oblige me to go very near in my dealing. To be sure, of late years I have been a great sufferer by the parliament. Three thousand pounds would hardly make me amends. The act for destroying the Mint was a severe cut upon our business. 'Till then, if a customer stepped out of the way—we knew where to have her. No doubt you know Mrs. Coaxer—there's a wench now (till to-day) with a good suit of clothes of mine upon her back, and I could never set eyes upon her for three months together.—Since the act too against imprisonment for small sums, my loss there too hath been very considerable; and it must be so, when a lady can borrow a handsome petticoat, or a clean gown, and I not have the least hank upon her! And, o' my conscience, now-a-days most ladies take a delight in cheating, when they can do it with safety.

PEACH.   Madam, you had a handsome gold watch of us t'other day for seven guineas. Considering we must have our profit—to a gentleman upon the road, a gold watch will be scarce worth the taking.

TRAPES.   Consider, Mr. Peachum, that watch was remark-able and not of very safe sale. If you have any black velvet scarfs—they are a handsome winter wear, and take with most gentlemen who deal with my customers. 'Tis I that put the ladies upon a good foot. 'Tis not youth or beauty that fixes their price. The gentlemen always pay according to their dress, from half a crown to two guineas; and yet those hussies make nothing of bilking of me. Then, too, allowing for acci-dents—I have eleven fine customers now down under the sur-geon's hands; what with fees and other expenses, there are great goings-out, and no comings-in, and not a farthing to pay for at least a month's clothing. We run great risks—great risks indeed.

PEACH.   As I remember, you said something just now of Mrs. Coaxer.

TRAPES.   Yes, Sir. To be sure, I stripped her of a suit of my own clothes about two hours ago, and have left her as she should be, in her shift, with a lover of hers, at my house. She called him upstairs, and he was going to Marybone in a hackney coach. And I hope, for her own sake and mine, she will persuade the captain to redeem her, for the captain is very generous to the ladies.

LOCK. What captain?

TRAPES. He thought I did not know him. An intimate acquaintance of yours, Mr. Peachum—only Captain Macheath—as fine as a lord.

PEACH. To-morrow, dear Mrs. Dye, you shall set your own price upon any of the goods you like. We have at least half a dozen velvet scarfs, and all at your service. Will you give me leave to make you a present of this suit of nightclothes for your own wearing? But are you sure it is Captain Macheath?

TRAPES. Though he thinks I have forgot him; nobody knows him better. I have taken a great deal of the captain's money in my time at second hand, for he always loved to have his ladies well dressed.

PEACH. Mr. Lockit and I have a little business with the captain—you understand me—and we will satisfy you for Mrs. Coaxer's debt.

LOCK. Depend upon it—we will deal like men of honour.

TRAPES. I don't enquire after your affairs—so whatever happens, I wash my hands on't. It hath always been my maxim, that one friend should assist another. But if you please, I'll take one of the scarfs home with me: 'tis always good to have something in hand. (*Exeunt*)

SCENE VII

SCENE: *Newgate*

LUCY

Jealousy, rage, love and fear are at once tearing me to pieces. How I am weatherbeaten and shattered with distresses!

AIR XLVII. *One evening, having lost my way*
I'm like a skiff on the ocean toss'd,
　　Now high, now low, with each billow borne,
With her rudder broke, and her anchor lost,
　　Deserted and all forlorn.
While thus I lie rolling and tossing all night,
That Polly lies sporting on seas of delight!
　　Revenge, revenge, revenge,
Shall appease my restless sprite.

I have the ratsbane ready. I run no risk, for I can lay her death upon the gin, and so many die of that naturally that I shall never be called in question. But say I were to be hanged—I never could be hanged for anything that would give me greater comfort than the poisoning that slut.

Enter FILCH

FILCH.   Madam, here's our Miss Polly come to wait upon you.

LUCY.   Show her in.   (*Exit* FILCH)

SCENE VIII

LUCY, POLLY

LUCY.   Dear Madam, your servant. I hope you will pardon my passion, when I was so happy to see you last. I was so overrun with the spleen, that I was perfectly out of myself. And really, when one hath the spleen everything is to be excused by a friend.

AIR XLVIII. *Now Roger, I'll tell thee, because thou'rt my son*

> When a wife's in her pout,
> (As she's sometimes, no doubt),
> The good husband, as meek as a lamb,
> Her vapours to still,
> First grants her her will,
> And the quieting draught is a dram.
> Poor man! And the quieting draught is a dram.

—I wish all our quarrels might have so comfortable a reconciliation.

POLLY.   I have no excuse for my own behaviour, Madam, but my misfortunes. And really, Madam, I suffer too upon your account.

LUCY.   But, Miss Polly—in the way of friendship, will you give me leave to propose a glass of cordial to you?

POLLY.   Strong waters are apt to give me the headache—I hope, Madam, you will excuse me.

LUCY.   Not the greatest lady in the land could have better in her closet, for her own private drinking. You seem mighty low in spirits, my dear.

POLLY.   I am sorry, Madam, my health will not allow me to accept of your offer. I should not have left you in the rude

manner I did when we met last, Madam, had not my papa
hauled me away so unexpectedly. I was indeed somewhat
provoked, and perhaps might use some expressions that were
disrespectful. But really, Madam, the captain treated me with
so much contempt and cruelty that I deserved your pity,
rather than your resentment.

LUCY.   But since his escape no doubt all matters are made
up again. Ah Polly! Polly! 'tis I am the unhappy wife, and
he loves you as if you were only his mistress.

POLLY.   Sure, Madam, you cannot think me so happy as
to be the object of your jealousy. A man is always afraid of
a woman who loves him too well—so that I must expect to be
neglected and avoided.

LUCY.   Then our cases, my dear Polly, are exactly alike.
Both of us, indeed, have been too fond.

AIR XLIX. *Oh, Bessy Bell*

POLLY.   A curse attends that woman's love,
              Who always would be pleasing.
LUCY.   The pertness of the billing dove,
              Like tickling, is but teasing.
POLLY.   What then in love can woman do?
LUCY.   If we grow fond they shun us.
POLLY.   And when we fly them, they pursue.
LUCY.   But leave us when they've won us.

LUCY.   Love is so very whimsical in both sexes, that it is
impossible to be lasting. But my heart is particular, and con-
tradicts my own observation.

POLLY.   But really, Mistress Lucy, by his last behaviour,
I think I ought to envy you. When I was forced from him,
he did not show the least tenderness. But perhaps he hath
a heart not capable of it.

AIR L. *Would fate to me Belinda give*

Among the men, coquets we find,
Who court by turns all womankind;
And we grant all their hearts desir'd,
When they are flatter'd and admir'd.

The coquets of both sexes are self-lovers, and that is a love
no other whatever can dispossess. I fear, my dear Lucy, our
husband is one of those.

LUCY.   Away with these melancholy reflections; indeed, my dear Polly, we are both of us a cup too low. Let me prevail upon you to accept of my offer.

AIR LI. *Come, sweet lass*

Come, sweet lass,
Let's banish sorrow
Till to-morrow;
Come, sweet lass,
Let's take a chirping glass.
Wine can clear
The vapours of despair;
And make us light as air;
Then drink, and banish care.

I can't bear, child, to see you in such low spirits. And I must persuade you to what I know will do you good. (*aside*) I shall now soon be even with the hypocritical strumpet.

(*Exit* LUCY)

SCENE IX

POLLY

All this wheedling of Lucy cannot be for nothing. At this time, too, when I know she hates me! The dissembling of a woman is always the forerunner of mischief. By pouring strong waters down my throat, she thinks to pump some secrets out of me. I'll be upon my guard, and won't taste a drop of her liquor, I'm resolved.

SCENE X

LUCY, *with strong waters.* POLLY

LUCY.   Come, Miss Polly.

POLLY.   Indeed, child, you have given yourself trouble to no purpose. You must, my dear, excuse me.

LUCY.   Really, Miss Polly, you are so squeamishly affected about taking a cup of strong waters as a lady before company. I vow, Polly, I shall take it monstrously ill if you refuse me. Brandy and men (though women love them never so well) are always taken by us with some reluctance—unless 'tis in private.

POLLY.   I protest, Madam, it goes against me.—— What

do I see! Macheath again in custody! Now every glimmering of happiness is lost. (*drops the glass of liquor on the ground*)

LUCY. (*aside*) Since things are thus, I'm glad the wench hath escaped: for by this event 'tis plain she was not happy enough to deserve to be poisoned.

SCENE XI

LOCKIT, MACHEATH, PEACHUM, LUCY, POLLY

LOCK. Set your heart to rest, Captain. You have neither the chance of love or money for another escape, for you are ordered to be called down upon your trial immediately.

PEACH. Away, hussies! This is not a time for a man to be hampered with his wives. You see, the gentleman is in chains already.

LUCY. O husband, husband, my heart longed to see thee; but to see thee thus distracts me!

POLLY. Will not my dear husband look upon his Polly? Why hadst thou not flown to me for protection? with me thou hadst been safe.

AIR LII. *The last time I went o'er the moor*

POLLY. Hither, dear husband, turn your eyes.

LUCY. Bestow one glance to cheer me.

POLLY. Think, with that look, thy Polly dies.

LUCY. Oh, shun me not—but hear me.

POLLY. 'Tis Polly sues.

LUCY. ——'Tis Lucy speaks.

POLLY. Is thus true love requited?

LUCY. My heart is bursting.

POLLY. ——Mine too breaks.

LUCY. Must I

POLLY. ——Must I be slighted?

MACH. What would you have me say, ladies? You see, this affair will soon be at an end, without my disobliging either of you.

PEACH. But the settling this point, Captain, might prevent a law-suit between your two widows.

AIR LIII. *Tom Tinker's my true love*

MACH. Which way shall I turn me? how can I decide?
Wives, the day of our death, are as fond as a bride.

One wife is too much for most husbands to hear,
But two at a time there's no mortal can bear.
This way, and that way, and which way I will,
What would comfort the one, t'other wife would
    take ill.

POLLY.   But if his own misfortunes have made him insensible to mine, a father sure will be more compassionate.—
Dear, dear Sir, sink the material evidence, and bring him off
at his trial—Polly upon her knees begs it of you.

AIR LIV. *I am a poor shepherd undone*

When my hero in court appears,
    And stands arraign'd for his life;
Then think of poor Polly's tears;
    For ah! poor Polly's his wife.
Like the sailor he holds up his hand,
    Distress'd on the dashing wave.
To die a dry death at land,
    Is as bad as a wat'ry grave.
And alas, poor Polly!
    Alack, and well-a-day!
Before I was in love,
    Oh! every month was May.

LUCY.   If Peachum's heart is hardened, sure you, Sir, will
have more compassion on a daughter. I know the evidence
is in your power. How then can you be a tyrant to me?
(*kneeling*)

AIR LV. *Ianthe the lovely*

When he holds up his hand arraign'd for his life,
Oh think of your daughter, and think I'm his wife!
What are cannons, or bombs, or clashing of swords?
For death is more certain by witnesses' words.
Then nail up their lips; that dread thunder allay;
And each month of my life will hereafter be May.

LOCK.   Macheath's time is come, Lucy. We know our own
affairs, therefore let us have no more whimpering or whining.

AIR LVI. *A cobbler there was*

Ourselves, like the great, to secure a retreat,
  When matters require it, must give up our gang.
    And good reason why,
    Or, instead of the fry,
    Ev'n Peachum and I,
  Like poor petty rascals, might hang, hang;
  Like poor petty rascals might hang.

PEACH. Set your heart at rest, Polly. Your husband is to
die to-day. Therefore, if you are not already provided, 'tis
high time to look about for another. There's comfort for you,
you slut.

LOCK. We are ready, Sir, to conduct you to the Old Bailey.

AIR LVII. *Bonny Dundee*

MACH. The charge is prepar'd; the lawyers are met,
    The judges all rang'd (a terrible show!)
  I go, undismay'd—for death is a debt,
    A debt on demand. So, take what I owe.
  Then farewell, my love—dear charmers, adieu!
  Contented I die—'tis the better for you.
    Here ends all dispute the rest of our lives,
    For this way at once I please all my wives.

Now, gentlemen, I am ready to attend you.

SCENE XII

LUCY, POLLY, FILCH

POLLY. Follow them, Filch, to the court. And when the
trial is over, bring me a particular account of his behaviour,
and of everything that happened. You'll find me here with
Miss Lucy.   (*Exit* FILCH)
But why is all this music?

LUCY. The prisoners whose trials are put off till next session are diverting themselves.

POLLY. Sure there is nothing so charming as music! I'm
fond of it to distraction! But alas! now, all mirth seems an
insult upon my affliction.—— Let us retire, my dear Lucy, and
indulge our sorrows. The noisy crew, you see, are coming
upon us.   (*Exeunt*)
(*a dance of prisoners in chains, etc.*)

SCENE XIII

SCENE: *The condemned hold*

MACHEATH, *in a melancholy posture*

AIR LVIII. *Happy groves*

O cruel, cruel, cruel case!
Must I suffer this disgrace?

AIR LIX. *Of all the girls that are so smart*

Of all the friends in time of grief,
    When threat'ning death looks grimmer,
Not one so sure can bring relief,
    As this best friend, a brimmer.   (*drinks*)

AIR LX. *Britons, strike home*

Since I must swing—I scorn, I scorn to wince or whine.
                                        (*rises*)

AIR LXI. *Chevy Chase*

But now again my spirits sink;
I'll raise them high with wine.
                        (*drinks a glass of wine*)

AIR LXII. *To old Sir Simon the King*

But valour the stronger grows,
The stronger liquor we're drinking.
And how can we feel our woes,
When we've lost the trouble of thinking?   (*drinks*)

AIR LXIII. *Joy to great Cæsar*

If thus—— A man can die
Much bolder with brandy.
                (*pours out a bumper of brandy*)

AIR LXIV. *There was an old woman*

So I drink off this bumper.—— And now I can stand the test.
And my comrades shall see that I die as brave as the best.
                                        (*drinks*)

AIR LXV. *Did you ever hear of a gallant sailor*

But can I leave my pretty hussies,
Without one tear, or tender sigh?

AIR LXVI. *Why are mine eyes still flowing*

Their eyes, their lips, their busses,
Recall my love.—Ah, must I die!

AIR LXVII. *Greensleeves*

Since laws were made for ev'ry degree,
To curb vice in others, as well as me,
I wonder we han't better company,
    Upon Tyburn tree!
But gold from law can take out the sting;
And if rich men like us were to swing,
'Twould thin the land, such numbers to string
    Upon Tyburn tree!

Enter Jailor

JAILOR.   Some friends of yours, Captain, desire to be admitted. I leave you together.   (*Exit*)

SCENE XIV

MACHEATH, BEN BUDGE, MATT OF THE MINT

MACH.   For my having broke prison, you see, gentlemen, I am ordered immediate execution. The sheriff's officers, I believe, are now at the door. That Jemmy Twitcher should peach me, I own surprised me! 'Tis a plain proof that the world is all alike, and that even our gang can no more trust one another than other people. Therefore, I beg you, gentlemen, look well to yourselves, for in all probability you may live some months longer.

MATT.   We are heartily sorry, Captain, for your misfortune. But 'tis what we must all come to.

MACH.   Peachum and Lockit, you know, are infamous scoundrels. Their lives are as much in your power, as yours are in theirs. Remember your dying friend!—'tis my last request. Bring those villains to the gallows before you, and I am satisfied.

MATT.   We'll do't.

Enter Jailor

JAILOR.   Miss Polly and Miss Lucy intreat a word with you.

MACH.   Gentlemen, adieu.

SCENE XV

LUCY, MACHEATH, POLLY

MACH.   My dear Lucy—my dear Polly—whatsoever hath passed between us is now at an end. If you are fond of marrying again, the best advice I can give you is to ship yourselves off for the West Indies, where you'll have a fair chance of getting a husband apiece; or by good luck, two or three, as you like best.

POLLY.   How can I support this sight!

LUCY.   There is nothing moves one so much as a great man in distress.

AIR LXVIII. *All you that must take a leap*

LUCY.   Would I might be hanged!
POLLY.   ——And I would so too!
LUCY.   To be hanged with you
POLLY.   ——My dear, with you.
MACH.   Oh, leave me to thought! I fear! I doubt!
         I tremble! I droop!—See, my courage is out.
                         (*turns up the empty bottle*)
POLLY.   No token of love?
MACH.   ——See, my courage is out.
                         (*turns up the empty pot*)
LUCY.   No token of love?
POLLY.   ——Adieu!
LUCY.   ——Farewell!
MACH.   But hark! I hear the toll of the bell!
CHORUS.   Tol de rol lol, etc.

Re-enter Jailor

JAILOR.   Four women more, Captain, with a child apiece! See, here they come.

Enter Women and Children

MACH.   What—four wives more! This is too much.——Here—tell the sheriff's officers I am ready.
                         (*Exit* MACHEATH *guarded*)

SCENE XVI

To them enter PLAYER *and* BEGGAR

PLAY.   But, honest friend, I hope you don't intend that Macheath shall be really executed.

BEG.   Most certainly, Sir. To make the piece perfect, I
was for doing strict poetical justice. Macheath is to be
hanged; and for the other personages of the drama, the audience must have supposed they were all either hanged or
transported.

PLAY.   Why then, friend, this is a downright deep tragedy. The catastrophe is manifestly wrong, for an opera must
end happily.

BEG.   Your objection, Sir, is very just and is easily removed. For you must allow that in this kind of drama 'tis no
matter how absurdly things are brought about.—— So—you
rabble there—run and cry a reprieve!—let the prisoner be
brought back to his wives in triumph.

PLAY.   All this we must do, to comply with the taste of
the town.

BEG.   Through the whole piece you may observe such a
similitude of manners in high and low life, that it is difficult
to determine whether (in the fashionable vices) the fine gentlemen imitate the gentlemen of the road, or the gentlemen
of the road the fine gentlemen. Had the play remained as I
at first intended, it would have carried a most excellent moral.
'Twould have shown that the lower sort of people have their
vices in a degree as well as the rich; and that they are punished for them.

SCENE XVII

To them MACHEATH, *with rabble, etc.*

MACH.   So, it seems, I am not left to my choice, but must
have a wife at last.—— Look ye, my dears, we will have no
controversy now. Let us give this day to mirth, and I am
sure she who thinks herself my wife will testify her joy by
a dance.

ALL.   Come, a dance—a dance.

MACH.   Ladies, I hope you will give me leave to present
a partner to each of you. And (if I may without offence) for
this time, I take Polly for mine. (*to* POLLY) And for life, you
slut—for we were really married.—— As for the rest—— But at
present keep your own secret.   (*a dance*)

AIR LXIX. *Lumps of pudding*

Thus I stand like the Turk, with his doxies around;
From all sides their glances his passion confound:
For black, brown, and fair, his inconstancy burns,

And the different beauties subdue him by turns:
Each calls forth her charms, to provoke his desires:
Though willing to all, with but one he retires.
But think of this maxim, and put off your sorrow,
The wretch of to-day may be happy to-morrow.
    CHORUS.   But think of this maxim, etc.

The Tragedy of Tragedies;

OR,

The Life and Death of Tom Thumb the Great

With the Annotations of
H. Scriblerus Secundus

BY HENRY FIELDING

H. SCRIBLERUS SECUNDUS; HIS PREFACE

The town hath seldom been more divided in its opinion than concerning the merit of the following scenes. Whilst some publicly affirmed that no author could produce so fine a piece but Mr. Pope, others have with as much vehemence insisted that no one could write anything so bad but Mr. Fielding.

Nor can we wonder at this dissension about its merit, when

the learned world have not unanimously decided even the
very nature of this tragedy. For though most of the univer-
sities in Europe have honoured it with the name of *Egregium
et maximi pretii opus, tragœdiis tam antiquis quam novis
longe anteponendum;*[1] nay, Dr. Bentley hath pronounced,
*Citius Mævii Æneadem quam Scribleri istius tragœdiam hanc
crediderim, cujus auctorem Senecam ipsum tradidisse haud
dubitarim;*[2] and the great Professor Burman hath styled *Tom
Thumb, Heroum omnium tragicorum facile principem.*[3] Nay,
though it hath, among other languages, been translated into
Dutch, and celebrated with great applause at Amsterdam
(where burlesque never came) by the title of *Mynheer Van-
der Thumb,* the burgomasters receiving it with that reverent
and silent attention which becometh an audience at a deep
tragedy: notwithstanding all this, there have not been wanting some who have represented these scenes in a ludicrous
light; and Mr. Dennis hath been heard to say, with some
concern, that he wondered a tragical and Christian nation
would permit a representation on its theatre so visibly designed to ridicule and extirpate everything that is great and
solemn among us.

This learned critic and his followers were led into so great
an error by that surreptitious and piratical copy which stole
last year into the world—with what injustice and prejudice to
our author, I hope will be acknowledged by everyone who
shall happily peruse this genuine and original copy. Nor can
I help remarking, to the great praise of our author, that, however imperfect the former was, still did even that faint resemblance of the true *Tom Thumb* contain sufficient beauties to
give it a run of upwards of forty nights, to the politest audi-
ences. But, notwithstanding that applause which it received
from all the best judges, it was as severely censured by some
few bad ones and, I believe, rather maliciously than ignorantly
reported to have been intended a burlesque on the loftiest
parts of tragedy and designed to banish what we generally
call "fine things" from the stage.

Now, if I can set my country right in an affair of this importance, I shall lightly esteem any labour which it may cost.
And this I the rather undertake, first, as it is indeed in some
measure incumbent on me to vindicate myself from that sur-

[1] An outstanding and most precious work, much to be put before ancient
as well as modern tragedies.
[2] I might sooner believe Mævius wrote the Æneid than this Scriblerus this
tragedy, the author of which, no doubt, Seneca himself recorded.
[3] Tom Thumb, of all tragic heroes easily the chief.

reptitious copy before mentioned, published by some ill-meaning people under my name; secondly, as knowing myself more capable of doing justice to our author than any other man, as I have given myself more pains to arrive at a thorough understanding of this little piece, having for ten years together read nothing else; in which time I think I may modestly presume, with the help of my English dictionary, to comprehend all the meanings of every word in it.

But should any error of my pen awaken Clariss. Bentleium to enlighten the world with his annotations on our author, I shall not think that the least reward or happiness arising to me from these my endeavours.

I shall waive at present what hath caused such feuds in the learned world, whether this piece was originally written by Shakespeare, though certainly that, were it true, must add a considerable share to its merit, especially with such who are so generous as to buy and to commend what they never read, from an implicit faith in the author only—a faith which our age abounds in as much as it can be called deficient in any other.

Let it suffice that the *Tragedy of Tragedies, or, The Life and Death of Tom Thumb,* was written in the reign of Queen Elizabeth. Nor can the objection made by Mr. Dennis that the tragedy must then have been antecedent to the history, have any weight, when we consider that though the *History of Tom Thumb,* printed by and for Edward Midwinter, at the Looking-Glass on London Bridge, be of a later date; still must we suppose this history to have been transcribed from some other, unless we suppose the writer thereof to be inspired, a gift very faintly contended for by the writers of our age. As to this history's not bearing the stamp of second, third, or fourth edition, I see but little in that objection, editions being very uncertain lights to judge of books by; and perhaps Mr. Midwinter may have joined twenty editions in one, as Mr. Curll hath ere now divided one into twenty.

Nor doth the other argument, drawn from the little care our author hath taken to keep up to the letter of the history, carry any greater force. Are there not instances of plays wherein the history is so perverted that we can know the heroes whom they celebrate by no other marks than their names? Nay, do we not find the same character placed by different poets in such different lights that we can discover not the least sameness or even likeness in the features? The Sophonisba of Mairet and of Lee is a tender, passionate, amorous mistress of

Massinissa. Corneille and Mr. Thomson give her no other passion but the love of her country, and make her as cool in her affection to Massinissa as to Syphax. In the two latter she resembles the character of Queen Elizabeth; in the two former, she is the picture of Mary, Queen of Scotland. In short, the one Sophonisba is as different from the other as the Brutus of Voltaire is from the Marius, Jun. of Otway, or as the Minerva is from the Venus of the ancients.

Let us now proceed to a regular examination of the tragedy before us, in which I shall treat separately of the fable, the moral, the characters, the sentiments, and the diction. And first of the

Fable, which I take to be the most simple imaginable, and, to use the words of an eminent author, "One, regular, and uniform, not charged with a multiplicity of incidents, and yet affording several revolutions of fortune; by which the passions may be excited, varied, and driven to their full tumult of emotion." Nor is the action of this tragedy less great than uniform. The spring of all is the love of Tom Thumb for Huncamunca, which causeth the quarrel between their majesties in the first act; the passion of Lord Grizzle in the second; the rebellion, fall of Lord Grizzle and Glumdalca, devouring of Tom Thumb by the cow, and that bloody catastrophe, in the third.

Nor is the *moral* of this excellent tragedy less noble than the *fable:* it teaches these two instructive lessons, *viz.:* that human happiness is exceeding transient, and that death is the certain end of all men; the former whereof is inculcated by the fatal end of Tom Thumb, the latter by that of all the other personages.

The *characters* are, I think, sufficiently described in the *Dramatis Personæ,* and I believe we shall find few plays where greater care is taken to maintain them throughout and to preserve in every speech that characteristical mark which distinguishes them from each other. "But," says Mr. Dennis, "how well doth the character of Tom Thumb, whom we must call the hero of this tragedy, if it hath any hero, agree with the precepts of Aristotle, who defineth tragedy to be the imitation of a short but perfect action containing a just greatness in itself, etc. What greatness can be in a fellow whom history relateth to have been no higher than a span?" This gentleman seemeth to think, with Sergeant Kite, that the greatness of a man's soul is in proportion to that of his body, the contrary of which is affirmed by our English physiognomical writers. Besides, if I understand Aristotle right, he speaketh only of the greatness of the action, and not of the person.

As for the *sentiments* and the *diction,* which now only remain to be spoken to: I thought I could afford them no stronger justification than by producing parallel passages out of the best of our English writers. Whether this sameness of thought and expression which I have quoted from them proceeded from an agreement in their way of thinking, or whether they have borrowed from our author, I leave the reader to determine. I shall adventure to affirm this of the sentiments of our author, that they are generally the most familiar which I have ever met with and at the same time delivered with the highest dignity of phrase; which brings me to speak of his *diction.* Here I shall only beg one postulatum, *viz.:* that the greatest perfection of the language of a tragedy is, that it is not to be understood; which granted (as I think it must be), it will necessarily follow that the only way to avoid this is by being too high or too low for the understanding, which will comprehend everything within its reach. Those two extremities of style Mr. Dryden illustrates by the familiar image of two inns, which I shall term the aërial and the subterrestrial.

Horace goeth farther, and showeth when it is proper to call at one of these inns, and when at the other:

Telephus et Peleus, cum pauper et exul uterque,
Projicit ampullas et sesquipedalia verba.[1]

That he approveth of the *sesquipedalia verba* is plain; for had not Telephus and Peleus used this sort of diction in prosperity, they could not have dropped it in adversity. The aërial inn, therefore, says Horace, is proper only to be frequented by princes and other great men in the highest affluence of fortune; the subterrestrial is appointed for the entertainment of the poorer sort of people only, whom Horace advises *dolere sermone pedestri;*[2] the true meaning of both which citations is, that bombast is the proper language for joy and doggerel for grief, the latter of which is literally implied in the *sermo pedestris* as the former is in the *sesquipedalia verba.*

Cicero recommendeth the former of these. *Quid est tam furiosum vel tragicum quam verborum sonitus inanis, nullâ subjectâ sententiâ neque scientiâ.* "What can be so proper for tragedy as a set of big-sounding words, so contrived together

[1] Telephus and Peleus, when poor and in exile, spurned rant and sesquipedalian words.
[2] To utter woe in plain speech.

as to convey no meaning?"—which I shall one day or other prove to be the sublime of Longinus. Ovid declareth absolutely for the latter inn:

Omne genus scripti gravitate tragœdia vincit.[1]

Tragedy hath of all writings the greatest share in the bathos, which is the profound of Scriblerus.

I shall not presume to determine which of these two styles be properer for tragedy. It sufficeth that our author excelleth in both. He is very rarely within sight through the whole play, either rising higher than the eye of your understanding can soar or sinking lower than it careth to stoop. But here it may perhaps be observed that I have given more frequent instances of authors who have imitated him in the sublime than in the contrary. To which I answer: First, bombast being properly a redundancy of genius, instances of this nature occur in poets whose names do no more honour to our author than the writers in the doggerel which proceeds from a cool, calm, weighty way of thinking—instances whereof are most frequently to be found in authors of a lower class; secondly, that the works of such authors are difficultly found at all; thirdly, that it is a very hard task to read them, in order to extract these flowers from them; and lastly, it is very often difficult to transplant them at all, they being like some flowers of a very nice nature which will flourish in no soil but their own. For it is easy to transcribe a thought, but not the want of one. The *Earl of Essex*, for instance, is a little garden of choice rarities whence you can scarce transplant one line so as to preserve its original beauty. This must account to the reader for his missing the names of several of his acquaintance, which he had certainly found here had I ever read their works; for which, if I have not a just esteem, I can at least say with Cicero, *Quae non contemno, quippe quae nunquam legerim.*[2] However, that the reader may meet with due satisfaction in this point, I have a young commentator from the University who is reading over all the modern tragedies, at five shillings a dozen, and collecting all that they have stole from our author, which shall shortly be added as an appendix to this work.

---

1 Tragedy outdoes all other types of writing in seriousness.
2 I do not hold them in contempt, for I never read them.

DRAMATIS PERSONÆ

Men:

KING ARTHUR, *a passionate sort of king, husband to* QUEEN DOLLALLOLLA, *of whom he stands a little in fear; father to* HUNCAMUNCA, *whom he is very fond of; and in love with* GLUMDALCA

TOM THUMB THE GREAT, *a little hero with a great soul, something violent in his temper, which is a little abated by his love for* HUNCAMUNCA

GHOST OF GAFFER THUMB, *a whimsical sort of Ghost*

LORD GRIZZLE, *extremely zealous for the liberty of the subject, very choleric in his temper, and in love with* HUNCA-MUNCA

MERLIN, *a Conjurer, and in some sort father to* TOM THUMB

NOODLE, ⎱ *Courtiers in place, and consequently of that party*
DOODLE, ⎰ *that is uppermost*

FOODLE, *a Courtier that is out of place, and consequently of that party that is undermost*

BAILIFF *and* ⎱ *of the party of the plaintiff*
FOLLOWER, ⎰

PARSON, *of the side of the church*

Women:

QUEEN DOLLALLOLLA, *wife to* KING ARTHUR, *and mother to* HUNCAMUNCA, *a woman entirely faultless, saving that she is a little given to drink, a little too much a virago towards her husband, and in love with* TOM THUMB

THE PRINCESS HUNCAMUNCA, *daughter to their Majesties* KING ARTHUR *and* QUEEN DOLLALLOLLA, *of a very sweet, gentle, and amorous disposition, equally in love with* LORD GRIZZLE *and* TOM THUMB, *and desirous to be married to them both*

GLUMDALCA, *of the giants, a captive queen, beloved by the king, but in love with* TOM THUMB

CLEORA ⎱ *Maids of honour,* ⎱ NOODLE
MUSTACHA ⎰ *in love with* ⎰ DOODLE

Courtiers, Guards, Rebels, Drums, Trumpets, Thunder and Lightning

SCENE: *The Court of King Arthur, and a Plain thereabouts*

THE TRAGEDY OF TRAGEDIES

OR

THE LIFE AND DEATH OF TOM THUMB

THE GREAT

With the Annotations of

H. SCRIBLERUS SECUNDUS

ACT I

SCENE I

SCENE: *The Palace*

DOODLE, NOODLE

DOOD. Sure such a day[1] as this was never seen!
The sun himself, on this auspicious day,
Shines like a beau in a new birthday suit:
This down the seams embroider'd, that the beams.
All nature wears one universal grin.

[1] Corneille recommends some very remarkable day, wherein to fix the action of a tragedy. This the best of our tragical writers have understood to mean a day remarkable for the serenity of the sky, or what we generally call a fine summer's day: so that, according to this their exposition, the same months are proper for tragedy which are proper for pastoral. Most of our celebrated English tragedies as *Cato, Mariamne, Tamerlane,* &c., begin with their observations on the morning. Lee seems to have come the nearest to this beautiful description of our author's:

> The morning dawns with an unwonted crimson,
> The flowers all odorous seem, the garden birds
> Sing louder, and the *laughing* sun ascends
> The gaudy earth with an unusual brightness;
> All nature smiles. *Cæs. Borg.*

Massinissa, in the new *Sophonisba*, is also a favourite of the sun:

> ——The sun too seems
> As conscious of my joy, with broader eye
> To look abroad the world, and all things smile
> Like Sophonisba.

Memnon, in the *Persian Princess*, makes the sun decline rising, that he may not peep on objects which would profane his brightness:

> ——The morning rises slow,
> And all those ruddy streaks that us'd to paint
> The day's approach are lost in clouds, as if
> The horrors of the night had sent 'em back,
> To warn the sun he should not leave the sea,
> To peep, &c.

247

NOOD.   This day, O Mr. Doodle, is a day
Indeed,[2] a day we never saw before.
The mighty Thomas Thumb[3] victorious comes;
Millions of giants crowd his chariot wheels,
Giants![4] to whom the giants in Guildhall
Are infant dwarfs. They frown, and foam, and roar,
While Thumb, regardless of their noise, rides on.
So some cock-sparrow in a farmer's yard,
Hops at the head of an huge flock of turkeys.

DOOD.   When Goody Thumb first brought this Thomas forth,
The Genius of our land triumphant reign'd;
Then, then, O Arthur! did thy Genius reign.

NOOD.   They tell me it is whisper'd[5] in the books

[2] This line is highly conformable to the beautiful simplicity of the ancients. It hath been copied by almost every modern:

> Not to be is not to be in woe.
>
> *State of Innocence.*
>
> Love is not sin but where 'tis sinful love.
>
> *Don Sebastian.*
>
> Nature is nature, Lælius.
>
> *Sophonisba.*
>
> Men are but men, we did not make ourselves.
>
> *Revenge.*

[3] Dr. Bentley reads, The mighty Tall-mast Thumb. Mr. D——s, The mighty Thumping Thumb. Mr. T——d reads, Thundering. I think Thomas more agreeable to the great simplicity so apparent in our author.

[4] That learned historian Mr. Salmon, in the third number of his criticism on our author, takes great pains to explode this passage. "It is," says he, "difficult to guess what giants are here meant, unless the giant Despair in the *Pilgrim's Progress*, or the giant Greatness in the *Royal Villain;* for I have heard of no other sort of giants in the reign of King Arthur." Petrus Burmanus makes three Tom Thumbs, one whereof he supposes to have been the same person whom the Greeks called Hercules, and that by these giants are to be understood the Centaurs slain by that hero. Another Tom Thumb he contends to have been no other than the Hermes Trismegistus of the ancients. The third Tom Thumb he places under the reign of King Arthur; to which third Tom Thumb, says he, the actions of the other two were attributed. Now, though I know that this opinion is supported by an assertion of Justus Lipsius *"Thomam illum Thumbum non alium quam Herculem fuisse satis constat,"* [That Tom Thumb could have been no other than Hercules.] yet shall I venture to oppose one line of Mr. Midwinter against them all:

> In Arthur's court Tom Thumb did live.

"But then," says Dr. Bentley, "if we place Tom Thumb in the court of King Arthur, it will be proper to place that court out of Britain, where no giants were ever heard of." Spenser, in his *Fairy Queen,* is of another opinion, where, describing Albion, he says,

> ——Far within a salvage nation dwelt
> Of hideous giants.

And in the same canto,

> Then Elfar, with two brethren giants had,
> The one of which had two heads—the other three.

Risum teneatis, amici. [Don't laugh, friends.]

[5] "To whisper in books," says Mr. Dennis, "is errant nonsense." I am afraid this learned man does not sufficiently understand the extensive meaning of the word whisper. If he had rightly understood what is meant by the "senses

Of all our sages, that this mighty hero,
By Merlin's art begot, hath not a bone
Within his skin, but is a lump of gristle.

    DOOD.   Then 'tis a gristle of no mortal kind;
Some god, my Noodle, stept into the place
Of Gaffer Thumb, and more than half begot[6]
This mighty Tom.

    NOOD.   —Sure he was sent express[7]
From heav'n to be the pillar of our state.
Though small his body be, so very small
A chairman's leg is more than twice as large,
Yet is his soul like any mountain big;
And as a mountain once brought forth a mouse,
So doth this mouse contain a mighty mountain.[8]

    DOOD.   Mountain indeed! So terrible his name,
The giant nurses frighten children with it,[9]
And cry Tom Thumb is come, and if you are
Naughty, will surely take the child away.

    NOOD.   But hark! these trumpets[10] speak the king's approach.

    DOOD.   He comes most luckily for my petition.   (*flourish*)

---

whisp'ring the soul," in the *Persian Princess*, or what "whisp'ring like winds" is in *Aurengzebe*, or like thunder in another author, he would have understood this. Emmeline in Dryden sees a voice, but she was born blind, which is an excuse Panthea cannot plead in *Cyrus*, who hears a sight:

             ——Your description will surpass
            All fiction, painting, or dumb show of horror,
            That ever ears yet heard, or eyes beheld.

When Mr. Dennis understands these, he will understand whispering in books.
 6 ——Some ruffian stept into his father's place,
    And more than half begot him.

                             Mary Queen of Scots.

 7 ——For Ulamar seems *sent express from heaven,*
    To civilize this rugged Indian clime.

                             Liberty Asserted.

 8 *Omne majus continet in se minus, sed minus non in se majus continere potest,* [Every greater contains in itself the lesser, but the lesser cannot contain in itself the greater.] says Scaliger in *Thumbo.*—I suppose he would have cavilled at these beautiful lines in the *Earl of Essex:*
             ——Thy most inveterate soul,
             That looks through the foul prison of thy body.
And at those of Dryden:
             The palace is without too well design'd,
             Conduct me in, for I will view thy mind.

                             Aurengzebe.

 9 Mr. Banks hath copied this almost verbatim:
             It was enough to say, here's Essex come,
             And nurses still'd their children with the fright.

                             Earl of Essex.

 10 The trumpet in a tragedy is generally as much as to say *Enter King,* which makes Mr. Banks, in one of his plays, call it "the trumpet's formal sound."

SCENE II

KING, QUEEN, GRIZZLE, NOODLE, DOODLE, FOODLE

KING.   Let nothing but a face of joy appear;[11]
The man who frowns this day shall lose his head,
That he may have no face to frown withal.
Smile, Dollallolla—Ha! what wrinkled sorrow
Hangs, sits, lies, frowns[12] upon thy knitted brow?
Whence flow those tears fast down thy blubber'd cheeks,
Like a swoln gutter, gushing through the streets?
QUEEN.   Excess of joy, my Lord, I've heard folks[13] say,
Gives tears as certain as excess of grief.
KING.   If it be so, let all men cry for joy,
Till my whole court be drowned with their tears;[14]

[11] Phraortes, in the *Captives,* seems to have been acquainted with King
Arthur:

> Proclaim a festival for seven days' space,
> Let the court shine in all its pomp and lustre,
> Let all our streets resound with shouts of joy;
> Let music's care-dispelling voice be heard;
> The sumptuous banquet and the flowing goblet
> Shall warm the cheek and fill the heart with gladness.
> Astarbe shall sit mistress of the feast.

[12] Repentance *frowns* on thy contracted brow.

Sophonisba.

> Hung on his clouded brow, I mark'd despair.

Ibid.

> ——A sullen gloom
> Scowls on his brow.

Busiris.

[13] Plato is of this opinion, and so is Mr. Banks:

> Behold these tears sprung from fresh pain and joy.

Earl of Essex.

[14] These floods are very frequent in the tragic authors:

> Near to some murmuring brook I'll lay me down,
> Whose waters, if they should too shallow flow,
> My tears shall swell them up till I will drown.

LEE'S *Sophonisba.*

> Pouring forth tears at such a lavish rate,
> That were the world on fire they might have drown'd
> The wrath of heav'n, and quench'd the mighty ruin.

Mithridates.

One author changes the waters of grief to those of joy:

> ——These tears, that sprung from tides of grief,
> Are now augmented to a flood of joy.

Cyrus the Great.

Another:

> Turns all the *streams* of heat, and makes them flow
> In pity's channel.

Royal Villain.

One drowns himself:

> ——Pity like a torrent *pours* me down,
> Now I am drowning all within a deluge.

Anna Bullen.

Cyrus drowns the whole world,

> Our swelling grief
> Shall melt into a deluge, and the world
> Shall drown in tears.

Cyrus the Great.

Nay, till they overflow my utmost land,
And leave me nothing but the sea to rule.

   DOOD.   My liege, I a petition have here got.

   KING.   Petition me no petitions, Sir, to-day;
Let other hours be set apart for business.
To-day it is our pleasure to be drunk,[15]
And this our queen shall be as drunk as we.

   QUEEN.   (Though I already half seas over[16] am)
If the capacious goblet overflow
With arrack punch—'fore George! I'll see it out:
Of rum, and brandy, I'll not taste a drop.

   KING.   Though rack, in punch, eight shillings be a quart,
And rum and brandy be no more than six,
Rather than quarrel you shall have your will.

(trumpets)

But, ha! the warrior comes—the great Tom Thumb—
The little hero, giant-killing boy,
Preserver of my kingdom, is arrived.

SCENE III

TOM THUMB to them, with Officers, Prisoners,
and Attendants

   KING.   Oh! welcome most, most welcome to my arms.[17]
What gratitude can thank away the debt
Your valour lays upon me?

---

[15] An expression vastly beneath the dignity of tragedy, says Mr. Dennis, yet we find the word he cavils at in the mouth of Mithridates less properly used, and applied to a more terrible idea:

> I would be drunk with death.
>
> Mithridates.

The author of the new Sophonisba taketh hold of this monosyllable, and uses it pretty much to the same purpose:

> The Carthaginian sword with Roman blood
> Was drunk.

I would ask Mr. Dennis which gives him the best idea, a drunken king, or a drunken sword?

Mr. Tate dresses up King Arthur's resolution in heroics:

> Merry, my lord, o' th' captain's humour right,
> I am resolv'd to be dead drunk to-night.

Lee also uses this charming word:

> Love's the drunkenness of the mind.
>
> Gloriana.

[16] Dryden hath borrowed this, and applied it improperly:

> I'm half seas o'er in death.
>
> Cleom.

[17] This figure is in great use among the tragedians:

> 'Tis therefore, therefore 'tis.
>
> Victim.

> I long, repent, repent, and long again.
>
> Busiris.

QUEEN (*aside*).   ——Oh! ye gods![18]

THUMB.   When I'm not thank'd at all, I'm thank'd enough;
I've done my duty, and I've done no more.[19]

QUEEN (*aside*).   Was ever such a godlike creature seen!

KING.   Thy modesty's a candle[20] to thy merit,
It shines itself, and shows thy merit too.
But say, my boy, where didst thou leave the giants?

THUMB.   My liege, without the castle gates they stand,
The castle gates too low for their admittance.

KING.   What look they like?

THUMB.   Like nothing but themselves.

QUEEN (*aside*).   And sure thou art like nothing but thyself.[21]

KING.   Enough! the vast idea fills my soul.
I see them, yes, I see them now before me:
The monstrous, ugly, barb'rous sons of whores.
But ha! what form majestic strikes our eyes?
So perfect, that it seems to have been drawn
By all the gods in council: so fair she is,
That surely at her birth the council paus'd,
And then at length cried out, "This is a woman!"[22]

THUMB.   Then were the gods mistaken. She is not
A woman, but a giantess—whom we,
With much ado, have made a shift to haul[23]

---

[18] A tragical exclamation.

[19] This line is copied verbatim in the *Captives.*

[20] We find a candlestick for this candle in two celebrated authors:
          ——Each star withdraws
     His golden head, and burns within the socket.
                                             Nero.

     A soul grown old and sunk into the socket.
                                             Sebastian.

[21] This simile occurs very frequently among the dramatic writers of both
kinds.

[22] Mr. Lee hath stolen this thought from our author:
          ——This perfect face, drawn by the gods in council,
     Which they were long a making.
                              Lucius Junius Brutus.
          ——At his birth the heavenly council paus'd,
          And then at last cried out, "This is a man!"
Dryden hath improved this hint to the utmost perfection:
     So perfect, that the very gods who form'd you, wonder'd
     At their own skill, and cried, "A lucky hit
     Has mended our design!" Their envy hinder'd,
     Or you had been immortal, and a pattern,
     When heaven would work for ostentation sake,
     To copy out again.   *All for Love.*
Banks prefers the works of Michael Angelo to that of the gods:
     A pattern for the gods to make a man by,
     Or Michael Angelo to form a statue.

[23] It is impossible, says Mr. W——— sufficiently to admire this natural easy
line.

Within the town: for she is by a foot[24]
Shorter than all her subject giants were.

    GLUM.   We yesterday were both a queen and wife,
One hundred thousand giants own'd our sway,
Twenty whereof were married to ourself.

    QUEEN.   Oh! happy state of giantism—where husbands
Like mushrooms grow, whilst hapless we are forc'd
To be content, nay, happy thought, with one.

    GLUM.   But then to lose them all in one black day,
That the same sun which, rising, saw me wife
To twenty giants, setting, should behold
Me widowed of them all. My worn-out heart,
That ship, leaks fast, and the great heavy lading,
My soul, will quickly sink.[25]

    QUEEN.   Madam, believe
I view your sorrows with a woman's eye;
But learn to bear them with what strength you may,
To-morrow we will have our grenadiers
Drawn out before you, and you then shall choose
What husbands you think fit.

    GLUM.   Madam, I am
Your most obedient and most humble servant.[26]

    KING.   Think, mighty princess, think this court your own,
Nor think the landlord me, this house my inn;
Call for whate'er you will, you'll nothing pay.
I feel a sudden pain within my breast,
Nor know I whether it arise from love
Or only the wind-colic.[27] Time must show.
O Thumb! What do we to thy valour owe!
Ask some reward, great as we can bestow.

    THUMB.   I ask not kingdoms, I can conquer those;[28]

---

[24] This tragedy, which in most points resembles the ancients, differs from them in this—that it assigns the same honour to lowness of stature which they did to height. The gods and heroes in Homer and Virgil are continually described higher by the head than their followers, the contrary of which is observed by our author. In short, to exceed on either side is equally admirable, and a man of three foot is as wonderful a sight as a man of nine.

[25] My blood leaks fast, and the great heavy lading
    My soul will quickly sink.   *Mithridates.*
    My soul is like a ship.   *Injured Love.*

[26] This well-bred line seems to be copied in the *Persian Princess:*
        To be your humblest and most faithful slave.

[27] This doubt of the king puts me in mind of a passage in the *Captives,* where the noise of feet is mistaken for the rustling of leaves.
      ——Methinks I hear
    The sound of feet:
    No; 'twas the wind that shook yon cypress boughs.

[28] Mr. Dryden seems to have had this passage in his eye in the first page of *Love Triumphant.*

I ask not money, money I've enough;
For what I've done, and what I mean to do,
For giants slain, and giants yet unborn,
Which I will slay—if this be call'd a debt,
Take my receipt in full—I ask but this,
To sun myself[29] in Huncamunca's eyes.

    KING.   Prodigious bold request.

    QUEEN (*aside*).   ——Be still, my soul.[30]

    THUMB.   My heart is at the threshold of your mouth,
And waits its answer there.—Oh! do not frown.
I've tried, to reason's tune, to tune my soul,
But love did overwind and crack the string.
Though Jove in thunder had cried out, YOU SHAN'T,
I should have lov'd her still—for oh, strange fate!
Then when I lov'd her least, I lov'd her most![31]

    KING.   It is resolv'd—the princess is your own.

    THUMB.   Oh! happy, happy, happy, happy[32] Thumb!

    QUEEN.   Consider, Sir; reward your soldier's merit,
But give not Huncamunca to Tom Thumb.

    KING.   Tom Thumb! Odzooks! my wide-extended realm
Knows not a name so glorious as Tom Thumb.
Let Macedonia Alexander boast,
Let Rome her Cæsars and her Scipios show,
Her Messieurs France, let Holland boast Mynheers,
Ireland her O's, her Macs let Scotland boast,
Let England boast no other than Tom Thumb.

    QUEEN.   Though greater yet his boasted merit was,
He shall not have my daughter, that is pos'.

---

[29] Don Carlos, in the *Revenge*, suns himself in the charms of his mistress:
          While in the lustre of her charms I lay.

[30] A tragical phrase much in use.

[31] This speech hath been taken to pieces by several tragical authors, who seem to have rifled it, and shared its beauties among them.

    My soul waits at the portal of thy breast,
    To ravish from thy lips the welcome news.

                      Anna Bullen.

    My soul stands list'ning at my ears.

                      Cyrus the Great.

    Love to his tune my jarring heart would bring,
    But reason overwinds, and cracks the string.

                      Duke of Guise.

    ——I should have loved,
    Though Jove, in muttering thunder, had forbid it.

                      New Sophonisba.

And when it (*my heart*) wild resolves to love no more,
Then is the triumph of excessive love.   *Ibidem.*

[32] Massinissa is one-fourth less happy than Tom Thumb:
          Oh! happy, happy, happy! *New Sophonisba.*

KING.   Ha! sayest thou, Dollallolla?

QUEEN.   ——I say he shan't.

KING.   Then by our royal self[33] we swear you lie.

QUEEN.   Who but a dog, who but a dog[34]
Would use me as thou dost? Me, who have lain
These twenty years so loving by thy side![35]
But I will be reveng'd. I'll hang myself.
Then tremble all who did this match persuade,
For, riding on a cat, from high I'll fall,
And squirt down royal vengeance on you all.[36]

FOOD.   Her majesty the queen is in a passion.[37]

KING.   Be she, or be she not,[38] I'll to the girl
And pave thy way, O Thumb.—Now by ourself,
We were indeed a pretty king of clouts
To truckle to her will. For when by force
Or art the wife her husband overreaches,
Give him the petticoat, and her the breeches.

THUMB.   Whisper ye winds, that Huncamunca's mine!
Echoes repeat, that Huncamunca's mine!
The dreadful business of the war is o'er,
And beauty, heav'nly beauty! crowns my toils!
I've thrown the bloody garment now aside,
And hymeneal sweets invite my bride.

So when some chimney-sweeper all the day
Hath through dark paths pursu'd the sooty way,
At night, to wash his hands and face he flies,
And in his t'other shirt with his Brickdusta lies.[39]

33 No, by myself.   *Anna Bullen.*

34 ———————————— Who caus'd
   This dreadful revolution in my fate,
   Ulamar.   Who but a dog, who but a dog?

                                         Liberty Asserted.

35 ———————————— A bride,
   Who twenty years lay loving by your side.

                                                    BANKS.

36 For, borne upon a cloud, from high I'll fall,
   And rain down royal vengeance on you all.

                                         Albion Queens.

37 An information very like this we have in the *Tragedy of Love,* where,
Cyrus having stormed in the most violent manner, Cyaxares observes very
calmly,
              Why, nephew Cyrus—you are mov'd.

38 'Tis in your choice:
   Love me, or love me not.

                                      Conquest of Granada.

39 There is not one beauty in this charming speech but hath been borrowed
by almost every tragic writer.

SCENE IV

GRIZZLE *solus*

Where art thou, Grizzle?[40] where are now thy glories?
Where are the drums that waken thee to honour?
Greatness is a lac'd coat from Monmouth-street,
Which fortune lends us for a day to wear,
To-morrow puts it on another's back.
The spiteful sun but yesterday survey'd
His rival high as Saint Paul's cupola;
Now may he see me as Fleet-ditch laid low.

SCENE V

QUEEN, GRIZZLE

QUEEN.   Teach me to scold, prodigious-minded Grizzle.[41]
Mountain of treason, ugly as the devil,
Teach this confunded hateful mouth of mine
To spout forth words malicious as thyself,
Words which might shame all Billingsgate to speak.
    GRIZ.   Far be it from my pride to think my tongue
Your royal lips can in that art instruct,
Where in you so excel. But may I ask,
Without offence, wherefore my queen would scold?
    QUEEN.   Wherefore? Oh! Blood and thunder! ha'n't you
        heard
(What ev'ry corner of the court resounds)
That little Thumb will be a great man made?
    GRIZ.   I heard it, I confess—for who, alas!
Can always stop his ears?[42]—but would my teeth,
By grinding knives, had first been set on edge.
    QUEEN.   Would I had heard, at the still noon of night,
The hallaloo of fire in every street!
Odsbobs! I have a mind to hang myself,

---

[40] Mr. Banks has (I wish I could not say too servilely) imitated this of
Grizzle in his *Earl of Essex:*
                    Where art thou, Essex, &c.
[41] The Countess of Nottingham, in the *Earl of Essex,* is apparently acquainted with Dollallolla.
[42] Grizzle was not probably possessed of that glue of which Mr. Banks speaks
in his *Cyrus:*
                    I'll glue my ears to ev'ry word.

To think I should a grandmother be made
By such a rascal!—Sure the king forgets
When in a pudding, by his mother put,
The bastard, by a tinker, on a stile
Was dropp'd.—O, good lord Grizzle! can I bear
To see him from a pudding mount the throne?
Or can, oh can! my Huncamunca bear
To take a pudding's offspring to her arms?

    GRIZ.   O horror! horror! horror! cease, my queen;
Thy voice, like twenty screech-owls,[43] wracks my brain.

    QUEEN.   Then rouse thy spirit—we may yet prevent
This hated match.

    GRIZ.   We will; not fate itself,[44]
Should it conspire with Thomas Thumb, should cause it.
I'll swim through seas; I'll ride upon the clouds;
I'll dig the earth; I'll blow out every fire;
I'll rave; I'll rant; I'll rise; I'll rush; I'll roar;
Fierce as the man whom smiling dolphins[45] bore
From the prosaic to poetic shore.
I'll tear the scoundrel into twenty pieces.

    QUEEN.   Oh, no! prevent the match, but hurt him not;
For, though I would not have him have my daughter,
Yet can we kill the man that kill'd the giants?

    GRIZ.   I tell you, Madam, it was all a trick;
He made the giants first, and then he kill'd them;
As fox-hunters bring foxes to the wood,
And then with hounds they drive them out again.

    QUEEN.   How! have you seen no giants? Are there not
Now, in the yard, ten thousand proper giants?

    GRIZ.   Indeed I cannot positively tell,
But firmly do believe there is not one.[46]

---

[43] Screech-owls, dark ravens, and amphibious monsters,
    Are screaming in that voice.   *Mary Queen of Scots.*
[44] The reader may see all the beauties of this speech in a late ode, called the
Naval Lyric.
[45] This epithet to a dolphin doth not give one so clear an idea as were to
be wished, a smiling fish seeming a little more difficult to be imagined than a
flying fish. Mr. Dryden is of opinion that smiling is the property of reason, and
that no irrational creature can smile:
    Smiles not allow'd to beasts from reason move.
                  State of Innocence.
[46] These lines are written in the same key with those in the *Earl of Essex:*
    Why, say'st thou so? I love thee well, indeed
    I do, and thou shalt find by this, 'tis true.
Or with this in *Cyrus:*
    The most heroic mind that ever was.
And with above half of the modern tragedies.

QUEEN.   Hence! from my sight! thou traitor, hie away;
By all my stars! thou enviest Tom Thumb.
Go, Sirrah! go, hie away! hie![47]—thou art
A setting dog: begone!

GRIZ.   Madam, I go.
Tom Thumb shall feel the vengeance you have rais'd:
So, when two dogs are fighting in the streets,
With a third dog one of the two dogs meets,
With angry teeth he bites him to the bone,
And this dog smarts for what that dog had done.

SCENE VI

QUEEN *sola*

And whither shall I go? Alack-a-day!
I love Tom Thumb—but must not tell him so;
For what's a woman, when her virtue's gone?
A coat without its lace; wig out of buckle;
A stocking with a hole in't—I can't live
Without my virtue, or without Tom Thumb.
Then let me weigh them in two equal scales;[48]
In this scale put my virtue, that, Tom Thumb.
Alas! Tom Thumb is heavier than my virtue.
But hold!—perhaps I may be left a widow:
This match prevented, then Tom Thumb is mine:
In that dear hope I will forget my pain.

So, when some wench to Tothill-Bridewell's sent,
With beating hemp and flogging she's content:
She hopes in time to ease her present pain,
At length is free, and walks the streets again.

---

[47] Aristotle, in that excellent work of his which is very justly styled his masterpiece, earnestly recommends using the terms of art, however coarse or even indecent they may be. Mr. Tate is of the same opinion.

> *Bru.* Do not, like young hawks, fetch a course about;
> 　　　Your game flies fair.
> *Fra.* Do not fear it.
> 　　　He answers you in your own hawking phrase.
>
> 　　　　　　　　　　　　　　　　　　*Injured Love.*

I think these two great authorities are sufficient to justify Dollallolla in the use of the phrase, "Hie away, hie!" when in the same line she says she is speaking to a setting dog.

[48] We meet with such another pair of scales in Dryden's *King Arthur:*

> 　　　Arthur and Oswald, and their different fates,
> 　　　Are weighing now within the scales of heav'n.

Also in *Sebastian:*

> 　　　This hour my lot is weighing in the scales.

ACT II

SCENE I

SCENE: *The street*

BAILIFF, FOLLOWER

BAIL.   Come on, my trusty follower, come on;
This day discharge thy duty, and at night
A double mug of beer, and beer shall glad thee.
Stand here by me, this way must Noodle pass.

FOL.   No more, no more, O bailiff! every word
Inspires my soul with virtue. Oh! I long
To meet the enemy in the street—and nab him;
To lay arresting hands upon his back,
And drag him trembling to the spunging-house.

BAIL.   There when I have him, I will spunge upon him.
Oh! glorious thought! by the sun, moon, and stars,
I will enjoy it, though it be in thought![49]
Yes, yes, my follower, I will enjoy it.

FOL.   Enjoy it then some other time, for now
Our prey approaches.

BAIL.   Let us retire.

SCENE II

TOM THUMB, NOODLE, BAILIFF, FOLLOWER

THUMB.   Trust me, my Noodle, I am wondrous sick;
For, though I love the gentle Huncamunca,
Yet at the thought of marriage I grow pale;
For, oh! but swear thou'lt keep it ever secret,
I will unfold a tale will make thee stare.[50]

NOOD.   I swear by lovely Huncamunca's charms.

THUMB.   Then know—my grandmamma hath often said,
"Tom Thumb, beware of marriage."[51]

NOOD.   Sir, I blush
To think a warrior, great in arms as you,

[49] Mr. Rowe is generally imagined to have taken some hints from this scene in his character of Bajazet; but as he, of all the tragic writers, bears the least resemblance to our author in his diction, I am unwilling to imagine he would condescend to copy him in this particular.

[50] This method of surprising an audience, by raising their expectation to the highest pitch, and then baulking it, hath been practised with great success by most of our tragical authors.

[51] Almeyda, in *Sebastian*, is in the same distress:
Sometimes methinks I hear the groan of ghosts,
Thin hollow sounds and lamentable screams;
Then, like a dying echo from afar,
My mother's voice that cries, "Wed not, Almeyda;
Forewarn'd, Almeyda, marriage is thy crime."

Should be affrighted by his grandmamma.
Can an old woman's empty dreams deter
The blooming hero from the virgin's arms?
Think of the joy that will your soul alarm,
When in her fond embraces clasp'd you lie,
While on her panting breast, dissolv'd in bliss,
You pour out all Tom Thumb in every kiss.

THUMB.   Oh! Noodle, thou hast fir'd my eager soul;
Spite of my grandmother she shall be mine;
I'll hug, caress, I'll eat her up with love.
Whole days, and nights, and years shall be too short
For our enjoyment; every sun shall rise
Blushing to see us in our bed together.[52]

NOOD.   O, Sir! this purpose of your soul pursue.

BAIL.   O, Sir! I have an action against you.

NOOD.   At whose suit is it?

BAIL.   At your tailor's, Sir.
Your tailor put this warrant in my hands,
And I arrest you, Sir, at his commands.

THUMB.   Ha! dogs! Arrest my friend before my face!
Think you Tom Thumb will suffer this disgrace?
But let vain cowards threaten by their word,
Tom Thumb shall show his anger by his sword.
                    (*kills the Bailiff and his Follower*)

BAIL.   Oh, I am slain!

FOL.   I am murder'd also
And to the shades, the dismal shades below,
My bailiff's faithful follower I go.

NOOD.   Go then to hell, like rascals as you are,
And give our service to the bailiffs there.[53]

---

[52] "As very well he may, if he hath any modesty in him," says Mr. Dennis.
The author of *Busiris* is extremely zealous to prevent the sun's blushing at any
indecent object; and therefore on all such occasions he addresses himself to
the sun, and desires him to keep out of the way.

> Rise never more, O sun! let night prevail,
> Eternal darkness close the world's wide scene.
>
>   *Busiris.*

> Sun, hide thy face, and put the world in mourning.
>
>   *Ibid.*

Mr. Banks makes the sun perform the office of Hymen, and therefore not
likely to be disgusted at such a sight:

> The sun sets forth like a gay brideman with you.
>
>   *Mary Queen of Scots.*

[53] Nourmahal sends the same message to heaven:

> For I would have you, when you upwards move,
> Speak kindly of us to our friends above.
>
>   *Aurengzebe.*

We find another "to hell," in the *Persian Princess:*

> Villain, get thee down
> To hell, and tell them that the fray's begun.

THUMB.   Thus perish all the bailiffs in the land,
Till debtors at noon-day shall walk the streets,
And no one fear a bailiff or his writ.

SCENE III

SCENE: *The Princess Huncamunca's apartment*

HUNCAMUNCA, CLEORA, MUSTACHA

HUNC.   [54]Give me some music—see that it be sad.

CLEORA *sings.*

I.

Cupid, ease a love-sick maid,
Bring thy quiver to her aid;
With equal ardor wound the swain,
Beauty should never sigh in vain.

II.

Let him feel the pleasing smart,
Drive thy arrow through his heart;
When one you wound, you then destroy;
When both you kill, you kill with joy.

HUNC.   O Tom Thumb! Tom Thumb! wherefore art thou
Tom Thumb?[55]
Why hadst thou not been born of royal race?
Why had not mighty Bantam been thy father?
Or else the King of Brentford, Old or New?
MUST.   I am surprised that your Highness can give your-
self a moment's uneasiness about that little insignificant fel-
low,[56] Tom Thumb the Great—one properer for a plaything
than a husband. Were he my husband, his horns should be
as long as his body. If you had fallen in love with a grenadier,
I should not have wondered at it. If you had fallen in love
with something; but to fall in love with nothing!
HUNC.   Cease, my Mustacha, on thy duty cease.

[54] Anthony gives the same command in the same words.
                                                       All for Love.
[55] Oh! Marius, Marius, wherefore art thou Marius?
                                                       Otway's Marius.
[56] Nothing is more common than these seeming contradictions; such as,
                         Haughty weakness.   *Victim.*
                         Great small world.   *Noah's Flood.*

The zephyr, when in flow'ry vales it plays,
Is not so soft, so sweet as Thummy's breath.
The dove is not so gentle to its mate.

MUST.   The dove is every bit as proper for a husband.
Alas! Madam, there's not a beau about the court looks so little
like a man. He is a perfect butterfly, a thing without substance, and almost without shadow too.

HUNC.   This rudeness is unseasonable: desist,
Or I shall think this railing comes from love.
Tom Thumb's a creature of that charming form,
That no one can abuse, unless they love him.

MUST.   Madam, the king.

SCENE IV

KING, HUNCAMUNCA

KING.   Let all but Huncamunca leave the room.
                    (*Exeunt* CLEORA *and* MUSTACHA)
Daughter, I have observ'd of late some grief
Unusual in your countenance—your eyes
[57]That, like two open windows, us'd to show
The lovely beauty of the rooms within,
Have now two blinds before them. What is the cause?
Say, have you not enough of meat and drink?
We've giv'n strict orders not to have you stinted.

HUNC.   Alas! my Lord, I value not myself
That once I eat two fowls and half a pig;
Small is that praise; but oh! a maid may want
What she can neither eat nor drink.[58]

KING.   What's that?

---

[57] Lee hath improved this metaphor:
> Dost thou not view joy peeping from my eyes,
>   The casements opened wide to gaze on thee,
> So Rome's glad citizens to windows rise,
>   When they some young triumpher fain would see.
>   *Gloriana.*

[58] Almahide hath the same contempt for these appetites:
> To eat and drink can no perfection be.
>   *Conquest of Granada.*

The Earl of Essex is of a different opinion, and seems to place the chief
happiness of a general therein:
> Were but commanders half so well rewarded,
>   Then they might eat.   BANK's *Earl of Essex.*

But, if we may believe one who knows more than either, the devil himself,
we shall find eating to be an affair of more moment than is generally imagined:
> Gods are immortal only by their food.
>   Lucifer, in the *State of Innocence.*

HUNC.   O spare my blushes; but I mean a husband.[59]

KING.   If that be all, I have provided one,
A husband great in arms, whose warlike sword
Streams with the yellow blood of slaughter'd giants,
Whose name in Terra Incognita is known,
Whose valour, wisdom, virtue make a noise
Great as the kettle-drums of twenty armies.

HUNC.   Whom does my royal father mean?

KING.   Tom Thumb.

HUNC.   Is it possible?

KING.   Ha! the window-blinds are gone;
A country-dance of joy is in your face,[60]
Your eyes spit fire, your cheeks grow red as beef.

HUNC.   Oh, there's a magic-music in that sound,
Enough to turn me into beef indeed!
Yes, I will own, since licens'd by your word,
I'll own Tom Thumb the cause of all my grief.
For him I've sigh'd, I've wept, I've gnawed my sheets.

KING.   Oh! thou shalt gnaw thy tender sheets no more;
A husband thou shalt have to mumble now.

HUNC.   Oh! happy sound! henceforth let no one tell
That Huncamunca shall lead apes in hell.
Oh! I am overjoy'd!

KING.   I see thou art.
Joy lightens in thy eyes, and thunders from thy brows;
Transports, like lightning, dart along thy soul,[61]
As small-shot through a hedge.

HUNC.   Oh! say not small.

KING.   This happy news shall on our tongue ride post,

---

[59] "This expression is enough of itself," says Mr. Dennis, "utterly to destroy the character of Huncamunca!" Yet we find a woman of no abandoned character in Dryden adventuring farther, and thus excusing herself:

> To speak our wishes first, forbid it pride,
> Forbid it modesty; true, they forbid it,
> But Nature does not. When we are athirst,
> Or hungry, will imperious Nature stay,
> Nor eat, nor drink, before 'tis bid fall on?
>
> *Cleomenes*

Cassandra speaks before she is asked: Huncamunca afterwards. Cassandra speaks her wishes to her lover: Huncamunca only to her father.

[60] Her eyes resistless magic bear;
> Angels, I see, and gods are dancing there.
>
> Lee's *Sophonisba.*

[61] Mr. Dennis, in that excellent tragedy called *Liberty Asserted*, which is thought to have given so great a stroke to the late French king, hath frequent imitations of this beautiful speech of King Arthur:

> Conquest light'ning in his eyes, and thund'ring in his arm.
> Joy lightened in her eyes.
> Joys like lightning dart along my soul.

Ourself we bear the happy news to Thumb.
Yet think not, daughter, that your powerful charms
Must still detain the hero from his arms;
Various his duty, various his delight;
Now is his turn to kiss, and now to fight;
And now to kiss again. So, mighty[62] Jove,
When with excessive thund'ring tir'd above,
Comes down to earth, and takes a bit—and then
Flies to his trade of thund'ring back again.

SCENE V

GRIZZLE, HUNCAMUNCA

    GRIZ. Oh! Huncamunca, Huncamunca, oh![63]
Thy pouting breasts, like kettle-drums of brass,
Beat everlasting loud alarms of joy;
As bright as brass they are, and oh, as hard;
Oh! Huncamunca, Huncamunca, oh!
    HUNC. Ha! dost thou know me, princess as I am,
That thus of me you dare to make your game?[64]
    GRIZ. O Huncamunca, well I know that you
A princess are, and a king's daughter, too.
But love no meanness scorns, no grandeur fears, ⎫
Love often lords into the cellar bears,   ⎬
And bids the sturdy porter come upstairs.   ⎭
For what's too high for love, or what's too low?
Oh! Huncamunca, Huncamunca, oh!
    HUNC. But, granting all you say of love were true,
My love, alas! is to another due!
In vain to me a-suitoring you come,
For I'm already promis'd to Tom Thumb.
    GRIZ. And can my princess such a durgen wed,
One fitter for your pocket than your bed!
Advis'd by me, the worthless baby shun,

---

[62] Jove, with excessive thund'ring tir'd above,
    Comes down for ease, enjoys a nymph, and then
    Mounts dreadful, and to thund'ring goes again.

                                     Gloriana.

[63] This beautiful line, which ought, says Mr. W——, to be written in gold,
is imitated in the *New Sophonisba:*
                Oh! Sophonisba, Sophonisba, oh!
                Oh! Narva, Narva, oh!
The author of a song called *Duke upon Duke* hath improved it:
                Alas! O Nick, O Nick, alas!
Where, by the help of a little false spelling, you have two meanings in the
repeated words.

[64] Edith, in the *Bloody Brother,* speaks to her lover in the same familiar
language:
                Your grace is full of game.

Or you will ne'er be brought to bed of one.
Oh, take me to thy arms, and never flinch,
Who am a man, by Jupiter! ev'ry inch.
Then, while in joys together lost we lie,
I'll press thy soul while gods stand wishing by.[65]

HUNC. If, Sir, what you insinuate you prove,
All obstacles of promise you remove;
For all engagements to a man must fall,
Whene'er that man is prov'd no man at all.

GRIZ. Oh! let him seek some dwarf, some fairy miss,
Where no joint-stool must lift him to the kiss.
But, by the stars and glory, you appear
Much fitter for a Prussian grenadier;
One globe alone on Atlas' shoulders rests,
Two globes are less than Huncamunca's breasts;
The milky way is not so white, that's flat,
And sure thy breasts are full as large as that.

HUNC. Oh, Sir, so strong your eloquence I find,
It is impossible to be unkind.

GRIZ. Ah! speak that o'er again, and let the sound
From one pole to another pole rebound;[66]
The earth and sky each be a battledore,
And keep the sound, that shuttlecock, up an hour;
To Doctors Commons for a license I,
Swift as an arrow from a bow, will fly.

HUNC. Oh, no! lest some disaster we should meet,
'Twere better to be married at the Fleet.

GRIZ. Forbid it, all ye powers, a princess should
By that vile place contaminate her blood;
My quick return shall to my charmer prove
I travel on the post-horses of love.

HUNC. Those post-horses to me will seem too slow
Though they should fly swift as the gods, when they
Ride on behind that post-boy, Opportunity.[87]

---

[65] Traverse the glittering chambers of the sky,
Borne on a cloud in view of fate I'll lie,
And press her soul while gods stand wishing by.

Hannibal.

[66] Let the four winds from distant corners meet,
And on their wings first bear it into France;
Then back again to Edina's proud walls,
Till victim to the sound th' aspiring city falls.

Albion Queens.

[87] I do not remember any metaphors so frequent in the tragic poets as those
borrowed from riding post:
The gods and opportunity ride post.

Hannibal.

SCENE VI

TOM THUMB, HUNCAMUNCA

THUMB.   Where is my princess, where's my Huncamunca?
Where are those eyes, those cardmatches of love,
That light up[68] all with love my waxen soul?
Where is that face with artful nature made
In the same moulds where Venus' self was cast?[69]
  HUNC.   Oh! what is music to the ear that's deaf,[70]

                          ——Let's rush together,
                  For death rides post.

                                        Cæsar Borgia.

                  Destruction gallops to thy murder post.

                                        Gloriana.

  [68] This image, too, very often occurs:
              ——Bright as when thy eye
          First lighted up our loves.

                                        Aurengzebe.
          'Tis not a crown alone lights up my name.

                                        Busiris.
  [69] There is great dissension among the poets concerning the method of
making man. One tells his mistress that the mould she was made in being lost,
heaven cannot form such another. Lucifer, in Dryden, gives a merry description
of his own formation:

              Whom heaven, neglecting, made and scarce design'd,
              But threw me in for number to the rest.

                                        State of Innocence.
In one place, the same poet supposes man to be made of metal:
                      ——I was form'd
          Of that coarse metal which, when she was made,
          The gods threw by for rubbish.

                                        All for Love.
In another, of dough:
          When the gods moulded up the paste of man,
          Some of their clay was left upon their hands,
          And so they made Egyptians.

                                        Cleomenes.
In another, of clay:
          ——Rubbish of remaining clay.

                                        Sebastian.
One makes the soul of wax:
          Her waxen soul begins to melt apace.

                                        Anna Bullen.
Another of flint:
          Sure our two souls have somewhere been acquainted
          In former beings, or, struck out together,
          One spark to Afric flew, and one to Portugal.

                                        Sebastian.
  To omit the great quantities of iron, brazen, and leaden souls which are so
plenty in modern authors—I cannot omit the dress of a soul as we find it in
Dryden:

          Souls shirted but with air.   *King Arthur.*
  Nor can I pass by a particular sort of soul in a particular sort of description
in the *New Sophonisba*:

          Ye mysterious powers,
          ——Whether through your gloomy depths I wander,
          Or on the mountains walk, give me the calm,
          The steady smiling soul, where wisdom sheds
          Eternal sunshine, and eternal joy.
  [70] This line Mr. Banks has plundered entire in his *Anna Bullen.*

Or a goose-pie to him that has no taste?
What are these praises now to me, since I
Am promis'd to another?

    THUMB.   Ha! promised?

    HUNC.   Too sure; it's written in the book of fate.

    THUMB.   Then I will tear away the leaf
Wherein it's writ, or, if fate won't allow
So large a gap within its journal-book,[71]
I'll blot it out at least.

SCENE VII

GLUMDALCA, TOM THUMB, HUNCAMUNCA

    GLUM.   I need not ask[72] if you are Huncamunca;
Your brandy nose proclaims——

    HUNC.   I am a princess;
Nor need I ask who you are.

    GLUM.   A giantess;
The queen of those who made and unmade queens.

    HUNC.   The man whose chief ambition is to be
My sweetheart hath destroy'd these mighty giants.

    GLUM.   Your sweetheart? dost thou think the man who once
Hath worn my easy chains will e'er wear thine?

    HUNC.   Well may your chains be easy, since, if fame
Says true, they have been tried on twenty husbands.
The glove or boot, so many times pull'd on,
May well sit easy on the hand or foot.[73]

    GLUM.   I glory in the number, and when I
Sit poorly down, like thee, content with one,
Heaven change this face for one as bad as thine.

    HUNC.   Let me see nearer what this beauty is

---

[71] Good heaven, the book of fate before me lay,
    But to tear out the journal of that day.
    Or, if the order of the world below
    Will not the gap of one whole day allow,
    Give me that minute when she made her vow.

Conquest of Granada.

[72] I know some of the commentators have imagined that Mr. Dryden, in the altercative scene between Cleopatra and Octavia, a scene which Mr. Addison inveighs against with great bitterness, is much beholden to our author. How just this their observation is I will not presume to determine.

[73] "A cobbling poet indeed," says Mr. Dennis; and yet I believe we may find as monstrous images in the tragic authors: I'll put down one:
    Untie your folded thoughts, and let them dangle loose as a bride's hair.

Injured Love.

Which line seems to have as much title to a milliner's shop as our author's to a shoemaker's.

That captivates the heart of men by scores.

(Holds a candle to her face)

Oh! heaven, thou art as ugly as the devil.

GLUM.   You'd give the best of shoes within your shop
To be but half so handsome.

HUNC.   Since you come
To that, I'll put my beauty to the test:[74]
Tom Thumb, I'm yours, if you with me will go.

GLUM.   Oh! stay, Tom Thumb, and you alone shall fill
That bed where twenty giants used to lie.

THUMB.   In the balcony that o'erhangs the stage,
I've seen a whore two 'prentices engage;
One half-a-crown does in his fingers hold,
The other shows a little piece of gold;
She the half-guinea wisely does purloin,
And leaves the larger and the baser coin.

GLUM.   Left, scorn'd, and loath'd for such a chit as this;
I feel the storm that's rising in my mind;
Tempests and whirlwinds rise, and roll, and roar.[75]
I'm all within a hurricane, as if
The world's four winds were pent within my carcase.[76]
Confusion, horror, murder, guts, and death![77]

SCENE VIII

KING, GLUMDALCA

KING.   [78]Sure never was so sad a king as I!
My life is worn as ragged as a coat
A beggar wears; a prince should put it off.[79]
To love a captive and a giantess!

[74] Mr. L—— takes occasion in this place to commend the great care of our author to preserve the metre of blank verse, in which Shakespeare, Jonson, and Fletcher were so notoriously negligent; and the moderns, in imitation of our author, so laudably observant:

——Then does
Your majesty believe that he can be
A traitor!   *Earl of Essex.*

Every page of *Sophonisba* gives us instances of this excellence.

[75] Love mounts and rolls about my stormy mind.

Aurengzebe.

Tempests and whirlwinds through my bosom move.

Cleomenes.

[76] With such a furious tempest on his brow,
As if the world's four winds were pent within
His blustering carcase.   *Anna Bullen.*

[77] Verba Tragica.

[78] This speech hath been terribly mauled by the poets.

[79] ——My life is worn to rags,
Not worth a prince's wearing.

Love Triumphant.

Oh love! oh love! how great a king art thou![80]
My tongue's thy trumpet, and thou trumpetest,
Unknown to me, within me. Oh, Glumdalca!
Heaven thee design'd a giantess to make,
But an angelic soul was shuffled in.[81]
I am a multitude of walking griefs,[82]
And only on her lips the balm is found
To spread a plaster that might cure them all.[83]

GLUM.   What do I hear?

KING.   What do I see?

GLUM.   Oh!

KING.   Ah!

GLUM.   [84]Ah! wretched queen!

KING.   Oh! wretched king!

GLUM.   Ah!

KING.   Oh![85]

SCENE IX

TOM THUMB, HUNCAMUNCA, PARSON

PAR.   Happy's the wooing that's not long a-doing;
For, if I guess aright, Tom Thumb this night

80 Must I beg the pity of my slave?
   Must a king beg! But love's a greater king,
   A tyrant, nay, a devil, that possesses me.
   He tunes the organ of my voice and speaks,
   Unknown to me, within me.   *Sebastian.*
81 When thou wert form'd heaven did a man begin;
   But a brute soul by chance was shuffled in.

                                                Aurengzebe.

82 ——I am a multitude
   Of walking griefs.
                                                New Sophonisba.

83 I will take thy scorpion blood,
   And lay it to my grief till I have ease.
                                                Anna Bullen.

84 Our author, who everywhere shows his great penetration into human nature, here outdoes himself: where a less judicious poet would have raised a
long scene of whining love, he, who understood the passions better, and that
so violent an affection as this must be too big for utterance, chooses rather to
send his characters off in this sullen and doleful manner, in which admirable
conduct he is imitated by the author of the justly celebrated *Eurydice*. Dr.
Young seems to point at this violence of passion:
                        ——Passion chokes
         Their words, and they're the statues of despair.
And Seneca tells us, *Curæ leves loquuntur, ingentes stupent.* [Light cares speak;
the heavy are mute.] The story of the Egyptian king in Herodotus is too well
known to need to be inserted; I refer the more curious reader to the excellent
Montaigne, who hath written an essay on this subject.
  85 To part is death.
            'Tis death to part.
                  Ah!
                        Oh!
                                                What D'ye Call It.

Shall give a being to a new Tom Thumb.

    THUMB.   It shall be my endeavour so to do.

    HUNC.   Oh! fie upon you, Sir, you make me blush.

    THUMB.   It is the virgin's sign, and suits you well:
I know not where, nor how, nor what I am;[86]
[87]I'm so transported, I have lost myself.

    HUNC.   Forbid it, all ye stars, for you're so small,
That were you lost, you'd find yourself no more.
So the unhappy sempstress once, they say,
Her needle in a pottle, lost, of hay;
In vain she look'd, and look'd, and made her moan,
For ah, the needle was forever gone.

    PAR.   Long may they live, and love, and propagate,

[86] Nor know I whether
    What am I, who, or where.

Busiris.

    I was I know not what, and am I know not how.

Gloriana.

[87] To understand sufficiently the beauty of this passage, it will be necessary
that we comprehend every man to contain two selfs. I shall not attempt to
prove this from philosophy, which the poets make so plainly evident.
    One runs away from the other:

                ——Let me demand your majesty,
                Why fly you from yourself?

Duke of Guise.

In a second, one self is a guardian to the other:
                Leave me the care of me.

Conquest of Granada.

Again:

                Myself am to myself less near.

Ibid.

In the same, the first self is proud of the second:
                I myself am proud of me.

State of Innocence.

In a third, distrustful of him:
                Fain I would tell, but whisper it in mine ear,
                That none besides might hear, nay, not myself.

Earl of Essex.

In a fourth, honours him:
                I honour Rome,
                But honour too myself.

Sophonisba.

In a fifth, at variance with him:
                Leave me not thus at variance with myself.

Busiris.

Again, in a sixth:
                I find myself divided from myself.

Medea.

    She seemed the sad effigies of herself.

Albion Queens.

    Assist me, Zulema, if thou wouldst be
    The friend thou seemest, assist me against me.

The Conquest of Granada.

From all which it appears that there are two selfs; and therefore Tom
Thumb's losing himself is no such solecism as it hath been represented by men
rather ambitious of criticizing than qualified to criticize.

Till the whole land be peopled with Tom Thumbs!
So, when the Cheshire cheese a maggot breeds,
Another and another still succeeds:
By thousands and ten thousands they increase,
Till one continu'd maggot fills the rotten cheese.[88]

SCENE X

NOODLE, *and then* GRIZZLE

NOOD. Sure, Nature means to break her solid chain,
Or else unfix the world, and in a rage
To hurl it from its axletree and hinges;
All things are so confus'd,[89] the king's in love,
The queen is drunk, the princess marry'd is.

GRIZ. Oh! Noodle, hast thou Huncamunca seen?

NOOD. I've seen a thousand sights this day, where none
Are by the wonderful bitch herself outdone.
The king, the queen, and all the court, are sights.

GRIZ. D—n your delay, you trifler, are you drunk, ha?
I will not hear one word but Huncamunca.[90]

NOOD. By this time she is marry'd to Tom Thumb.

GRIZ. [91]My Huncamunca!

NOOD.   Your Huncamunca,
Tom Thumb's Huncamunca, every man's Huncamunca

GRIZ. If this be true, all womankind are damn'd.

NOOD. If it be not, may I be so myself.

GRIZ. See where she comes! I'll not believe a word
Against that face, upon whose ample brow[92]
Sits innocence with majesty enthron'd.

---

88 Mr. Fielding imagines this parson to have been a Welsh one, from his
simile.

89 Our author hath been plundered here, according to custom:

> Great Nature, *break thy chain* that links together
> The fabric of the world, and make a chaos
> Like that within my soul.   *Love Triumphant.*
> ——Startle Nature, unfix the globe,
> And hurl it from its *axletree and hinges.*
>   *Albion Queens.*
> The tott'ring earth seems sliding off its props.
>   *The Persian Princess.*

90 D—n your delay, ye torturers, proceed;
I will not hear one word but Almahide.
                                 Conquest of Granada.

91 Mr. Dryden hath imitated this in *All for Love.*

92 This Miltonic style abounds in the *New Sophonisba:*
> ——And on her ample brow
> Sat majesty.

GRIZZLE, HUNCAMUNCA

GRIZ.   Where has my Huncamunca been? See here
The license in my hand!

HUNC.   Alas! Tom Thumb.

GRIZ.   Why dost thou mention him?

HUNC.   Ah, me! Tom Thumb.

GRIZ.   What means my lovely Huncamunca?

HUNC.   Hum!

GRIZ.   Oh! speak.

HUNC.   Hum!

GRIZ.   Ha! your every word is hum.
You force me still to answer you, Tom Thumb.[93]
Tom Thumb, I'm on the rack, I'm in a flame,
Tom Thumb, Tom Thumb, Tom Thumb, you love the name;[94]
So pleasing is that sound, that, were you dumb,
You still would find a voice to cry, "Tom Thumb."

HUNC.   Oh! be not hasty to proclaim my doom!
My ample heart for more than one has room:
A maid like me heaven form'd at least for two,
I married him, and now I'll marry you.[95]

GRIZ.   Ha! dost thou own thy falsehood to my face?
Think'st thou that I will share thy husband's place?
Since to that office one cannot suffice,
And since you scorn to dine one single dish on,
Go, get your husband put into commission,
Commissioners to discharge (ye gods! it fine is)
The duty of a husband to your Highness.
Yet think not long I will my rival bear,
Or unreveng'd the slighted willow wear;
The gloomy, brooding tempest, now confin'd
Within the hollow caverns of my mind,

---

[93] Your ev'ry answer still so ends in that,
   You force me still to answer you Morat.

Aurengzebe.

[94] Morat, Morat, Morat, you love the name.

Aurengzebe.

[95] "Here is a sentiment for the virtuous Huncamunca," says Mr. Dennis.
And yet, with the leave of this great man, the virtuous Panthea, in *Cyrus,* hath
an heart every whit as ample:

   For two I must confess are gods to me,
   Which is my Abradatus first, and thee.

Cyrus the Great.

Nor is the lady in *Love Triumphant* more reserved, though not so intelligible:

   ——I am so divided,
   That I grieve most for both, and love both most.

In dreadful whirl shall roll along the coasts, ⎫
Shall thin the land of all the men it boasts, ⎬
And cram up ev'ry chink of hell with ghosts.[96] ⎭
So have I seen, in some dark winter's day,
A sudden storm rush down the sky's highway,
Sweep through the streets with terrible ding dong,
Gush through the spouts, and wash whole crowds along.[97]
The crowded shops the thronging vermin screen, ⎫
Together cram the dirty and the clean, ⎬
And not one shoe-boy in the street is seen. ⎭

    HUNC.   Oh, fatal rashness! should his fury slay
My hapless bridegroom on his wedding-day,
I, who this morn of two chose which to wed,
May go again this night alone to bed.
So have I seen some wild unsettled fool,
Who had her choice of this and that joint-stool,
To give the preference to either loth,
And fondly coveting to sit on both,
While the two stools her sitting-part confound,
Between 'em both fall squat upon the ground.[98]

[96] A ridiculous supposition to any one who considers the great and extensive largeness of hell, says a commentator; but not so to those who consider the great expansion of immaterial substance. Mr. Banks makes one soul to be so expanded that heaven could not contain it:

      The heavens are all too narrow for her soul.
                         Virtue Betrayed.

The *Persian Princess* hath a passage not unlike the author of this:

      We will send such shoals of murder'd slaves,
      Shall glut hell's empty regions.

This threatens to fill hell, even though it were empty: Lord Grizzle only to fill up the chinks, supposing the rest already full.

[97] Mr. Addison is generally thought to have had this simile in his eye when he wrote that beautiful one at the end of the third act of his *Cato*.

[98] This beautiful simile is founded on a proverb which does honour to the English language:

      Between two stools the breech falls to the ground.

I am not so pleased with any written remains of the ancients as with those little aphorisms which verbal tradition hath delivered down to us under the title of proverbs. It were to be wished that, instead of filling their pages with the fabulous theology of the pagans, our modern poets would think it worth their while to enrich their works with the proverbial sayings of their ancestors. Mr. Dryden hath chronicled one in heroic:

      Two *ifs* scarce make one possibility.
                      Conquest of Granada.

My Lord Bacon is of opinion that, whatever is known of arts and sciences might be proved to have lurked in the Proverbs of Solomon. I am of the same opinion in relation to those above mentioned; at least I am confident that a more perfect system of ethics, as well as economy, might be compiled out of them than is at present extant, either in the works of the ancient philosophers, or those more valuable, as more voluminous, ones of the modern divines.

ACT III

SCENE I

SCENE: KING ARTHUR'S *palace*

GHOST (*solus*).   Hail! ye black horrors of midnight's mid-
        noon!
Ye fairies, goblins, bats, and screech-owls, hail!
And, oh! ye mortal watchmen, whose hoarse throats
Th' immortal ghosts' dread croakings counterfeit,
All hail![99]——Ye dancing phantoms, who, by day,
Are some condemn'd to fast, some feast in fire,
Now play in churchyards, skipping o'er the graves,
To the loud music of the silent bell,[100]
All hail!

SCENE II

KING *and* GHOST

KING.   What noise is this? What villain dares,
At this dread hour, with feet and voice profane,
Disturb our royal walls?
GHOST.   One who defies
Thy empty power to hurt him; one who dares
Walk in thy bedchamber.[101]

---

99 Of all the particulars in which the modern stage falls short of the ancient,
there is none so much to be lamented as the great scarcity of ghosts in the latter.
Whence this proceeds I will not presume to determine. Some are of opinion
that the moderns are unequal to that sublime language which a ghost ought to
speak. One says, ludicrously, that ghosts are out of fashion; another, that they
are properer for comedy; forgetting, I suppose, that Aristotle hath told us that a
ghost is the soul of tragedy; for so I render the $\psi v \chi \grave{\eta}$ $\acute{o}$ $\mu \hat{v} \theta o s$ $\tau \hat{\eta} s$ $\tau \rho a \gamma \omega \delta \acute{\iota} a s$
which M. Dacier, amongst others, hath mistaken; I suppose misled by not
understanding the *fabula* of the Latins, which signifies a ghost as well as a fable.
    ——*Te premet nox, fabulæque manes.* [Night presses thee down, and the
fabled spirits.]   *Horace.*
Of all the ghosts that have ever appeared on the stage, a very learned and
judicious foreign critic gives the preference to this of our author. These are
his words, speaking of this tragedy:—*Nec quidquam in illâ admirabilius quam
phasma quoddam horrendum, quod omnibus aliis spectris, quibuscum scatet
Anglorum tragœdia, longe (pace D—ysii V. Doctiss. dixerim) prætulerim.* [Nor
is there in it anything more admirable than that horrid ghost which I should
much prefer to all other ghosts with which English tragedy teems—despite the
opinion of the most learned Dionysius.]
    100 We have already given instances of this figure.
    101 Almanzor reasons in the same manner:
                    ——A ghost I'll be;
            And from a ghost, you know, no place is free.
                                            Conquest of Granada.

KING.   Presumptuous slave!
Thou diest.

   GHOST.   Threaten others with that word:
I am a ghost, and am already dead.[102]

   KING.   Ye stars! 'tis well. Were thy last hour to come,
This moment had been it; yet by thy shroud
I'll pull thee backward, squeeze thee to a bladder,
Till thou dost groan thy nothingness away.[103]   (*Ghost retires*)
Thou flyest! 'Tis well.
I thought what was the courage of a ghost![104]
Yet, dare not, on thy life—why say I that,
Since life thou hast not?—dare not walk again
Within these walls, on pain of the Red Sea.
For, if henceforth I ever find thee here,
As sure, sure as a gun, I'll have thee laid.

   GHOST.   Were the Red Sea a sea of Holland's gin,
The liquor (when alive) whose very smell
I did detest, did loathe—yet, for the sake
Of Thomas Thumb, I would be laid therein.

   KING.   Ha! said you?

   GHOST.   Yes, my liege, I said Tom Thumb,
Whose father's ghost I am—once not unknown
To mighty Arthur. But, I see, 'tis true,
The dearest friend, when dead, we all forget.

   KING.   'Tis he, it is the honest Gaffer Thumb.
Oh! let me press thee in my eager arms,
Thou best of ghosts! thou something more than ghost!

---

102 "The man who writ this wretched pun," says Mr. Dennis, "would have
picked your pocket": which he proceeds to show not only bad in itself, but
doubly so on so solemn an occasion. And yet, in that excellent play of *Liberty
Asserted*, we find something very much resembling a pun in the mouth of a
mistress, who is parting with the lover she is fond of:

> *Ul.* Oh, mortal woe! one kiss, and then farewell.
> *Irene.* The gods have given to others to fare well.
>   O! miserably must Irene fare.

Agamemnon, in the *Victim*, is full as facetious on the most solemn occasion,
that of sacrificing his daughter:

> Yes, daughter, yes; you will assist the priest;
> Yes, you must offer up your—vows for Greece.

103 I'll pull thee backwards by thy shroud to light,
   Or else I'll squeeze thee, like a bladder, there,
   And make thee groan thyself away to air.

                                   Conquest of Granada.

Snatch me, ye gods, this moment into nothing.

                                   Cyrus the Great.

104 So, art thou gone? Thou canst no conquest boast:
   I thought what was the courage of a ghost.

                                   Conquest of Granada.

King Arthur seems to be as brave a fellow as Almanzor, who says most hero-
ically,

             ——In spite of ghosts I'll on.

GHOST.   Would I were something more, that we again
Might feel each other in the warm embrace.
But now I have th' advantage of my king,
For I feel thee, whilst thou dost not feel me.[105]

KING.   But say, thou dearest air,[106] oh! say what dread,
Important business sends thee back to earth?

GHOST.   Oh! then prepare to hear—which but to hear
Is full enough to send thy spirit hence.
Thy subjects up in arms, by Grizzle led,
Will, ere the rosy-finger'd morn shall ope
The shutters of the sky, before the gate
Of this thy royal palace, swarming spread.
So have I seen the bees in clusters swarm,
So have I seen the stars in frosty nights,
So have I seen the sand in windy days,
So have I seen the ghosts on Pluto's shore,
So have I seen the flowers in spring arise,
So have I seen the leaves in autumn fall,
So have I seen the fruits in summer smile,
So have I seen the snow in winter frown.[107]

KING.   D—n all thou'st seen! Dost thou, beneath the shape
Of Gaffer Thumb, come hither to abuse me
With similes, to keep me on the rack?
Hence—or, by all the torments of thy hell,
I'll run thee through the body, though thou'st none.[108]

GHOST.   Arthur, beware! I must this moment hence,
Not frighted by your voice, but by the cocks!
Arthur beware, beware, beware, beware!
Strive to avert thy yet impending fate;
For, if thou'rt killed to-day,
To-morrow all thy care will come too late.

---

[105] The ghost of Lausaria, in *Cyrus*, is a plain copy of this, and is therefore
worth reading:

> Ah, Cyrus!
> Thou may'st as well grasp water, or fleet air,
> As think of touching my immortal shade.
>
> *Cyrus the Great.*

[106] Thou better part of heavenly air.

Conquest of Granada.

[107] "A string of similes," says one, "proper to be hung up in the cabinet of
a prince."

[108] This passage hath been understood several different ways by the commentators. For my part, I find it difficult to understand it at all. Mr. Dryden
says:

> I've heard something how two bodies meet,
> But how two souls join I know not.

So that, till the body of a spirit be better understood, it will be difficult to
understand how it is possible to run him through it.

SCENE III

KING (*solus*).   Oh! stay, and leave me not uncertain thus!
And whilst thou tellest me what's like my fate,
Oh, teach me how I may avert it too!
Curst be the man who first a simile made!
Curst ev'ry bard who writes! So have I seen
Those whose comparisons are just and true,
And those who liken things not like at all.
The devil is happy that the whole creation
Can furnish out no simile to his fortune.

SCENE IV

KING, QUEEN

QUEEN.   What is the cause, my Arthur, that you steal
Thus silently from Dollallolla's breast?
Why dost thou leave me in the dark alone,
When well thou know'st I am afraid of sprites?[109]
    KING.   Oh, Dollallolla! do not blame my love!
I hop'd the fumes of last night's punch had laid
Thy lovely eyelids fast. But, oh! I find
There is no power in drams to quiet wives;
Each morn, as the returning sun, they wake,
And shine upon their husbands.
    QUEEN.   Think, oh think!
What a surprise it must be to the sun,
Rising, to find the vanish'd world away.
What less can be the wretched wife's surprise
When, stretching out her arms to fold thee fast,
She folds her useless bolster in her arms.
Think, think, on that.[110] Oh! think, think well on that!
I do remember also to have read
In Dryden's *Ovid's Metamorphoses*,[111]
That Jove in form inanimate did lie
With beauteous Danaë; and, trust me, love,
I fear'd the bolster might have been a Jove.[112]

[109] Cydaria is of the same fearful temper with Dollallolla.
    I never durst in darkness be alone.
                                        Indian Emperor.

[110] Think well of this, think that, think every way.
                                        Sophonisba.

[111] These quotations are more usual in the comic than in the tragic writers.
[112] "This distress," says Mr. Dennis, "I must allow to be extremely beautiful, and tends to heighten the virtuous character of Dollallolla, who is so exceeding delicate, that she is in the highest apprehension from the inanimate embrace of a bolster. An example worthy of imitation from all our writers of tragedy."

KING. Come to my arms, most virtuous of thy sex;
O, Dollallolla! were all wives like thee,
So many husbands never had worn horns.
Should Huncamunca of thy worth partake,
Tom Thumb indeed were blest.——Oh, fatal name!
For didst thou know one quarter what I know,
Then wouldst thou know—alas! what thou wouldst know!
    QUEEN. What can I gather hence? Why dost thou speak
Like men who carry raree-shows about?
"Now, you shall see, gentlemen, what you shall see."
O, tell me more, or thou hast told too much.

SCENE V

KING, QUEEN, NOODLE

    NOOD. Long life attend your majesties serene,
Great Arthur, king, and Dollallolla, queen!
Lord Grizzle, with a bold rebellious crowd,
Advances to the palace, threat'ning loud,
Unless the princess be deliver'd straight, ⎫
And the victorious Thumb, without his pate, ⎬
They are resolv'd to batter down the gate. ⎭

SCENE VI

KING, QUEEN, HUNCAMUNCA, NOODLE

    KING. See where the princess comes! Where is Tom
Thumb?
    HUNC. Oh! Sir, about an hour and half ago
He sally'd out to encounter with the foe,
And swore, unless his fate had him mis'ed, ⎫
From Grizzle's shoulders to cut off his head, ⎬
And serve't up with your chocolate in bed. ⎭
    KING. 'Tis well, I find one devil told us both.
Come, Dollallolla, Huncamunca, come;
Within we'll wait for the victorious Thumb;
In peace and safety we secure may stay,
While to his arm we trust the bloody fray;
Though men and giants should conspire with gods,
He is alone equal to all these odds.[113]
    QUEEN. He is, indeed, a helmet to us all;

[113]   "Credat Judæus Appella,
                   Non ego,"
says Mr. Dennis. "For, passing over the absurdity of being equal to odds, can
we possibly suppose a little insignificant fellow—I say again, a little insignificant
fellow—able to vie with a strength which all the Samsons and Herculeses of

While he supports, we need not fear to fall;[114]
His arm dispatches all things to our wish,
And serves up every foe's head in a dish.
Void is the mistress of the house of care,
While the good cook presents the bill of fare;
Whether the cod, that northern king of fish,
Or duck, or goose, or pig, adorn the dish,
No fears the number of her guests afford,
But at her hour she sees the dinner on the board.

SCENE VII

SCENE: *A plain*

LORD GRIZZLE, FOODLE, *and Rebels*

GRIZ.   Thus far our arms with victory are crown'd;
For, though we have not fought, yet we have found
No enemy to fight withal.[115]

FOOD.   Yet I,
Methinks, would willingly avoid this day,
This first of April, to engage our foes.

GRIZ.   This day, of all the days of th' year, I'd choose,[116]

---

antiquity would be unable to encounter?" I shall refer this incredulous critic to
Mr. Dryden's defence of his Almanzor; and, lest that should not satisfy him, I
shall quote a few lines from the speech of a much braver fellow than Almanzor,
Mr. Johnson's Achilles:

> Though human race rise in embattled hosts,
> To force her from my arms—Oh! son of Atreus!
> By that immortal pow'r, whose deathless spirit
> Informs this earth, *I will oppose them all.*

Victim.

114 "I have heard of being supported by a staff," says Mr. Dennis, "but never
of being supported by an helmet." I believe he never heard of sailing with
wings, which he may read in no less a poet than Mr. Dryden:

> Unless we borrow wings, and sail thro' air.

Love Triumphant.

What will he say to a kneeling valley?

> ——I'll stand
> Like a safe valley, that low bends the knee
> To some aspiring mountain.   *Injured Love.*

I am ashamed of so ignorant a carper, who doth not know that an epithet in
tragedy is very often no other than an expletive. Do not we read in the *New
Sophonisba* of "grinding chains, blue plagues, white occasions, and blue serenity"? Nay, 'tis not the adjective only, but sometimes half a sentence is put by
way of expletive, as, "Beauty pointed high with spirit," in the same play; and,
"In the lap of blessing, to be most curst," in the *Revenge.*

115 A victory like that of Almanzor:

> Almanzor is victorious without fight.

Conquest of Granada.

116 Well have we chose an happy day for fight,
For every man, in course of time, has found
Some days are lucky, some unfortunate.

King Arthur.

For on this day my grandmother was born.
Gods! I will make Tom Thumb an April fool;
Will teach his wit an errand it ne'er knew,
And send it post to the Elysian shades.[117]

    FOOD.   I'm glad to find our army is so stout,
Nor does it move my wonder less than joy.

    GRIZ.   What friends we have, and how we came so strong,
I'll softly tell you as we march along.[118]

SCENE VIII

Thunder and Lightning

TOM THUMB, GLUMDALCA, *cum suis*

    THUMB.   Oh, Noodle! hast thou seen a day like this?
The unborn thunder rumbles o'er our heads,[119]
As if the gods meant to unhinge the world;
And heaven and earth in wild confusion hurl;
Yet will I boldly tread the tott'ring ball.[120]

    MERL. (*offstage*)   Tom Thumb!
    THUMB.   What voice is this I hear?
    MERL. (*offstage*)   Tom Thumb!
    THUMB.   Again it calls.
    MERL. (*offstage*)   Tom Thumb!
    GLUM.   It calls again.
    THUMB.   Appear, whoe'er thou art, I fear thee not.
    MERL. (*enters*)   Thou hast no cause to fear, I am thy friend,
Merlin by name, a conjurer by trade,
And to my art thou dost thy being owe.

    THUMB.   How!
    MERL.   Hear then the mystic getting of Tom Thumb.
    His father was a ploughman plain,
    His mother milk'd the cow;[121]
    And yet the way to get a son
    This couple knew not how.

[117] We read of such another in Lee:
    Teach his rude wit a flight she never made,
    And send her post to the Elysian shade.
Gloriana.

[118] These lines are copied verbatim in the *Indian Emperor.*
[119] Unborn thunder rolling in a cloud.
Conquest of Granada.

[120] Were heaven and earth in wild confusion hurl'd,
    Should the rash gods unhinge the rolling world,
    Undaunted would I tread the tott'ring ball,
    Crush'd, but unconquer'd, in the dreadful fall.
Female Warrior.

[121] See the *History of Tom Thumb*, page 2.

Until such time the good old man
    To learned Merlin goes,
And there to him, in great distress,
    In secret manner shows;
How in his heart he wish'd to have
    A child, in time to come,
To be his heir, though it might be
    No bigger than his thumb:
Of which old Merlin was foretold
    That he his wish should have;
And so a son of stature small
    The charmer to him gave.
Thou'st heard the past, look up and see the future.

THUMB.   Lost in amazement's gulf, my senses sink;[122]
See there, Glumdalca, see another me![123]

GLUM.   O sight of horror! see, you are devour'd
By the expanded jaws of a red cow.

MERL.   Let not these sights deter thy noble mind,
For, lo! a sight more glorious courts thy eyes:
See from afar a theatre arise;
There ages, yet unborn, shall tribute pay
To the heroic actions of this day:
Then buskin tragedy at length shall choose
Thy name the best supporter of her muse.[124]

THUMB.   Enough, let every warlike music sound,
We fall contented, if we fall renown'd.

SCENE IX

LORD GRIZZLE, FOODLE, *Rebels, on one side;*
TOM THUMB, GLUMDALCA, *on the other*

FOOD.   At length the enemy advances nigh,
I hear them with my ear, and see them with my eye.[125]

---

122 ——Amazement swallows up my sense,
    And in th' impetuous whirl of circling fate
    Drinks down my reason.
                                            Persian Princess.

123   ——I have outfac'd myself.
        What! am I two? Is there another me?
                                            King Arthur.

124 The character of Merlin is wonderful throughout, but most so in this prophetic part. We find several of these prophecies in the tragic authors, who frequently take this opportunity to pay a compliment to their country, and sometimes to their prince. None but our author (who seems to have detested the least appearance of flattery) would have passed by such an opportunity of being a political prophet.

125 I saw the villain, Myron; with these eyes I saw him.
                                            Busiris.

In both which places it is intimated that it is sometimes possible to see with other eyes than your own.

GRIZ.   Draw all your swords: for liberty we fight,
And liberty the mustard is of life.[126]

THUMB.   Are you the man whom men fam'd Grizzle name?

GRIZ.   Are you the much more fam'd Tom Thumb?[127]

THUMB.   The same.

GRIZ.   Come on; our worth upon ourselves we'll prove;
For liberty I fight.

THUMB.   And I for love.

(*A bloody engagement between the two armies here,
drums beating, trumpets sounding, thunder and lightning.—They fight off and on several times. Some fall.*
GRIZZLE *and* GLUMDALCA *remain.*)

GLUM.   Turn, coward, turn, nor from a woman fly.

GRIZ.   Away—thou art too ignoble for my arm.

GLUM.   Have at thy heart.

GRIZ.   Nay, then I thrust at thine.

GLUM.   You push too well; you've run me through the guts,
And I am dead.

GRIZ.   Then there's an end of one.

THUMB.   When thou art dead, then there's an end of two,
Villain.

GRIZ.   Tom Thumb!

THUMB.   Rebel!

GRIZ.   Tom Thumb!

THUMB.   Hell!

GRIZ.   Huncamunca![128]

THUMB.   Thou hast it there.

GRIZ.   Too sure I feel it.

THUMB.   To hell then, like a rebel as you are,
And give my service to the rebels there.

GRIZ.   Triumph not, Thumb, nor think thou shalt enjoy
Thy Huncamunca undisturb'd; I'll send

[126] "This mustard," says Mr. Dennis, "is enough to turn one's stomach. I
would be glad to know what idea the author had in his head when he wrote it."
This will be, I believe, best explained by a line of Mr. Dennis's:

And gave him liberty, the salt of life.

Liberty Asserted.

The understanding that can digest the one will not rise at the other.

[127] *Han.* Are you the chief whom men fam'd Scipio call?
Scip. Are you the much more famous Hannibal?

Hannibal.

[128] Dr. Young seems to have copied this engagement in his *Busiris:*
Myr. Villain!
Mem. Myron!
Myr. Rebel!
Mem. Myron!
Myr. Hell!
Mem. Mandane!

My ghost to fetch her to the other world;[129]
It shall but bait at heaven, and then return.[130]
But, ha! I feel death rumbling in my brains:[131]
Some kinder sprite knocks softly at my soul, [132]
And gently whispers it to haste away;
I come, I come, most willingly I come.
So, when some city wife, for country air,
To Hampstead or to Highgate does repair,
Her to make haste her husband does implore,
And cries, "My dear, the coach is at the door":
With equal wish, desirous to be gone,
She gets into the coach, and then she cries—"Drive on!"[133]

    THUMB.   With those last words he vomited his soul,[134]
Which, like whipt cream,[135] the devil will swallow down.
Bear off the body, and cut off the head,
Which I will to the king in triumph lug;
Rebellion's dead, and now I'll go to breakfast.

SCENE X

KING, QUEEN, HUNCAMUNCA, *and Courtiers*

    KING.   Open the prisons, set the wretched free,
And bid our treasurer disburse six pounds
To pay their debts. Let no one weep to-day.
Come, Dollallolla; curse that odious name!
It is so long, it asks an hour to speak it.
By heavens! I'll change it into Doll, or Loll,

---

[129] This last speech of my Lord Grizzle hath been of great service to our poets:

> ——I'll hold it fast
> As life, and when life's gone I'll hold this last;
> And if thou tak'st it from me when I'm slain,
> I'll send my ghost, and fetch it back again.
>
>   *Conquest of Granada.*

[130]   My soul should with such speed obey,
> It should not bait at heaven to stop its way.

> Lee seems to have had this last in his eye:
> 'Twas not my purpose, Sir, to tarry there;
> I would but go to heaven to take the air.
>
>   *Gloriana.*

[131]   A rising *vapour rumbling* in my brains.
>   *Cleomenes.*

[132]   Some kind sprite knocks softly at my soul,
> To tell me fate's at hand.   *Sebastian.*

[133] Mr. Dryden seems to have had this simile in his eye, when he says,
> My soul is packing up, and just on wing.
>   *Conquest of Granada.*

[134]   And in a purple vomit pour'd his soul.
>   *Cleomenes.*

[135]   The devil swallows vulgar souls
> Like whipt cream.   *Sebastian.*

Or any other civil monosyllable,
That will not tire my tongue.[136]——Come, sit thee down.
Here seated, let us view the dancers' sports;
Bid 'em advance. This is the wedding-day
Of Princess Huncamunca and Tom Thumb;
Tom Thumb! who wins two victories[137] to-day,
And this way marches, bearing Grizzle's head.

A dance here

NOOD.   Oh! monstrous, dreadful, terrible. Oh! Oh!
Deaf be my ears, for ever blind my eyes!
Dumb be my tongue! feet lame! all senses lost!
Howl wolves, grunt bears, hiss snakes, shriek all ye ghosts![138]
KING.   What does the blockhead mean?
NOOD.   I mean, my liege,
Only to grace my tale with decent horror.[139]
Whilst from my garret, twice two stories high,
I look'd abroad into the streets below,
I saw Tom Thumb attended by the mob;
Twice twenty shoe-boys, twice two dozen links,
Chairmen and porters, hackney-coachmen, whores.
Aloft he bore the grizzly head of Grizzle;
When of a sudden thro' the streets there came
A cow, of larger than the usual size,
And in a moment—guess, oh! guess the rest!—
And in a moment swallow'd up Tom Thumb.
KING.   Shut up again the prisons, bid my treasurer
Not give three farthings out—hang all the culprits,
Guilty or not—no matter—ravish virgins;
Go bid the schoolmasters whip all their boys;
Let lawyers, parsons, and physicians loose
To rob, impose on, and to kill the world.
NOOD.   Her majesty the queen is in a swoon.

[136]   How I could curse my name of Ptolemy!
            It is so long, it asks an hour to write it.
            By heav'n! I'll change it into Jove or Mars,
            Or any other civil monosyllable,
            That will not tire my hand.   *Cleomenes.*
[137] Here is a visible conjunction of two days in one, by which our author
may have either intended an emblem of a wedding, or to insinuate that men
in the honey-moon are apt to imagine time shorter than it is. It brings into my
mind a passage in the comedy called *The Coffee-House Politician:*
            We will celebrate this day at my house to-morrow.
[138] These beautiful phrases are all to be found in one single speech of *King
Arthur, or The British Worthy.*
[139]   I was but teaching him to grace his tale
            With decent horror.   *Cleomenes.*

QUEEN.   Not so much in a swoon but I have still
Strength to reward the messenger of ill news.

(kills NOODLE*)*

NOOD.   Oh! I am slain.

CLE.   My lover's kill'd, I will revenge him so.

(kills the QUEEN*)*

HUNC.   My mamma kill'd! vile murderess, beware.

(kills CLEORA*)*

DOOD.   This for an old grudge to thy heart.

(kills HUNCAMUNCA*)*

MUST.   And this
I drive to thine, O Doodle! for a new one.

(kills DOODLE*)*

KING.   Ha! murderess vile, take that.

(kills MUSTACHA*)*

And take thou this.   *(kills himself, and falls)*
So when the child, whom nurse from danger guards,
Sends Jack for mustard with a pack of cards,
Kings, queens, and knaves, throw one another down,
Till the whole pack lies scatter'd and o'erthrown;
So all our pack upon the floor is cast,
And all I boast is—that I fall the last.[140]   *(dies)*

[140] We may say with Dryden,
> Death did at length so many slain forget,
> And left the tale, and took them by the great.
>
> *Conquest of Granada.*

I know of no tragedy which comes nearer to this charming and bloody catastrophe than *Cleomenes*, where the curtain covers five principal characters dead
on the stage. These lines too—
> I ask no questions then, of who killed who:
> The bodies tell the story as they lie—

seem to have belonged more properly to this scene of our author; nor can I
help imagining they were originally his. *The Rival Ladies*, too, seem beholden
to this scene:
> We're now a chain of lovers link'd in death:
> Julia goes first, Gonsalvo hangs on her,
> And Angelina hangs upon Gonsalvo,
> As I on Angelina.

No scene, I believe, ever received greater honours than this. It was applauded
by several encores, a word very unusual in tragedy. And it was very difficult
for the actors to escape without a second slaughter. This I take to be a lively
assurance of that fierce spirit of liberty which remains among us, and which
Mr. Dryden, in his *Essay on Dramatic Poetry*, hath observed: "Whether custom," says he, "hath so insinuated itself into our countrymen, or nature hath so
formed them to fierceness, I know not, but they will scarcely suffer combats
and other objects of horror to be taken from them." And indeed I am for having
them encouraged in this martial disposition: nor do I believe our victories over
the French have been owing to anything more than to those bloody spectacles
daily exhibited in our tragedies, of which the French stage is so entirely clear.

The London Merchant:

OR,

The History of George Barnwell

BY GEORGE LILLO

> Learn to be wise from others' harm,
> And you shall do full well.
> > Old Ballad of *The Lady's Fall.*

TO SIR JOHN EYLES, BART., MEMBER OF PARLIAMENT FOR, AND
ALDERMAN OF, THE CITY OF LONDON, AND SUB-GOVERNOR
OF THE SOUTH-SEA COMPANY

SIR,

If tragic poetry be, as Mr. Dryden has somewhere said, the
most excellent and most useful kind of writing, the more ex-
tensively useful the moral of any tragedy is, the more excellent
that piece must be of its kind.

I hope I shall not be thought to insinuate that this, to which
I have presumed to prefix your name, is such; that depends on

its fitness to answer the end of tragedy, the exciting of the passions in order to the correcting such of them as are criminal, either in their nature, or through their excess. Whether the following scenes do this in any tolerable degree, is, with the deference that becomes one who would not be thought vain, submitted to your candid and impartial judgment.

What I would infer is this, I think, evident truth; that tragedy is so far from losing its dignity by being accommodated to the circumstances of the generality of mankind, that it is more truly august in proportion to the extent of its influence and the numbers that are properly affected by it, as it is more truly great to be the instrument of good to many who stand in need of our assistance, than to a very small part of that number.

If princes, etc., were alone liable to misfortunes arising from vice or weakness in themselves or others, there would be good reason for confining the characters in tragedy to those of superior rank; but, since the contrary is evident, nothing can be more reasonable than to proportion the remedy to the disease.

I am far from denying that tragedies, founded on any instructive and extraordinary events in history, or well-invented fables, where the persons introduced are of the highest rank, are without their use, even to the bulk of the audience. The strong contrast between a Tamerlane and a Bajazet may have its weight with an unsteady people, and contribute to the fixing of them in the interest of a prince of the character of the former, when, through their own levity or the arts of designing men, they are rendered factious and uneasy, though they have the highest reason to be satisfied. The sentiments and example of a Cato may inspire his spectators with a just sense of the value of liberty, when they see that honest patriot prefer death to an obligation from a tyrant who would sacrifice the constitution of his country, and the liberties of mankind, to his ambition or revenge. I have attempted, indeed, to enlarge the province of the graver kind of poetry, and should be glad to see it carried on by some abler hand. Plays founded on moral tales in private life may be of admirable use, by carrying conviction to the mind with such irresistible force as to engage all the faculties and powers of the soul in the cause of virtue, by stifling vice in its first principles. They who imagine this to be too much to be attributed to tragedy, must be strangers to the energy of that noble species of poetry. Shakespeare, who has given such amazing proofs of his genius, in that as well as in comedy, in his *Hamlet* has the following lines:

Had he the motive and the cause for passion
That I have, he would drown the stage with tears
And cleave the general ear with horrid speech;
Make mad the guilty, and appall the free,
Confound the ign'rant, and amaze indeed
The very faculty of eyes and ears.

And farther, in the same speech:

I've heard that guilty creatures at a play
Have, by the very cunning of the scene,
Been so struck to the soul, that presently
They have proclaim'd their malefactions.

Prodigious! yet strictly just. But I shan't take up your valuable time with my remarks; only give me leave just to observe that he seems so firmly persuaded of the power of a well-wrote piece to produce the effect here ascribed to it, as to make Hamlet venture his soul on the event, and rather trust that than a messenger from the other world, though it assumed, as he expresses it, his *noble father's form,* and assured him that it was his *spirit.* "I'll have," says Hamlet, "grounds more relative.

. . . The play's the thing,
Wherein I'll catch the conscience of the king."

Such plays are the best answers to them who deny the lawfulness of the stage.

Considering the novelty of this attempt, I thought it would be expected from me to say something in its excuse; and I was unwilling to lose the opportunity of saying something of the usefulness of tragedy in general, and what may be reasonably expected from the farther improvement of this excellent kind of poetry.

Sir, I hope you will not think I have said too much of an art, a mean specimen of which I am ambitious enough to recommend to your favour and protection. A mind conscious of superior worth as much despises flattery as it is above it. Had I found in myself an inclination to so contemptible a vice, I should not have chose Sir John Eyles for my patron. And indeed the best-writ panegyric, though strictly true, must place you in a light much inferior to that in which you have long been fixed by the love and esteem of your fellow citizens, whose choice of you for one of their representatives in Parliament has sufficiently declared their sense of your merit. Nor hath the knowledge of your worth been confined to the City. The proprietors in the South-Sea Company, in which are in-

cluded numbers of persons as considerable for their rank, fortune, and understanding as any in the kingdom, gave the
greatest proof of their confidence in your capacity and probity
when they chose you sub-governor of their company at a time
when their affairs were in the utmost confusion and their
properties in the greatest danger. Neither is the Court insensible of your importance. I shall not therefore attempt a character so well known nor pretend to add anything to a reputation so well established.

Whatever others may think of a dedication wherein there is
so much said of other things, and so little of the person to
whom it is addressed, I have reason to believe that you will
the more easily pardon it on that very account.

I am, Sir,

Your most obedient

Humble servant,

George Lillo.

PROLOGUE

The Tragic Muse, sublime, delights to show
Princes distrest and scenes of royal woe;
In awful pomp, majestic, to relate
The fall of nations or some hero's fate,
That scepter'd chiefs may by example know
The strange vicissitudes of things below,
What dangers on security attend,
How pride and cruelty in ruin end:
Hence Providence supreme to know, and own
Humanity adds glory to a throne.
    In ev'ry former age and foreign tongue
With native grandeur thus the goddess sung.
Upon our stage, indeed, with wish'd success,
You've sometimes seen her in a humbler dress—
Great only in distress. When she complains
In Southern's, Rowe's, or Otway's moving strains,
The brilliant drops that fall from each bright eye
The absent pomp with brighter gems supply.
Forgive us then, if we attempt to show,
In artless strains, a tale of private woe.
A London 'prentice ruin'd, is our theme,
Drawn from the fam'd old song that bears his name.
We hope your taste is not so high to scorn

A moral tale, esteem'd ere you were born;
Which, for a century of rolling years,
Has fill'd a thousand thousand eyes with tears.
   If thoughtless youth to warn, and shame the age
From vice destructive, well becomes the stage;
If this example innocence insure,
Prevent our guilt, or by reflection cure;
If Millwood's dreadful crimes and sad despair
Commend the virtue of the good and fair:
Tho' art be wanting, and our numbers fail,
Indulge the attempt, in justice to the tale!

DRAMATIS PERSONÆ

Men:

THOROWGOOD
BARNWELL, *uncle to* GEORGE
GEORGE BARNWELL
TRUEMAN
BLUNT

Women:

MARIA THOROWGOOD
MILLWOOD
LUCY

Officers with their Attendants, Keeper, and Footmen

SCENE: *London, and an adjacent village*

THE LONDON MERCHANT

OR

THE HISTORY OF GEORGE BARNWELL

ACT I

SCENE I

SCENE: *A room in* THOROWGOOD's *house*

Enter THOROWGOOD *and* TRUEMAN

TR. Sir, the packet from Genoa is arrived.

(gives letters)

THOR. Heav'n be praised! The storm that threatened our royal mistress, pure religion, liberty and laws, is for a time diverted; the haughty and revengeful Spaniard, disappointed of the loan on which he depended from Genoa, must now attend the slow return of wealth from his new world to supply his empty coffers ere he can execute his purposed invasion of our happy island; by which means time is gained to make such preparations on our part as may, heav'n concurring, prevent his malice, or turn the meditated mischief on himself.

TR. He must be insensible, indeed, who is not affected when the safety of his country is concerned. Sir, may I know by what means—if I am too bold——

THOR. Your curiosity is laudable, and I gratify it with the greater pleasure, because from thence you may learn how honest merchants, as such, may sometimes contribute to the safety of their country, as they do at all times to its happiness; that if hereafter you should be tempted to any action that has the appearance of vice or meanness in it, upon reflecting upon the dignity of our profession, you may, with honest scorn, reject whatever is unworthy of it.

TR. Should Barnwell, or I, who have the benefit of your example, by our ill conduct bring any imputation on that honourable name, we must be left without excuse.

THOR. You compliment, young man. (TRUEMAN *bows re-*

spectfully.) Nay, I'm not offended. As the name of merchant never degrades the gentleman, so by no means does it exclude him; only take heed not to purchase the character of complaisant at the expense of your sincerity.——But to answer your question. The bank of Genoa had agreed, at excessive interest and on good security, to advance the King of Spain a sum of money sufficient to equip his vast Armado; of which our peerless Elizabeth (more than in name the mother of her people) being well informed, sent Walsingham, her wise and faithful secretary, to consult the merchants of this loyal city, who all agreed to direct their several agents to influence, if possible, the Genoese to break their contract with the Spanish court. 'Tis done; the state and bank of Genoa, having maturely weighed and rightly judged of their true interest, prefer the friendship of the merchants of London to that of a monarch who proudly styles himself King of both Indies.

TR. Happy success of prudent councils! What an expense of blood and treasure is here saved! Excellent queen! Oh, how unlike those princes who make the danger of foreign enemies a pretence to oppress their subjects by taxes great and grievous to be borne.

THOR. Not so our gracious queen, whose richest exchequer is her people's love, as their happiness her greatest glory.

TR. On these terms to defend us is to make our protection a benefit worthy her who confers it, and well worth our acceptance.—— Sir, have you any commands for me at this time?

THOR. Only look carefully over the files to see whether there are any tradesmen's bills unpaid; if there are, send and discharge 'em. We must not let artificers lose their time, so useful to the public and their families, in unnecessary attendance.   (*Exit* TRUEMAN)

Enter MARIA

Well, Maria, have you given orders for the entertainment? I would have it in some measure worthy the guests. Let there be plenty, and of the best, that the courtiers may at least commend our hospitality.

MA. Sir, I have endeavoured not to wrong your well-known generosity by an ill-timed parsimony.

THOR. Nay, 'twas a needless caution; I have no cause to doubt your prudence.

MA. Sir, I find myself unfit for conversation; I should but increase the number of the company without adding to their satisfaction.

THOR. Nay, my child! this melancholy must not be indulged.

MA. Company will but increase it: I wish you would dispense with my absence; solitude best suits my present temper.

THOR. You are not insensible that it is chiefly on your account these noble lords do me the honour so frequently to grace my board; should you be absent, the disappointment may make them repent their condescension and think their labour lost.

MA. He that shall think his time or honour lost in visiting you can set no real value on your daughter's company, whose only merit is that she is yours. The man of quality who chooses to converse with a gentleman and merchant of your worth and character may confer honour by so doing, but he loses none.

THOR. Come, come, Maria, I need not tell you that a young gentleman may prefer your conversation to mine, yet intend me no disrespect at all; for, though he may lose no honour in my company, 'tis very natural for him to expect more pleasure in yours. I remember the time when the company of the greatest and wisest man in the kingdom would have been insipid and tiresome to me if it had deprived me of an opportunity of enjoying your mother's.

MA. Yours no doubt was as agreeable to her, for generous minds know no pleasure in society but where 'tis mutual.

THOR. Thou know'st I have no heir, no child but thee: the fruits of many years' successful industry must all be thine. Now, it would give me pleasure great as my love to see on whom you would bestow it. I am daily solicited by men of the greatest rank and merit for leave to address you, but I have hitherto declined it, in hopes that by observation I should learn which way your inclination tends; for, as I know love to be essential to happiness in the marriage state, I had rather my approbation should confirm your choice than direct it.

MA. What can I say? How shall I answer as I ought this tenderness, so uncommon even in the best of parents? But you are without example; yet had you been less indulgent, I had been most wretched. That I look on the crowd of courtiers that visit here with equal esteem but equal indifference, you have observed, and I must needs confess; yet had you asserted your authority, and insisted on a parent's right to be obeyed, I had submitted, and to my duty sacrificed my peace.

THOR. From your perfect obedience in every other instance I feared as much, and therefore would leave you with-

out a bias in an affair wherein your happiness is so immediately concerned.

MA.   Whether from a want of that just ambition that would
become your daughter, or from some other cause, I know not,
but I find high birth and titles don't recommend the man who
owns them to my affections.

THOR.   I would not that they should, unless his merit recommends him more. A noble birth and fortune, though they
make not a bad man good, yet they are a real advantage to a
worthy one, and place his virtues in the fairest light.

MA.   I cannot answer for my inclinations, but they shall
ever be submitted to your wisdom and authority; and, as you
will not compel me to marry where I cannot love, love shall
never make me act contrary to my duty.——Sir, have I your
permission to retire?

THOR.   I'll see you to your chamber.   (*Exeunt*)

SCENE II

SCENE: *A room in* MILLWOOD's *house*

MILLWOOD *at her toilet.* LUCY, *waiting*

MILL.   How do I look to-day, Lucy?

LUCY.   Oh, killingly, Madam! A little more red, and you'll
be irresistible! But why this more than ordinary care of your
dress and complexion? What new conquest are you aiming at?

MILL.   A conquest would be new indeed!

LUCY.   Not to you, who make 'em every day—but to me—
well! 'tis what I'm never to expect, unfortunate as I am. But
your wit and beauty——

MILL.   First made me a wretch, and still continue me so.
Men, however generous or sincere to one another, are all sel-
fish hypocrites in their affairs with us. We are no otherwise
esteemed or regarded by them but as we contribute to their
satisfaction.

LUCY.   You are certainly, Madam, on the wrong side in
this argument. Is not the expense all theirs? And I am sure 'tis
our own fault if we ha'n't our share of the pleasure.

MILL.   We are but slaves to men.

LUCY.   Nay, 'tis they that are slaves most certainly; for
we lay them under contribution.

MILL.   Slaves have no property—no, not even in themselves. All is the victor's.

LUCY.   You are strangely arbitrary in your principles,
Madam.

MILL.   I would have my conquests complete, like those of the Spaniards in the New World, who first plundered the natives of all the wealth they had, and then condemned the wretches to the mines for life to work for more.

LUCY.   Well, I shall never approve of your scheme of government; I should think it much more politic, as well as just, to find my subjects an easier employment.

MILL.   It's a general maxim among the knowing part of mankind, that a woman without virtue, like a man without honour or honesty, is capable of any action, though never so vile; and yet what pains will they not take, what arts not use, to seduce us from our innocence, and make us contemptible and wicked, even in their own opinions! Then is it not just, the villains, to their cost, should find us so? But guilt makes them suspicious, and keeps them on their guard; therefore we can take advantage only of the young and innocent part of the sex, who, having never injured women, apprehend no injury from them.

LUCY.   Ay, they must be young indeed.

MILL.   Such a one, I think, I have found. As I've passed through the City, I have often observed him, receiving and paying considerable sums of money; from thence I conclude he is employed in affairs of consequence.

LUCY.   Is he handsome?

MILL.   Ay, ay, the stripling is well made and has a good face.

LUCY.   About——

MILL.   Eighteen.

LUCY.   Innocent, handsome, and about eighteen! You'll be vastly happy. Why, if you manage well, you may keep him to yourself these two or three years.

MILL.   If I manage well, I shall have done with him much sooner. Having long had a design on him, and meeting him yesterday, I made a full stop, and, gazing wishfully on his face, asked him his name. He blushed, and bowing very low, answered: "George Barnwell." I begged his pardon for the freedom I had taken, and told him that he was the person I had long wished to see, and to whom I had an affair of importance to communicate at a proper time and place. He named a tavern; I talked of honour and reputation, and invited him to my house. He swallowed the bait, promised to come, and this is the time I expect him. (*knocking at the door*) Somebody knocks;—d'ye hear; I am at home to nobody to-day but him.   (*Exit* LUCY)

——Less affairs must give way to those of more consequence, and I am strangely mistaken if this does not prove of great importance to me and him too, before I have done with him. Now, after what manner shall I receive him? Let me consider—what manner of person am I to receive? He is young, innocent, and bashful: therefore I must take care not to put him out of countenance at first. But then, if I have any skill in physiognomy, he is amorous, and, with a little assistance, will soon get the better of his modesty. I'll e'en trust to Nature, who does wonders in these matters. If to seem what one is not, in order to be the better liked for what one really is; if to speak one thing, and mean the direct contrary, be art in a woman—I know nothing of nature.

Enter BARNWELL, *bowing very low.* LUCY *at a distance*

MILL.   Sir! the surprise and joy——

BARN.   Madam——

MILL.   (*advancing*) This is such a favour——

BARN.   Pardon me, Madam——

MILL.   (*still advances*) So unhoped for—(BARNWELL *salutes her, and retires in confusion.*)—to see you here. Excuse the confusion——

BARN.   I fear I am too bold.

MILL.   Alas, Sir! I may justly apprehend you think me so. Please, Sir, to sit. I am as much at a loss how to receive this honour as I ought, as I am surprised at your goodness in conferring it.

BARN.   I thought you had expected me: I promised to come.

MILL.   That is the more surprising; few men are such religious observers of their word.

BARN.   All who are honest are.

MILL.   To one another. But we simple women are seldom thought of consequence enough to gain a place in your remembrance.

(*laying her hand on his, as by accident*)

BARN.   (*aside*) Her disorder is so great, she don't perceive she has laid her hand on mine. Heavens! how she trembles! What can this mean?

MILL.   The interest I have in all that relates to you (the reason of which you shall know hereafter), excites my curiosity; and, were I sure you would pardon my presumption, I should desire to know your real sentiments on a very particular subject.

BARN. Madam, you may command my poor thoughts on any subject; I have none that I would conceal.

MILL. You'll think me bold.

BARN. No, indeed.

MILL. What then are your thoughts of love?

BARN. If you mean the love of women, I have not thought of it at all. My youth and circumstances make such thoughts improper in me yet. But if you mean the general love we owe to mankind, I think no one has more of it in his temper than myself. I don't know that person in the world whose happiness I don't wish and wouldn't promote, were it in my power. In an especial manner I love my uncle and my master, but, above all, my friend.

MILL. You have a friend then whom you love?

BARN. As he does me, sincerely.

MILL. He is, no doubt, often blessed with your company and conversation.

BARN. We live in one house, and both serve the same worthy merchant.

MILL. Happy, happy youth! Whoe'er thou art, I envy thee, and so must all who see and know this youth. What have I lost, by being formed a woman! I hate my sex, myself. Had I been a man, I might, perhaps, have been as happy in your friendship, as he who now enjoys it. But, as it is—oh!

BARN. (*aside*) I never observed women before, or this is sure the most beautiful of her sex!——You seem disordered, Madam! May I know the cause?

MILL. Do not ask me—I can never speak it, whatever is the cause. I wish for things impossible. I would be a servant, bound to the same master, to live in one house with you.

BARN. (*aside*) How strange, and yet how kind, her words and actions are! And the effect they have on me is as strange. I feel desires I never knew before. I must be gone, while I have power to go.——Madam, I humbly take my leave.

MILL. You will not, sure, leave me so soon!

BARN. Indeed, I must.

MILL. You cannot be so cruel! I have prepared a poor supper, at which I promised myself your company.

BARN. I am sorry I must refuse the honour you designed me, but my duty to my master calls me hence. I never yet neglected his service; he is so gentle, and so good a master, that, should I wrong him, though he might forgive me, I never should forgive myself.

MILL. Am I refused, by the first man, the second favour

I ever stooped to ask? Go then, thou proud, hard-hearted youth! But know, you are the only man that could be found who would let me sue twice for greater favours.

BARN. What shall I do! How shall I go or stay!

MILL. Yet do not, do not, leave me! I with my sex's pride would meet your scorn, but when I look upon you—when I behold those eyes—oh! spare my tongue, and let my blushes—(this flood of tears to that will force its way) declare—what woman's modesty should hide.

BARN. Oh, heavens! she loves me, worthless as I am; her looks, her words, her flowing tears confess it. And can I leave her, then? Oh, never, never!——Madam, dry up your tears! You shall command me always; I will stay here forever, if you'd have me.

LUCY. (*aside*) So! She has wheedled him out of his virtue of obedience already, and will strip him of all the rest, one after another, till she has left him as few as her ladyship or myself.

MILL. Now you are kind, indeed; but I mean not to detain you always. I would have you shake off all slavish obedience to your master, but you may serve him still.

LUCY. (*aside*) "Serve him still"! Ay, or he'll have no opportunity of fingering his cash, and then he'll not serve your end, I'll be sworn.

Enter BLUNT

BLUNT. Madam, supper's on the table.

MILL. Come, Sir, you'll excuse all defects. My thoughts were too much employed on my guest to observe the entertainment. (*Exeunt* MILLWOOD *and* BARNWELL)

BLUNT. What! is all this preparation, this elegant supper, variety of wines, and music, for the entertainment of that young fellow?

LUCY. So it seems.

BLUNT. What! is our mistress turned fool at last? She's in love with him, I suppose.

LUCY. I suppose not; but she designs to make him in love with her if she can.

BLUNT. What will she get by that? He seems under age, and can't be supposed to have much money.

LUCY. But his master has, and that's the same thing, as she'll manage it.

BLUNT. I don't like this fooling with a handsome young

fellow; while she's endeavouring to ensnare him, she may be caught herself.

LUCY.   Nay, were she like me, that would certainly be the consequence, for, I confess, there is something in youth and innocence that moves me mightily.

BLUNT.   Yes, so does the smoothness and plumpness of a partridge move a mighty desire in the hawk to be the destruction of it.

LUCY.   Why, birds are their prey, as men are ours—though, as you observed, we are sometimes caught ourselves; but that, I dare say, will never be the case with our mistress.

BLUNT.   I wish it may prove so, for you know we all depend upon her. Should she trifle away her time with a young fellow that there's nothing to be got by, we must all starve.

LUCY.   There's no danger of that, for I am sure she has no view in this affair but interest.

BLUNT.   Well, and what hopes are there of success in that?

LUCY.   The most promising that can be. 'Tis true, the youth has his scruples; but she'll soon teach him to answer them by stifling his conscience. Oh, the lad is in a hopeful way, depend upon't.   (*Exeunt*)

SCENE *draws and discovers* BARNWELL *and* MILLWOOD *at supper. An entertainment of music and singing after which they come forward.*

BARN.   What can I answer? All that I know is, that you are fair and I am miserable.

MILLWOOD.   We are both so, and yet the fault is in ourselves.

BARN.   To ease our present anguish by plunging into guilt is to buy a moment's pleasure with an age of pain.

MILL.   I should have thought the joys of love as lasting as they are great; if ours prove otherwise, 'tis your inconstancy must make them so.

BARN.   The law of heaven will not be reversed, and that requires us to govern our passions.

MILL.   To give us sense of beauty and desires, and yet forbid us to taste and be happy, is cruelty to nature. Have we passions only to torment us?

BARN.   To hear you talk, though in the cause of vice; to gaze upon your beauty, press your hand, and see your snow-white bosom heave and fall, inflames my wishes; my pulse beats high; my senses all are in a hurry, and I am on the rack

of wild desire. Yet, for a moment's guilty pleasure, shall I
lose my innocence, my peace of mind, and hopes of solid
happiness?

    MILL.   Chimeras all! Come on with me and prove
No joys like womankind, no heav'n like love.

    BARN.   I would not, yet must on.
Reluctant thus, the merchant quits his ease,
And trusts to rocks, and sands, and stormy seas;
In hopes some unknown golden coast to find,
Commits himself, tho' doubtful, to the wind;
Longs much for joys to come, yet mourns those left behind.
                                    (*Exeunt*)

ACT II

SCENE I

SCENE: *A room in Thorowgood's house*

Enter BARNWELL

    BARN.   How strange are all things round me! Like some
thief, who treads forbidden ground and fain would lurk unseen, fearful I enter each apartment of this well-known house.
To guilty love, as if that were too little, already have I added
breach of trust. —— A thief! —— Can I know myself that
wretched thing, and look my honest friend and injured master in the face? Though hypocrisy may a while conceal my
guilt, at length it will be known, and public shame and ruin
must ensue. In the meantime, what must be my life? ever to
speak a language foreign to my heart; hourly to add to the
number of my crimes in order to conceal 'em! Sure, such was
the condition of the grand apostate, when first he lost his
purity; like me, disconsolate he wandered, and, while yet in
heaven, bore all his future hell about him.

Enter TRUEMAN

    TR.   Barnwell! Oh, how I rejoice to see you safe! so will
our master and his gentle daughter, who during your absence
often enquired after you.

    BARN.   (*aside*)   Would he were gone; his officious love will
pry into the secrets of my soul.

    TR.   Unless you knew the pain the whole family has felt
on your account, you can't conceive how much you are beloved. But why thus cold and silent? When my heart is full
of joy for your return, why do you turn away? why thus avoid

me? what have I done? how am I altered since you saw me last? Or rather, what have you done? and why are you thus changed, for I am still the same.

BARN. (*aside*) What have I done, indeed!

TR. Not speak!—nor look upon me!

BARN. (*aside*) By my face he will discover all I would conceal; methinks already I begin to hate him.

TR. I cannot bear this usage from a friend; one whom till now I ever found so loving, whom yet I love, though this unkindness strikes at the root of friendship, and might destroy it in any breast but mine.

BARN. (*turning to him*) I am not well. Sleep has been a stranger to these eyes since you beheld them last.

TR. Heavy they look indeed, and swollen with tears— now they o'erflow. Rightly did my sympathizing heart forbode last night, when thou wast absent, something fatal to our peace.

BARN. Your friendship engages you too far. My troubles, whate'er they are, are mine alone; you have no interest in them, nor ought your concern for me give you a moment's pain.

TR. You speak as if you knew of friendship nothing but the name. Before I saw your grief I felt it. Since we parted last I have slept no more than you, but pensive in my chamber sat alone and spent the tedious night in wishes for your safety and return; e'en now, though ignorant of the cause, your sorrow wounds me to the heart.

BARN. 'Twill not be always thus. Friendship and all engagements cease, as circumstances and occasions vary; and, since you once may hate me, perhaps it might be better for us both that now you loved me less.

TR. Sure, I but dream! without a cause would Barnwell use me thus? Ungenerous and ungrateful youth, farewell! I shall endeavour to follow your advice. (*going*) (*aside*)—— Yet stay; perhaps I am too rash, and angry when the cause demands compassion. Some unforeseen calamity may have befallen him, too great to bear.

BARN. (*aside*) What part am I reduced to act! 'Tis vile and base to move his temper thus—the best of friends and men!

TR. I am to blame; prithee, forgive me, Barnwell! Try to compose your ruffled mind, and let me know the cause that thus transports you from yourself. My friendly counsel may restore your peace.

BARN. All that is possible for man to do for man, your generous friendship may effect; but here even that's in vain.

TR. Something dreadful is labouring in your breast. Oh, give it vent, and let me share your grief; 'twill ease your pain, should it admit no cure, and make it lighter by the part I bear.

BARN. Vain supposition! My woes increase by being observed; should the cause be known, they would exceed all bounds.

TR. So well I know thy honest heart, guilt cannot harbour there.

BARN. (*aside*) Oh, torture insupportable!

TR. Then why am I excluded? have I a thought I would conceal from you?

BARN. If still you urge me on this hated subject, I'll never enter more beneath this roof nor see your face again.

TR. 'Tis strange. But I have done; say but you hate me not.

BARN. Hate you! I am not that monster yet.

TR. Shall our friendship still continue?

BARN. It's a blessing I never was worthy of, yet now must stand on terms, and but upon conditions can confirm it.

TR. What are they?

BARN. Never hereafter, though you should wonder at my conduct, desire to know more than I am willing to reveal.

TR. 'Tis hard; but upon any conditions, I must be your friend.

BARN. Then, as much as one lost to himself can be another's, I am yours.   (*embracing*)

TR. Be ever so, and may heaven restore your peace!

BARN. Will yesterday return? We have heard the glorious sun, that till then incessant rolled, once stopped his rapid course, and once went back; the dead have risen, and parched rocks poured forth a liquid stream to quench a people's thirst; the sea divided and formed walls of water, while a whole nation passed in safety through its sandy bosom; hungry lions have refused their prey, and men unhurt have walked amidst consuming flames; but never yet did time, once past, return.

TR. Though the continued chain of time has never once been broke, nor ever will, but uninterrupted must keep on its course, till lost in eternity it ends there where it first begun; yet, as heaven can repair whatever evils time can bring upon us, we ought never to despair. —— But business requires our attendance—business, the youth's best preservative from ill, as idleness his worst of snares. Will you go with me?

BARN.   I'll take a little time to reflect on what has passed, and follow you.   (*Exit* TRUEMAN)
I might have trusted Trueman and engaged him to apply to my uncle to repair the wrong I have done my master. But what of Millwood? must I expose her too? Ungenerous and base! Then heaven requires it not. But heaven requires that I forsake her. What! never see her more! Does heaven require that? I hope I may see her, and heaven not be offended. Presumptuous hope—dearly already have I proved my frailty; should I once more tempt heaven, I may be left to fall never to rise again. Yet shall I leave her, forever leave her, and not let her know the cause?—she who loves me with such a boundless passion! Can cruelty be duty? I judge of what she then must feel by what I now endure. The love of life and fear of shame, opposed by inclination strong as death or shame, like wind and tide in raging conflict met, when neither can prevail, keep me in doubt. How then can I determine?

Enter THOROWGOOD

THOR.   Without a cause assigned, or notice given, to absent yourself last night was a fault, young man, and I came to chide you for it, but hope I am prevented. That modest blush, the confusion so visible in your face, speak grief and shame. When we have offended heaven, it requires no more; and shall man, who needs himself to be forgiven, be harder to appease? If my pardon or love be of moment to your peace, look up, secure of both.

BARN.   (*aside*)   This goodness has o'ercome me. O Sir! you know not the nature and extent of my offence, and I should abuse your mistaken bounty to receive it. Though I had rather die than speak my shame; though racks could not have forced the guilty secret from my breast, your kindness has.

THOR.   Enough, enough; whate'er it be, this concern shows you're convinced, and I am satisfied. (*aside*) How painful is the sense of guilt to an ingenuous mind!—some youthful folly which it were prudent not to enquire into. When we consider the frail condition of humanity, it may raise our pity, not our wonder, that youth should go astray when reason, weak at the best opposed to inclination, scarce formed and wholly unassisted by experience, faintly contends, or willingly becomes the slave of sense. The state of youth is much to be deplored, and the more so because they see it not, being then to danger most exposed when they are least prepared for their defence.

BARN. It will be known, and you recall your pardon and abhor me.

THOR. I never will. Yet be upon your guard in this gay, thoughtless season of your life; when the sense of pleasure's quick and passion high, the voluptuous appetites raging and fierce demand the strongest curb; take heed of a relapse. When vice becomes habitual, the very power of leaving it is lost.

BARN. Hear me on my knees confess——

THOR. Not a syllable more upon this subject; it were not mercy, but cruelty, to hear what must give you such torment to reveal.

BARN. This generosity amazes and distracts me.

THOR. This remorse makes thee dearer to me than if thou hadst never offended. Whatever is your fault, of this I'm certain; 'twas harder for you to offend than me to pardon.

(*Exit* THOROWGOOD)

BARN. Villain! villain! villain! basely to wrong so excellent a man! Should I again return to folly?—detested thought! But what of Millwood then? Why, I renounce her—I give her up. The struggle's over and virtue has prevailed. Reason may convince, but gratitude compels. This unlooked-for generosity has saved me from destruction. (*going*)

Enter a Footman

FOOT. Sir, two ladies from your uncle in the country desire to see you.

BARN. (*aside*) Who should they be?——Tell them I'll wait upon 'em. (*Exit Footman*) Methinks I dread to see 'em. Now everything alarms me. Guilt, what a coward hast thou made me! (*Exit*)

SCENE II

SCENE: *Another room in* THOROWGOOD's *house*

MILLWOOD *and* LUCY *discovered*

Enter Footman

FOOT. Ladies, he'll wait upon you immediately.

MILL. 'Tis very well. I thank you. (*Exit Footman*)

Enter BARNWELL

BARN. Confusion!——Millwood!

MILL. That angry look tells me that here I'm an unwelcome guest. I feared as much—the unhappy are so everywhere.

BARN. Will nothing but my utter ruin content you?

MILL. Unkind and cruel! Lost myself, your happiness is now my only care.

BARN. How did you gain admission?

MILL. Saying we were desired by your uncle to visit and deliver a message to you, we were received by the family without suspicion, and with much respect conducted here.

BARN. Why did you come at all?

MILL. I never shall trouble you more; I'm come to take my leave forever. Such is the malice of my fate. I go hopeless, despairing ever to return. This hour is all I have left. One short hour is all I have to bestow on love and you, for whom I thought the longest life too short.

BARN. Then we are met to part forever?

MILL. It must be so. Yet think not that time or absence shall ever put a period to my grief or make me love you less: though I must leave you, yet condemn me not!

BARN. Condemn you? No, I approve your resolution and rejoice to hear it; 'tis just, 'tis necessary. I have well weighed, and found it so.

LUCY. (*aside*) I'm afraid the young man has more sense than she thought he had.

BARN. Before you came, I had determined never to see you more.

MILL. (*aside*) Confusion!

LUCY. (*aside*) Ay! we are all out! This is a turn so unexpected that I shall make nothing of my part; they must e'en play the scene betwixt themselves.

MILL. 'Twas some relief to think, though absent, you would love me still; but to find, though Fortune had been indulgent, that you, more cruel and inconstant, had resolved to cast me off—this, as I never could expect, I have not learnt to bear.

BARN. I am sorry to hear you blame in me a resolution that so well becomes us both.

MILL. I have reason for what I do, but you have none.

BARN. Can we want a reason for parting, who have so many to wish we never had met?

MILL. Look on me, Barnwell: am I deformed or old, that satiety so soon succeeds enjoyment? Nay, look again; am I not she whom yesterday you thought the fairest and the kindest of her sex? whose hand, trembling with ecstasy, you pressed and moulded thus, while on my eyes you gazed with such delight, as if desire increased by being fed?

BARN. No more! let me repent my former follies, if possible, without remembering what they were.

MILL. Why?

BARN. Such is my frailty that 'tis dangerous.

MILL. Where is the danger, since we are to part?

BARN. The thought of that already is too painful.

MILL. If it be painful to part, then I may hope at least you do not hate me?

BARN. No—no—I never said I did. O my heart!——

MILL. Perhaps you pity me?

BARN. I do—I do—indeed, I do.

MILL. You'll think upon me?

BARN. Doubt it not, while I can think at all!

MILL. You may judge an embrace at parting too great a favour—though it would be the last. (*He draws back.*) A look shall then suffice—farewell—forever.

(*Exeunt* MILLWOOD *and* LUCY)

BARN. If to resolve to suffer be to conquer, I have conquered. Painful victory!

Re-enter MILLWOOD *and* LUCY

MILL. One thing I had forgot; I never must return to my own house again. This I thought proper to let you know, lest your mind should change and you should seek in vain to find me there. Forgive me this second intrusion; I only came to give you this caution, and that perhaps was needless.

BARN. I hope it was; yet it is kind, and I must thank you for it.

MILL. (*to* LUCY) My friend, your arm. Now I am gone forever. (*going*)

BARN. One thing more: sure, there's no danger in my knowing where you go? If you think otherwise——

MILL. (*weeping*) Alas!

LUCY (*aside*) We are right, I find; that's my cue.——Ah, dear Sir, she's going she knows not whither; but go she must.

BARN. Humanity obliges me to wish you well. Why will you thus expose yourself to needless troubles?

LUCY.   Nay, there's no help for it. She must quit the town immediately, and the kingdom as soon as possible; it was no small matter, you may be sure, that could make her resolve to leave you.

MILL.   No more, my friend, since he for whose dear sake alone I suffer, and am content to suffer, is kind and pities me. Whene'er I wander through wilds and deserts, benighted and forlorn, that thought shall give me comfort.

BARN.   For my sake? Oh, tell me how! which way am I so cursed as to bring such ruin on thee?

MILL.   No matter; I am contented with my lot.

BARN.   Leave me not in this incertainty!

MILL.   I have said too much.

BARN.   How, how am I the cause of your undoing?

MILL.   To know it will but increase your troubles.

BARN.   My troubles can't be greater than they are.

LUCY.   Well, well, Sir, if she won't satisfy you, I will.

BARN.   I am bound to you beyond expression.

MILL.   Remember, Sir, that I desired you not to hear it.

BARN.   Begin, and ease my racking expectation!

LUCY.   Why, you must know, my lady here was an only child; but her parents, dying while she was young, left her and her fortune (no inconsiderable one, I assure you) to the care of a gentleman who has a good estate of his own.

MILL.   Ay, ay, the barbarous man is rich enough; but what are riches when compared to love?

LUCY.   For a while he performed the office of a faithful guardian, settled her in a house, hired her servants—but you have seen in what manner she lived; so I need say no more of that.

MILL.   How I shall live hereafter, heaven knows!

LUCY.   All things went on as one could wish till, some time ago, his wife dying, he fell violently in love with his charge, and would fain have married her. Now, the man is neither old nor ugly, but a good, personable sort of a man; but I don't know how it was, she could never endure him. In short, her ill usage so provoked him, that he brought in an account of his executorship, wherein he makes her debtor to him.

MILL.   A trifle in itself, but more than enough to ruin me, whom, by his unjust account, he had stripped of all before.

LUCY.   Now, she having neither money nor friend, except me, who am as unfortunate as herself, he compelled her to pass his account, and give bond for the sum he demanded, but still provided handsomely for her and continued his court-ship till, being informed by his spies (truly I suspect some in her own family) that you were entertained at her house and stayed with her all night, he came this morning raving and storming like a madman; talks no more of marriage—so there's no hopes of making up matters that way—but vows her ruin unless she'll allow him the same favour that he supposes she granted you.

BARN. Must she be ruined or find her refuge in another's arms?

MILL. He gave me but an hour to resolve in. That's happily spent with you—and now I go.

BARN. To be exposed to all the rigours of the various seasons, the summer's parching heat, and winter's cold; unhoused to wander friendless through the unhospitable world, in misery and want, attended with fear and danger, and pursued by malice and revenge—wouldst thou endure all this for me, and can I do nothing, nothing to prevent it?

LUCY. 'Tis really a pity there can be no way found out.

BARN. Oh, where are all my resolutions now? Like early vapours, or the morning dew, chased by the sun's warm beams, they're vanished and lost, as though they had never been.

LUCY. Now, I advised her, Sir, to comply with the gentle-man; that would not only put an end to her troubles, but make her fortune at once.

BARN. Tormenting fiend, away! I had rather perish, nay, see her perish, than have her saved by him; I will myself prevent her ruin, though with my own. A moment's patience; I'll return immediately. (*Exit* BARNWELL)

LUCY. 'Twas well you came, or by what I can perceive you had lost him.

MILL. That, I must confess, was a danger I did not foresee; I was only afraid he should have come without money. You know a house of entertainment like mine is not kept without expense.

LUCY. That's very true. But then, you should be reasonable in your demands; 'tis pity to discourage a young man.

MILL. Leave that to me.

Re-enter BARNWELL *with a bag of money*

BARN. What am I about to do? Now you, who boast your reason all-sufficient, suppose yourselves in my condition, and determine for me whether it's right to let her suffer for my faults, or, by this small addition to my guilt, prevent the ill effects of what is past.

LUCY (*aside*) These young sinners think everything in the ways of wickedness so strange. But I could tell him that this is nothing but what's very common; for one vice as naturally begets another, as a father a son. But he'll find out that himself, if he lives long enough.

BARN. Here, take this, and with it purchase your deliverance; return to your house, and live in peace and safety.

MILL. So I may hope to see you there again?

BARN. Answer me not, but fly, lest, in the agonies of my remorse, I take again what is not mine to give, and abandon thee to want and misery!

MILL. Say but you'll come!

BARN. You are my fate, my heaven, or my hell. Only leave me now; dispose of me hereafter as you please.

(*Exeunt* MILLWOOD *and* LUCY)

What have I done? Were my resolutions founded on reason and sincerely made? Why then has heaven suffered me to fall? I sought not the occasion; and if my heart deceives me not, compassion and generosity were my motives. Is virtue inconsistent with itself, or are vice and virtue only empty names? Or do they depend on accidents, beyond our power to produce or to prevent—wherein we have no part, and yet must be determined by the event? But why should I attempt to reason? All is confusion, horror, and remorse. I find I am lost, cast down from all my late erected hopes, and plunged again in guilt, yet scarce know how or why:

Such undistinguish'd horrors make my brain,
Like hell, the seat of darkness and of pain.   (*Exit*)

ACT III

SCENE I

SCENE: *A room in* THOROWGOOD's *house*

Enter THOROWGOOD *and* TRUEMAN

THOR. Methinks I would not have you only learn the method of merchandise and practise it hereafter, merely as a means of getting wealth; 'twill be well worth your pains to study it as a science, to see how it is founded in reason and the nature of things; how it promotes humanity, as it has opened and yet keeps up an intercourse between nations far remote from one another in situation, customs and religion;

promoting arts, industry, peace and plenty; by mutual benefits diffusing mutual love from pole to pole.

TR. Something of this I have considered, and hope, by your assistance, to extend my thoughts much farther. I have observed those countries where trade is promoted and encouraged do not make discoveries to destroy, but to improve, mankind; by love and friendship to tame the fierce and polish the most savage; to teach them the advantages of honest traffic by taking from them, with their own consent, their useless superfluities, and giving them in return what, from their ignorance in manual arts, their situation, or some other accident, they stand in need of.

THOR. 'Tis justly observed. The populous East, luxuriant, abounds with glittering gems, bright pearls, aromatic spices, and health-restoring drugs. The late-found western world's rich earth glows with unnumbered veins of gold and silver ore. On every climate and on every country heaven has bestowed some good peculiar to itself. It is the industrious merchant's business to collect the various blessings of each soil and climate, and, with the product of the whole, to enrich his native country. —— Well! I have examined your accounts. They are not only just, as I have always found them, but regularly kept and fairly entered. I commend your diligence. Method in business is the surest guide. He who neglects it frequently stumbles, and always wanders perplexed, uncertain, and in danger. Are Barnwell's accounts ready for my inspection? He does not use to be the last on these occasions.

TR. Upon receiving your orders he retired, I thought, in some confusion. If you please, I'll go and hasten him. I hope he hasn't been guilty of any neglect.

THOR. I'm now going to the Exchange; let him know, at my return I expect to find him ready. (*Exeunt*)

Enter MARIA *with a book; sits and reads*

MA. How forcible is truth! The weakest mind, inspired with love of that, fixed and collected in itself, with indifference beholds the united force of earth and hell opposing. Such souls are raised above the sense of pain, or so supported that they regard it not. The martyr cheaply purchases his heaven: small are his sufferings, great is his reward. Not so the wretch who combats love with duty, when the mind, weakened and dissolved by the soft passion, feeble and hopeless, opposes its own desires. What is an hour, a day, a year of pain, to a whole life of tortures such as these?

Enter TRUEMAN

TR. O Barnwell! O my friend, how art thou fallen!

MA. Ha! Barnwell! What of him? Speak—say, what of Barnwell!

TR. 'Tis not to be concealed. I've news to tell of him that will afflict your generous father, yourself, and all who know him.

MA. Defend us, heaven!

TR. I cannot speak it. See there.

(gives a letter. MARIA *reads)*

"Trueman,

I know my absence will surprise my honoured master and yourself, and the more when you shall understand that the reason of my withdrawing, is my having embezzled part of the cash with which I was entrusted. After this, 'tis needless to inform you that I intend never to return again. Though this might have been known by examining my accounts, yet, to prevent that unnecessary trouble, and to cut off all fruitless expectations of my return, I have left this from the lost

"George Barnwell."

TR. Lost indeed! Yet how he should be guilty of what he there charges himself withal, raises my wonder equal to my grief. Never had youth a higher sense of virtue. Justly he thought, and as he thought he practised; never was life more regular than his: an understanding uncommon at his years; an open, generous manliness of temper; his manners easy, unaffected, and engaging.

MA. This and much more you might have said with truth. He was the delight of every eye and joy of every heart that knew him.

TR. Since such he was, and was my friend, can I support his loss? See! the fairest and happiest maid this wealthy city boasts, kindly condescends to weep for thy unhappy fate, poor ruined Barnwell!

MA. Trueman, do you think a soul so delicate as his, so sensible of shame, can e'er submit to live a slave to vice?

TR. Never, never! So well I know him, I'm sure this act of his, so contrary to his nature, must have been caused by some unavoidable necessity.

MA. Is there no means yet to preserve him?

TR. Oh, that there were! But few men recover reputation

lost—a merchant, never. Nor would he, I fear, though I should find him, ever be brought to look his injured master in the face.

MA.   I fear as much, and therefore would never have my father know it.

TR.   That's impossible.

MA.   What's the sum?

TR.   'Tis considerable. I've marked it here, to show it, with the letter, to your father, at his return.

MA.   If I should supply the money, could you so dispose of that, and the account, as to conceal this unhappy mismanagement from my father?

TR.   Nothing more easy. But can you intend it? Will you save a helpless wretch from ruin? Oh! 'twere an act worthy such exalted virtue as Maria's. Sure, heaven in mercy to my friend inspired the generous thought!

MA.   Doubt not but I would purchase so great a happiness at a much dearer price:—but how shall he be found?

TR.   Trust to my diligence for that. In the meantime, I'll conceal his absence from your father, or find such excuses for it that the real cause shall never be suspected.

MA.   In attempting to save from shame one who we hope may yet return to virtue, to heaven and you, the only witnesses of this action, I appeal, whether I do anything misbecoming my sex and character.

TR.   Earth must approve the deed, and heaven, I doubt not, will reward it.

MA.   If heaven succeeds it, I am well rewarded. A virgin's fame is sullied by suspicion's lightest breath; and therefore as this must be a secret from my father and the world, for Barnwell's sake, for mine, let it be so to him!   (*Exeunt*)

SCENE II

SCENE: *A room in* MILLWOOD'S *house*

Enter LUCY *and* BLUNT

LUCY.   Well! what do you think of Millwood's conduct now?

BLUNT.   I own it is surprising: I don't know which to admire most, her feigned or his real passion, though I have sometimes been afraid that her avarice would discover her.

But his youth and want of experience make it the easier to impose on him.

LUCY. No, it is his love. To do him justice, notwithstanding his youth, he don't want understanding; but you men are much easier imposed on in these affairs than your vanity will allow you to believe. Let me see the wisest of you all as much in love with me as Barnwell is with Millwood, and I'll engage to make as great a fool of him.

BLUNT. And all circumstances considered, to make as much money of him too?

LUCY. I can't answer for that. Her artifice in making him rob his master at first, and the various stratagems by which she has obliged him to continue that course, astonish even me, who know her so well.

BLUNT. But then you are to consider that the money was his master's.

LUCY. There was the difficulty of it. Had it been his own, it had been nothing. Were the world his, she might have it for a smile. But those golden days are done; he's ruined, and Millwood's hope of farther profits there are at an end.

BLUNT. That's no more than we all expected.

LUCY. Being called by his master to make up his accounts, he was forced to quit his house and service, and wisely flies to Millwood for relief and entertainment.

BLUNT. I have not heard of this before! How did she receive him?

LUCY. As you would expect. She wondered what he meant; was astonished at his impudence; and, with an air of modesty peculiar to herself, swore so heartily that she never saw him before, that she put me out of countenance.

BLUNT. That's much, indeed! But how did Barnwell behave?

LUCY. He grieved, and, at length, enraged at this barbarous treatment, was preparing to be gone; when, making toward the door, he showed a sum of money which he had brought from his master's—the last he's ever like to have from thence.

BLUNT. But then Millwood?

LUCY. Ay, she, with her usual address, returned to her old arts of lying, swearing, and dissembling—hung on his neck, wept, and swore 'twas meant in jest, till the amorous youth melted into tears, threw the money into her lap, and swore he had rather die than think her false.

BLUNT.   Strange infatuation!

LUCY.   But what followed was stranger still. As doubts
and fears, followed by reconcilement, ever increase love
where the passion is sincere, so in him it caused so wild a
transport of excessive fondness, such joy, such grief, such
pleasure, and such anguish, that nature in him seemed sinking with the weight, and the charmed soul disposed to quit
his breast for hers. Just then, when every passion with lawless
anarchy prevailed, and reason was in the raging tempest lost,
the cruel, artful Millwood prevailed upon the wretched youth
to promise—what I tremble but to think on.

BLUNT.   I am amazed! What can it be?

LUCY.   You will be more so, to hear it is to attempt the life
of his nearest relation and best benefactor——

BLUNT.   His uncle! whom we have often heard him speak
of as a gentleman of a large estate and fair character in the
country where he lives.

LUCY.   The same. She was no sooner possessed of the last
dear purchase of his ruin, but her avarice, insatiate as the
grave, demanded this horrid sacrifice. Barnwell's near relation
and unsuspected virtue must give too easy means to seize the
good man's treasure, whose blood must seal the dreadful
secret and prevent the terrors of her guilty fears.

BLUNT.   Is it possible she could persuade him to do an act
like that? He is, by nature, honest, grateful, compassionate,
and generous; and though his love and her artful persuasions
have wrought him to practise what he most abhors, yet we all
can witness for him with what reluctance he has still com-
plied. So many tears he shed o'er each offence, as might, if
possible, sanctify theft, and make a merit of a crime.

LUCY.   'Tis true, at the naming the murder of his uncle he
started into rage, and, breaking from her arms, where she till
then had held him with well-dissembled love and false endear-
ments, called her "cruel, monster, devil," and told her she was
born for his destruction. She thought it not for her purpose
to meet his rage with rage, but affected a most passionate fit
of grief—railed at her fate and cursed her wayward stars, that
still her wants should force her to press him to act such deeds
as she must needs abhor as well as he: but told him necessity
had no law, and love no bounds; that therefore he never truly
loved, but meant, in her necessity, to forsake her; then
kneeled, and swore that since, by his refusal, he had given her
cause to doubt his love, she never would see him more, unless,

to prove it true, he robbed his uncle to supply her wants, and murdered him to keep it from discovery.

BLUNT.   I am astonished! What said he?

LUCY.   Speechless he stood; but in his face you might have read that various passions tore his very soul. Oft he, in anguish, threw his eyes towards heaven, and then as often bent their beams on her; then wept and groaned, and beat his troubled breast. At length, with horror not to be expressed, he cried: "Thou cursed fair! have I not given dreadful proofs of love? What drew me from my youthful innocence, to stain my then unspotted soul, but love? What caused me to rob my worthy gentle master, but cursed love? What makes me now a fugitive from his service, loathed by myself, and scorned by all the world, but love? What fills my eyes with tears, my soul with torture never felt on this side death before? Why, love, love, love! And why, above all, do I resolve" (for, tearing his hair, he cried, "I do resolve") "to kill my uncle?"

BLUNT.   Was she not moved? It makes me weep to hear the sad relation.

LUCY.   Yes—with joy, that she had gained her point. She gave him no time to cool, but urged him to attempt it instantly. He's now gone; if he performs it and escapes, there's more money for her; if not, he'll ne'er return, and then she's fairly rid of him.

BLUNT.   'Tis time the world were rid of such a monster.

LUCY.   If we don't do our endeavours to prevent this murder, we are as bad as she.

BLUNT.   I'm afraid it is too late.

LUCY.   Perhaps not. Her barbarity to Barnwell makes me hate her. We have run too great a length with her already. I did not think her or myself so wicked as I find, upon reflection, we are.

BLUNT.   'Tis true, we have all been too much so. But there is something so horrid in murder, that all other crimes seem nothing when compared to that. I would not be involved in the guilt of that for all the world.

LUCY.   Nor I, heaven knows; therefore, let us clear ourselves by doing all that is in our power to prevent it. I have just thought of a way that, to me, seems probable. Will you join with me to detect this cursed design?

BLUNT.   With all my heart. He who knows of a murder intended to be committed and does not discover it, in the eye of the law and reason is a murderer.

LUCY.   Let us lose no time; I'll acquaint you with the particulars as we go.

(*Exeunt*)

SCENE III

SCENE: *A walk at some distance from a country seat*

Enter BARNWELL

BARN.   A dismal gloom obscures the face of day; either the sun has slipped behind a cloud, or journeys down the west of heaven with more than common speed, to avoid the sight of what I'm doomed to act. Since I set forth on this accursed design, where'er I tread, methinks, the solid earth trembles beneath my feet. Yonder limpid stream, whose hoary fall has made a natural cascade, as I passed by, in doleful accents seemed to murmur "Murder." The earth, the air, and water, seemed concerned—but that's not strange; the world is punished, and nature feels a shock when Providence permits a good man's fall! Just heaven! Then what should I be? for him that was my father's only brother, and since his death has been to me a father, who took me up an infant, and an orphan; reared me with tenderest care, and still indulged me with most paternal fondness—yet here I stand avowed his destined murderer. I stiffen with horror at my own impiety. 'Tis yet unperformed. What if I quit my bloody purpose, and fly the place! (*going, then stops*) But whither, oh whither, shall I fly? My master's once friendly doors are ever shut against me; and without money Millwood will never see me more, and life is not to be endured without her. She's got such firm possession of my heart, and governs there with such despotic sway—ay, there's the cause of all my sin and sorrow! 'Tis more than love; 'tis the fever of the soul and madness of desire. In vain does nature, reason, conscience, all oppose it; the impetuous passion bears down all before it, and drives me on to lust, to theft, and murder. O conscience! feeble guide to virtue, thou only show'st us when we go astray, but wantest power to stop us in our course.——Ha, in yonder shady walk I see my uncle. He's alone. Now for my disguise! (*plucks out a vizor*) This is his hour of private meditation. Thus daily he prepares his soul for heaven, whilst I—but what have I to do with heaven? Ha! No struggles, conscience!

Hence, hence, remorse, and ev'ry thought that's good!
The storm that lust began must end in blood.

(*puts on the vizor, draws a pistol and exit*)

SCENE IV

SCENE: *A close walk in a wood*

Enter UNCLE

UN. If I were superstitious, I should fear some danger lurked unseen, or death were nigh. A heavy melancholy clouds my spirits; my imagination is filled with ghastly forms of dreary graves and bodies changed by death, when the pale, lengthened visage attracts each weeping eye, and fills the musing soul, at once, with grief and horror, pity and aversion. I will indulge the thought. The wise man prepares himself for death by making it familiar to his mind. When strong reflections hold the mirror near, and the living in the dead behold their future selves, how does each inordinate passion and desire cease, or sicken at the view! The mind scarce moves; the blood, curdling and chilled, creeps slowly through the veins —fixed, still, and motionless we stand, so like the solemn object of our thoughts, we are almost at present what we must be hereafter, till curiosity awakes the soul and sets it on inquiry.

Enter GEORGE BARNWELL *at a distance*

O Death, thou strange mysterious power, seen every day, yet never understood but by the incommunicative dead, what art thou? The extensive mind of man, that with a thought circles the earth's vast globe, sinks to the center, or ascends above the stars; that worlds exotic finds, or thinks it finds, thy thick clouds attempts to pass in vain: lost and bewildered in the horrid gloom, defeated she returns more doubtful than before, of nothing certain—but of labour lost.

(*During this speech,* BARNWELL *sometimes presents the pistol and draws it back again.*)

BARN. (*throwing down the pistol*)   Oh, 'tis impossible!

(*Uncle starts and attempts to draw his sword.*)

UN. A man is near me, armed and masked!

BARN. Nay, then there's no retreat.

(*plucks a poniard from his bosom, and stabs him*)

UN. Oh! I am slain! All-gracious heaven, regard the prayer of thy dying servant! Bless with the choicest blessings my dearest nephew; forgive my murderer, and take my fleeting soul to endless mercy!

(BARNWELL *throws off his mask, runs to him, and, kneeling by him, raises and chafes him.*)

BARN. Expiring saint! O murdered, martyred uncle! Lift
up your dying eyes, and view your nephew in your murderer!
Oh, do not look so tenderly upon me! Let indignation lighten
from your eyes, and blast me ere you die!—By heaven, he
weeps in pity of my woes. Tears—tears, for blood! The murdered, in the agonies of death, weeps for his murderer.——Oh,
speak your pious purpose—pronounce my pardon then, and
take me with you!——He would, but cannot.——Oh, why, with
such fond affection, do you press my murdering hand? What!
will you kiss me? (BARNWELL *kisses his uncle, who groans and
dies.*) Life, that hovered on his lips but till he had sealed my
pardon, in that kiss expired. He's gone forever—and oh! I follow. (*swoons away upon his uncle's dead body.*) Do I still
live to press the suffering bosom of the earth? Do I still
breathe, and taint with my infectious breath the wholesome
air? Let heaven from its high throne, in justice or in mercy,
now look down on that dear murdered saint and me the murderer, and, if his vengeance spares, let pity strike and end my
wretched being! Murder the worst of crimes, and parricide
the worst of murders, and this the worst of parricides! Cain,
who stands on record from the birth of time, and must to its
last final period, as accursed, slew a brother favoured above
him. Detested Nero by another's hand dispatched a mother
that he feared and hated. But I, with my own hand, have
murdered a brother, mother, father, and a friend most loving
and beloved. This execrable act of mine's without a parallel.
Oh, may it ever stand alone—the last of murders, as it is the
worst!

> The rich man thus, in torment and despair,
> Preferr'd his vain but charitable prayer.
> The fool, his own soul lost, would fain be wise
> For others' good; but heaven his suit denies.
> By laws and means well known we stand or fall,
> And one eternal rule remains for all.   (*Exit*)

ACT IV

SCENE I

SCENE: *A room in* THOROWGOOD's *house*

Enter MARIA

MA. How falsely do they judge who censure or applaud,
as we're afflicted or rewarded here! I know I am unhappy, yet

cannot charge myself with any crime more than the common frailties of our kind, that should provoke just heaven to mark me out for sufferings so uncommon and severe. Falsely to accuse ourselves, heaven must abhor; then it is just and right that innocence should suffer, for heaven must be just in all its ways. Perhaps by that we are kept from moral evils much worse than penal, or more improved in virtue; or may not the lesser ills that we sustain be made the means of greater good to others? Might all the joyless days and sleepless nights that I have passed but purchase peace for thee,

Thou dear, dear cause of all my grief and pain,
Small were the loss, and infinite the gain,
Though to the grave in secret love I pine,
So life and fame and happiness were thine.

Enter TRUEMAN

What news of Barnwell?

TR. None. I have sought him with the greatest diligence, but all in vain.

MA. Does my father yet suspect the cause of his absence?

TR. All appeared so just and fair to him, it is not possible he ever should; but his absence will no longer be concealed. Your father's wise; and, though he seems to hearken to the friendly excuses I would make for Barnwell, yet I am afraid he regards 'em only as such, without suffering them to influence his judgment.

MA. How does the unhappy youth defeat all our designs to serve him! Yet I can never repent what we have done. Should he return, 'twill make his reconciliation with my father easier, and preserve him from future reproach from a malicious, unforgiving world.

Enter THOROWGOOD *and* LUCY

THOR. This woman here has given me a sad, and (bating some circumstances) too probable account of Barnwell's defection.

LUCY. I am sorry, Sir, that my frank confession of my former unhappy course of life should cause you to suspect my truth on this occasion.

THOR. It is not that; your confession has in it all the appearance of truth. (*to them*) Among many other particulars, she informs me that Barnwell has been influenced to break his trust, and wrong me at several times of considerable sums of money; now, as I know this to be false, I would fain doubt the whole of her relation, too dreadful to be willingly believed.

MA. Sir, your pardon; I find myself on a sudden so indisposed that I must retire.—— (*aside*) Providence opposes all attempts to save him. Poor ruined Barnwell! Wretched, lost Maria! (*Exit* MARIA)

THOR. How am I distressed on every side! Pity for that unhappy youth, fear for the life of a much valued friend—and then my child, the only joy and hope of my declining life! Her melancholy increases hourly, and gives me painful apprehensions of her loss. O Trueman! this person informs me that your friend, at the instigation of an impious woman, is gone to rob and murder his venerable uncle.

TR. Oh, execrable deed! I am blasted with the horror of the thought.

LUCY. This delay may ruin all.

THOR. What to do or think I know not. That he ever wronged me, I know is false; the rest may be so too—there's all my hope.

TR. Trust not to that; rather suppose all true than lose a moment's time: even now the horrid deed may be a-doing—dreadful imagination!—or it may be done, and we be vainly debating on the means to prevent what is already past.

THOR. (*aside*) This earnestness convinces me that he knows more than he has yet discovered.——What ho! without there! who waits?

Enter a Servant

Order the groom to saddle the swiftest horse and prepare to set out with speed! An affair of life and death demands his diligence. (*Exit Servant*)
——(*to* LUCY) For you, whose behaviour on this occasion I have no time to commend as it deserves, I must engage your farther assistance. Return and observe this Millwood till I come. I have your directions, and will follow you as soon as possible. (*Exit* LUCY)
——Trueman, you, I am sure, will not be idle on this occasion. (*Exit* THOROWGOOD)

TR. He only who is a friend can judge of my distress. (*Exit*)

SCENE II

SCENE: MILLWOOD'S *house*

Enter MILLWOOD

MILL.   I wish I knew the event of his design; the attempt without success would ruin him. Well! what have I to apprehend from that? I fear too much. The mischief being only intended, his friends, in pity of his youth, turn all their rage on me. I should have thought of that before. Suppose the deed done—then, and then only, I shall be secure. Or what if he returns without attempting it at all?

Enter BARNWELL, *bloody*

But he is here, and I have done him wrong; his bloody hands show he has done the deed, but show he wants the prudence to conceal it.

BARN.   Where shall I hide me? whither shall I fly to avoid the swift, unerring hand of Justice?

MILL.   Dismiss your fears; though thousands had pursued you to the door, yet being entered here, you are safe as innocence. I have such a cavern, by art so cunningly contrived, that the piercing eyes of Jealousy and Revenge may search in vain, nor find the entrance to the safe retreat. There will I hide you if any danger's near.

BARN.   Oh, hide me—from myself if it be possible; for while I bear my conscience in my bosom, though I were hid where man's eye never saw nor light e'er dawned, 'twere all in vain. For oh! that inmate, that impartial judge, will try, convict, and sentence me for murder, and execute me with never-ending torments. Behold these hands all crimsoned o'er with my dear uncle's blood! Here's a sight to make a statue start with horror, or turn a living man into a statue.

MILL.   Ridiculous! Then it seems you are afraid of your own shadow, or, what's less than a shadow, your conscience.

BARN.   Though to man unknown I did the accursed act, what can we hide from heaven's all-seeing eye?

MILL.   No more of this stuff! What advantage have you made of his death, or what advantage may yet be made of it? Did you secure the keys of his treasure? those no doubt were about him. What gold, what jewels, or what else of value have you brought me?

BARN.   Think you I added sacrilege to murder? Oh! had you seen him as his life flowed from him in a crimson flood, and heard him praying for me by the double name of nephew and of murderer (alas, alas! he knew not then that his nephew was his murderer) how would you have wished, as I did, though you had a thousand years of life to come, to have given them all to have lengthened his one hour! But, being dead, I fled the sight of what my hands had done, nor could I, to have gained the empire of the world, have violated, by theft, his sacred corpse.

MILL. Whining, preposterous, canting villain, to murder your uncle, rob him of life, nature's first, last, dear prerogative, after which there's no injury; then fear to take what he no longer wanted, and bring to me your penury and guilt! Do you think I'll hazard my reputation—nay, my life, to entertain you?

BARN. O Millwood! this from thee!—but I have done; if you hate me, if you wish me dead, then are you happy—for oh! 'tis sure my grief will quickly end me.

MILL. (*aside*) In his madness he will discover all and involve me in his ruin. We are on a precipice from whence there's no retreat for both——then to preserve myself. (*pauses*) There is no other way—'tis dreadful; but reflection comes too late when danger's pressing—and there's no room for choice. It must be done. (*rings a bell*)

Enter a Servant

Fetch me an officer, and seize this villain: he has confessed himself a murderer; should I let him escape, I justly might be thought as bad as he. (*Exit Servant*)

BARN. O Millwood! sure you do not, cannot mean it. Stop the messenger!—upon my knees I beg you'd call him back! 'Tis fit I die indeed, but not by you. I will this instant deliver myself into the hands of justice, indeed I will; for death is all I wish. But thy ingratitude so tears my wounded soul, 'tis worse ten thousand times than death with torture.

MILL. Call it what you will, I am willing to live, and live secure, which nothing but your death can warrant.

BARN. If there be a pitch of wickedness that seats the author beyond the reach of vengeance, you must be secure. But what remains for me but a dismal dungeon, hard-galling fetters, an awful trial, and an ignominious death? justly to fall unpitied and abhorred? after death to be suspended between heaven and earth, a dreadful spectacle, the warning and horror of a gaping crowd? This I could bear, nay, wish not to avoid, had it but come from any hand but thine.

Enter BLUNT, *Officer and Attendants*

MILL.   Heaven defend me! Conceal a murderer? Here,
Sir; take this youth into your custody. I accuse him of murder, and will appear to make good my charge.

(*They seize him*)

BARN.   To whom of what, or how shall I complain? I'll not
accuse her: the hand of heaven is in it, and this the punishment of lust and parricide. Yet heaven, that justly cuts me off,
still suffers her to live, perhaps to punish others. Tremendous
mercy! so fiends are cursed with immortality, to be the exe-
cutioners of heaven.

Be warn'd, ye youths, who see my sad despair,
Avoid lewd women, false as they are fair;
By reason guided, honest joys pursue;   ⎫
The fair, to honour and to virtue true,   ⎬
Just to herself, will ne'er be false to you. ⎭
By my example learn to shun my fate;
(How wretched is the man who's wise too late!)
Ere innocence, and fame, and life, be lost,
Here purchase wisdom cheaply, at my cost!

(*Exeunt* BARNWELL, *Officer and Attendants*)

MILL.   Where's Lucy? why is she absent at such a time?

BLUNT.   Would I had been so too. Lucy will soon be here,
and, I hope, to thy confusion, thou devil!

MILL.   Insolent! This to me?

BLUNT.   The worst that we know of the devil is that he
first seduces to sin and then betrays to punishment.

(*Exit* BLUNT)

MILL.   They disapprove of my conduct then, and mean to
take this opportunity to set up for themselves. My ruin is resolved. I see my danger, but scorn both it and them; I was
not born to fall by such weak instruments.   (*going*)

Enter THOROWGOOD

THOR.   Where is the scandal of her own sex and curse of
ours?

MILL.   What means this insolence? Who do you seek?

THOR.   Millwood.

MILL.   Well, you have found her then. I am Millwood.

THOR.   Then you are the most impious wretch that e'er the
sun beheld.

MILL.   From your appearance I should have expected wisdom and moderation, but your manners belie your aspect.
What is your business here? I know you not.

THOR. Hereafter you may know me better; I am Barn-well's master.

MILL. Then you are master to a villain—which, I think, is not much to your credit.

THOR. Had he been as much above thy arts as my credit is superior to thy malice, I need not have blushed to own him.

MILL. My arts? I don't understand you, Sir! If he has done amiss, what's that to me? Was he my servant, or yours? You should have taught him better.

THOR. Why should I wonder to find such uncommon impudence in one arrived to such a height of wickedness? When innocence is banished, modesty soon follows. Know, sorceress, I'm not ignorant of any of thy arts by which you first deceived the unwary youth: I know how, step by step, you've led him on (reluctant and unwilling) from crime to crime, to this last horrid act, which you contrived and, by your cursed wiles, even forced him to commit.

MILL. (aside) Ha! Lucy has got the advantage and accused me first; unless I can turn the accusation and fix it upon her and Blunt, I am lost.

THOR. Had I known your cruel design sooner, it had been prevented; to see you punished as the law directs is all that now remains. Poor satisfaction! for he, innocent as he is, compared to you, must suffer too. But heaven, who knows our frame and graciously distinguishes between frailty and presumption, will make a difference, though man cannot, who sees not the heart, but only judges by the outward action.

MILL. I find, Sir, we are both unhappy in our servants. I was surprised at such ill treatment, without cause, from a gentleman of your appearance, and therefore too hastily returned it: for which I ask your pardon. I now perceive you have been so far imposed on as to think me engaged in a former correspondence with your servant, and, some way or other, accessary to his undoing.

THOR. I charge you as the cause, the sole cause, of all his guilt and all his suffering—of all he now endures, and must endure, till a violent and shameful death shall put a dreadful period to his life and miseries together.

MILL. 'Tis very strange; but who's secure from scandal and detraction? So far from contributing to his ruin, I never spoke to him till since that fatal accident, which I lament as much as you. 'Tis true, I have a servant, on whose account he has of late frequented my house; if she has abused my good opinion of her, am I to blame? Hasn't Barnwell done the same by you?

THOR. I hear you; pray, go on.

MILL. I have been informed he had a violent passion for her, and she for him; but till now I always thought it innocent; I know her poor, and given to expensive pleasures: now who can tell but she may have influenced the amorous youth to commit this murder, to supply her extravagancies? It must be so. I now recollect a thousand circumstances that confirm it. I'll have her, and a manservant that I suspect as an accomplice, secured immediately. I hope, Sir, you will lay aside your ill-grounded suspicions of me, and join to punish the real contrivers of this bloody deed.   (offers to go)

THOR. Madam, you pass not this way; I see your design, but shall protect them from your malice.

MILL. I hope you will not use your influence, and the credit of your name, to screen such guilty wretches. Consider, Sir, the wickedness of persuading a thoughtless youth to such a crime.

THOR. I do—and of betraying him when it was done.

MILL. That which you call betraying him, may convince you of my innocence. She who loves him, though she contrived the murder, would never have delivered him into the hands of justice, as I, struck with horror at his crimes, have done.

THOR. How should an unexperienced youth escape her snares? The powerful magic of her wit and form might betray the wisest to simple dotage, and fire the blood that age had froze long since. Even I, that with just prejudice came prepared, had, by her artful story, been deceived, but that my strong conviction of her guilt makes even a doubt impossible. ——Those whom subtilely you would accuse, you know are your accusers; and (which proves unanswerably their innocence and your guilt) they accused you before the deed was done, and did all that was in their power to prevent it.

MILL. Sir, you are very hard to be convinced; but I have such a proof which, when produced, will silence all objections.

(*Exit* MILLWOOD)

Enter LUCY, TRUEMAN, BLUNT, *Officers, etc.*

LUCY. Gentlemen, pray place yourselves, some on one side of that door, and some on the other; watch her entrance, and act as your prudence shall direct you.——(*to* THOROW-

GOOD) This way! and note her behaviour. I have observed her; she's driven to the last extremity, and is forming some desperate resolution. I guess at her design.

Re-enter MILLWOOD *with a pistol.* TRUEMAN
secures her

TR. Here thy power of doing mischief ends, deceitful, cruel, bloody woman!

MILL. Fool, hypocrite, villain—man! thou canst not call me that.

TR. To call thee woman were to wrong thy sex, thou devil!

MILL. That imaginary being is an emblem of thy cursed sex collected—a mirror, wherein each particular man may see his own likeness and that of all mankind.

THOR. Think not by aggravating the faults of others to extenuate thy own, of which the abuse of such uncommon perfections of mind and body is not the least.

MILL. If such I had, well may I curse your barbarous sex, who robbed me of 'em ere I knew their worth; then left me, too late, to count their value by their loss. Another and another spoiler came, and all my gain was poverty and reproach. My soul disdained, and yet disdains, dependence and contempt. Riches, no matter by what means obtained, I saw, secured the worst of men from both. I found it therefore necessary to be rich, and to that end I summoned all my arts. You call 'em wicked; be it so! they were such as my conversation with your sex had furnished me withal.

THOR. Sure, none but the worst of men conversed with thee.

MILL. Men of all degrees and all professions I have known, yet found no difference but in their several capacities; all were alike wicked to the utmost of their power. In pride, contention, avarice, cruelty and revenge, the reverend priesthood were my unerring guides. From suburb-magistrates, who live by ruined reputations, as the unhospitable natives of Cornwall do by shipwrecks, I learned that to charge my innocent neighbours with my crimes was to merit their protection; for to screen the guilty is the less scandalous when many are suspected, and detraction, like darkness and death, blackens all objects and levels all distinction. Such are your venal magistrates, who favour none but such as, by their office, they are sworn to punish. With them, not to be guilty is the worst of crimes, and large fees privately paid are every needful virtue.

THOR.   Your practice has sufficiently discovered your contempt of laws, both human and divine; no wonder then that you should hate the officers of both.

MILL.   I know you and I hate you all; I expect no mercy and I ask for none; I followed my inclinations, and that the best of you do every day. All actions seem alike natural and indifferent to man and beast, who devour, or are devoured, as they meet with others weaker or stronger than themselves.

THOR.   What pity it is, a mind so comprehensive, daring, and inquisitive, should be a stranger to religion's sweet and powerful charms!

MILL.   I am not fool enough to be an atheist, though I have known enough of men's hypocrisy to make a thousand simple women so. Whatever religion is in itself, as practised by mankind it has caused the evils you say it was designed to cure. War, plague, and famine, have not destroyed so many of the human race as this pretended piety has done, and with such barbarous cruelty, as if the only way to honour heaven were to turn the present world into hell.

THOR.   Truth is truth, though from an enemy and spoke in malice. You bloody, blind, and superstitious bigots, how will you answer this?

MILL.   What are your laws, of which you make your boast, but the fool's wisdom and the coward's valour? the instrument and screen of all your villainies, by which you punish in others what you act yourselves, or would have acted had you been in their circumstances. The judge who condemns the poor man for being a thief had been a thief himself had he been poor. Thus you go on deceiving and being deceived, harassing, plaguing, and destroying one another; but women are your universal prey.

Women, by whom you are, the source of joy,
With cruel arts you labour to destroy;
A thousand ways our ruin you pursue,
Yet blame in us those arts first taught by you.
Oh may, from hence, each violated maid,
By flatt'ring, faithless, barb'rous man betray'd,
When robbed of innocence and virgin fame,
From your destruction raise a nobler name;
To right their sex's wrongs devote their mind,
And future Millwoods prove, to plague mankind!

(*Exeunt*)

ACT V

SCENE I

SCENE: *A room in a prison*

Enter THOROWGOOD, BLUNT *and* LUCY

THOR. I have recommended to Barnwell a reverend divine, whose judgment and integrity I am well acquainted with; nor has Millwood been neglected, but she, unhappy woman, still obstinate, refuses his assistance.

LUCY. This pious charity to the afflicted well becomes your character; yet pardon me, Sir, if I wonder you were not at their trial.

THOR. I knew it was impossible to save him, and I and my family bear so great a part in his distress, that to have been present would but have aggravated our sorrows without relieving his.

BLUNT. It was mournful, indeed. Barnwell's youth and modest deportment, as he passed, drew tears from every eye. When placed at the bar and arraigned before the reverend judges, with many tears and interrupting sobs he confessed and aggravated his offences, without accusing or once reflecting on Millwood, the shameless author of his ruin; who, dauntless and unconcerned, stood by his side, viewing with visible pride and contempt the vast assembly, who all with sympathizing sorrow wept for the wretched youth. Millwood, when called upon to answer, loudly insisted upon her innocence, and made an artful and a bold defence; but, finding all in vain, the impartial jury and the learned bench concurring to find her guilty, how did she curse herself, poor Barnwell, us, her judges, all mankind! But what could that avail? she was condemned, and is this day to suffer with him.

THOR. The time draws on; I am going to visit Barnwell, as you are Millwood.

LUCY. We have not wronged her, yet I dread this interview. She's proud, impatient, wrathful, and unforgiving. To be the branded instruments of vengeance, to suffer in her shame and sympathize with her in all she suffers, is the tribute we must pay for our former ill-spent lives and long confederacy with her in wickedness.

THOR. Happy for you it ended when it did! What you

have done against Millwood, I know proceeded from a just abhorrence of her crimes, free from interest, malice, or revenge. Proselytes to virtue should be encouraged; pursue your purposed reformation, and know me hereafter for your friend.

LUCY. This is a blessing as unhoped for as unmerited; but heaven, that snatched us from impending ruin, sure intends you as its instrument to secure us from apostasy.

THOR. With gratitude to impute your deliverance to heaven, is just. Many, less virtuously disposed than Barnwell was, have never fallen in the manner he has done—may not such owe their safety rather to Providence than to themselves? With pity and compassion let us judge him. Great were his faults, but strong was the temptation. Let his ruin learn us diffidence, humanity, and circumspection; for we, who wonder at his fate, perhaps, had we like him been tried, like him we had fallen too. (*Exeunt*)

SCENE II

SCENE: *A dungeon. A table and lamp*

BARNWELL, *reading. Enter* THOROWGOOD *at a distance*

THOR. There see the bitter fruits of passion's detested reign and sensual appetite indulged—severe reflections, penitence, and tears.

BARN. My honoured, injured master, whose goodness has covered me a thousand times with shame, forgive this last unwilling disrespect; indeed, I saw you not.

THOR. 'Tis well; I hope you were better employed in viewing of yourself. Your journey's long, your time for preparation almost spent. I sent a reverend divine to teach you to improve it, and should be glad to hear of his success.

BARN. The word of truth, which he recommended for my constant companion in this my sad retirement, has at length removed the doubts I laboured under. From thence I've learned the infinite extent of heavenly mercy; that my offences, though great, are not unpardonable; and that 'tis not my interest only, but my duty, to believe and to rejoice in that hope: so shall heaven receive the glory, and future penitents the profit of my example.

THOR. Proceed.

BARN. 'Tis wonderful that words should charm despair, speak peace and pardon to a murderer's conscience; but truth and mercy flow in every sentence, attended with force and energy divine. How shall I describe my present state of mind? I hope in doubt, and trembling I rejoice; I feel my grief increase, even as my fears give way. Joy and gratitude now supply more tears than the horror and anguish of despair before.

THOR.   These are the genuine signs of true repentance, the only preparatory, the certain way to everlasting peace. Oh, the joy it gives to see a soul formed and prepared for heaven! For this the faithful minister devotes himself to meditation, abstinence, and prayer, shunning the vain delights of sensual joys, and daily dies that others may live forever. For this he turns the sacred volumes o'er, and spends his life in painful search of truth. The love of riches and the lust of power, he looks upon with just contempt and detestation, who only counts for wealth the souls he wins, and whose highest ambition is to serve mankind. If the reward of all his pains be to preserve one soul from wandering, or turn one from the error of his ways, how does he then rejoice, and own his little labours overpaid!

BARN.   What do I owe for all your generous kindness? But though I cannot, heaven can and will reward you.

THOR.   To see thee thus is joy too great for words. Farewell! heaven strengthen thee! Farewell!

BARN.   O Sir! there's something I would say if my sad, swelling heart would give me leave.

THOR.   Give it vent a while and try.

BARN.   I had a friend—'tis true I am unworthy, yet methinks your generous example might persuade—could I not see him once before I go from whence there's no return?

THOR.   He's coming, and as much thy friend as ever. (aside) But I'll not anticipate his sorrow; too soon he'll see the sad effect of his contagious ruin. This torrent of domestic misery bears too hard upon me; I must retire to indulge a weakness I find impossible to overcome.——Much loved, and much lamented youth, farewell! Heaven strengthen thee! Eternally farewell!

BARN.   The best of masters and of men, farewell! While I live, let me not want your prayers!

THOR.   Thou shalt not: thy peace being made with heaven, death's already vanquished; bear a little longer the pains that attend this transitory life, and cease from pain forever.

(*Exit* THOROWGOOD)

BARN. Perhaps I shall. I find a power within that bears my soul above the fears of death, and, spite of conscious shame and guilt, gives me a taste of pleasure more than mortal.

Enter TRUEMAN *and Keeper*

KEEP. Sir, there's the prisoner.   (*Exit Keeper*)

BARN. Trueman—my friend, whom I so wished to see! yet now he's here I dare not look upon him. (*weeps*)

TR. O Barnwell! Barnwell!

BARN. Mercy, mercy, gracious heaven! for death, but not for this, I was prepared.

TR. What have I suffered since I saw you last! What pain hath absence given me! But oh! to see thee thus!

BARN. I know it is dreadful! I feel the anguish of thy generous soul—but I was born to murder all who love me. (*both weep*)

TR. I came not to reproach you; I thought to bring you comfort, but I'm deceived, for I have none to give; I came to share thy sorrow, but cannot bear my own.

BARN. My sense of guilt, indeed, you cannot know; 'tis what the good and innocent, like you, can ne'er conceive. But other griefs at present I have none but what I feel for you. In your sorrow I read you love me still; but yet methinks 'tis strange, when I consider what I am.

TR. No more of that! I can remember nothing but thy virtues, thy honest, tender friendship, our former happy state, and present misery. Oh, had you trusted me when first the fair seducer tempted you, all might have been prevented.

BARN. Alas, thou knowest not what a wretch I've been! Breach of friendship was my first and least offence: so far was I lost to goodness, so devoted to the author of my ruin, that, had she insisted on my murdering thee, I think I should have done it.

TR. Prithee, aggravate thy faults no more!

BARN. I think I should!—thus good and generous as you are, I should have murdered you!

TR. We have not yet embraced, and may be interrupted. Come to my arms!

BARN. Never! never will I taste such joys on earth; never will I so soothe my just remorse. Are these honest arms and faithful bosom fit to embrace and to support a murderer? These iron fetters only shall clasp, and flinty pavement bear me (*throwing himself on the ground*)—even these too good for such a bloody monster.

TR. Shall fortune sever those whom friendship joined? Thy miseries cannot lay thee so low but love will find thee. Here will we offer to stern calamity, this place the altar, and ourselves the sacrifice! Our mutual groans shall echo to each other through the dreary vault; our sighs shall number the moments as they pass, and mingling tears communicate such anguish as words were never made to express.

BARN. Then be it so! (*rising*) Since you propose an intercourse of woe, pour all your griefs into my breast, and in exchange take mine! (*embracing*) Where's now the anguish that you promised? You've taken mine and make me no return. Sure, peace and comfort dwell within these arms, and sorrow can't approach me while I'm here. This too is the work of heaven, which, having before spoke peace and pardon to me, now sends thee to confirm it. Oh, take, take some of the joy that overflows my breast!

TR. I do, I do. Almighty Power, how hast thou made us capable to bear, at once, the extremes of pleasure and of pain!

Enter Keeper

KEEP. Sir.

TR. I come.   (*Exit Keeper*)

BARN. Must you leave me? Death would soon have parted us forever.

TR. O my Barnwell! there's yet another task behind; again your heart must bleed for others' woes.

BARN. To meet and part with you, I thought was all I had to do on earth. What is there more for me to do or suffer?

TR. I dread to tell thee, yet it must be known. Maria——

BARN. Our master's fair and virtuous daughter?

TR. The same.

BARN. No misfortune, I hope, has reached that lovely maid! Preserve her, heaven, from every ill, to show mankind that goodness is your care!

TR. Thy, thy misfortunes, my unhappy friend, have reached her. Whatever you and I have felt, and more, if more be possible, she feels for you.

BARN. (*aside*) I know he doth abhor a lie and would not trifle with his dying friend.——This is, indeed, the bitterness of death!

TR.   You must remember, for we all observed it, for some time past a heavy melancholy weighed her down. Disconsolate she seemed, and pined and languished from a cause unknown, till, hearing of your dreadful fate, the long stifled flame blazed out: she wept, she wrung her hands, and tore her hair, and in the transport of her grief discovered her own lost state whilst she lamented yours.

BARN.   Will all the pain I feel restore thy ease, lovely, unhappy maid? (*weeping*) Why did you not let me die and never know it?

TR.   It was impossible; she makes no secret of her passion for you, and is determined to see you ere you die. She waits for me to introduce her.   (*Exit* TRUEMAN)

BARN.   Vain, busy thoughts, be still! What avails it to think on what I might have been? I now am—what I've made myself.

Enter TRUEMAN *with* MARIA

TR.   Madam, reluctant I lead you to this dismal scene. This is the seat of misery and guilt. Here awful justice reserves her public victims. This is the entrance to shameful death.

MA.   To this sad place, then no improper guest, the abandoned, lost Maria brings despair—and see the subject and the cause of all this world of woe! Silent and motionless he stands, as if his soul had quitted her abode and the lifeless form alone was left behind, yet that so perfect that beauty and death, ever at enmity, now seem united there.

BARN.   I groan but murmur not. Just heaven, I am your own; do with me what you please.

MA.   Why are your streaming eyes still fixed below, as though thou'dst give the greedy earth thy sorrows and rob me of my due? Were happiness within your power, you should bestow it where you pleased; but in your misery I must and will partake.

BARN.   Oh! say not so, but fly, abhor, and leave me to my fate! Consider what you are—how vast your fortune, and how bright your fame; have pity on your youth, your beauty, and unequalled virtue, for which so many noble peers have sighed in vain! Bless with your charms some honourable lord; adorn with your beauty and by your example improve the English court, that justly claims such merit; so shall I quickly be to you—as though I had never been.

MA. When I forget you, I must be so, indeed. Reason, choice, virtue, all forbid it. Let women like Millwood, if there are more such women, smile in prosperity and in adversity forsake. Be it the pride of virtue to repair, or to partake, the ruin such have made.

TR. Lovely, ill-fated maid! Was there ever such generous distress before? How must this pierce his grateful heart, and aggravate his woes!

BARN. Ere I knew guilt or shame, when fortune smiled, and when my youthful hopes were at the highest—if then to have raised my thoughts to you had been presumption in me, never to have been pardoned, think how much beneath yourself you condescend, to regard me now!

MA. Let her blush who, proffering love, invades the freedom of your sex's choice, and meanly sues in hopes of a return! Your inevitable fate hath rendered hope impossible as vain. Then why should I fear to avow a passion so just and so disinterested?

TR. If any should take occasion from Millwood's crimes to libel the best and fairest part of the creation, here let them see their error! The most distant hopes of such a tender passion from so bright a maid might add to the happiness of the most happy, and make the greatest proud. Yet here 'tis lavished in vain: though by the rich present the generous donor is undone, he on whom it is bestowed receives no benefit.

BARN. So the aromatic spices of the East, which all the living covet and esteem, are, with unavailing kindness, wasted on the dead.

MA. Yes, fruitless is my love, and unavailing all my sighs and tears. Can they save thee from approaching death—from such a death? Oh, terrible idea! What is her misery and distress, who sees the first, last object of her love, for whom alone she'd live—for whom she'd die a thousand, thousand deaths, if it were possible—expiring in her arms? Yet she is happy when compared to me. Were millions of worlds mine, I'd gladly give them in exchange for her condition. The most consummate woe is light to mine. The last of curses to other miserable maids is all I ask for my relief, and that's denied me.

TR. Time and reflection cure all ills.

MA. All but this; his dreadful catastrophe, virtue herself abhors. To give a holiday to suburb slaves, and passing entertain the savage herd, who, elbowing each other for a sight, pursue and press upon him like his fate! A mind with piety

and resolution armed may smile on death. But public ig-
nominy, everlasting shame—shame, the death of souls, to die
a thousand times, and yet survive even death itself, in never-
dying infamy—is this to be endured? Can I, who live in him,
and must, each hour of my devoted life, feel all these woes
renewed—can I endure this?

TR. Grief has so impaired her spirits, she pants as in the
agonies of death.

BARN. Preserve her, heaven, and restore her peace, nor
let her death be added to my crimes! (*Bell tolls*) I am summoned to my fate.

Enter Keeper and Officers

KEEP. Sir, the officers attend you; Millwood is already
summoned.

BARN. Tell 'em I'm ready.——And now, my friend, farewell! (*embracing*) Support and comfort the best you can this
mourning fair. No more! Forget not to pray for me!——
(*turning to* MARIA) Would you, bright excellence, permit me
the honour of a chaste embrace, the last happiness this world
could give were mine. (*She inclines toward him; they embrace*) Exalted goodness! Oh, turn your eyes from earth and
me to heaven, where virtue like yours is ever heard. Pray for
the peace of my departing soul! Early my race of wickedness
began, and soon reached the summit. Ere nature has finished
her work and stamped me man—just at the time that others
begin to stray—my course is finished. Though short my span
of life, and few my days, yet count my crimes for years, and
I have lived whole ages. Thus justice, in compassion to mankind, cuts off a wretch like me, by one such example to secure
thousands from future ruin. Justice and mercy are in heaven
the same: its utmost severity is mercy to the whole, thereby to
cure man's folly and presumption, which else would render
even infinite mercy vain and ineffectual.

> If any youth, like you, in future times,
> Shall mourn my fate, tho' he abhor my crimes;
> Or tender maid, like you, my tale shall hear,
> And to my sorrows give a pitying tear:
> To each such melting eye and throbbing heart
> Would gracious heaven this benefit impart,
> Never to know my guilt nor feel my pain, ⎫
> Then must you own, you ought not to complain; ⎬
> Since you nor weep, nor shall I die, in vain. ⎭

(*Exeunt*)

SCENE THE LAST

SCENE: *The place of execution. The gallows and ladders at
the farther end of the stage. A crowd of spectators*
BLUNT *and* LUCY

LUCY.   Heavens! What a throng!

BLUNT.   How terrible is death when thus prepared!

LUCY.   Support them, heaven; thou only canst support
them; all other help is vain.

OFFICER. (*within*)   Make way there; make way, and give
the prisoners room!

LUCY.   They are here: observe them well. How humble
and composed young Barnwell seems! But Millwood looks
wild, ruffled with passion, confounded and amazed.

Enter BARNWELL, MILLWOOD, *Officers and Executioner*

BARN.   See, Millwood, see, our journey's at an end. Life,
like a tale that's told, is passed away; that short, but dark and
unknown passage, death, is all the space 'tween us and endless joys, or woes eternal.

MILL.   Is this the end of all my flattering hopes? Were
youth and beauty given me for a curse, and wisdom only to
insure my ruin? They were, they were. Heaven, thou hast
done thy worst. Or if thou hast in store some untried plague,
somewhat that's worse than shame, despair and death, unpitied death, confirmed despair and soul-confounding shame
—something that men and angels can't describe, and only
fiends, who bear it, can conceive—now, pour it now, on this
devoted head, that I may feel the worst thou canst inflict and
bid defiance to thy utmost power.

BARN.   Yet ere we pass the dreadful gulf of death, yet ere
you're plunged in everlasting woe, oh, bend your stubborn
knees and harder heart, humbly to deprecate the wrath divine.
Who knows but heaven, in your dying moments, may bestow
that grace and mercy which your life despised?

MILL.   Why name you mercy to a wretch like me? Mercy's
beyond my hope, almost beyond my wish. I can't repent, nor
ask to be forgiven.

BARN.   Oh, think what 'tis to be for ever, ever miserable;
nor with vain pride oppose a power that's able to destroy you.

MILL.   That will destroy me: I feel it will. A deluge of
wrath is pouring on my soul. Chains, darkness, wheels, racks,

sharp stinging scorpions, molten lead, and seas of sulphur are light to what I feel.

BARN. Oh! add not to your vast account despair—a sin more injurious to heaven than all you've yet committed.

MILL. Oh! I have sinned beyond the reach of mercy.

BARN. Oh, say not so: 'tis blasphemy to think it. As yon bright roof is higher than the earth, so and much more does heaven's goodness pass our apprehension. Oh, what created being shall presume to circumscribe mercy, that knows no bounds?

MILL. This yields no hope. Though mercy may be boundless, yet 'tis free: and I was doomed, before the world began, to endless pains, and thou to joys eternal.

BARN. O gracious heaven! extend thy pity to her: let thy rich mercy flow in plenteous streams to chase her fears and heal her wounded soul.

MILL. It will not be. Your prayers are lost in air, or else returned perhaps with double blessings to your bosom, but me they help not.

BARN. Yet hear me, Millwood!

MILL. Away! I will not hear thee: I tell thee, youth, I am by heaven devoted a dreadful instance of its power to punish. (BARNWELL *seems to pray*) If thou wilt pray, pray for thyself, not me.——How doth his fervent soul mount with his words, and both ascend to heaven! that heaven, whose gates are shut with adamantine bars against my prayers, had I the will to pray. I cannot bear it—sure, 'tis the worst of torments to behold others enjoy that bliss that we must never taste.

OFFICER. The utmost limit of your time's expired.

MILL. Encompassed with horror, whither must I go? I would not live—nor die. That I could cease to be!—or ne'er had been!

BARN. Since peace and comfort are denied her here, may she find mercy where she least expects it, and this be all her hell. From our example may all be taught to fly the first approach of vice; but, if o'ertaken

By strong temptation, weakness, or surprise,
Lament their guilt, and by repentance rise.
Th' impenitent alone die unforgiven;
To sin's like man, and to forgive like heaven.

(BARNWELL *and* MILLWOOD *are conducted toward the gallows*)

Enter TRUEMAN

LUCY.   Heart-breaking sight! O wretched, wretched Mill-wood!

TR.   How is she disposed to meet her fate?

BLUNT.   Who can describe unutterable woe?

LUCY.   She goes to death encompassed with horror, loathing life, and yet afraid to die; no tongue can tell her anguish and despair.

TR.   Heaven be better to her than her fears! May she prove a warning to others, a monument of mercy in herself!

LUCY.   Oh, sorrow insupportable! break, break, my heart!

TR.   In vain
With bleeding hearts and weeping eyes we show
A human, gen'rous sense of others' woe,
Unless we mark what drew their ruin on,
And, by avoiding that—prevent our own.   (*Exeunt*)

EPILOGUE

Written by COLLEY CIBBER, ESQ., POET LAUREATE, *and spoken by* MARIA

Since fate has robb'd me of the hapless youth
For whom my heart had hoarded up its truth,
By all the laws of love and honour, now
I'm free again to choose—and one of you.
  But soft—with caution first I'll round me peep;
Maids, in my case, should look before they leap.
Here's choice enough, of various sorts and hue,
The cit, the wit, the rake cocked up in cue,
The fair, spruce mercer, and the tawny Jew.
  Suppose I search the sober gallery—no,
There's none but prentices—and cuckolds all a-row;
And these, I doubt (*pointing to the boxes*), are those that
    make 'em so.
  'Tis very well, enjoy the jest! But you,
Fine, powdered sparks—nay, I'm told 'tis true—
Your happy spouses—can make cuckolds too.
'Twixt you and them, the diff'rence this perhaps:
The cit's asham'd whene'er his duck he traps;
But you, when madam's tripping, let her fall,
Cock up your hats, and take no shame at all.

What if some favour'd poet I could meet,
Whose love would lay his laurels at my feet?
No; painted passion real love abhors:
His flame would prove the suit of creditors.

Not to detain you, then, with longer pause,
In short, my heart to this conclusion draws:
I yield it to the hand that's loudest in applause.

She Stoops to Conquer:

OR,

The Mistakes of a Night

BY OLIVER GOLDSMITH

PROLOGUE

By DAVID GARRICK, ESQ.

Enter CAPTAIN ABSOLUTE,

Dressed in black, and holding a handkerchief to his eyes

Excuse me, sirs, I pray—I can't yet speak—
I'm crying now—and have been all the week!
'Tis not alone this mourning suit, good masters;
I've that within—for which there are no plasters!
Pray would you know the reason why I'm crying?

The Comic Muse, long sick, is now a-dying!
And if she goes, my tears will never stop;
For, as a play'r, I can't squeeze out one drop:
I am undone, that's all—shall lose my bread—
I'd rather, but that's nothing—lose my head.
When the sweet maid is laid upon the bier,
Shuter and *I* shall be chief mourners here.
To *her* a mawkish drab of spurious breed,
Who deals in *sentimentals,* will succeed!
Poor *Ned* and *I* are dead to all intents,
We can as soon speak *Greek* as *sentiments!*
Both nervous grown, to keep our spirits up,
We now and then take down a hearty cup.
What shall we do?—If Comedy forsake us!
They'll turn us out, and no one else will take us,
But why can't I be moral?—Let me try—
My heart thus pressing—fix'd my face and eye—
With a sententious look, that nothing means
(Faces are blocks in sentimental scenes),
Thus I begin—— *All is not gold that glitters,*
Pleasure seems sweet, but proves a glass of bitters.
When ign'rance enters, folly is at hand;
Learning is better far than house and land.
Let not your virtue trip, who trips may stumble,
And virtue is not virtue, if she tumble.
    I give it up—morals won't do for me;
To make you laugh, I must play tragedy.
One hope remains—hearing the maid was ill,
A *doctor* comes this night to show his skill.
To cheer her heart, and give your muscles motion,
He, in *five draughts* prepared, presents a potion:
A kind of magic charm—for, be assur'd,
If you will *swallow it,* the maid is cur'd:
But desp'rate the Doctor, and her case is,
If you reject the dose, and make wry faces!
This truth he boasts, will boast it while he lives,
No *pois'nous drugs* are mix'd in what he gives.
Should he succeed, you'll give him his degree;
If not, within he will receive no fee!
The college *you,* must his pretensions back,
Pronounce him *regular,* or dub him *quack.*

DRAMATIS PERSONÆ

Men:

SIR CHARLES MARLOW
CHARLES MARLOW (*his Son*)
RICHARD HARDCASTLE
GEORGE HASTINGS
TONY LUMPKIN
DIGGORY

Women:

MRS. HARDCASTLE
MISS KATE HARDCASTLE
MISS CONSTANCE NEVILLE
MAID

Landlords, Servants, &c., &c.

SHE STOOPS TO CONQUER

OR

THE MISTAKES OF A NIGHT

ACT I

SCENE I

SCENE: *A chamber in an old-fashioned house*

Enter MRS. HARDCASTLE *and* MR. HARDCASTLE

MRS. HARD. I vow, Mr. Hardcastle, you're very particular. Is there a creature in the whole country, but ourselves, that does not take a trip to town now and then, to rub off the rust a little? There's the two Miss Hoggs, and our neighbour, Mrs. Grigsby, go to take a month's polishing every winter.

HARD. Ay, and bring back vanity and affectation to last them the whole year. I wonder why London cannot keep its own fools at home. In my time, the follies of the town crept slowly among us, but now they travel faster than a stage-coach. Its fopperies come down, not only as inside passengers, but in the very basket.

MRS. HARD. Ay, *your* times were fine times indeed; you have been telling us of *them* for many a long year. Here we live in an old rumbling mansion, that looks for all the world like an inn, but that we never see company. Our best visitors are old Mrs. Oddfish, the curate's wife, and little Cripplegate, the lame dancing-master: and all our entertainment your old stories of Prince Eugene and the Duke of Marlborough. I hate such old-fashioned trumpery.

HARD. And I love it. I love everything that's old: old friends, old times, old manners, old books, old wine; and, I believe, Dorothy (*taking her hand*) you'll own I have been pretty fond of an old wife.

MRS. HARD. Lord, Mr. Hardcastle, you're forever at your Dorothy's and your old wife's. You may be a Darby, but I'll be no Joan, I promise you. I'm not so old as you'd make me,

347

by more than one good year. Add twenty to twenty, and make money of that.

HARD. Let me see; twenty added to twenty—makes just fifty and seven.

MRS. HARD. It's false, Mr. Hardcastle: I was but twenty when I was brought to bed of Tony, that I had by Mr. Lumpkin, my first husband; and he's not come to years of discretion yet.

HARD. Nor ever will, I dare answer for him. Ay, you have taught *him* finely!

MRS. HARD. No matter. Tony Lumpkin has a good fortune. My son is not to live by his learning. I don't think a boy wants much learning to spend fifteen hundred a year.

HARD. Learning, quotha! A mere composition of tricks and mischief.

MRS. HARD. Humour, my dear; nothing but humour. Come, Mr. Hardcastle, you must allow the boy a little humour.

HARD. I'd sooner allow him a horse-pond. If burning the footmen's shoes, frighting the maids, and worrying the kittens, be humour, he has it. It was but yesterday he fastened my wig to the back of my chair, and when I went to make a bow, I popped my bald head in Mrs. Frizzle's face.

MRS. HARD. And am I to blame? The poor boy was always too sickly to do any good. A school would be his death. When he comes to be a little stronger, who knows what a year or two's Latin may do for him?

HARD. Latin for him! A cat and fiddle! No, no, the alehouse and the stable are the only schools he'll ever go to.

MRS. HARD. Well, we must not snub the poor boy now, for I believe we shan't have him long among us. Anybody that looks in his face may see he's consumptive.

HARD. Ay, if growing too fat be one of the symptoms.

MRS. HARD. He coughs sometimes.

HARD. Yes, when his liquor goes the wrong way.

MRS. HARD. I'm actually afraid of his lungs.

HARD. And truly, so am I; for he sometimes whoops like a speaking trumpet—(TONY *hallooing behind the scenes*)— Oh, there he goes——A very consumptive figure, truly!

Enter TONY, *crossing the stage*

MRS. HARD. Tony, where are you going, my charmer? Won't you give papa and I a little of your company, lovee?

TONY. I'm in haste, Mother, I cannot stay.

MRS. HARD. You shan't venture out this raw evening, my dear: you look most shockingly.

TONY. I can't stay, I tell you. "The Three Pigeons" expects me down every moment. There's some fun going forward.

HARD. Ay; the ale-house, the old place: I thought so.

MRS. HARD. A low, paltry set of fellows.

TONY. Not so low, neither. There's Dick Muggins, the exciseman; Jack Slang, the horse-doctor; little Aminadab, that grinds the music-box; and Tom Twist, that spins the pewter platter.

MRS. HARD. Pray, my dear, disappoint them for one night at least.

TONY. As for disappointing *them*, I should not so much mind; but I can't abide to disappoint *myself*.

MRS. HARD. (*detaining him*) You shan't go.

TONY. I will, I tell you.

MRS. HARD. I say you shan't.

TONY. We'll see which is strongest, you or I.

(*Exit, hauling her out*)

HARDCASTLE *solus*

HARD. Ay, there goes a pair that only spoil each other. But is not the whole age in a combination to drive sense and discretion out of doors? There's my pretty darling, Kate; the fashions of the times have almost infected her too. By living a year or two in town, she is as fond of gauze, and French frippery, as the best of them.

Enter MISS HARDCASTLE

Blessings on my pretty innocence! Dressed out as usual, my Kate. Goodness! what a quantity of superfluous silk hast thou got about thee, girl! I could never teach the fools of this age that the indigent world could be clothed out of the trimmings of the vain.

MISS HARD. You know our agreement, Sir. You allow me the morning to receive and pay visits, and to dress in my own manner; and in the evening, I put on my housewife's dress to please you.

HARD. Well, remember, I insist on the terms of our agreement; and, by the bye, I believe I shall have occasion to try your obedience this very evening.

MISS HARD. I protest, Sir, I don't comprehend your meaning.

HARD. Then, to be plain with you, Kate, I expect the

young gentleman I have chosen to be your husband from town this very day. I have his father's letter, in which he informs me his son is set out, and that he intends to follow himself shortly after.

MISS HARD.   Indeed! I wish I had known something of this before. Bless me, how shall I behave? It's a thousand to one I shan't like him; our meeting will be so formal, and so like a thing of business, that I shall find no room for friendship or esteem.

HARD.   Depend upon it, child, I'll never control your choice; but Mr. Marlow, whom I have pitched upon, is the son of my old friend, Sir Charles Marlow, of whom you have heard me talk so often. The young gentleman has been bred a scholar, and is designed for an employment in the service of his country. I am told he's a man of an excellent understanding.

MISS HARD.   Is he?

HARD.   Very generous.

MISS HARD.   I believe I shall like him.

HARD.   Young and brave.

MISS HARD.   I'm sure I shall like him.

HARD.   And very handsome.

MISS HARD.   My dear papa, say no more, (*kissing his hand*) he's mine, I'll have him!

HARD.   And, to crown all, Kate, he's one of the most bashful and reserved young fellows in all the world.

MISS HARD.   Eh! you have frozen me to death again. That word "reserved" has undone all the rest of his accomplishments. A reserved lover, it is said, always makes a suspicious husband.

HARD.   On the contrary, modesty seldom resides in a breast that is not enriched with nobler virtues. It was the very feature in his character that first struck me.

MISS HARD.   He must have more striking features to catch me, I promise you. However, if he be so young, so handsome, and so everything, as you mention, I believe he'll do still. I think I'll have him.

HARD.   Ay, Kate, but there is still an obstacle. It's more than an even wager he may not have *you*.

MISS HARD.   My dear papa, why will you mortify one so? —— Well, if he refuses, instead of breaking my heart at his indifference, I'll only break my glass for its flattery, set my cap to some new fashion, and look out for some less difficult admirer.

HARD.   Bravely resolved! In the meantime, I'll go prepare the servants for his reception; as we seldom see company, they want as much training as a company of recruits the first day's muster.   (*Exit*)

MISS HARDCASTLE *sola*

MISS HARD.   Lud, this news of papa's puts me all in a flutter. "Young, handsome"; these he put last, but I put them foremost. "Sensible, good-natured"; I like all that. But then, "reserved," and "sheepish"; that's much against him. Yet, can't he be cured of his timidity by being taught to be proud of his wife? Yes, and can't I—— But I vow I'm disposing of the husband, before I have secured the lover.

Enter MISS NEVILLE

MISS HARD.   I'm glad you're come, Neville, my dear. Tell me, Constance, how do I look this evening? Is there anything whimsical about me? Is it one of my well-looking days, child? Am I in face to-day?

MISS NEV.   Perfectly, my dear. Yet, now I look again— bless me!—sure, no accident has happened among the canary birds or the gold-fishes? Has your brother or the cat been meddling? Or has the last novel been too moving?

MISS HARD.   No; nothing of all this. I have been threat-ened—I can scarce get it out—I have been threatened with a lover.

MISS NEV.   And his name——

MISS HARD.   Is Marlow.

MISS NEV.   Indeed!

MISS HARD.   The son of Sir Charles Marlow.

MISS NEV.   As I live, the most intimate friend of Mr. Hastings, *my* admirer. They are never asunder. I believe you must have seen him when we lived in town.

MISS HARD.   Never.

MISS NEV.   He's a very singular character, I assure you. Among women of reputation and virtue, he is the modestest man alive; but his acquaintance give him a very different character among creatures of another stamp: you understand me.

MISS HARD.   An odd character, indeed! I shall never be able to manage him. What shall I do? Pshaw, think no more of him, but trust to occurrences for success. But how goes on your own affair, my dear? Has my mother been courting you for my brother Tony, as usual?

MISS NEV. I have just come from one of our agreeable *tête-à-têtes*. She has been saying a hundred tender things, and setting off her pretty monster as the very pink of perfection.

MISS HARD. And her partiality is such that she actually thinks him so. A fortune like yours is no small temptation. Besides, as she has the sole management of it, I'm not surprised to see her unwilling to let it go out of the family.

MISS NEV. A fortune like mine, which chiefly consists in jewels, is no such mighty temptation. But at any rate, if my dear Hastings be but constant, I make no doubt to be too hard for her at last. However, I let her suppose that I am in love with her son, and she never once dreams that my affections are fixed upon another.

MISS HARD. My good brother holds out stoutly. I could almost love him for hating you so.

MISS NEV. It is a good-natured creature at bottom, and I'm sure would wish to see me married to anybody but himself. But my aunt's bell rings for our afternoon's walk round the improvements. *Allons.* Courage is necessary, as our affairs are critical.

MISS HARD. Would it were bedtime, and all were well.

(*Exeunt*)

SCENE II

SCENE: *An ale-house room*

Several shabby fellows with punch and tobacco. TONY *at the head of the table, a little higher than the rest: a mallet in his hand*

OMNES. Hurrea, hurrea, hurrea, bravo!

FIRST FELLOW. Now, gentlemen, silence for a song. The 'Squire is going to knock himself down for a song.

OMNES. Ay, a song, a song.

TONY. Then I'll sing you, gentlemen, a song I made upon this ale-house, "The Three Pigeons."

SONG

Let schoolmasters puzzle their brain,
    With grammar, and nonsense, and learning;
Good liquor, I stoutly maintain,
    Gives *genus* a better discerning.
Let them brag of their heathenish gods,
    Their Lethes, their Styxes, and Stygians;
Their Quis, and their Quæs, and their Quods,
    They're all but a parcel of pigeons.
            Toroddle, toroddle, toroll!

When Methodist preachers come down,
 A-preaching that drinking is sinful,
I'll wager the rascals a crown,
 They always preach best with a skinful.
But when you come down with your pence,
 For a slice of their scurvy religion,
I'll leave it to all men of sense,
 But you, my good friend, are the pigeon.
       Toroddle, toroddle, toroll!

Then come, put the jorum about,
 And let us be merry and clever,
Our hearts and our liquors are stout,
 Here's the Three Jolly Pigeons forever.
Let some cry up woodcock or hare,
 Your bustards, your ducks, and your widgeons;
But of all the birds in the air,
 Here's a health to the Three Jolly Pigeons.
       Toroddle, toroddle, toroll!

OMNES. Bravo, bravo!

FIRST FELLOW. The 'Squire has got spunk in him.

SECOND FEL. I loves to hear him sing, bekeays he never gives us nothing that's *low.*

THIRD FEL. Oh, damn anything that's *low,* I cannot bear it!

FOURTH FEL. The genteel thing is the genteel thing at any time; if so be that a gentleman bees in a concatenation accordingly.

THIRD FEL. I like the maxum of it, Master Muggins. What, though I am obligated to dance a bear, a man may be a gentleman for all that. May this be my poison, if my bear ever dances but to the very genteelest of tunes: *Water Parted,* or the minuet in *Ariadne.*

SECOND FEL. What a pity it is the 'Squire is not come to his own. It would be well for all the publicans within ten miles round of him.

TONY. Ecod, and so it would, Master Slang. I'd then show what it was to keep choice of company.

SECOND FEL. Oh, he takes after his own father for that. To be sure, old 'Squire Lumpkin was the finest gentleman I ever set my eyes on. For winding the straight horn, or beating a thicket for a hare, or a wench, he never had his fellow. It was a saying in the place, that he kept the best horses, dogs, and girls, in the whole county.

TONY. Ecod, and when I'm of age I'll be no bastard, I promise you. I have been thinking of Bet Bouncer and the miller's grey mare to begin with. But come, my boys, drink about and be merry, for you pay no reckoning. Well, Stingo, what's the matter?

Enter Landlord

LAND.   There be two gentlemen in a post-chaise at the door. They have lost their way upo' the forest; and they are talking something about Mr. Hardcastle.

TONY.   As sure as can be, one of them must be the gentleman that's coming down to court my sister. Do they seem to be Londoners?

LAND.   I believe they may. They look woundily like Frenchmen.

TONY.   Then desire them to step this way, and I'll set them right in a twinkling. (*Exit Landlord*) Gentlemen, as they mayn't be good enough company for you, step down for a moment, and I'll be with you in the squeezing of a lemon.   (*Exeunt mob*)

TONY *solus*

TONY.   Father-in-law has been calling me whelp, and hound, this half year. Now, if I pleased, I could be so re-venged upon the old grumbletonian. But then I'm afraid— afraid of what! I shall soon be worth fifteen hundred a year, and let him frighten me out of *that* if he can.

Enter Landlord, conducting MARLOW *and* HASTINGS

MARL.   What a tedious, uncomfortable day have we had of it! We were told it was but forty miles across the country, and we have come above threescore.

HAST.   And all, Marlow, from that unaccountable reserve of yours, that would not let us enquire more frequently on the way.

MARL.   I own, Hastings, I am unwilling to lay myself un-der an obligation to everyone I meet, and often stand the chance of an unmannerly answer.

HAST.   At present, however, we are not likely to receive any answer.

TONY.   No offence, gentlemen. But I'm told you have been enquiring for one Mr. Hardcastle, in these parts. Do you know what part of the country you are in?

HAST.   Not in the least, Sir, but should thank you for in-formation.

TONY. Nor the way you came?

HAST. No, Sir; but if you can inform us——

TONY. Why, gentlemen, if you know neither the road you are going, nor where you are, nor the road you came, the first thing I have to inform you is, that—you have lost your way.

MARL. We wanted no ghost to tell us that.

TONY. Pray, gentlemen, may I be so bold as to ask the place from whence you came?

MARL. That's not necessary towards directing us where we are to go.

TONY. No offence; but question for question is all fair, you know. Pray, gentlemen, is not this same Hardcastle a cross-grained, old-fashioned, whimsical fellow, with an ugly face, a daughter, and a pretty son?

HAST. We have not seen the gentleman, but he has the family you mention.

TONY. The daughter, a tall, trapesing, trolloping, talkative maypole—the son, a pretty, well-bred, agreeable youth, that everybody is fond of.

MARL. Our information differs in this. The daughter is said to be well-bred, and beautiful; the son, an awkward booby, reared up and spoiled at his mother's apron-string.

TONY. He-he-hem—— Then, gentlemen, all I have to tell you is, that you won't reach Mr. Hardcastle's house this night, I believe.

HAST. Unfortunate!

TONY. It's a damned long, dark, boggy, dirty, dangerous way. Stingo, tell the gentlemen the way to Mr. Hardcastle's; (*winking upon the Landlord*) Mr. Hardcastle's, of Quagmire Marsh, you understand me.

LAND. Master Hardcastle's! Lack-a-daisy, my masters, you're come a deadly deal wrong! When you came to the bottom of the hill, you should have crossed down Squash-lane.

MARL. Cross down Squash-lane!

LAND. Then you were to keep straight forward, till you came to four roads.

MARL. Come to where four roads meet!

TONY. Ay; but you must be sure to take only one of them.

MARL. O Sir, you're facetious.

TONY. Then, keeping to the right, you are to go sideways till you come upon Crack-skull Common: there you must look sharp for the track of the wheel, and go forward, till you come to farmer Murrain's barn. Coming to the farmer's barn, you are to turn to the right, and then to the left, and then to the right about again, till you find out the old mill——

MARL. Zounds, man! we could as soon find out the longitude!

HAST. What's to be done, Marlow?

MARL. This house promises but a poor reception; though perhaps the landlord can accommodate us.

LAND. Alack, Master, we have but one spare bed in the whole house.

TONY. And to my knowledge, that's taken up by three lodgers already. (*after a pause, in which the rest seem disconcerted*) I have hit it. Don't you think, Stingo, our landlady could accommodate the gentlemen by the fireside, with —three chairs and a bolster?

HAST. I hate sleeping by the fireside.

MARL. And I detest your three chairs and a bolster.

TONY. You do, do you?—then, let me see—what—if you go on a mile further, to the Buck's Head; the old Buck's Head on the hill, one of the best inns in the whole county?

HAST. O ho! so we have escaped an adventure for this night, however.

LAND. (*apart to* TONY) Sure, you ben't sending them to your father's as an inn, be you?

TONY. Mum, you fool you. Let *them* find that out. (*to them*) You have only to keep on straight forward, till you come to a large old house by the roadside. You'll see a pair of large horns over the door. That's the sign. Drive up the yard, and call stoutly about you.

HAST. Sir, we are obliged to you. The servants can't miss the way?

TONY. No, no: but I tell you, though, the landlord is rich, and going to leave off business; so he wants to be thought a gentleman, saving your presence, he! he! he! He'll be for giving you his company; and, ecod, if you mind him, he'll persuade you that his mother was an alderman, and his aunt a justice of peace.

LAND. A troublesome old blade, to be sure; but 'a keeps as good wines and beds as any in the whole country.

MARL. Well, if he supplies us with these, we shall want no further connection. We are to turn to the right, did you say?

TONY.   No, no; straight forward. I'll just step myself, and show you a piece of the way. (*to the Landlord*) Mum!

LAND.   Ah, bless your heart, for a sweet, pleasant—damned mischievous son of a whore.   (*Exeunt*)

ACT II

SCENE: *An old-fashioned house*

Enter HARDCASTLE, *followed by three or four awkward Servants*

HARD.   Well, I hope you're perfect in the table exercise I have been teaching you these three days. You all know your posts and your places, and can show that you have been used to good company, without ever stirring from home.

OMNES.   Ay, ay.

HARD.   When company comes, you are not to pop out and stare, and then run in again, like frighted rabbits in a warren.

OMNES.   No, no.

HARD.   You, Diggory, whom I have taken from the barn, are to make a show at the side-table; and you, Roger, whom I have advanced from the plough, are to place yourself behind *my* chair. But you're not to stand so, with your hands in your pockets. Take your hands from your pockets, Roger; and from your head, you blockhead, you. See how Diggory carries his hands. They're a little too stiff, indeed, but that's no great matter.

DIGG.   Ay, mind how I hold them. I learned to hold my hands this way, when I was upon drill for the militia. And so being upon drill——

HARD.   You must not be so talkative, Diggory. You must be all attention to the guests. You must hear us talk, and not think of talking; you must see us drink, and not think of drinking; you must see us eat, and not think of eating.

DIGG.   By the laws, your worship, that's parfectly unpossible. Whenever Diggory sees yeating going forward, ecod, he's always wishing for a mouthful himself.

HARD.   Blockhead! Is not a bellyful in the kitchen as good as a bellyful in the parlour? Stay your stomach with that reflection.

DIGG.   Ecod, I thank your worship, I'll make a shift to stay my stomach with a slice of cold beef in the pantry.

HARD. Diggory, you are too talkative. Then, if I happen to say a good thing, or tell a good story at table, you must not all burst out a-laughing, as if you made part of the company.

DIGG. Then, ecod, your worship must not tell the story of Ould Grouse in the gun-room: I can't help laughing at that—he! he! he!—for the soul of me. We have laughed at that these twenty years—ha! ha! ha!

HARD. Ha! ha! ha! The story is a good one. Well, honest Diggory, you may laugh at that—but still remember to be attentive. Suppose one of the company should call for a glass of wine, how will you behave? A glass of wine, Sir, if you please (*to* DIGGORY)——Eh, why don't you move?

DIGG. Ecod, your worship, I never have courage till I see the eatables and drinkables brought upo' the table, and then I'm as bauld as a lion.

HARD. What, will nobody move?

FIRST SERV. I'm not to leave this pleace.

SECOND SERV. I'm sure it's no pleace of mine.

THIRD SERV. Nor mine, for sartain.

DIGG. Wauns, and I'm sure it canna be mine.

HARD. You numskulls! and so while, like your betters, you are quarrelling for places, the guests must be starved. O you dunces! I find I must begin all over again.——But don't I hear a coach drive into the yard? To your posts, you blockheads! I'll go in the meantime, and give my old friend's son a hearty reception at the gate.   (*Exit* HARDCASTLE)

DIGG. By the elevens, my pleace is gone quite out my head!

ROGER. I know that my pleace is to be everywhere.

FIRST SERV. Where the devil is mine?

SECOND SERV. My pleace is to be nowhere at all; and so J'ze go about my business.

(*Exeunt Servants, running about as if frighted, different ways*)

Enter ROGER *with candles, showing in* MARLOW *and* HASTINGS

SERV. Welcome, gentlemen, very welcome. This way.

HAST. After the disappointments of the day, welcome once more, Charles, to the comforts of a clean room and a good fire. Upon my word, a very well-looking house; antique but creditable.

MARL. The usual fate of a large mansion. Having first

ruined the master by good housekeeping, it at last comes to
levy contributions as an inn.

HAST.   As you say, we passengers are to be taxed to pay
all these fineries. I have often seen a good sideboard, or a
marble chimney-piece, though not actually put in the bill,
enflame a reckoning confoundedly.

MARL.   Travellers, George, must pay in all places. The
only difference is that, in good inns, you pay dearly for lux-
uries; in bad inns, you are fleeced and starved.

HAST.   You have lived pretty much among them. In truth,
I have been often surprised that you, who have seen so much
of the world, with your natural good sense, and your many
opportunities, could never yet acquire a requisite share of
assurance.

MARL.   The Englishman's malady. But tell me, George,
where could I have learned that assurance you talk of? My
life has been chiefly spent in a college, or an inn, in seclusion
from that lovely part of the creation that chiefly teach men
confidence. I don't know that I was ever familiarly acquainted
with a single modest woman—except my mother. But among
females of another class, you know——

HAST.   Ay, among them you are impudent enough, of all
conscience.

MARL.   They are of *us*, you know.

HAST.   But in the company of women of reputation I
never saw such an idiot, such a trembler; you look for all the
world as if you wanted an opportunity of stealing out of the
room.

MARL.   Why, man, that's because I *do* want to steal out
of the room. Faith, I have often formed a resolution to break
the ice, and rattle away at any rate. But I don't know how,
a single glance from a pair of fine eyes has totally overset
my resolution. An impudent fellow may counterfeit modesty,
but I'll be hanged if a modest man can ever counterfeit
impudence.

HAST.   If you could but say half the fine things to them
that I have heard you lavish upon the bar-maid of an inn,
or even a college bed-maker——

MARL.   Why, George, I can't say fine things to them. They
freeze, they petrify me. They may talk of a comet, or a burning mountain, or some such bagatelle; but to me a modest
woman, dressed out in all her finery, is the most tremendous
object of the whole creation.

HAST. Ha! ha! ha! At this rate, man, how can you ever expect to marry?

MARL. Never; unless, as among kings and princes, my bride were to be courted by proxy. If, indeed, like an Eastern bridegroom, one were to be introduced to a wife he never saw before, it might be endured. But to go through all the terrors of a formal courtship, together with the episode of aunts, grandmothers, and cousins, and at last to blurt out the broad, staring question of, *Madam, will you marry me?* No, no, that's a strain much above me, I assure you.

HAST. I pity you. But how do you intend behaving to the lady you are come down to visit at the request of your father?

MARL. As I behave to all other ladies. Bow very low; answer yes, or no, to all her demands. But for the rest, I don't think I shall venture to look in her face till I see my father's again.

HAST. I'm surprised that one who is so warm a friend can be so cool a lover.

MARL. To be explicit, my dear Hastings, my chief inducement down was to be instrumental in forwarding your happiness, not my own. Miss Neville loves you; the family don't know you; as my friend, you are sure of a reception; and let honour do the rest.

HAST. My dear Marlow! But I'll suppress the emotion. Were I a wretch, meanly seeking to carry off a fortune, you should be the last man in the world I would apply to for assistance. But Miss Neville's person is all I ask, and that is mine, both from her deceased father's consent, and her own inclination.

MARL. Happy man! you have talents and art to captivate any woman. I'm doomed to adore the sex, and yet to converse with the only part of it I despise. This stammer in my address, and this awkward, unprepossessing visage of mine, can never permit me to soar above the reach of a milliner's 'prentice, or one of the duchesses of Drury Lane. Pshaw! this fellow here to interrupt us.

Enter HARDCASTLE

HARD. Gentlemen, once more you are heartily welcome. Which is Mr. Marlow? Sir, you're heartily welcome. It's not my way, you see, to receive my friends with my back to the fire. I like to give them a hearty reception, in the old style, at my gate. I like to see their horses and trunks taken care of.

MARL. (*aside*) He has got our names from the servants

already. (*to him*) We approve your caution and hospitality, Sir. (*to* HASTINGS) I have been thinking, George, of changing our travelling dresses in the morning. I am grown confoundedly ashamed of mine.

HARD.   I beg, Mr. Marlow, you'll use no ceremony in this house.

HAST.   I fancy, Charles, you're right: the first blow is half the battle. I intend opening the campaign with the white and gold.

HARD.   Mr. Marlow—Mr. Hastings—gentlemen—pray be under no constraint in this house. This is Liberty Hall, gentlemen. You may do just as you please here.

MARL.   Yet, George, if we open the campaign too fiercely at first, we may want ammunition before it is over. I think to reserve the embroidery to secure a retreat.

HARD.   Your talking of a retreat, Mr. Marlow, puts me in mind of the Duke of Marlborough, when we went to besiege Denain. He first summoned the garrison——

MARL.   Don't you think the *ventre d'or* waistcoat will do with the plain brown?

HARD.   He first summoned the garrison, which might consist of about five thousand men——

HAST.   I think not: brown and yellow mix but very poorly.

HARD.   I say, gentlemen, as I was telling you, he summoned the garrison, which might consist of about five thousand men——

MARL.   The girls like finery.

HARD.   Which might consist of about five thousand men, well appointed with stores, ammunition, and other implements of war. "Now," says the Duke of Marlborough to George Brooks, that stood next to him—you must have heard of George Brooks—"I'll pawn my dukedom," says he, "but I take that garrison without spilling a drop of blood." So——

MARL.   What, my good friend, if you gave us a glass of punch in the meantime; it would help us to carry on the siege with vigour.

HARD.   Punch, Sir! (*aside*) This is the most unaccountable kind of modesty I ever met with!

MARL.   Yes, Sir, punch. A glass of warm punch, after our journey, will be comfortable. This is Liberty Hall, you know.

HARD.   Here's cup, Sir.

MARL.   (*aside*) So this fellow, in his Liberty Hall, will only let us have just what he pleases.

HARD.   (*taking the cup*)   I hope you'll find it to your mind.

I have prepared it with my own hands, and I believe you'll own the ingredients are tolerable. Will you be so good as to pledge me, Sir? Here, Mr. Marlow, here is to our better acquaintance. *(drinks)*

MARL. *(aside)* A very impudent fellow this! But he's a character, and I'll humour him a little. Sir, my service to you. *(drinks)*

HAST. *(aside)* I see this fellow wants to give us his company, and forgets that he's an innkeeper before he has learned to be a gentleman.

MARL. From the excellence of your cup, my old friend, I suppose you have a good deal of business in this part of the country. Warm work, now and then, at elections, I suppose.

HARD. No, Sir, I have long given that work over. Since our betters have hit upon the expedient of electing each other, there's no business *for us that sell ale.*

HAST. So, then, you have no turn for politics, I find.

HARD. Not in the least. There was a time, indeed, I fretted myself about the mistakes of government, like other people; but finding myself every day grow more angry, and the government growing no better, I left it to mend itself. Since that, I no more trouble my head about Hyder Ally, or Ally Cawn, than about *Ally Croaker.* Sir, my service to you.

HAST. So that with eating above stairs, and drinking below, with receiving your friends within, and amusing them without, you lead a good, pleasant, bustling life of it.

HARD. I do stir about a great deal, that's certain. Half the differences of the parish are adjusted in this very parlour.

MARL. *(after drinking)* And you have an argument in your cup, old gentleman, better than any in Westminster Hall.

HARD. Ay, young gentleman, that, and a little philosophy.

MARL. *(aside)* Well, this is the first time I ever heard of an innkeeper's philosophy.

HAST. So, then, like an experienced general, you attack them on every quarter. If you find their reason manageable, you attack it with your philosophy; if you find they have no reason, you attack them with this. Here's your health, my philosopher. *(drinks)*

HARD. Good, very good, thank you; ha! ha! Your generalship puts me in mind of Prince Eugene, when he fought the Turks at the battle of Belgrade. You shall hear——

MARL. Instead of the battle of Belgrade, I believe it's

almost time to talk about supper. What has your philosophy got in the house for supper?

HARD. For supper, Sir! (*aside*) Was ever such a request to a man in his own house!

MARL. Yes, Sir, supper, Sir; I begin to feel an appetite. I shall make devilish work to-night in the larder, I promise you.

HARD. (*aside*) Such a brazen dog sure never my eyes beheld. (*to him*) Why, really, Sir, as for supper, I can't well tell. My Dorothy and the cook-maid settle these things between them. I leave these kind of things entirely to them.

MARL. You do, do you?

HARD. Entirely. By the bye, I believe they are in actual consultation upon what's for supper this moment in the kitchen.

MARL. Then I beg they'll admit *me* as one of their privy council. It's a way I have got. When I travel, I always choose to regulate my own supper. Let the cook be called. No offence, I hope, Sir.

HARD. Oh no, Sir, none in the least; yet I don't know how: our Bridget, the cook-maid, is not very communicative upon these occasions. Should we send for her, she might scold us all out of the house.

HAST. Let's see your list of the larder, then. I ask it as a favour. I always match my appetite to my bill of fare.

MARL. (*to* HARDCASTLE, *who looks at them with surprise*) Sir, he's very right, and it's my way, too.

HARD. Sir, you have a right to command here. Here, Roger, bring us the bill of fare for to-night's supper; I believe it's drawn out.   (*Exit* ROGER)
Your manner, Mr. Hastings, puts me in mind of my uncle, Colonel Wallop. It was a saying of his, that no man was sure of his supper till he had eaten it.

HAST. (*aside*) All upon the high ropes! His uncle a colonel! We shall soon hear of his mother being a justice of peace.   (*enter* ROGER *carrying bill of fare*)
But let's hear the bill of fare.

MARL. (*perusing*) What's here? For the first course; for the second course; for the dessert. The devil, Sir, do you think we have brought down the whole Joiners' Company, or the Corporation of Bedford, to eat up such a supper? Two or three little things, clean and comfortable, will do.

HAST. But let's hear it.

MARL. (*reading*) For the first course, at the top, a pig, and pruin sauce.

HAST. Damn your pig, I say!

MARL. And damn your pruin sauce, say I!

HARD. And yet, gentlemen, to men that are hungry, pig with pruin sauce is very good eating.

MARL. At the bottom, a calf's tongue and brains.

HAST. Let your brains be knocked out, my good Sir; I don't like them.

MARL. Or you may clap them on a plate by themselves. I do.

HARD. (*aside*) Their impudence confounds me. (*to them*) Gentlemen, you are my guests; make what alterations you please. Is there anything else you wish to retrench or alter, gentlemen?

MARL. Item: a pork pie, a boiled rabbit and sausages, a florentine, a shaking pudding, and a dish of tiff—taff—taffety cream!

HAST. Confound your made dishes! I shall be as much at a loss in this house as at a green and yellow dinner at the French Ambassador's table. I'm for plain eating.

HARD. I'm sorry, gentlemen, that I have nothing you like; but if there be anything you have a particular fancy to——

MARL. Why, really, Sir, your bill of fare is so exquisite, that any one part of it is full as good as another. Send us what you please. So much for supper. And now to see that our beds are aired, and properly taken care of.

HARD. I entreat you'll leave all that to me. You shall not stir a step.

MARL. Leave that to you! I protest, Sir, you must excuse me; I always look to these things myself.

HARD. I must insist, Sir, you'll make yourself easy on that head.

MARL. You see I'm resolved on it. (*aside*) A very troublesome fellow this, as ever I met with.

HARD. Well, Sir, I'm resolved at least to attend you. (*aside*) This may be modern modesty, but I never saw anything look so like old-fashioned impudence.

(*Exeunt* MARLOW *and* HARDCASTLE)

HASTINGS *solus*

HAST. So I find this fellow's civilities begin to grow troublesome. But who can be angry at those assiduities which are meant to please him? Ha! what do I see? Miss Neville, by all that's happy!

Enter MISS NEVILLE

MISS NEV.   My dear Hastings! To what unexpected good fortune, to what accident, am I to ascribe this happy meeting?

HAST.   Rather let me ask the same question, as I could never have hoped to meet my dearest Constance at an inn.

MISS NEV.   An inn! sure you mistake! My aunt, my guardian, lives here. What could induce you to think this house an inn?

HAST.   My friend, Mr. Marlow, with whom I came down, and I, have been sent here as to an inn, I assure you. A young fellow, whom we accidentally met at a house hard by, directed us hither.

MISS NEV.   Certainly it must be one of my hopeful cousin's tricks, of whom you have heard me talk so often; ha! ha! ha! ha!

HAST.   He whom your aunt intends for you? He of whom I have such just apprehensions?

MISS NEV.   You have nothing to fear from him, I assure you. You'd adore him if you knew how heartily he despises me. My aunt knows it too, and has undertaken to court me for him, and actually begins to think she has made a conquest.

HAST.   Thou dear dissembler! You must know, my Constance, I have just seized this happy opportunity of my friend's visit here to get admittance into the family. The horses that carried us down are now fatigued with their journey, but they'll soon be refreshed; and then, if my dearest girl will trust in her faithful Hastings, we shall soon be landed in France, where even among slaves the laws of marriage are respected.

MISS NEV.   I have often told you that, though ready to obey you, I yet should leave my little fortune behind with reluctance. The greatest part of it was left me by my uncle, the India director, and chiefly consists in jewels. I have been for some time persuading my aunt to let me wear them. I fancy I'm very near succeeding. The instant they are put into my possession, you shall find me ready to make them and myself yours.

HAST.   Perish the baubles! Your person is all I desire. In the meantime, my friend Marlow must not be let into his mistake. I know the strange reserve of his temper is such that, if abruptly informed of it, he would instantly quit the house before our plan was ripe for execution.

MISS NEV. But how shall we keep him in the deception? Miss Hardcastle is just returned from walking; what if we still continue to deceive him? This, this way—— (*They confer*)

Enter MARLOW

MARL. The assiduities of these good people tease me beyond bearing. My host seems to think it ill manners to leave me alone, and so he claps not only himself but his old-fashioned wife on my back. They talk of coming to sup with us too; and then, I suppose, we are to run the gauntlet through all the rest of the family——What have we got here?

HAST. My dear Charles! Let me congratulate you!—The most fortunate accident!—Who do you think is just alighted?

MARL. Cannot guess.

HAST. Our mistresses, boy, Miss Hardcastle and Miss Neville. Give me leave to introduce Miss Constance Neville to your acquaintance. Happening to dine in the neighborhood, they called, on their return to take fresh horses, here. Miss Hardcastle has just stepped into the next room, and will be back in an instant. Wasn't it lucky? eh!

MARL. (*aside*) I have just been mortified enough of all conscience, and here comes something to complete my embarrassment.

HAST. Well! but wasn't it the most fortunate thing in the world?

MARL. Oh! yes. Very fortunate—a most joyful encounter ——But our dresses, George, you know, are in disorder—— What if we should postpone the happiness till to-morrow?— to-morrow at her own house. It will be every bit as convenient —and rather more respectful. To-morrow let it be.

(*offering to go*)

HAST. By no means, Sir. Your ceremony will displease her. The disorder of your dress will show the ardour of your impatience. Besides, she knows you are in the house, and will permit you to see her.

MARL. O! the devil! how shall I support it? Hem! hem! Hastings, you must not go. You are to assist me, you know. I shall be confoundedly ridiculous. Yet, hang it, I'll take courage! Hem!

HAST. Pshaw, man! it's but the first plunge, and all's over! She's but a woman, you know.

MARL.   And of all women, she that I dread most to encounter!

Enter MISS HARDCASTLE, *as returned from walking, a bonnet, &c.*

HAST.   (*introducing them*)   Miss Hardcastle, Mr. Marlow; I'm proud of bringing two persons of such merit together, that only want to know, to esteem each other.

MISS HARD.   (*aside*)   Now for meeting my modest gentleman with a demure face, and quite in his own manner. (*after a pause, in which he appears very uneasy and disconcerted*) I'm glad of your safe arrival, Sir—I'm told you had some accidents by the way.

MARL.   Only a few, Madam. Yes, we had some. Yes, Madam, a good many accidents, but should be sorry—Madam —or rather glad of any accidents—that are so agreeably concluded. Hem!

HAST.   (*to him*)   You never spoke better in your whole life. Keep it up, and I'll insure you the victory.

MISS HARD.   I'm afraid you flatter, Sir. You that have seen so much of the finest company can find little entertainment in an obscure corner of the country.

MARL.   (*gathering courage*)   I have lived, indeed, in the world, Madam; but I have kept very little company. I have been but an observer upon life, Madam, while others were enjoying it.

MISS NEV.   But that, I am told, is the way to enjoy it at last.

HAST.   (*to him*)   Cicero never spoke better. Once more, and you are confirmed in assurance forever.

MARL.   (*to him*)   Hem! stand by me then, and when I'm down, throw in a word or two to set me up again.

MISS HARD.   An observer, like you, upon life, were, I fear, disagreeably employed, since you must have had much more to censure than to approve.

MARL.   Pardon me, Madam. I was always willing to be amused. The folly of most people is rather an object of mirth than uneasiness.

HAST.   (*to him*)   Bravo, bravo. Never spoke so well in your whole life. Well, Miss Hardcastle, I see that you and Mr. Marlow are going to be very good company. I believe our being here will but embarrass the interview.

MARL.   Not in the least, Mr. Hastings. We like your company of all things. (*to him*) Zounds! George, sure you won't go? How can you leave us?

HAST. Our presence will but spoil conversation, so we'll retire to the next room. (*to him*) You don't consider, man, that we are to manage a little *tête-à-tête* of our own.

(*Exeunt* HASTINGS *and* MISS NEVILLE)

MISS HARD. (*after a pause*) But you have not been wholly an observer, I presume, Sir: the ladies, I should hope, have employed some part of your addresses.

MARL. (*relapsing into timidity*) Pardon me, Madam, I—I—I—as yet have studied—only—to—deserve them.

MISS HARD. And that, some say, is the very worst way to obtain them.

MARL. Perhaps so, Madam. But I love to converse only with the more grave and sensible part of the sex.——But I'm afraid I grow tiresome.

MISS HARD. Not at all, Sir; there is nothing I like so much as grave conversation myself; I could hear it forever. Indeed I have often been surprised how a man of *sentiment* could ever admire those light, airy pleasures, where nothing reaches the heart.

MARL. It's—a disease—of the mind, Madam. In the variety of tastes there must be some who, wanting a relish—for—um—a—um——

MISS HARD. I understand you, Sir. There must be some who, wanting a relish for refined pleasures, pretend to despise what they are incapable of tasting.

MARL. My meaning, Madam, but infinitely better expressed. And I can't help observing—a——

MISS HARD. (*aside*) Who could ever suppose this fellow impudent upon some occasions! (*to him*) You were going to observe, Sir——

MARL. I was observing, Madam—I protest, Madam, I forget what I was going to observe.

MISS HARD. (*aside*) I vow and so do I. (*to him*) You were observing, Sir, that in this age of hypocrisy—something about hypocrisy, Sir.

MARL. Yes, Madam. In this age of hypocrisy there are few who upon strict enquiry do not—a—a—a——

MISS HARD. I understand you perfectly, Sir.

MARL. (*aside*) Egad! and that's more than I do myself.

MISS HARD. You mean that in this hypocritical age there are few that do not condemn in public what they practise in private; and think they pay every debt to virtue when they praise it.

MARL. True, Madam; those who have most virtue in their

mouths have least of it in their bosoms. But I'm sure I tire you, Madam.

MISS HARD. Not in the least, Sir; there's something so agreeable and spirited in your manner, such life and force—pray, Sir, go on.

MARL. Yes, Madam, I was saying—that there are some occasions—when a total want of courage, Madam, destroys all the—and puts us—upon—a—a—a——

MISS HARD. I agree with you entirely; a want of courage upon some occasions assumes the appearance of ignorance, and betrays us when we most want to excel. I beg you'll proceed.

MARL. Yes, Madam. Morally speaking, Madam——But I see Miss Neville expecting us in the next room. I would not intrude for the world.

MISS HARD. I protest, Sir, I never was more agreeably entertained in all my life. Pray go on.

MARL. Yes, Madam. I was——But she beckons us to join her. Madam, shall I do myself the honour to attend you?

MISS HARD. Well, then, I'll follow.

MARL. (*aside*) This pretty smooth dialogue has done for me. (*Exit*)

MISS HARDCASTLE *sola*

MISS HARD. Ha! ha! ha! Was there ever such a sober, sentimental interview? I'm certain he scarce looked in my face the whole time. Yet the fellow, but for his unaccountable bashfulness, is pretty well, too. He has good sense, but then so buried in his fears, that it fatigues one more than ignorance. If I could teach him a little confidence, it would be doing somebody that I know of a piece of service. But who is that somebody?—that, faith, is a question I can scarce answer. (*Exit*)

Enter TONY *and* MISS NEVILLE, *followed by* MRS.
HARDCASTLE *and* HASTINGS

TONY. What do you follow me for, Cousin Con? I wonder you're not ashamed to be so very engaging.

MISS NEV. I hope, Cousin, one may speak to one's own relations, and not be to blame.

TONY. Ay, but I know what sort of a relation you want to make me, though; but it won't do. I tell you, Cousin Con, it won't do; so I beg you'll keep your distance. I want no nearer relationship.

(*She follows, coquetting him to the back scene*)

MRS. HARD.   Well! I vow, Mr. Hastings, you are very entertaining. There's nothing in the world I love to talk of so
much as London, and the fashions, though I was never there
myself.

HAST.   Never there! You amaze me! From your air and
manner, I concluded you had been bred all your life either at
Ranelagh, St. James's, or Tower Wharf.

MRS. HARD.   O! Sir, you're only pleased to say so. We country persons can have no manner at all. I'm in love with the
town, and that serves to raise me above some of our neigh-
bouring rustics; but who can have a manner, that has never
seen the Pantheon, the Grotto Gardens, the Borough, and
such places, where the nobility chiefly resort? All I can do is
to enjoy London at second-hand. I take care to know every
tête-à-tête from the *Scandalous Magazine*, and have all the
fashions, as they come out, in a letter from the two Miss
Rickets of Crooked Lane. Pray, how do you like this head,
Mr. Hastings?

HAST.   Extremely elegant and *degagée*, upon my word,
Madam. Your *friseur* is a Frenchman, I suppose?

MRS. HARD.   I protest, I dressed it myself from a print in
the *Ladies' Memorandum-book* for the last year.

HAST.   Indeed! Such a head in a side-box, at the play-
house, would draw as many gazers as my Lady Mayoress at a
City Ball.

MRS. HARD.   I vow, since inoculation began, there is no
such thing to be seen as a plain woman; so one must dress a
little particular or one may escape in the crowd.

HAST.   But that can never be your case, Madam, in any
dress.   (*bowing*)

MRS. HARD.   Yet, what signifies *my* dressing, when I have
such a piece of antiquity by my side as Mr. Hardcastle? All I
can say will never argue down a single button from his clothes.
I have often wanted him to throw off his great flaxen wig, and
where he was bald, to plaster it over, like my Lord Pately,
with powder.

HAST.   You are right, Madam; for, as among the ladies
there are none ugly, so among the men there are none old.

MRS. HARD.   But what do you think his answer was? Why,
with his usual Gothic vivacity, he said I only wanted him to
throw off his wig to convert it into a *tête* for my own wearing.

HAST.   Intolerable! At your age you may wear what you
please, and it must become you.

MRS. HARD. Pray, Mr. Hastings, what do you take to be the most fashionable age about town?

HAST. Some time ago forty was all the mode; but I'm told the ladies intend to bring up fifty for the ensuing winter.

MRS. HARD. Seriously? Then I shall be too young for the fashion.

HAST. No lady begins now to put on jewels till she's past forty. For instance, Miss there, in a polite circle, would be considered as a child, as a mere maker of samplers.

MRS. HARD. And yet, Mrs. Niece thinks herself as much a woman, and is as fond of jewels, as the oldest of us all.

HAST. Your niece, is she? And that young gentleman—a brother of yours, I should presume?

MRS. HARD. My son, Sir. They are contracted to each other. Observe their little sports. They fall in and out ten times a day, as if they were man and wife already. (*to them*) Well, Tony, child, what soft things are you saying to your Cousin Constance this evening?

TONY. I have been saying no soft things; but that it's very hard to be followed about so. Ecod! I've not a place in the house now that's left to myself but the stable.

MRS. HARD. Never mind him, Con, my dear. He's in another story behind your back.

MISS NEV. There's something generous in my cousin's manner. He falls out before faces, to be forgiven in private.

TONY. That's a damned confounded—crack.

MRS. HARD. Ah, he's a sly one! Don't you think they're like each other about the mouth, Mr. Hastings? The Blenkinsop mouth to a T. They're of a size, too. Back to back, my pretties, that Mr. Hastings may see you. Come, Tony.

TONY. You had as good not make me, I tell you.

                                              (*measuring*)

MISS NEV. O lud! he has almost cracked my head.

MRS. HARD. Oh the monster! For shame, Tony. You a man, and behave so!

TONY. If I'm a man, let me have my fortin. Ecod! I'll not be made a fool of no longer.

MRS. HARD. Is this, ungrateful boy, all that I'm to get for the pains I have taken in your education? I that have rocked you in your cradle, and fed that pretty mouth with a spoon! Did not I work that waistcoat to make you genteel? Did not I prescribe for you every day, and weep while the receipt was operating?

TONY. Ecod! you had reason to weep, for you have been dosing me ever since I was born. I have gone through every receipt in *The Complete Huswife* ten times over; and you have thoughts of coursing me through *Quincy* next spring. But, ecod! I tell you, I'll not be made a fool of no longer.

MRS. HARD. Wasn't it all for your good, viper? Wasn't it all for your good?

TONY. I wish you'd let me and my good alone, then. Snubbing this way when I'm in spirits! If I'm to have any good, let it come of itself; not to keep dinging it, dinging it into one so.

MRS. HARD. That's false; I never see you when you're in spirits. No, Tony, you then go to the ale-house or kennel. I'm never to be delighted with your agreeable wild notes, unfeeling monster!

TONY. Ecod! Mamma, your own notes are the wildest of the two.

MRS. HARD. Was ever the like? But I see he wants to break my heart, I see he does.

HAST. Dear Madam, permit me to lecture the young gentleman a little. I'm certain I can persuade him to his duty.

MRS. HARD. Well! I must retire. Come, Constance, my love. You see, Mr. Hastings, the wretchedness of my situation. Was ever poor woman so plagued with a dear, sweet, pretty, provoking, undutiful boy?

(*Exeunt* MRS. HARDCASTLE *and* MISS NEVILLE)

HASTINGS, TONY

TONY (*singing*). *There was a young man riding by, and fain would have his will. Rang do didlo dee.*——Don't mind her. Let her cry. It's the comfort of her heart. I have seen her and sister cry over a book for an hour together, and they said they liked the book the better the more it made them cry.

HAST. Then you're no friend to the ladies, I find, my pretty young gentleman?

TONY. That's as I find 'um.

HAST. Not to her of your mother's choosing, I dare answer? And yet she appears to me a pretty, well-tempered girl.

TONY. That's because you don't know her as well as I. Ecod! I know every inch about her; and there's not a more bitter, cantankerous toad in all Christendom.

HAST. (*aside*) Pretty encouragement, this, for a lover!

TONY. I have seen her since the height of that. She has as many tricks as a hare in a thicket, or a colt the first day's breaking.

HAST. To me she appears sensible and silent.

TONY. Ay, before company. But when she's with her play-mates, she's as loud as a hog in a gate.

HAST. But there is a meek modesty about her that charms me.

TONY. Yes, but curb her never so little, she kicks up, and you're flung in a ditch.

HAST. Well, but you must allow her a little beauty.—Yes, you must allow her some beauty.

TONY. Bandbox! She's all a made-up thing, mun. Ah! could you but see Bet Bouncer of these parts, you might then talk of beauty. Ecod! she has two eyes as black as sloes, and cheeks as broad and red as a pulpit cushion. She'd make two of she.

HAST. Well, what say you to a friend that would take this bitter bargain off your hands?

TONY. Anon!

HAST. Would you thank him that would take Miss Neville, and leave you to happiness and your dear Betsy?

TONY. Ay; but where is there such a friend, for who would take *her*?

HAST. I am he. If you but assist me, I'll engage to whip her off to France, and you shall never hear more of her.

TONY. Assist you! Ecod, I will, to the last drop of my blood. I'll clap a pair of horses to your chaise that shall trundle you off in a twinkling, and maybe get you a part of her fortin beside, in jewels, that you little dream of.

HAST. My dear 'Squire, this looks like a lad of spirit.

TONY. Come along then, and you shall see more of my spirit before you have done with me. (*singing*)

> *We are the boys*
> *That fears no noise*
> *Where the thundering cannons roar.*

(*Exeunt*)

ACT III

SCENE: *The same house*

Enter HARDCASTLE *solus*

HARD. What could my old friend Sir Charles mean by recommending his son as the modestest young man in town? To me he appears the most impudent piece of brass that ever

spoke with a tongue. He has taken possession of the easy chair
by the fireside already. He took off his boots in the parlour,
and desired me to see them taken care of. I'm desirous to
know how his impudence affects my daughter. She will certainly be shocked at it.

Enter MISS HARDCASTLE, *plainly dressed*

HARD. Well, my Kate, I see you have changed your dress,
as I bid you; and yet, I believe, there was no great occasion.

MISS HARD. I find such a pleasure, Sir, in obeying your
commands, that I take care to observe them without ever debating their propriety.

HARD. And yet, Kate, I sometimes give you some cause,
particularly when I recommended my *modest* gentleman to you
as a lover to-day.

MISS HARD. You taught me to expect something extraordinary, and I find the original exceeds the description.

HARD. I was never so surprised in my life! He has quite
confounded all my faculties!

MISS HARD. I never saw anything like it: and a man of the
world, too!

HARD. Ay, he learned it all abroad—what a fool was I, to
think a young man could learn modesty by travelling. He
might as soon learn wit at a masquerade.

MISS HARD. It seems all natural to him.

HARD. A good deal assisted by bad company and a French
dancing-master.

MISS HARD. Sure, you mistake, Papa! A French dancing-
master could never have taught him that timid look—that
awkward address—that bashful manner.

HARD. Whose look? whose manner? child!

MISS HARD. Mr. Marlow's: his *mauvaise honte,* his timidity, struck me at the first sight.

HARD. Then your first sight deceived you; for I think him
one of the most brazen first sights that ever astonished my
senses.

MISS HARD. Sure, Sir, you rally! I never saw any one so
modest.

HARD. And can you be serious! I never saw such a bounc-
ing, swaggering puppy since I was born. Bully Dawson was
but a fool to him.

MISS HARD. Surprising! He met me with a respectful bow,
a stammering voice, and a look fixed on the ground.

HARD.   He met me with a loud voice, a lordly air, and a familiarity that made my blood freeze again.

MISS HARD.   He treated me with diffidence and respect; censured the manners of the age; admired the prudence of girls that never laughed; tired me with apologies for being tiresome; then left the room with a bow, and "Madam, I would not for the world detain you."

HARD.   He spoke to me as if he knew me all his life before; asked twenty questions, and never waited for an answer; interrupted my best remarks with some silly pun; and when I was in my best story of the Duke of Marlborough and Prince Eugene, he asked if I had not a good hand at making punch. Yes, Kate, he asked your father if he was a maker of punch!

MISS HARD.   One of us must certainly be mistaken.

HARD.   If he be what he has shown himself, I'm determined he shall never have my consent.

MISS HARD.   And if he be the sullen thing I take him, he shall never have mine.

HARD.   In one thing then we are agreed—to reject him.

MISS HARD.   Yes—but upon conditions. For if you should find him less impudent, and I more presuming; if you find him more respectful, and I more importunate—I don't know— the fellow is well enough for a man— Certainly we don't meet many such at a horse-race in the country.

HARD.   If we should find him so— But that's impossible. The first appearance has done my business. I'm seldom deceived in that.

MISS HARD.   And yet there may be many good qualities under that first appearance.

HARD.   Ay, when a girl finds a fellow's outside to her taste, she then sets about guessing the rest of his furniture. With her, a smooth face stands for good sense, and a genteel figure for every virtue.

MISS HARD.   I hope, Sir, a conversation begun with a compliment to my good sense won't end with a sneer at my understanding?

HARD.   Pardon me, Kate. But if young Mr. Brazen can find the art of reconciling contradictions, he may please us both, perhaps.

MISS HARD.   And as one of us must be mistaken, what if we go to make further discoveries?

HARD.   Agreed. But depend on't I'm in the right.

MISS HARD.   And depend on't I'm not much in the wrong.
                                              (*Exeunt*)

Enter TONY, *running in with a casket*

TONY. Ecod! I have got them. Here they are. My cousin Con's necklaces, bobs and all. My mother shan't cheat the poor souls out of their fortin neither. O! my genus, is that you?

Enter HASTINGS

HAST. My dear friend, how have you managed with your mother? I hope you have amused her with pretending love for your cousin, and that you are willing to be reconciled at last? Our horses will be refreshed in a short time, and we shall soon be ready to set off.

TONY. And here's something to bear your charges by the way (*giving the casket*)—your sweetheart's jewels. Keep them, and hang those, I say, that would rob you of one of them!

HAST. But how have you procured them from your mother?

TONY. Ask me no questions, and I'll tell you no fibs. I procured them by the rule of thumb. If I had not a key to every drawer in mother's bureau, how could I go to the ale-house so often as I do? An honest man may rob himself of his own at any time.

HAST. Thousands do it every day. But to be plain with you, Miss Neville is endeavouring to procure them from her aunt this very instant. If she succeeds, it will be the most delicate way, at least, of obtaining them.

TONY. Well, keep them, till you know how it will be. But I know how it will be well enough; she'd as soon part with the only sound tooth in her head.

HAST. But I dread the effects of her resentment, when she finds she has lost them.

TONY. Never you mind her resentment; leave *me* to manage that. I don't value her resentment the bounce of a cracker. Zounds! here they are! Morrice! Prance! (*Exit* HASTINGS)

TONY, MRS. HARDCASTLE, MISS NEVILLE

MRS. HARD. Indeed, Constance, you amaze me. Such a girl as you want jewels? It will be time enough for jewels, my dear, twenty years hence, when your beauty begins to want repairs.

MISS NEV. But what will repair beauty at forty, will certainly improve it at twenty, Madam.

MRS. HARD. Yours, my dear, can admit of none. That

natural blush is beyond a thousand ornaments. Besides, child, jewels are quite out at present. Don't you see half the ladies of our acquaintance, my Lady Kill-day-light, and Mrs. Crump, and the rest of them, carry their jewels to town, and bring nothing but paste and marcasites back?

MISS NEV. But who knows, Madam, but somebody that shall be nameless would like me best with all my little finery about me?

MRS. HARD. Consult your glass, my dear, and then see if, with such pair of eyes, you want any better sparklers. What do you think, Tony, my dear? Does your cousin Con want any jewels, in your eyes, to set off her beauty?

TONY. That's as thereafter may be.

MISS NEV. My dear Aunt, if you knew how it would oblige me.

MRS. HARD. A parcel of old-fashioned rose and table-cut things. They would make you look like the court of King Solomon at a puppet-show. Besides, I believe I can't readily come at them. They may be missing, for aught I know to the contrary.

TONY. (*apart to* MRS. HARDCASTLE) Then why don't you tell her so at once, as she's so longing for them? Tell her they're lost. It's the only way to quiet her. Say they're lost, and call me to bear witness.

MRS. HARD. (*apart to* TONY) You know, my dear, I'm only keeping them for you. So if I say they're gone, you'll bear me witness, will you? He! he! he!

TONY. Never fear me. Ecod! I'll say I saw them taken out with my own eyes.

MISS NEV. I desire them but for a day, Madam, just to be permitted to show them as relics, and then they may be locked up again.

MRS. HARD. To be plain with you, my dear Constance, if I could find them you should have them. They're missing, I assure you. Lost, for aught I know; but we must have patience, wherever they are.

MISS NEV. I'll not believe it; this is but a shallow pretence to deny me. I know they're too valuable to be so slightly kept, and as you are to answer for the loss——

MRS. HARD. Don't be alarmed, Constance. If they be lost, I must restore an equivalent. But my son knows they are missing, and not to be found.

TONY. That I can bear witness to. They are missing, and not to be found, I'll take my oath on't.

MRS. HARD.   You must learn resignation, my dear; for though we lose our fortune, yet we should not lose our patience. See me, how calm I am.

MISS NEV.   Ay, people are generally calm at the misfortunes of others.

MRS. HARD.   Now, I wonder a girl of your good sense should waste a thought upon such trumpery. We shall soon find them; and in the meantime you shall make use of my garnets till your jewels be found.

MISS NEV.   I detest garnets!

MRS. HARD.   The most becoming things in the world to set off a clear complexion. You have often seen how well they look upon me. You *shall* have them.

MISS NEV.   I dislike them of all things. You shan't stir. (*Exit* MRS. HARDCASTLE)——Was ever anything so provoking—to mislay my own jewels, and force me to wear her trumpery?

TONY.   Don't be a fool. If she gives you the garnets take what you can get. The jewels are your own already. I have stolen them out of her bureau, and she does not know it. Fly to your spark, he'll tell you more of the matter. Leave me to manager *her*.

MISS NEV.   My dear Cousin!

TONY.   Vanish. She's here, and has missed them already. (*Exit* MISS NEVILLE.) Zounds! how she fidgets and spits about like a Catherine wheel.

Enter MRS. HARDCASTLE

MRS. HARD.   Confusion! thieves! robbers! We are cheated, plundered, broke open, undone!

TONY.   What's the matter, what's the matter, Mamma? I hope nothing has happened to any of the good family?

MRS. HARD.   We are robbed. My bureau has been broke open, the jewels taken out, and I'm undone!

TONY.   Oh! is that all? Ha! ha! ha! By the laws, I never saw it better acted in my life. Ecod, I thought you was ruined in earnest, ha, ha, ha!

MRS. HARD.   Why, boy, I *am* ruined in earnest. My bureau has been broke open, and all taken away.

TONY.   Stick to that; ha, ha, ha! stick to that. I'll bear witness, you know, call me to bear witness.

MRS. HARD.   I tell you, Tony, by all that's precious, the jewels are gone, and I shall be ruined forever.

TONY.   Sure I know they're gone, and I am to say so.

MRS. HARD. My dearest Tony, but hear me. They're gone, I say.

TONY. By the laws, Mamma, you make me for to laugh, ha! ha! I know who took them well enough, ha! ha! ha!

MRS. HARD. Was there ever such a blockhead, that can't tell the difference between jest and earnest? I can tell you I'm not in jest, booby.

TONY. That's right, that's right! You must be in a bitter passion, and then nobody will suspect either of us. I'll bear witness that they are gone.

MRS. HARD. Was there ever such a cross-grained brute, that won't hear me! Can you bear witness that you're no better than a fool? Was ever poor woman so beset with fools on one hand, and thieves on the other?

TONY. I can bear witness to that.

MRS. HARD. Bear witness again, you blockhead, you, and I'll turn you out of the room directly. My poor niece, what will become of *her!* Do you laugh, you unfeeling brute, as if you enjoyed my distress?

TONY. I can bear witness to that.

MRS. HARD. Do you insult me, monster? I'll teach you to vex your mother, I will!

TONY. I can bear witness to that.

(He runs off; she follows him)

Enter MISS HARDCASTLE *and* MAID

MISS HARD. What an unaccountable creature is that brother of mine, to send them to the house as an inn! ha! ha! I don't wonder at his impudence.

MAID. But what is more, Madam, the young gentleman, as you passed by in your present dress, asked me if you were the bar-maid. He mistook you for the bar-maid, Madam!

MISS HARD. Did he? Then, as I live, I'm resolved to keep up the delusion. Tell me, Pimple, how do you like my present dress? Don't you think I look something like Cherry in *The Beaux' Stratagem?*

MAID. It's the dress, Madam, that every lady wears in the country, but when she visits or receives company.

MISS HARD. And are you sure he does not remember my face or person?

MAID. Certain of it.

MISS HARD. I vow I thought so; for though we spoke for some time together, yet his fears were such that he never once

looked up during the interview. Indeed, if he had, my bonnet
would have kept him from seeing me.

MAID. But what do you hope from keeping him in his mistake?

MISS HARD. In the first place, I shall be *seen*, and that is no
small advantage to a girl who brings her face to market. Then
I shall perhaps make an acquaintance, and that's no small victory gained over one who never addresses any but the wildest
of her sex. But my chief aim is to take my gentleman off his
guard, and, like an invisible champion of romance, examine
the giant's force before I offer to combat.

MAID. But are you sure you can act your part, and disguise your voice so that he may mistake that, as he has already mistaken your person?

MISS HARD. Never fear me. I think I have got the true bar
cant.—— Did your honour call?—— Attend the Lion there.——
Pipes and tobacco for the Angel.—— The Lamb has been out-
rageous this half hour!

MAID. It will do, Madam. But he's here.　　　(*Exit Maid*)

Enter MARLOW

MARL. What a bawling in every part of the house; I have
scarce a moment's repose. If I go to the best room, there I find
my host and his story. If I fly to the gallery, there we have my
hostess with her curtesy down to the ground. I have at last got
a moment to myself, and now for recollection.

(walks and muses)

MISS HARD. Did you call, Sir? Did your honour call?

MARL. (*musing*) As for Miss Hardcastle, she's too grave
and sentimental for me.

MISS HARD. Did your honour call?

(She still places herself before him, he turning away.)

MARL. No, child. (*musing*) Besides, from the glimpse I
had of her, I think she squints.

MISS HARD. I'm sure, Sir, I heard the bell ring.

MARL. No, no. (*musing*) I have pleased my father, however, by coming down, and I'll to-morrow please myself by
returning.

(taking out his tablets and perusing)

MISS HARD. Perhaps the other gentleman called, Sir?

MARL. I tell you, no.

MISS HARD. I should be glad to know, Sir. We have such a
parcel of servants.

MARL. No, no, I tell you. (*looks full in her face*) Yes, child, I think I did call. I wanted—I wanted—I vow, child, you are vastly handsome.

MISS HARD. O la, Sir, you'll make one ashamed.

MARL. Never saw a more sprightly, malicious eye. Yes, yes, my dear, I did call. Have you got any of your—a—what d'ye call it, in the house?

MISS HARD. No, Sir, we have been out of that these ten days.

MARL. One may call in this house, I find, to very little purpose. Suppose I should call for a taste, just by way of trial, of the nectar of your lips; perhaps I might be disappointed in that too.

MISS HARD. Nectar! nectar! That's a liquor there's no call for in these parts. French, I suppose. We keep no French wines here, Sir.

MARL. Of true English growth, I assure you.

MISS HARD. Then it's odd I should not know it. We brew all sorts of wines in this house, and I have lived here these eighteen years.

MARL. Eighteen years! Why, one would think, child, you kept the bar before you were born. How old are you?

MISS HARD. O! Sir, I must not tell my age. They say women and music should never be dated.

MARL. To guess at this distance, you can't be much above forty. (*approaching*) Yet nearer, I don't think so much. (*approaching*) By coming close to some women, they look younger still; but when we come very close indeed——

(*attempting to kiss her*)

MISS HARD. Pray, Sir, keep your distance. One would think you wanted to know one's age as they do horses, by mark of mouth.

MARL. I protest, child, you use me extremely ill. If you keep me at this distance, how is it possible you and I can be ever acquainted?

MISS HARD. And who wants to be acquainted with you? I want no such acquaintance, not I. I'm sure you did not treat Miss Hardcastle, that was here a while ago, in this obstropalous manner. I'll warrant me, before her you looked dashed, and kept bowing to the ground, and talked, for all the world, as if you was before a justice of peace.

MARL. (*aside*) Egad! she has hit it, sure enough. (*to her*) In awe of her, child? Ha! ha! ha! A mere awkward, squinting thing! No, no. I find you don't know me. I laughed and rallied her a little; but I was unwilling to be too severe. No, I could not be too severe, *curse me!*

MISS HARD.   O! then, Sir, you are a favourite, I find, among the ladies?

MARL.   Yes, my dear, a great favourite. And yet, hang me, I don't see what they find in me to follow. At the Ladies' Club in town, I'm called their agreeable Rattle. Rattle, child, is not my real name, but one I'm known by. My name is Solomons. Mr. Solomons, my dear, at your service.

(*offering to salute her*)

MISS HARD.   Hold, Sir, you are introducing me to your club, not to yourself. And you're so great a favourite there, you say?

MARL.   Yes, my dear. There's Mrs. Mantrap, Lady Betty Blackleg, the Countess of Sligo, Mrs. Langhorns, old Miss Biddy Buckskin, and your humble servant, keep up the spirit of the place.

MISS HARD.   Then it's a very merry place, I suppose?

MARL.   Yes, as merry as cards, suppers, wine, and old women can make us.

MISS HARD.   And their agreeable Rattle, ha! ha! ha!

MARL. (*aside*)   Egad! I don't quite like this chit. She looks knowing, methinks.— You laugh, child?

MISS HARD.   I can't but laugh to think what time they all have for minding their work or their family.

MARL. (*aside*)   All's well; she don't laugh at me. (*to her*) Do *you* ever work, child?

MISS HARD.   Ay, sure. There's not a screen or a quilt in the whole house but what can bear witness to that.

MARL.   Odso! then you must show me your embroidery. I embroider and draw patterns myself a little. If you want a judge of your work you must apply to me.

(*seizing her hand*)

Enter HARDCASTLE, *who stands in surprise*

MISS HARD.   Ay, but the colours don't look well by candle-light. You shall see all in the morning.   (*struggling*)

MARL.   And why not now, my angel? Such beauty fires beyond the power of resistance. — Pshaw! the father here! My old luck: I never nicked seven that I did not throw ames ace three times following.   (*Exit* MARLOW)

HARD.   So, Madam! So I find *this* is your *modest* lover. This is your humble admirer that kept his eyes fixed on the ground, and only adored at humble distance. Kate, Kate, art thou not ashamed to deceive your father so?

MISS HARD. Never trust me, dear Papa, but he's still the modest man I first took him for; you'll be convinced of it as well as I.

HARD. By the hand of my body, I believe his impudence is infectious! Didn't I see him seize your hand? Didn't I see him haul you about like a milkmaid? and now you talk of his respect and his modesty, forsooth!

MISS HARD. But if I shortly convince you of his modesty, that he has only the faults that will pass off with time, and the virtues that will improve with age, I hope you'll forgive him.

HARD. The girl would actually make one run mad! I tell you I'll not be convinced. I am convinced. He has scarcely been three hours in the house, and he has already encroached on all my prerogatives. You may like his impudence, and call it modesty. But my son-in-law, Madam, must have very different qualifications.

MISS HARD. Sir, I ask but this night to convince you.

HARD. You shall not have half the time, for I have thoughts of turning him out this very hour.

MISS HARD. Give me that hour, then, and I hope to satisfy you.

HARD. Well, an hour let it be then. But I'll have no trifling with your father. All fair and open, do you mind me?

MISS HARD. I hope, Sir, you have ever found that I considered your commands as my pride; for your kindness is such, that my duty as yet has been inclination.

(*Exeunt*)

ACT IV

SCENE: *The same house.*

Enter HASTINGS *and* MISS NEVILLE

HAST. You surprise me! Sir Charles Marlow expected here this night? Where have you had your information?

MISS NEV. You may depend upon it. I just saw his letter to Mr. Hardcastle, in which he tells him he intends setting out a few hours after his son.

HAST. Then, my Constance, all must be completed before he arrives. He knows me; and should he find me here, would discover my name, and perhaps my designs, to the rest of the family.

MISS NEV. The jewels, I hope, are safe?

HAST. Yes, yes. I have sent them to Marlow, who keeps the keys of our baggage. In the meantime, I'll go to prepare matters for our elopement. I have had the 'Squire's promise of a fresh pair of horses; and, if I should not see him again, will write him further directions.   (*Exit*)

MISS NEV. Well, success attend you! In the meantime, I'll go amuse my aunt with the old pretence of a violent passion for my cousin.   (*Exit*)

Enter MARLOW, *followed by a Servant*

MARL. I wonder what Hastings could mean by sending me so valuable a thing as a casket to keep for him, when he knows the only place I have is the seat of a post-coach at an inn-door. Have you deposited the casket with the landlady, as I ordered you? Have you put it into her own hands?

SERV. Yes, your honour.

MARL. She said she'd keep it safe, did she?

SERV. Yes; she said she'd keep it safe enough; she asked me how I came by it; and she said she had a great mind to make me give an account of myself.   (*Exit Servant*)

MARL. Ha! ha! ha! They're safe, however. What an unaccountable set of beings have we got amongst! This little barmaid, though, runs in my head most strangely, and drives out the absurdities of all the rest of the family. She's mine, she must be mine, or I'm greatly mistaken.

Enter HASTINGS

HAST. Bless me! I quite forgot to tell her that I intended to prepare at the bottom of the garden. Marlow here, and in spirits too!

MARL. Give me joy, George! Crown me, shadow me with laurels! Well, George, after all, we modest fellows don't want for success among the women.

HAST. Some women, you mean. But what success has your honour's modesty been crowned with now, that it grows so insolent upon us?

MARL. Didn't you see the tempting, brisk, lovely little thing that runs about the house with a bunch of keys to its girdle?

HAST. Well, and what then?

MARL. She's mine, you rogue, you. Such fire, such motion, such eyes, such lips—but, egad! she would not let me kiss them though

HAST.   But are you so sure, so very sure of her?

MARL.   Why, man, she talked of showing me her work above-stairs, and I am to improve the pattern.

HAST.   But how can *you*, Charles, go about to rob a woman of her honour?

MARL.   Pshaw! pshaw! We all know the honour of the bar-maid of an inn. I don't intend to *rob* her, take my word for it; there's nothing in this house I shan't honestly *pay* for.

HAST.   I believe the girl has virtue.

MARL.   And if she has, I should be the last man in the world that would attempt to corrupt it.

HAST.   You have taken care, I hope, of the casket I sent you to lock up? It's in safety?

MARL.   Yes, yes; it's safe enough. I have taken care of it. But how could you think the seat of a post-coach at an inn-door a place of safety? Ah! numbskull! I have taken better precautions for you than you did for yourself. I have——

HAST.   What?

MARL.   I have sent it to the landlady to keep for you.

HAST.   To the landlady!

MARL.   The landlady.

HAST.   You did!

MARL.   I did. She's to be answerable for its forthcoming, you know.

HAST.   Yes, she'll bring it forth, with a witness.

MARL.   Wasn't I right? I believe you'll allow that I acted prudently upon this occasion?

HAST.   (*aside*)   He must not see my uneasiness.

MARL.   You seem a little disconcerted, though, methinks. Sure nothing has happened?

HAST.   No, nothing. Never was in better spirits in all my life. And so you left it with the landlady, who, no doubt, very readily undertook the charge.

MARL.   Rather too readily. For she not only kept the casket, but, through her great precaution, was going to keep the messenger too. Ha! ha! ha!

HAST.   He! he! he! They're safe, however.

MARL.   As a guinea in a miser's purse.

HAST.   (*aside*)   So now all hopes of fortune are at an end, and we must set off without it. (*to him*) Well, Charles, I'll leave you to your meditations on the pretty bar-maid, and he! he! he! may you be as successful for yourself as you have been for me.   (*Exit*)

MARL.   Thank ye, George! I ask no more. Ha! ha! ha!

Enter HARDCASTLE

HARD. I no longer know my own house. It's turned all topsy-turvy. His servants have got drunk already. I'll bear it no longer, and yet, from my respect for his father, I'll be calm. (*to him*) Mr. Marlow, your servant. I'm your very humble servant.   (*bowing low*)

MARL. Sir, your humble servant. (*aside*) What's to be the wonder now?

HARD. I believe, Sir, you must be sensible, Sir, that no man alive ought to be more welcome than your father's son, Sir. I hope you think so?

MARL. I do from my soul, Sir. I don't want much entreaty. I generally make my father's son welcome wherever he goes.

HARD. I believe you do, from my soul, Sir. But though I say nothing to your own conduct, that of your servants is insufferable. Their manner of drinking is setting a very bad example in this house, I assure you.

MARL. I protest, my very good Sir, that's no fault of mine. If they don't drink as they ought, *they* are to blame. I ordered them not to spare the cellar. I did, I assure you. (*to the side-scene*) Here, let one of my servants come up. (*to him*) My positive directions were, that as I did not drink myself, they should make up for my deficiencies below.

HARD. Then they had your orders for what they do? I'm satisfied!

MARL. They had, I assure you. You shall hear from one of themselves.

Enter JEREMY, *drunk*

MARL. You, Jeremy! Come forward, Sirrah! What were my orders? Were you not told to drink freely, and call for what you thought fit, for the good of the house?

HARD. (*aside*) I begin to lose my patience.

JEREMY. Please your honour, liberty and Fleet Street forever! Though I'm but a servant, I'm as good as another man. I'll drink for no man before supper, Sir, damme! Good liquor will sit upon a good supper, but a good supper will not sit upon—hiccup—upon my conscience, Sir.   (*Exit*)

MARL. You see, my old friend, the fellow is as drunk as he can possibly be. I don't know what you'd have more, unless you'd have the poor devil soused in a beer-barrel.

HARD. (*aside*) Zounds! he'll drive me distracted, if I con-

tain myself any longer. —— Mr. Marlow—Sir! I have submitted to your insolence for more than four hours, and I see
no likelihood of its coming to an end. I'm now resolved to
be master here, Sir, and I desire that you and your drunken
pack may leave my house directly.

MARL.   Leave your house!—Sure you jest, my good friend?
What, when I'm doing what I can to please you!

HARD.   I tell you, Sir, you don't please me; so I desire
you'll leave my house.

MARL.   Sure you cannot be serious? At this time o' night,
and such a night? You only mean to banter me.

HARD.   I tell you, Sir, I'm serious; and now that my passions are roused, I say this house is mine, Sir; this house is
mine, and I command you to leave it directly.

MARL.   Ha! ha! ha! A puddle in a storm. I shan't stir a
step, I assure you. (*in a serious tone*) This your house, fellow! It's my house. This is my house. Mine, while I choose to
stay. What right have you to bid me leave this house, Sir?
I never met with such impudence, curse me, never in my
whole life before.

HARD.   Nor I, confound me if ever I did! To come to my
house, to call for what he likes, to turn me out of my own
chair, to insult the family, to order his servants to get drunk,
and then to tell me, *This house is mine, Sir!* By all that's impudent, it makes me laugh. Ha! ha! ha! Pray, Sir, (*bantering*)
as you take the house, what think you of taking the rest of
the furniture? There's a pair of silver candle-sticks, and there's
a fire-screen, and here's a pair of brazen-nosed bellows; perhaps you may take a fancy to them?

MARL.   Bring me your bill, Sir; bring me your bill, and
let's make no more words about it.

HARD.   There are a set of prints, too. What think you of
The Rake's Progress for your own apartment?

MARL.   Bring me your bill, I say, and I'll leave you and
your infernal house directly.

HARD.   Then there's a mahogany table that you may see
your face in.

MARL.   My bill, I say.

HARD.   I had forgot the great chair, for your own particular slumbers, after a hearty meal.

MARL.   Zounds! bring me my bill, I say, and let's hear no
more on't.

HARD.   Young man, young man, from your father's letter
to me, I was taught to expect a well-bred, modest man as a

visitor here, but now I find him no better than a coxcomb and a bully; but he will be down here presently, and shall hear more of it.   (*Exit*)

MARL.   How's this! Sure I have not mistaken the house! Everything looks like an inn; the servants cry "Coming"; the attendance is awkward; the bar-maid, too, to attend us. But she's here, and will further inform me. Whither so fast, child? A word with you.

Enter MISS HARDCASTLE

MISS HARD.   Let it be short, then. I'm in a hurry. (*aside*) I believe he begins to find out his mistake, but it's too soon quite to undeceive him.

MARL.   Pray, child, answer me one question. What are you, and what may your business in this house be?

MISS HARD.   A relation of the family, Sir.

MARL.   What! a poor relation?

MISS HARD.   Yes, Sir. A poor relation appointed to keep the keys, and to see that the guests want nothing in my power to give them.

MARL.   That is, you act as the bar-maid of this inn.

MISS HARD.   Inn! O law!—— What brought that into your head? One of the best families in the county keep an inn! Ha! ha! ha! old Mr. Hardcastle's house an inn!

MARL.   Mr. Hardcastle's house! Is this house Mr. Hardcastle's house, child?

MISS HARD.   Ay, sure. Whose else should it be?

MARL.   So, then, all's out, and I have been damnably imposed on. Oh, confound my stupid head, I shall be laughed at over the whole town. I shall be stuck up in caricatura in all the print-shops—the *Dullissimo Macaroni*. To mistake this house of all others for an inn, and my father's old friend for an innkeeper! What a swaggering puppy must he take me for! What a silly puppy do I find myself! There again, may I be hanged, my dear, but I mistook you for the bar-maid.

MISS HARD.   Dear me! dear me! I'm sure there's nothing in my *behavour* to put me upon a level with one of that stamp.

MARL.   Nothing, my dear, nothing. But I was in for a list of blunders, and could not help making you a subscriber. My stupidity saw everything the wrong way. I mistook your assiduity for assurance, and your simplicity for allurement. But it's over—this house I no more show *my* face in.

MISS HARD.   I hope, Sir, I have done nothing to disoblige you. I'm sure I should be sorry to affront any gentleman who has been so polite, and said so many civil things to me. I'm sure I should be sorry (*pretending to cry*) if he left the family upon my account. I'm sure I should be sorry people said anything amiss, since I have no fortune but my character.

MARL. (*aside*) By heaven, she weeps! This is the first mark of tenderness I ever had from a modest woman, and it touches me. (*to her*) Excuse me, my lovely girl, you are the only part of the family I leave with reluctance. But to be plain with you, the difference of our birth, fortune, and education, make an honourable connexion impossible; and I can never harbour a thought of seducing simplicity that trusted in my honour, or bringing ruin upon one whose only fault was being too lovely.

MISS HARD. (*aside*) Generous man! I now begin to admire him. (*to him*) But I'm sure my family is as good as Miss Hardcastle's, and though I'm poor, that's no great misfortune to a contented mind, and, until this moment, I never thought that it was bad to want fortune.

MARL. And why now, my pretty simplicity?

MISS HARD. Because it puts me at a distance from one that, if I had a thousand pound, I would give it all to.

MARL. (*aside*) This simplicity bewitches me, so that if I stay I'm undone. I must make one bold effort, and leave her. (*to her*) Your partiality in my favour, my dear, touches me most sensibly, and were I to live for myself alone, I could easily fix my choice. But I owe too much to the opinion of the world, too much to the authority of a father, so that—I can scarcely speak it—it affects me! Farewell. (*Exit*)

MISS HARD. I never knew half his merit till now. He shall not go if I have power or art to detain him. I'll still preserve the character in which I *stooped to conquer,* but will undeceive my papa, who, perhaps, may laugh him out of his resolution. (*Exit*)

Enter TONY *and* MISS NEVILLE

TONY. Ay, you may steal for yourselves the next time. I have done my duty. She has got the jewels again, that's a sure thing; but she believes it was all a mistake of the servants.

MISS NEV. But, my dear Cousin, sure you won't forsake us in this distress? If she in the least suspects that I am going off, I shall certainly be locked up, or sent to my aunt Pedigree's, which is ten times worse.

TONY. To be sure, aunts of all kinds are damned bad

things. But what can I do? I have got you a pair of horses that will fly like Whistlejacket, and I'm sure you can't say but I have courted you nicely before her face. Here she comes; we must court a bit or two more, for fear she should suspect us.   (*They retire and seem to fondle*)

Enter MRS. HARDCASTLE

MRS. HARD.   Well, I was greatly fluttered, to be sure. But my son tells me it was all a mistake of the servants. I shan't be easy, however, till they are fairly married, and then let her keep her own fortune. But what do I see! Fondling together, as I'm alive. I never saw Tony so sprightly before. Ah! have I caught you, my pretty doves? What, billing, exchanging stolen glances, and broken murmurs! Ah!

TONY.   As for murmurs, Mother, we grumble a little now and then, to be sure. But there's no love lost between us.

MRS. HARD.   A mere sprinkling, Tony, upon the flame, only to make it burn brighter.

MISS NEV.   Cousin Tony promises to give us more of his company at home. Indeed, he shan't leave us any more. It won't leave us, Cousin Tony, will it?

TONY.   Oh! it's a pretty creature. No, I'd sooner leave my horse in a pound, than leave you when you smile upon one so. Your laugh makes you so becoming.

MISS NEV.   Agreeable Cousin! Who can help admiring that natural humour, that pleasant, broad, red, thoughtless (*patting his cheek*)—ah! it's a bold face!

MRS. HARD.   Pretty innocence.

TONY.   I'm sure I always loved Cousin Con's hazel eyes, and her pretty long fingers, that she twists this way and that, over the haspicholls, like a parcel of bobbins.

MRS. HARD.   Ah! he would charm the bird from the tree. I was never so happy before. My boy takes after his father, poor Mr. Lumpkin, exactly. The jewels, my dear Con, shall be yours incontinently. You shall have them. Isn't he a sweet boy, my dear? You shall be married to-morrow, and we'll put off the rest of his education, like Dr. Drowsy's sermons, to a fitter opportunity.

Enter DIGGORY

DIGG.   Where's the 'Squire? I have got a letter for your worship.

TONY.   Give it to my mamma. She reads all my letters first.

DIGG.   I had orders to deliver it into your own hands.

TONY.   Who does it come from?

DIGG.   Your worship mun ask that o' the letter itself.

(*Exit* DIGGORY)

TONY.   I could wish to know, though.

(*turning the letter and gazing on it*)

MISS NEV. (*aside*)   Undone, undone! A letter to him from Hastings. I know the hand. If my aunt sees it, we are ruined forever. I'll keep her employed a little if I can. (*to* MRS. HARDCASTLE) But I have not told you, Madam, of my cousin's smart answer just now to Mr. Marlow. We so laughed—you must know, Madam——this way a little, for he must not hear us.   (*They confer*)

TONY. (*still gazing*)   A damned cramp piece of penmanship as ever I saw in my life. I can read your print-hand very well. But here there are such handles, and shanks, and dashes, that one can scarce tell the head from the tail. *To Anthony Lumpkin, Esquire.* It's very odd, I can read the outside of my letters, where my own name is, well enough. But when I come to open it, it's all—buzz. That's hard, very hard; for the inside of the letter is always the cream of the correspondence.

MRS. HARD.   Ha! ha! ha! Very well, very well. And so my son was too hard for the philosopher.

MISS NEV.   Yes, Madam; but you must hear the rest, Madam. A little more this way, or he may hear us. You'll hear how he puzzled him again.

MRS. HARD.   He seems strangely puzzled now himself, methinks.

TONY (*still gazing*)   A damned up-and-down hand, as if it was disguised in liquor. (*reading*) *Dear Sir,*——Ay, that's that. Then there's an *M*, and a *T*, and an *S*, but whether the next be an *izzard* or an *R*, confound me, I cannot tell!

MRS. HARD.   What's that, my dear? Can I give you any assistance?

MISS NEV.   Pray, Aunt, let me read it. Nobody reads a cramp hand better than I. (*twitching the letter from her*) Do you know who it is from?

TONY.   Can't tell, except from Dick Ginger, the feeder.

MISS NEV.   Ay, so it is. (*pretending to read*) DEAR 'SQUIRE, Hoping that you're in health, as I am at this present. The gentlemen of the Shake-bag club has cut the gentlemen of Goose-green quite out of feather. The odds—um—odd battle— um—long fighting—um—here, here, it's all about cocks, and fighting; it's of no consequence; here, put it up, put it up.

(*thrusting the crumpled letter upon him*)

TONY. But I tell you, Miss, it's of all the consequence in the world! I would not lose the rest of it for a guinea. Here, Mother, do you make it out. Of no consequence!

(*giving* MRS. HARDCASTLE *the letter*)

MRS. HARD. How's this! (*reads*)

Dear 'Squire, I'm now waiting for Miss Neville with a post-chaise and pair, at the bottom of the garden, but I find my horses yet unable to perform the journey. I expect you'll assist us with a pair of fresh horses, as you promised. Dispatch is necessary, as the hag—ay, the hag—your mother, will otherwise suspect us. Yours, Hastings.

Grant me patience. I shall run distracted! My rage chokes me.

MISS NEV. I hope, Madam, you'll suspend your resentment for a few moments, and not impute to me any impertinence, or sinister design that belongs to another.

MRS. HARD. (*curtseying very low*) Fine spoken, Madam, you are most miraculously polite and engaging, and quite the very pink of courtesy and circumspection, Madam. (*changing her tone*) And you, you great ill-fashioned oaf, with scarce sense enough to keep your mouth shut—were you too joined against me? But I'll defeat all your plots in a moment. As for you, Madam, since you have got a pair of fresh horses ready, it would be cruel to disappoint them. So, if you please, instead of running away with your spark, prepare, this very moment, to run off with *me*. Your old aunt Pedigree will keep you secure, I'll warrant me. You, too, Sir, may mount your horse, and guard us upon the way. Here, Thomas, Roger, Diggory! I'll show you that I wish you better than you do yourselves. (*Exit*)

MISS NEV. So now I'm completely ruined.

TONY. Ay, that's a sure thing.

MISS NEV. What better could be expected from being connected with such a stupid fool—and after all the nods and signs I made him!

TONY. By the laws, Miss, it was your own cleverness, and not my stupidity, that did your business. You were so nice and so busy with your Shake-bags and Goose-greens that I thought you could never be making believe.

Enter HASTINGS

HAST. So, Sir, I find by my servant that you have shown my letter, and betrayed us. Was this well done, young gentleman?

TONY. Here's another. Ask Miss, there, who betrayed you. Ecod! it was her doing, not mine.

Enter MARLOW

MARL. So I have been finely used here among you. Rendered contemptible, driven into ill-manners, despised, insulted, laughed at.

TONY. Here's another. We shall have old Bedlam broke loose presently.

MISS NEV. And there, Sir, is the gentleman to whom we all owe every obligation.

MARL. What can I say to him, a mere boy, an idiot, whose ignorance and age are a protection!

HAST. A poor contemptible booby, that would but disgrace correction.

MISS NEV. Yet with cunning and malice enough to make himself merry with all our embarrassments.

HAST. An insensible cub.

MARL. Replete with tricks and mischief.

TONY. Baw! damme, but I'll fight you both, one after the other—with baskets.

MARL. As for him, he's below resentment. But your conduct, Mr. Hastings, requires an explanation. You knew of my mistakes, yet would not undeceive me.

HAST. Tortured as I am with my own disappointments, is this a time for explanations? It is not friendly, Mr. Marlow.

MARL. But, Sir——

MISS NEV. Mr. Marlow, we never kept on your mistake, till it was too late to undeceive you. Be pacified.

Enter Servant

SERV. My mistress desires you'll get ready immediately, Madam. The horses are putting to. Your hat and things are in the next room. We are to go thirty miles before morning.

(Exit Servant)

MISS NEV. Well, well; I'll come presently.

MARL. *(to* HASTINGS*)* Was it well done, Sir, to assist in rendering me ridiculous? To hang me out for the scorn of all my acquaintance? Depend upon it, Sir, I shall expect an explanation.

HAST. Was it well done, Sir, if you're upon that subject, to deliver what I entrusted to yourself, to the care of another, Sir?

MISS NEV. Mr. Hastings! Mr. Marlow! Why will you increase my distress by this groundless dispute? I implore, I entreat you——

Enter Servant

SERV. Your cloak, Madam. My mistress is impatient.

MISS NEV. I come. (*Exit Servant*) Pray, be pacified. If I leave you thus, I shall die with apprehension.

Enter Servant

SERV. Your fan, muff, and gloves, Madam. The horses aie waiting.   (*Exit Servant*)

MISS NEV. O, Mr. Marlow! if you knew what a scene of constraint and ill-nature lies before me, I'm sure it would convert your resentment into pity.

MARL. I'm so distracted with a variety of passions, that I don't know what I do. Forgive me, Madam. George, forgive me. You know my hasty temper, and should not exasperate it.

HAST. The torture of my situation is my only excuse.

MISS NEV. Well, my dear Hastings, if you have that esteem for me that I think, that I am sure you have, your constancy for three years will but increase the happiness of our future connexion. If——

MRS. HARD. (*within*) Miss Neville! Constance! why, Constance, I say!

MISS NEV. I'm coming! Well, constancy. Remember, constancy is the word.   (*Exit*)

HAST. My heart! How can I support this! To be so near happiness, and such happiness!

MARL. (*to* TONY) You see now, young gentleman, the effects of your folly What might be amusement to you is here disappointment, and even distress.

TONY. (*from a reverie*) Ecod, I have hit it. It's here! Your hands. Yours, and yours, my poor Sulky. My boots there, ho! Meet me two hours hence at the bottom of the garden; and if you don't find Tony Lumpkin a more good-natured fellow than you thought for, I'll give you leave to take my best horse, and Bet Bouncer into the bargain. Come along. My boots, ho!   (*Exeunt*)

ACT V

SCENE I

Scene continues

Enter HASTINGS *and Servant*

HAST.   You saw the old lady and Miss Neville drive off, you say?

SERV.   Yes, your honour. They went off in a post-coach, and the young 'Squire went on horseback. They're thirty miles off by this time.

HAST.   Then all my hopes are over.

SERV.   Yes, Sir. Old Sir Charles is arrived. He and the old gentleman of the house have been laughing at Mr. Marlow's mistake this half hour. They are coming this way.   (*Exit*)

HAST.   Then I must not be seen. So now to my fruitless appointment at the bottom of the garden. This is about the time.   (*Exit*)

Enter SIR CHARLES MARLOW *and* HARDCASTLE

HARD.   Ha! ha! ha! The peremptory tone in which he sent forth his sublime commands!

SIR CHAS.   And the reserve with which I suppose he treated all your advances.

HARD.   And yet he might have seen something in me above a common innkeeper, too.

SIR CHAS.   Yes, Dick, but he mistook you for an uncommon innkeeper, ha! ha! ha!

HARD.   Well, I'm in too good spirits to think of anything but joy. Yes, my dear friend, this union of our families will make our personal friendships hereditary; and though my daughter's fortune is but small——

SIR CHAS.   Why, Dick, will you talk of fortune to *me*? My son is possessed of more than a competence already, and can want nothing but a good and virtuous girl to share his happiness and increase it. If they like each other, as you say they do——

HARD.   *If*, man! I tell you they *do* like each other. My daughter as good as told me so.

SIR CHAS.   But girls are apt to flatter themselves, you know.

HARD.   I saw him grasp her hand in the warmest manner myself; and here he comes to put you out of your *ifs*, I warrant him.

Enter MARLOW

MARL. I come, Sir, once more, to ask pardon for my strange conduct. I can scarce reflect on my insolence without confusion.

HARD. Tut, boy, a trifle. You take it too gravely. An hour or two's laughing with my daughter will set all to rights again. She'll never like you the worse for it.

MARL. Sir, I shall be always proud of her approbation.

HARD. Approbation is but a cold word, Mr. Marlow; if I am not deceived, you have something more than approbation thereabouts. You take me?

MARL. Really, Sir, I have not that happiness.

HARD. Come, boy, I'm an old fellow, and know what's what as well as you that are younger. I know what has passed between you; but mum.

MARL. Sure, Sir, nothing has passed between us but the most profound respect on my side, and the most distant reserve on hers. You don't think, Sir, that my impudence has been passed upon all the rest of the family?

HARD. Impudence! No, I don't say that—not quite impudence—though girls like to be played with, and rumpled a little, too, sometimes. But she has told no tales, I assure you.

MARL. I never gave her the slightest cause.

HARD. Well, well, I like modesty in its place well enough; but this is overacting, young gentleman. You *may* be open. Your father and I will like you the better for it.

MARL. May I die, Sir, if I ever——

HARD. I tell you she don't dislike you; and as I am sure you like her——

MARL. Dear Sir—I protest, Sir——

HARD. I see no reason why you should not be joined as fast as the parson can tie you.

MARL. But hear me, Sir——

HARD. Your father approves the match; I admire it; every moment's delay will be doing mischief; so——

MARL. But why won't you hear me? By all that's just and true, I never gave Miss Hardcastle the slightest mark of my attachment, or even the most distant hint to suspect me of affection. We had but one interview, and that was formal, modest, and uninteresting.

HARD. (*aside*) This fellow's formal, modest impudence is beyond bearing.

SIR CHAS.   And you never grasped her hand, or made any protestations!

MARL.   As heaven is my witness, I came down in obedience to your commands. I saw the lady without emotion, and parted without reluctance. I hope you'll exact no further proofs of my duty, nor prevent me from leaving a house in which I suffer so many mortifications.   (*Exit*)

SIR CHAS.   I'm astonished at the air of sincerity with which he parted.

HARD.   And I'm astonished at the deliberate intrepidity of his assurance.

SIR CHAS.   I dare pledge my life and honour upon his truth.

HARD.   Here comes my daughter, and I would stake my happiness upon her veracity.

Enter MISS HARDCASTLE

HARD.   Kate, come hither, child. Answer us sincerely, and without reserve: has Mr. Marlow made you any professions of love and affection?

MISS HARD.   The question is very abrupt, Sir. But since you require unreserved sincerity, I think he has.

HARD. (*to* SIR CHARLES)   You see.

SIR CHAS.   And pray, Madam, have you and my son had more than one interview?

MISS HARD.   Yes, Sir, several.

HARD. (*to* SIR CHARLES)   You see.

SIR CHAS.   But did he profess any attachment?

MISS HARD.   A lasting one.

SIR CHAS.   Did he talk of love?

MISS HARD.   Much, Sir.

SIR CHAS.   Amazing! And all this formally?

MISS HARD.   Formally.

HARD.   Now, my friend, I hope you are satisfied.

SIR CHAS.   And how did he behave, Madam?

MISS HARD.   As most professed admirers do—said some civil things of my face, talked much of his want of merit, and the greatness of mine; mentioned his heart, gave a short tragedy speech, and ended with pretended rapture.

SIR CHAS.   Now I'm perfectly convinced, indeed. I know his conversation among women to be modest and submissive. This forward, canting, ranting manner by no means describes him, and I am confident he never sat for the picture.

MISS HARD.   Then what, Sir, if I should convince you to your face of my sincerity? If you and my papa, in about half an hour, will place yourselves behind that screen, you shall hear him declare his passion to me in person.

SIR CHAS.   Agreed. And if I find him what you describe, all my happiness in him must have an end.   (*Exit*)

MISS HARD.   And if you don't find him what I describe—I fear my happiness must never have a beginning.   (*Exeunt*)

SCENE II

Scene changes to the back of the garden

Enter HASTINGS

HAST.   What an idiot am I, to wait here for a fellow who probably takes a delight in mortifying me. He never intended to be punctual, and I'll wait no longer. What do I see? It is he, and perhaps with news of my Constance.

Enter TONY, *booted and spattered*

HAST.   My honest 'Squire! I now find you a man of your word. This looks like friendship.

TONY.   Ay, I'm your friend, and the best friend you have in the world, if you knew but all. This riding by night, by the bye, is cursedly tiresome. It has shook me worse than the basket of a stage-coach.

HAST.   But how? Where did you leave your fellow travellers? Are they in safety? Are they housed?

TONY.   Five and twenty miles in two hours and a half is no such bad driving. The poor beasts have smoked for it: rabbit me, but I'd rather ride forty miles after a fox, than ten with such *varment.*

HAST.   Well, but where have you left the ladies? I die with impatience.

TONY.   Left them! Why, where should I leave them but where I found them?

HAST.   This is a riddle.

TONY.   Riddle me this, then. What's that goes round the house, and round the house, and never touches the house?

HAST.   I'm still astray.

TONY.   Why, that's it, mon. I have led them astray. By jingo, there's not a pond or slough within five miles of the place but they can tell the taste of.

HAST.   Ha! ha! ha! I understand; you took them in a

round, while they supposed themselves going forward. And so you have at last brought them home again.

TONY.   You shall hear. I first took them down Featherbed Lane, where we stuck fast in the mud. I then rattled them crack over the stones of Up-and-down Hill. I then introduced them to the gibbet on Heavy-tree Heath; and from that, with a circumbendibus, I fairly lodged them in the horse-pond at the bottom of the garden.

HAST.   But no accident, I hope?

TONY.   No, no; only mother is confoundedly frightened. She thinks herself forty miles off. She's sick of the journey, and the cattle can scarce crawl. So if your own horses be ready, you may whip off with Cousin, and I'll be bound that no soul here can budge a foot to follow you.

HAST.   My dear friend, how can I be grateful?

TONY.   Ay, now it's "dear friend," "noble 'Squire." Just now, it was all "idiot," "cub," and "run me through the guts." Damn *your* way of fighting, I say. After we take a knock in this part of the country, we kiss and be friends. But if you had run me through the guts, then I should be dead, and you might go kiss the hangman.

HAST.   The rebuke is just. But I must hasten to relieve Miss Neville; if you keep the old lady employed, I promise to take care of the young one.

TONY.   Never fear me. Here she comes. Vanish!

(*Exit* HASTINGS)

She's got from the pond, and draggled up to the waist like a mermaid.

Enter MRS. HARDCASTLE

MRS. HARD.   Oh, Tony, I'm killed! Shook! Battered to death! I shall never survive it. That last jolt that laid us against the quickset hedge has done my business.

TONY.   Alack, Mama, it was all your own fault. You would be for running away by night, without knowing one inch of the way.

MRS. HARD.   I wish we were at home again. I never met so many accidents in so short a journey. Drenched in the mud, overturned in a ditch, stuck fast in a slough, jolted to a jelly, and at last to lose our way! Whereabouts do you think we are, Tony?

TONY.   By my guess we should be upon Crackskull Common, about forty miles from home.

MRS. HARD.   O lud! O lud! The most notorious spot in all

the country. We only want a robbery to make a complete, night on't.

TONY. Don't be afraid, Mama, don't be afraid. Two of the five that kept here are hanged, and the other three may not find us. Don't be afraid. Is that a man that's galloping behind us? No, it's only a tree. Don't be afraid.

MRS. HARD. The fright will certainly kill me.

TONY. Do you see anything like a black hat moving behind the thicket?

MRS. HARD. O death!

TONY. No, it's only a cow. Don't be afraid, Mama, don't be afraid.

MRS. HARD. As I'm alive, Tony, I see a man coming towards us. Ah! I'm sure on't. If he perceives us, we are undone.

TONY (*aside*) Father-in-law, by all that's unlucky, come to take one of his night walks. (*to her*) Ah, it's a highwayman, with pistols as long as my arm. A damned ill-looking fellow.

MRS. HARD. Good heaven defend us! He approaches.

TONY. Do you hide yourself in that thicket, and leave me to manage him. If there be any danger, I'll cough and cry hem. When I cough be sure to keep close.

(MRS. HARDCASTLE *hides behind a tree in the back scene.*)

Enter HARDCASTLE

HARD. I'm mistaken, or I heard voices of people in want of help. Oh, Tony, is that you? I did not expect you so soon back. Are your mother and her charge in safety?

TONY. Very safe, Sir, at my aunt Pedigree's. Hem.

MRS. HARD. (*from behind*) Ah, death! I find there's danger.

HARD. Forty miles in three hours; sure that's too much, my youngster.

TONY. Stout horses and willing minds make short journeys, as they say. Hem.

MRS. HARD. (*from behind*) Sure he'll do the dear boy no harm.

HARD. But I heard a voice here; I should be glad to know from whence it came?

TONY. It was I, Sir, talking to myself, Sir. I was saying that forty miles in four hours was very good going. Hem. As to be sure it was. Hem. I have got a sort of cold by being out in the air. We'll go in, if you please. Hem.

HARD.   But if you talked to yourself, you did not answer yourself. I am certain I heard two voices, and am resolved (*raising his voice*) to find the other out.

MRS. HARD.   (*from behind*)   Oh! he's coming to find me out. Oh!

TONY.   What need you go, Sir, if I tell you? Hem. I'll lay down my life for the truth—hem—I'll tell you all, Sir.

(*detaining him*)

HARD.   I tell you I will not be detained. I insist on seeing. It's in vain to expect I'll believe you.

MRS. HARD.   (*running forward from behind*)   O lud! he'll murder my poor boy, my darling! Here, good gentleman, whet your rage upon me. Take my money, my life, but spare that young gentleman, spare my child, if you have any mercy.

HARD.   My wife! as I'm a Christian. From whence can she come, or what does she mean?

MRS. HARD.   (*kneeling*)   Take compassion on us, good Mr. Highwayman. Take our money, our watches, all we have, but spare our lives. We will never bring you to justice, indeed we won't, good Mr. Highwayman.

HARD.   I believe the woman's out of her senses. What, Dorothy, don't you know *me?*

MRS. HARD.   Mr. Hardcastle, as I'm alive! My fears blinded me. But who, my dear, could have expected to meet you here, in this frightful place, so far from home? What has brought you to follow us?

HARD.   Sure, Dorothy, you have not lost your wits? So far from home, when you are within forty yards of your own door! (*to him*) This is one of your old tricks, you graceless rogue, you! (*to her*) Don't you know the gate, and the mulberry tree; and don't you remember the horse-pond, my dear?

MRS. HARD.   Yes, I shall remember the horse-pond as long as I live; I have caught my death in it. (*to* TONY) And is it to you, you graceless varlet, I owe all this? I'll teach you to abuse your mother, I will.

TONY.   Ecod, Mother, all the parish says you have spoiled me, and so you may take the fruits on't.

MRS. HARD.   I'll spoil you, I will.

(*Follows him off the stage*)

HARD.   There's morality, however, in his reply.   (*Exit*)

Enter HASTINGS *and* MISS NEVILLE

HAST.   My dear Constance, why will you deliberate thus? If we delay a moment, all is lost forever. Pluck up a little resolution, and we shall soon be out of the reach of her malignity.

MISS NEV.   I find it impossible. My spirits are so sunk with the agitations I have suffered, that I am unable to face any new danger. Two or three years' patience will at last crown us with happiness.

HAST.   Such a tedious delay is worse than inconstancy. Let us fly, my charmer. Let us date our happiness from this very moment. Perish fortune. Love and content will increase what we possess beyond a monarch's revenue. Let me prevail.

MISS NEV.   No, Mr. Hastings, no. Prudence once more comes to my relief, and I will obey its dictates. In the moment of passion, fortune may be despised, but it ever produces a lasting repentance. I'm resolved to apply to Mr. Hardcastle's compassion and justice for redress.

HAST.   But though he had the will, he has not the power to relieve you.

MISS NEV.   But he has influence, and upon that I am resolved to rely.

HAST.   I have no hopes. But since you persist, I must reluctantly obey you.   (*Exeunt*)

SCENE III

SCENE: *Another room in the house*

Enter SIR CHARLES *and* MISS HARDCASTLE

SIR CHAS.   What a situation am I in! If what you say appears, I shall then find a guilty son. If what he says be true, I shall then lose one that, of all others, I most wished for a daughter.

MISS HARD.   I am proud of your approbation, and to show I merit it, if you place yourselves as I directed, you shall hear his explicit declaration. But he comes.

SIR CHAS.   I'll to your father, and keep him to the appointment.   (*Exit* SIR CHARLES)

Enter MARLOW

MARL.   Though prepared for setting out, I come once more to take leave, nor did I, till this moment, know the pain I feel in the separation.

MISS HARD.   (*in her own natural manner*)   I believe these sufferings cannot be very great, Sir, which you can so easily remove. A day or two longer, perhaps, might lessen your uneasiness, by showing the little value of what you now think proper to regret.

MARL. (*aside*) This girl every moment improves upon me. (*to her*) It must not be, Madam. I have already trifled too long with my heart. My very pride begins to submit to my passion. The disparity of education and fortune, the anger of a parent, and the contempt of my equals begin to lose their weight; and nothing can restore me to myself but this painful effort of resolution.

MISS HARD. Then go, Sir; I'll urge nothing more to detain you. Though my family be as good as hers you came down to visit, and my education, I hope, not inferior, what are these advantages without equal affluence? I must remain contented with the slight approbation of imputed merit; I must have only the mockery of your addresses, while all your serious aims are fixed on fortune.

Enter HARDCASTLE *and* SIR CHARLES *from behind*

SIR CHAS. Here, behind this screen.

HARD. Ay, ay, make no noise. I'll engage my Kate covers him with confusion at last.

MARL. By heavens, Madam, fortune was ever my smallest consideration. Your beauty at first caught my eye; for who could see that without emotion? But every moment that I converse with you, steals in some new grace, heightens the picture, and gives it stronger expression. What at first seemed rustic plainness, now appears refined simplicity. What seemed forward assurance, now strikes me as the result of courageous innocence and conscious virtue.

SIR CHAS. What can it mean? He amazes me!

HARD. I told you how it would be. Hush!

MARL. I am now determined to stay, Madam, and I have too good an opinion of my father's discernment, when he sees you, to doubt his approbation.

MISS HARD. No, Mr. Marlow, I will not, cannot detain you. Do you think I could suffer a connexion in which there is the smallest room for repentance? Do you think I would take the mean advantage of a transient passion, to load you with confusion? Do you think I could ever relish that happiness which was acquired by lessening yours?

MARL. By all that's good, I can have no happiness but what's in your power to grant me. Nor shall I ever feel repentance but in not having seen your merits before. I will stay, even contrary to your wishes; and though you should persist to shun me, I will make my respectful assiduities atone for the levity of my past conduct.

MISS HARD.   Sir, I must entreat you'll desist. As our acquaintance began, so let it end, in indifference. I might have given an hour or two to levity; but seriously, Mr. Marlow, do you think I could ever submit to a connexion where *I* must appear mercenary, and *you* imprudent? Do you think I could ever catch at the confident addresses of a secure admirer?

MARL.   (*kneeling*)   Does this look like security? Does this look like confidence? No, Madam, every moment that shows me your merit, only serves to increase my diffidence and confusion. Here let me continue——

SIR CHAS.   I can hold it no longer. Charles, Charles, how hast thou deceived me! Is this your indifference, your uninteresting conversation!

HARD.   Your cold contempt! your formal interview! What have you to say now?

MARL.   That I'm all amazement! What can it mean?

HARD.   It means that you can say and unsay things at pleasure; that you can address a lady in private, and deny it in public; that you have one story for us, and another for my daughter.

MARL.   Daughter!—this lady your daughter?

HARD.   Yes, Sir, my only daughter—my Kate; whose else should she be?

MARL.   Oh, the devil!

MISS HARD.   Yes, Sir, that very identical tall, squinting lady you were pleased to take me for (*curtseying*); she that you addressed as the mild, modest, sentimental man of gravity, and the bold, forward, agreeable Rattle of the Ladies' Club. Ha! ha! ha!

MARL.   Zounds! there's no bearing this; it's worse than death.

MISS HARD.   In which of your characters, Sir, will you give us leave to address you? As the faltering gentleman, with looks on the ground, that speaks just to be heard, and hates hypocrisy; or the loud, confident creature, that keeps it up with Mrs. Mantrap, and old Miss Biddy Buckskin, till three in the morning? Ha! ha! ha!

MARL.   Oh, curse on my noisy head! I never attempted to be impudent yet, that I was not taken down. I must be gone.

HARD.   By the hand of my body, but you shall not. I see

it was all a mistake, and I am rejoiced to find it. You shall not, Sir, I tell you. I know she'll forgive you. Won't you forgive him, Kate? We'll all forgive you. Take courage, man.

(*They retire, she tormenting him, to the back scene*)

Enter MRS. HARDCASTLE *and* TONY

MRS. HARD. So, so, they're gone off. Let them go, I care not.

HARD. Who gone?

MRS. HARD. My dutiful niece and her gentleman, Mr. Hastings, from town. He who came down with our modest visitor here.

SIR CHAS. Who, my honest George Hastings! As worthy a fellow as lives, and the girl could not have made a more prudent choice.

HARD. Then, by the hand of my body, I'm proud of the connexion.

MRS. HARD. Well, if he has taken away the lady, he has not taken her fortune; that remains in this family to console us for her loss.

HARD. Sure, Dorothy, you would not be so mercenary?

MRS. HARD. Ay, that's my affair, not yours.

HARD. But you know if your son, when of age, refuses to marry his cousin, her whole fortune is then at her own disposal.

MRS. HARD. Ay, but he's not of age, and she has not thought proper to wait for his refusal.

Enter HASTINGS *and* MISS NEVILLE

MRS. HARD. (*aside*) What, returned so soon? I begin not to like it.

HAST. (*to* HARDCASTLE) For my late attempt to fly off with your niece, let my present confusion be my punishment. We are now come back, to appeal from your justice to your humanity. By her father's consent, I first paid her my addresses, and our passions were first founded in duty.

MISS NEV. Since his death, I have been obliged to stoop to dissimulation to avoid oppression. In an hour of levity, I was ready even to give up my fortune to secure my choice. But I'm now recovered from the delusion, and hope from your tenderness what is denied me from a nearer connexion.

MRS. HARD. Pshaw, pshaw! this is all but the whining end of a modern novel.

HARD. Be it what it will, I'm glad they're come back to reclaim their due. Come hither, Tony, boy. Do you refuse this lady's hand whom I now offer you?

TONY. What signifies my refusing? You know I can't refuse her till I'm of age, Father.

HARD. While I thought concealing your age, boy, was likely to conduce to your improvement, I concurred with your mother's desire to keep it secret. But since I find she turns it to a wrong use, I must now declare, you have been of age these three months.

TONY. Of age! Am I of age, Father?

HARD. Above three months.

TONY. Then you'll see the first use I'll make of my liberty. (*taking* MISS NEVILLE's *hand*) Witness all men, by these presents, that I, Anthony Lumpkin, Esquire, of BLANK place, refuse you, Constantia Neville, spinster, of no place at all, for my true and lawful wife. So Constance Neville may marry whom she pleases, and Tony Lumpkin is his own man again!

SIR CHAS. O brave 'Squire!

HAST. My worthy friend!

MRS. HARD. My undutiful offspring!

MARL. Joy, my dear George, I give you joy sincerely. And could I prevail upon my little tyrant here to be less arbitrary, I should be the happiest man alive, if you would return me the favour.

HAST. (*to* MISS HARDCASTLE) Come, Madam, you are now driven to the very last scene of all your contrivances. I know you like him, I'm sure he loves you, and you must and shall have him.

HARD. (*joining their hands*) And I say so, too. And, Mr. Marlow, if she makes as good a wife as she has a daughter, I don't believe you'll ever repent your bargain. So now to supper; to-morrow we shall gather all the poor of the parish about us, and the Mistakes of the Night shall be crowned with a merry morning; so, boy, take her; and as you have been mistaken in the mistress, my wish is, that you may never be mistaken in the wife.

EPILOGUE

By DR. GOLDSMITH

Spoken by MISS HARDCASTLE

Well, having stoop'd to conquer with success,
And gain'd a husband without aid from dress,
Still as a bar-maid, I could wish it too,
As I have conquer'd him to conquer you:
And let me say, for all your resolution,
That pretty bar-maids have done execution.
Our life is all a play, compos'd to please;
"We have our exits and our entrances."
The first act shows the simple country maid,
Harmless and young, of ev'rything afraid;
Blushes when hir'd, and with unmeaning action,
"I hopes as how to give you satisfaction."
Her second act displays a livelier scene—
Th' unblushing bar-maid of a country inn,
Who whisks about the house, at market caters,
Talks loud, coquets the guests, and scolds the waiters.
Next the scene shifts to town, and there she soars,
The chop-house toast of ogling connoisseurs.
On 'Squires and Cits she there displays her arts,
And on the gridiron broils her lovers' hearts—
And as she smiles, her triumphs to complete,
E'en Common Councilmen forget to eat.
The fourth act shows her wedded to the 'Squire,
And Madam now begins to hold it higher;
Pretends to taste, at Operas cries *caro!*
And quits her *Nancy Dawson* for *Che Faro;*
Dotes upon dancing, and in all her pride,
Swims round the room, the Heinel of Cheapside;
Ogles and leers, with artificial skill,
Till, having lost in age the power to kill,
She sits all night at cards, and ogles at spadille.
Such, tho' our lives, th' eventful history—
The fifth and last act still remains for me.
The bar-maid now for your protection prays,
Turns female barrister, and pleads for Bayes.

The

Rivals

BY RICHARD BRINSLEY SHERIDAN

PROLOGUE

By THE AUTHOR

*Enter Serjeant-at-Law and Attorney following and
giving a paper*

SERJ.   What's here—a vile cramp hand! I cannot see
Without my spectacles.
    ATT. (*aside*)   He means his fee.——
Nay, Mr. Serjeant, good Sir, try again. (*gives money*)
    SERJ.   The scrawl improves. (*more*) O come, 'tis pretty
        plain.

Hey! how's this?—*Dibble!*—sure it cannot be!
A poet's brief! A poet and a fee!

    ATT.   Yea, Sir!—though *you* without reward, I know,
Would gladly plead the Muses' cause——

    SERJ.   So-so!

    ATT.   And if the fee offends—your wrath should fall
On me——

    SERJ.   Dear Dibble, no offence at all—

    ATT.   *Some sons of Phœbus*—in the courts we meet.

    SERJ.   And fifty sons of Phœbus in the Fleet!

    ATT.   Nor pleads he worse, who with a decent sprig
Of bays adorns his legal waste of wig.

    SERJ.   Full-bottom'd heroes thus, on signs, unfurl
A leaf of laurel—in a grove of curl!
Yet tell your client, that, in adverse days,
This wig is warmer than a bush of bays.

    ATT.   Do you, then, Sir, my client's place supply,
Profuse of robe, and prodigal of tie—
Do you, with all those blushing pow'rs of face,⎫
And wonted bashful hesitating grace,   ⎬
Rise in the court, and flourish on the case. ⎭   (*Exit*)

    SERJ.   For practice, then, suppose—this brief will show it—
Me, Serjeant *Woodward*—counsel for the poet.
Us'd to the ground—I know 'tis hard to deal
With this dread *court*, from whence there's *no appeal;*
No *tricking* here, to blunt the edge of *law,*
Or, damned in *equity*—escape by *flaw:*
But *judgment* given—*your sentence* must remain;
No *writ of error* lies—to *Drury Lane!*

    Yet, when so kind you seem—'tis past dispute
We gain some favour, if not *costs of suit.*
No spleen is here! I see no hoarded fury;
—I think I never faced a milder jury!
Sad else our plight!—where frowns are transportation,
A hiss the gallows, and a groan, damnation!
But such the public candour, without fear
My client waives all *right of challenge* here.
No newsman from *our* session is dismiss'd,
Nor wit nor critic *we* scratch off the list;
His faults can never hurt another's ease,
His crime at worst—a *bad attempt* to please:
Thus, all respecting, he appeals to all,
And by the general voice will *stand* or *fall.*

PROLOGUE

By THE AUTHOR

Spoken on the Tenth Night, by JULIA

Granted our cause, our suit and trial o'er,
The worthy serjeant need appear no more:
In pleasing I a different client choose;
He served the poet—I would serve the Muse:
Like him, I'll try to merit your applause,
A female counsel in a female's cause.

    Look on this form*—where Humour, quaint and sly,
Dimples the cheek, and points the beaming eye;
Where gay Invention seems to boast its wiles
In amorous hint, and half-triumphant smiles;
While her light masks or covers Satire's strokes,
All hides the conscious blush her wit provokes.
Look on her well—does she seem form'd to teach?
Should you *expect* to hear this lady preach?
Is grey experience suited to her youth?
Do solemn sentiments become that mouth?
Bid her be grave, those lips should rebel prove
To every theme that slanders mirth or love.

    Yet, thus adorn'd with every graceful art
To charm the fancy and yet reach the heart—
Must we displace her, and instead advance
The goddess of the woeful countenance—
The sentimental Muse?—Her emblems view,
The Pilgrim's Progress, and a sprig of rue!
View her—too chaste to look like flesh and blood—
Primly portrayed on emblematic wood!
There, fix'd in usurpation, should she stand,
She'll snatch the dagger from her sister's hand;
And having made her votaries *weep a flood,*
Good heav'n! she'll end her comedies in blood—
Bid Harry Woodward (CAPTAIN ABSOLUTE) break poor Dunstal's (DAVID'S) crown!
Imprison Quick (ACRES), and knock Ned Shuter (SIR ANTHONY ABSOLUTE) down;
While sad Barsanti (LYDIA LANGUISH), weeping o'er the scene,
Shall stab herself—or poison Mrs. Green (MRS. MALAPROP).

   * *Pointing to the figure of* COMEDY.

Such dire encroachments to prevent in time,
Demands the critic's voice—the poet's rhyme.
Can our light scenes add strength to holy laws?
Such puny patronage but hurts the cause:
Fair Virtue scorns our feeble aid to ask;
And moral Truth disdains the trickster's mask.
For here their fav'rite stands,* whose brow—severe
And sad—claims Youth's respect, and Pity's tear;
Who, when oppressed by foes her worth creates,
Can point a poniard at the guilt she hates.

DRAMATIS PERSONÆ

Men:

SIR ANTHONY ABSOLUTE
CAPT. ABSOLUTE
FAULKLAND
ACRES
SIR LUCIUS O'TRIGGER
FAG
DAVID
COACHMAN

Women:

MRS. MALAPROP
LYDIA LANGUISH
JULIA
LUCY

Maid, Boy, Servants, &c.

SCENE: *Bath*

TIME OF ACTION, WITHIN ONE DAY

* *Pointing to* TRAGEDY.

THE RIVALS

ACT I

SCENE I

SCENE: *A street in Bath*

Coachman crosses the stage.—Enter FAG,
looking after him

FAG. What!—Thomas!—Sure, 'tis he?—What!—Thomas!—Thomas!

COACH. Hey!—Odd's life!—Mr. Fag!—give us your hand, my old fellow-servant.

FAG. Excuse my glove, Thomas:—I'm dev'lish glad to see you, my lad: why, my prince of charioteers, you look as hearty!—but who the deuce thought of seeing you in Bath!

COACH. Sure, Master, Madam Julia, Harry, Mrs. Kate, and the postilion be all come!

FAG. Indeed!

COACH. Aye! Master thought another fit of the gout was coming to make him a visit: so he'd a mind to gi't the slip, and whip! we were all off at an hour's warning.

FAG. Aye, aye! hasty in everything, or it would not be Sir Anthony Absolute!

COACH. But tell us, Mr. Fag, how does young master? Odd! Sir Anthony will stare to see the Captain here!

FAG. I do not serve Captain Absolute now.

COACH. Why sure!

FAG. At present I am employed by Ensign Beverley.

COACH. I doubt, Mr. Fag, you ha'n't changed for the better.

FAG. I have not changed, Thomas.

COACH. No! why, didn't you say you had left young master?

FAG. No.——Well, honest Thomas, I must puzzle you no farther: briefly then—Captain Absolute and Ensign Beverley are one and the same person.

COACH. The devil they are!

FAG. So it is indeed, Thomas; and the *Ensign*-half of my master being on guard at present—the *Captain* has nothing to do with me.

COACH. So, so!—What, this is some freak, I warrant!——Do tell us, Mr. Fag, the meaning o't—you know I ha' trusted you.

FAG. You'll be secret, Thomas?

COACH. As a coach-horse.

FAG. Why then the cause of all this is—LOVE—Love, Thomas, who (as you may get read to you) has been a masquerader ever since the days of Jupiter.

COACH. Aye, aye;—I guessed there was a lady in the case: but pray, why does your master pass only for *Ensign?* Now if he had shammed *General,* indeed——

FAG. Ah! Thomas, there lies the mystery o' the matter. Hark'ee, Thomas, my master is in love with a lady of a very singular taste: a lady who likes him better as a *half-pay Ensign* than if she knew he was son and heir to Sir Anthony Absolute, a baronet of three thousand a year!

COACH. That is an odd taste indeed!—but has she got the stuff, Mr. Fag? is she rich, hey?

FAG. Rich!—why, I believe she owns half the stocks—Z——ds! Thomas, she could pay the national debt as easily as I could my washerwoman! She has a lap-dog that eats out of gold—she feeds her parrot with small pearls—and all her thread-papers are made of bank-notes!

COACH. Bravo!—Faith!—Odd! I warrant she has a set of thousands at least. But does she draw kindly with the Captain?

FAG. As fond as pigeons.

COACH. May one hear her name?

FAG. Miss Lydia Languish. But there is an old tough aunt in the way; though, by the bye, she has never seen my master, for he got acquainted with Miss while on a visit in Gloucestershire.

COACH. Well—I wish they were once harnessed together in matrimony.——But pray, Mr. Fag, what kind of a place is this Bath? I ha' heard a deal of it—here's a mort o' merry-making, hey?

FAG. Pretty well, Thomas, pretty well—'tis a good lounge. In the morning we go to the Pump-room (though neither my master nor I drink the waters); after breakfast we saunter on the Parades, or play a game at billiards; at night we dance: but d——n the place, I'm tired of it: their regular hours stupefy me —not a fiddle nor a card after eleven! However, Mr. Faulk-

land's gentleman and I keep it up a little in private parties—
I'll introduce you there, Thomas: you'll like him much.

COACH.   Sure I know Mr. Du-Peigne—you know his master
is to marry Madam Julia.

FAG.   I had forgot.——But Thomas, you must polish a little
—indeed you must. Here now—this wig! what the devil do you
do with a *wig*, Thomas?—none of the London whips of any
degree of *ton* wear *wigs* now.

COACH.   More's the pity! more's the pity, I say—Odd's life!
when I heard how the lawyers and doctors had took to their
own hair, I thought how 'twould go next:—Odd rabbit it!
when the fashion had got foot on the Bar, I guessed 'twould
mount to the Box! But 'tis all out of character, believe me, Mr.
Fag: and look'ee, I'll never gi' up mine—the lawyers and doctors may do as they will.

FAG.   Well, Thomas, we'll not quarrel about that.

COACH.   Why, bless you, the gentlemen of they professions
ben't all of a mind—for in our village now, tho'ff *Jack Gauge,*
the *exciseman,* has ta'en to his carrots, there's little Dick, the
farrier, swears he'll never forsake his *bob,* tho' all the college
should appear with their own heads!

FAG.   Indeed! well said, Dick! But hold—mark! mark!
Thomas.

COACH.   Zooks! 'tis the Captain!—Is that the lady with
him?

FAG.   No! no! that is Madam Lucy—my master's mistress's
maid. They lodge at that house—but I must after him to tell
him the news.

COACH.   Odd! he's giving her money!——Well, Mr. Fag——

FAG.   Good-bye, Thomas.—I have an appointment in
Gyde's Porch this evening at eight; meet me there, and we'll
make a little party.   (*Exeunt severally*)

SCENE II

SCENE: *A dressing-room in* MRS. MALAPROP'S
lodgings

LYDIA *sitting on a sofa, with a book in her hand.*
LUCY, *as just returned from a message*

LUCY.   Indeed, Ma'am, I traversed half the town in search
of it: I don't believe there's a circulating library in Bath I
ha'n't been at.

LYD.   And could not you get *The Reward of Constancy?*

LUCY.   No, indeed, Ma'am.

LYD.   Nor *The Fatal Connection?*

LUCY.   No, indeed, Ma'am.

LYD.   Nor *The Mistakes of the Heart?*

LUCY.   Ma'am, as ill-luck would have it, Mr. Bull said Miss Sukey Saunter had just fetched it away.

LYD.   Heigh-ho! Did you inquire for *The Delicate Distress?*

LUCY.   Or *The Memoirs of Lady Woodford?* Yes, indeed, Ma'am. I asked everywhere for it; and I might have brought it from Mr. Frederick's, but Lady Slattern Lounger, who had just sent it home, had so soiled and dog's-eared it, it wa'n't fit for a Christian to read.

LYD.   Heigh-ho!—Yes, I always know when Lady Slattern has been before me. She has a most observing thumb; and I believe cherishes her nails for the convenience of making marginal notes.——Well, child, what *have* you brought me?

LUCY.   Oh! here, Ma'am. (*taking books from under her cloak, and from her pockets*) This is *The Gordian Knot,* and this *Peregrine Pickle.* Here are *The Tears of Sensibility* and *Humphry Clinker.* This is *The Memoirs of a Lady of Quality, written by herself,* and here the second volume of *The Sentimental Journey.*

LYD.   Heigh-ho!—What are those books by the glass?

LUCY.   The great one is only *The Whole Duty of Man*— where I press a few blonds, Ma'am.

LYD.   Very well—give me the *sal volatile.*

LUCY.   Is it in a blue cover, Ma'am?

LYD.   My smelling bottle, you simpleton!

LUCY.   Oh, the drops!—Here, Ma'am.

LYD.   Hold!—here's some one coming——quick! see who it is.   (*Exit* LUCY)

Surely I heard my cousin Julia's voice!

Re-enter LUCY

LUCY.   Lud! Ma'am, here is Miss Melville.

LYD.   Is it possible!——

Enter JULIA

LYD.   My dearest Julia, how delighted am I!—(*Embrace.*) How unexpected was this happiness!

JUL.   True, Lydia—and our pleasure is the greater; but what has been the matter?—you were denied to me at first!

LYD.   Ah! Julia, I have a thousand things to tell you! But

first inform me what has conjured you to Bath? Is Sir Anthony here?

JUL.   He is—we are arrived within this hour, and I suppose he will be here to wait on Mrs. Malaprop as soon as he is dressed.

LYD.   Then, before we are interrupted, let me impart to you some of my distress! I know your gentle nature will sympathize with me, though your prudence may condemn me! My letters have informed you of my whole connexion with Beverley—but I have lost him, Julia! My aunt has discovered our intercourse by a note she intercepted, and has confined me ever since! Yet, would you believe it? she has fallen absolutely in love with a tall Irish baronet she met one night since we have been here, at Lady Macshuffle's rout.

JUL.   You jest, Lydia!

LYD.   No, upon my word. She really carries on a kind of correspondence wth him, under a feigned name though, till she chooses to be known to him; but it is a *Delia* or a *Celia,* I assure you.

JUL.   Then surely she is now more indulgent to her niece.

LYD.   Quite the contrary. Since she has discovered her own frailty she is become more suspicious of mine. Then I must inform you of another plague! That odious Acres is to be in Bath to-day; so that I protest I shall be teased out of all spirits!

JUL.   Come, come, Lydia, hope the best. Sir Anthony shall use his interest with Mrs. Malaprop.

LYD.   But you have not heard the worst. Unfortunately I had quarreled with my poor Beverley just before my aunt made the discovery, and I have not seen him since to make it up.

JUL.   What was his offence?

LYD.   Nothing at all! But, I don't know how it was, as often as we had been together we had never had a quarrel! And, somehow, I was afraid he would never give me an opportunity. So last Thursday I wrote a letter to myself to inform myself that Beverley was at that time paying his addresses to another woman. I signed it *your friend unknown,* showed it to Beverley, charged him with his falsehood, put myself in a violent passion, and vowed I'd never see him more.

JUL.   And you let him depart so, and have not seen him since?

LYD.   'Twas the next day my aunt found the matter out. I intended only to have teased him three days and a half, and now I've lost him forever!

JUL.   If he is as deserving and sincere as you have represented him to me, he will never give you up so. Yet consider,
Lydia, you tell me he is but an ensign, and you have thirty
thousand pounds!

LYD.   But you know I lose most of my fortune if I marry
without my aunt's consent, till of age; and that is what I have
determined to do ever since I knew the penalty. Nor could I
love the man who would wish to wait a day for the alterna-
tive.

JUL.   Nay, this is caprice!

LYD.   What, does Julia tax me with caprice? I thought her
lover Faulkland had enured her to it.

JUL.   I do not love even *his* faults.

LYD.   But a-propos—you have sent to him, I suppose?

JUL.   Not yet, upon my word, nor has he the least idea of
my being in Bath. Sir Anthony's resolution was so sudden I
could not inform him of it.

LYD.   Well, Julia, you are your own mistress (though under the protection of Sir Anthony), yet have you for this long
year been a slave to the caprice, the whim, the jealousy of this
ungrateful Faulkland, who will ever delay assuming the right
of a husband, while you suffer him to be equally imperious as
a lover.

JUL.   Nay, you are wrong entirely. We were contracted
before my father's death. That, and some consequent embarrassments, have delayed what I know to be my Faulkland's
most ardent wish. He is too generous to trifle on such a point.
And for his character, you wrong him there too. No, Lydia, he
is too proud, too noble to be jealous: if he is captious, 'tis without dissembling; if fretful, without rudeness. Unused to the
fopperies of love, he is negligent of the little duties expected
from a lover—but being unhackneyed in the passion, his affection is ardent and sincere; and as it engrosses his whole soul,
he expects every thought and emotion of his mistress to move
in unison with his. Yet, though his pride calls for this full return, his humility makes him undervalue those qualities in
him which would entitle him to it; and not feeling why he
should be loved to the degree he wishes, he still suspects that
he is not loved enough. This temper, I must own, has cost me
many unhappy hours; but I have learned to think myself his
debtor for those imperfections which arise from the ardour of
his attachment.

LYD.   Well, I cannot blame you for defending him. But
tell me candidly, Julia, had he never saved your life, do you

think you should have been attached to him as you are? Believe me, the rude blast that overset your boat was a prosperous gale of love to him.

JUL.   Gratitude may have strengthened my attachment to Mr. Faulkland, but I loved him before he had preserved me; yet surely that alone were an obligation sufficient——

LYD.   Obligation! Why, a water-spaniel would have done as much! Well, I should never think of giving my heart to a man because he could swim!

JUL.   Come, Lydia, you are too inconsiderate.

LYD.   Nay, I do but jest.—— What's here?

Enter LUCY in a hurry

LUCY.   O Ma'am, here is Sir Anthony Absolute just come home with your aunt.

LYD.   They'll not come here.—— Lucy, do you watch.

(*Exit* LUCY)

JUL.   Yet I must go. Sir Anthony does not know I am here, and if we meet, he'll detain me, to show me the town. I'll take another opportunity of paying my respects to Mrs. Malaprop, when she shall treat me, as long as she chooses, with her select words so ingeniously *misapplied,* without being *mispronounced.*

Re-enter LUCY

LUCY.   O Lud! Ma'am, they are both coming upstairs.

LYD.   Well, I'll not detain you, coz. Adieu, my dear Julia. I'm sure you are in haste to send to Faulkland. There—through my room you'll find another stair-case.

JUL.   Adieu.——(*embrace*)   (*Exit* JULIA)

LYD.   Here, my dear Lucy, hide these books. Quick, quick! Fling *Peregrine Pickle* under the toilet—throw *Roderick Random* into the closet—put *The Innocent Adultery* into *The Whole Duty of Man*—thrust *Lord Aimworth* under the sofa—cram *Ovid* behind the bolster—there—put *The Man of Feeling* into your pocket—so, so,—now lay *Mrs. Chapone* in sight, and leave *Fordyce's Sermons* open on the table.

LUCY.   Oh burn it, Ma'am! the hair-dresser has torn away as far as *Proper Pride.*

LYD.   Never mind—open at *Sobriety.*—Fling me *Lord Chesterfield's Letters.*—Now for 'em.

Enter MRS. MALAPROP, and SIR ANTHONY ABSOLUTE

MRS. MAL.   There, Sir Anthony, there sits the deliberate

simpleton who wants to disgrace her family, and lavish herself on a fellow not worth a shilling!

LYD. Madam, I thought you once——

MRS. MAL. You thought, Miss! I don't know any business you have to think at all. Thought does not become a young woman. But the point we would request of you is, that you will promise to forget this fellow—to illiterate him, I say, quite from your memory.

LYD. Ah! Madam! our memories are independent of our wills. It is not so easy to forget.

MRS. MAL. But I say it is, Miss; there is nothing on earth so easy as to *forget*, if a person chooses to set about it. I'm sure I have as much forgot your poor dear uncle as if he had never existed—and I thought it my duty so to do; and let me tell you, Lydia, these violent memories don't become a young woman.

SIR ANTH. Why sure she won't pretend to remember what she's ordered not!—aye, this comes of her reading!

LYD. What crime, Madam, have I committed to be treated thus?

MRS. MAL. Now don't attempt to extirpate yourself from the matter; you know I have proof controvertible of it. But tell me, will you promise to do as you're bid? Will you take a husband of your friend's choosing?

LYD. Madam, I must tell you plainly, that had I no preference for anyone else, the choice you have made would be my aversion.

MRS. MAL. What business have you, Miss, with *preference* and *aversion?* They don't become a young woman; and you ought to know, that as both always wear off, 'tis safest in matrimony to begin with a little *aversion.* I am sure I hated your poor dear uncle before marriage as if he'd been a blackamoor—and yet, Miss, you are sensible what a wife I made!—and when it pleased heaven to release me from him, 'tis unknown what tears I shed! But suppose we were going to give you another choice, will you promise us to give up this Beverley?

LYD. Could I belie my thoughts so far as to give that promise, my actions would certainly as far belie my words.

MRS. MAL. Take yourself to your room. You are fit company for nothing but your own ill-humours.

LYD. Willingly, Ma'am—I cannot change for the worse.

(*Exit* LYDIA)

MRS. MAL. There's a little intricate hussy for you!

SIR ANTH. It is not to be wondered at, Ma'am—all this is

the natural consequence of teaching girls to read. Had I a thousand daughters, by heaven! I'd as soon have them taught the black art as their alphabet!

MRS. MAL. Nay, nay, Sir Anthony, you are an absolute misanthropy.

SIR ANTH. In my way hither, Mrs. Malaprop, I observed your niece's maid coming forth from a circulating library! She had a book in each hand—they were half-bound volumes, with marble covers! From that moment I guessed how full of duty I should see her mistress!

MRS. MAL. Those are vile places, indeed!

SIR ANTH. Madam, a circulating library in a town is as an evergreen tree of diabolical knowledge! It blossoms through the year! And depend on it, Mrs. Malaprop, that they who are so fond of handling the leaves, will long for the fruit at last.

MRS. MAL. Fie, fie, Sir Anthony, you surely speak laconically!

SIR ANTH. Why, Mrs. Malaprop, in moderation, now, what would you have a woman know?

MRS. MAL. Observe me, Sir Anthony. I would by no means wish a daughter of mine to be a progeny of learning; I don't think so much learning becomes a young woman; for instance —I would never let her meddle with Greek, or Hebrew, or Algebra, or Simony, or Fluxions, or Paradoxes, or such inflammatory branches of learning—neither would it be necessary for her to handle any of your mathematical, astronomical, diabolical instruments;—but, Sir Anthony, I would send her, at nine years old, to a boarding-school, in order to learn a little ingenuity and artifice. Then, Sir, she should have a supercilious knowledge in accounts—and as she grew up, I would have her instructed in geometry, that she might know something of the contagious countries—but above all, Sir Anthony, she should be mistress of orthodoxy, that she might not misspell, and mispronounce words so shamefully as girls usually do; and likewise that she might reprehend the true meaning of what she is saying. This, Sir Anthony, is what I would have a woman know—and I don't think there is superstitious article in it.

SIR ANTH. Well, well, Mrs. Malaprop, I will dispute the point no further with you; though I must confess that you are a truly moderate and polite arguer, for almost every third word you say is on my side of the question. But, Mrs. Malaprop, to the more important point in debate—you say you have no objection to my proposal.

MRS. MAL.   None, I assure you. I am under no positive engagement with Mr. Acres, and as Lydia is so obstinate against
him, perhaps your son may have better success.

SIR ANTH.   Well, Madam, I will write for the boy directly.
He knows not a syllable of this yet, though I have for some
time had the proposal in my head. He is at present with his
regiment.

MRS. MAL.   We have never seen your son, Sir Anthony;
but I hope no objection on his side.

SIR ANTH.   Objection!—let him object if he dare! No, no,
Mrs. Malaprop, Jack knows that the least demur puts me in a
frenzy directly. My process was always very simple—in their
younger days, 'twas "Jack do this";—if he demurred—I
knocked him down—and if he grumbled at that—I always sent
him out of the room.

MRS. MAL.   Aye, and the properest way, o' my conscience!
—nothing is so conciliating to young people as severity. Well,
Sir Anthony, I shall give Mr. Acres his discharge, and prepare
Lydia to receive your son's invocations; and I hope you will
represent *her* to the Captain as an object not altogether
illegible.

SIR ANTH.   Madam, I will handle the subject prudently.
Well, I must leave you—and let me beg you, Mrs. Malaprop,
to enforce this matter roundly to the girl; take my advice—
keep a tight hand; if she rejects this proposal—clap her under
lock and key—and if you were just to let the servants forget to
bring her dinner for three or four days, you can't conceive
how she'd come about!   (*Exit* SIR ANTHONY)

MRS. MAL.   Well, at any rate I shall be glad to get her
from under my intuition. She has somehow discovered my
partiality for Sir Lucius O'Trigger—sure, Lucy can't have betrayed me! No, the girl is such a simpleton, I should have
made her confess it.—— (*calls*) Lucy!—Lucy—Had she been
one of your artificial ones, I should never have trusted her.

Enter LUCY

LUCY.   Did you call, Ma'am?

MRS. MAL.   Yes, girl. Did you see Sir Lucius while you
was out?

LUCY.   No, indeed, Ma'am, not a glimpse of him.

MRS. MAL.   You are sure, Lucy, that you never mentioned——

LUCY.   O Gemini! I'd sooner cut my tongue out.

MRS. MAL.   Well, don't let your simplicity be imposed on.

LUCY. No, Ma'am.

MRS. MAL. So, come to me presently, and I'll give you another letter to Sir Lucius; but mind, Lucy—if ever you betray what you are intrusted with (unless it be other people's secrets to me) you forfeit my malevolence forever, and your being a simpleton shall be no excuse for your locality.

(*Exit* MRS. MALAPROP)

LUCY. Ha! ha! ha!—So, my dear *simplicity,* let me give you a little respite—(*altering her manner*)—let girls in my station be as fond as they please of appearing expert, and knowing in their trusts—commend me to a mask of *silliness,* and a pair of sharp eyes for my own interest under it! Let me see to what account have I turned my *simplicity* lately—(*looks at a paper*) For *abetting Miss Lydia Languish in a design of running away with an Ensign!—in money—sundry times—twelve pound twelve—gowns, five—hats, ruffles, caps, &c., &c.—numberless! From the said Ensign, within this last month, six guineas and a half.*—About a quarter's pay!—Item, *from Mrs. Malaprop, for betraying the young people to her*—when I found matters were likely to be discovered—*two guineas, and a black padusoy.*—Item, *from Mr. Acres, for carrying divers letters*—which I never delivered—*two guineas, and a pair of buckles.*—Item, *from Sir Lucius O'Trigger—three crowns—two gold pocket-pieces—and a silver snuff-box!*—Well done, *simplicity!*—Yet I was forced to make my Hibernian believe that he was corresponding, not with the *aunt,* but with the *niece:* for, though not overrich, I found he had too much pride and delicacy to sacrifice the feelings of a gentleman to the necessities of his fortune.   (*Exit*)

ACT II

SCENE I

SCENE: CAPTAIN ABSOLUTE's *lodgings*

CAPTAIN ABSOLUTE *and* FAG

FAG. Sir, while I was there Sir Anthony came in: I told him you had sent me to inquire after his health, and to know if he was at leisure to see you.

ABS. And what did he say on hearing I was at Bath?

FAG. Sir, in my life I never saw an elderly gentleman more astonished! He started back two or three paces, rapped out a dozen interjectoral oaths, and asked what the devil had brought you here!

ABS. Well, Sir, and what did you say?

FAG. O, I lied, Sir—I forget the precise lie; but you may depend on't, he got no truth from me. Yet, with submission, for fear of blunders in future, I should be glad to fix what *has* brought us to Bath, in order that we may lie a little consistently. Sir Anthony's servants were curious, Sir, very curious indeed.

ABS. You have said nothing to them?

FAG. Oh, not a word, Sir—not a word. Mr. Thomas, indeed, the coachman (whom I take to be the discreetest of whips)——

ABS. 'Sdeath!—you rascal! you have not trusted him!

FAG. Oh, *no,* Sir!—no—no—not a syllable, upon my veracity! He was, indeed, a little inquisitive; but I was sly, Sir—devilish sly!—My master (said I), honest Thomas (you know, Sir, one says *honest* to one's inferiors), is come to Bath to *recruit*—yes, Sir—I said, *to recruit*—and whether for men, money, or constitution, you know, Sir, is nothing to him, nor anyone else.

ABS. Well—*recruit* will do—let it be so——

FAG. Oh, Sir, recruit will do surprisingly—indeed, to give the thing an air, I told Thomas that your Honour had already enlisted five disbanded chairmen, seven minority waiters, and thirteen billiard markers.

ABS. You blockhead, never say more than is necessary.

FAG. I beg pardon, Sir—I beg pardon—— But with submission, a lie is nothing unless one supports it. Sir, whenever I draw on my invention for a good current lie, I always forge indorsements, as well as the bill.

ABS. Well, take care you don't hurt your credit by offering too much security. Is Mr. Faulkland returned?

FAG. He is above, Sir, changing his dress.

ABS. Can you tell whether he has been informed of Sir Anthony's and Miss Melville's arrival?

FAG. I fancy not, Sir; he has seen no one since he came in but his gentleman, who was with him at Bristol.——I think, Sir, I hear Mr. Faulkland coming down——

ABS. Go tell him I am here.

FAG. Yes, Sir (*going*). I beg pardon, Sir, but should Sir Anthony call, you will do me the favour to remember that we are *recruiting*, if you please.

ABS. Well, well.

FAG.   And in tenderness to my character, if your Honour could bring in the chairmen and waiters, I shall esteem it as an obligation; for though I never scruple a lie to serve my master, yet it hurts one's conscience to be found out.   (*Exit*)

ABS.   Now for my whimsical friend—if he does not know that his mistress is here, I'll tease him a little before I tell him——

Enter FAULKLAND

Faulkland, you're welcome to Bath again; you are punctual in your return.

FAULK.   Yes; I had nothing to detain me when I had finished the business I went on. Well, what news since I left you? How stand matters between you and Lydia?

ABS.   Faith, much as they were; I have not seen her since our quarrel; however, I expect to be recalled every hour.

FAULK.   Why don't you persuade her to go off with you at once?

ABS.   What, and lose two-thirds of her fortune? You forget that, my friend. No, no, I could have brought her to that long ago.

FAULK.   Nay then, you trifle too long—if you are sure of *her,* propose to the aunt *in your own character,* and write to Sir Anthony for his consent.

ABS.   Softly, softly, for though I am convinced my little Lydia would elope with me as Ensign Beverley, yet am I by no means certain that she would take me with the impediment of our friend's consent, a regular humdrum wedding, and the reversion of a good fortune on my side; no, no, I must prepare her gradually for the discovery, and make myself necessary to her, before I risk it.——Well, but Faulkland, you'll dine with us to-day at the hotel?

FAULK.   Indeed, I cannot: I am not in spirits to be of such a party.

ABS.   By heavens! I shall forswear your company. You are the most teasing, captious, incorrigible lover! Do love like a man!

FAULK.   I own I am unfit for company.

ABS.   Am not *I* a lover; aye, and a romantic one too? Yet do I carry everywhere with me such a confunded farrago of doubts, fears, hopes, wishes, and all the flimsy furniture of a country miss's brain!

FAULK.   Ah! Jack, your heart and soul are not, like mine, fixed immutably on one only object. You throw for a large stake, but losing—you could stake, and throw again. But I have set my sum of happiness on this cast, and not to succeed were to be stripped of all.

ABS.   But, for heaven's sake! what grounds for apprehension can your whimsical brain conjure up at present?

FAULK.   What grounds for apprehension did you say? Heavens! are there not a thousand! I fear for her spirits—her health—her life. My absence may fret her; her anxiety for my return, her fears for me, may oppress her gentle temper. And for her health—does not every hour bring me cause to be alarmed? If it rains, some shower may even then have chilled her delicate frame! If the wind be keen, some rude blast may have affected her! The heat of noon, the dews of the evening, may endanger the life of her, for whom only I value mine. O! Jack, when delicate and feeling souls are separated, there is not a feature in the sky, not a movement of the elements, not an aspiration of the breeze, but hints some cause for a lover's apprehension!

ABS.   Aye, but we may choose whether we will take the hint or not. So then, Faulkland, if you were convinced that Julia were well and in spirits, you would be entirely content?

FAULK.   I should be happy beyond measure—I am anxious only for that.

ABS.   Then to cure your anxiety at once—Miss Melville is in perfect health, and is at this moment in Bath!

FAULK.   Nay, Jack—don't trifle with me.

ABS.   She is arrived here with my father within this hour.

FAULK.   Can you be serious?

ABS.   I thought you knew Sir Anthony better than to be surprised at a sudden whim of this kind. Seriously then, it is as I tell you—upon my honour.

FAULK.   My dear friend!—Hollo, Du-Peigne! my hat—my dear Jack—now nothing on earth can give me a moment's uneasiness.

Enter FAG

FAG.   Sir, Mr. Acres just arrived is below.

ABS.   Stay, Faulkland, this Acres lives within a mile of Sir Anthony, and he shall tell you how your mistress has been ever since you left her.—— Fag, show the gentleman up.

(*Exit* FAG)

FAULK.   What, is he much acquainted in the family?

ABS.   Oh, very intimate. I insist on your not going: besides, his character will divert you.

FAULK.   Well, I should like to ask him a few questions.

ABS.   He is likewise a rival of mine—that is of my *other self's,* for he does not think his friend Captain Absolute ever saw the lady in question; and it is ridiculous enough to hear him complain to me of *one Beverley,* a concealed skulking rival, who——

FAULK.   Hush! He's here.

Enter ACRES

ACRES.   Hah! my dear friend, noble captain, and honest Jack, how dost thou? Just arrived, faith, as you see. Sir, your humble servant. Warm work on the roads, Jack!—Odds whips and wheels! I've travelled like a comet, with a tail of dust all the way as long as the Mall.

ABS.   Ah! Bob, you are indeed an eccentric planet, but we know your attraction hither. Give me leave to introduce Mr. Faulkland to you; Mr. Faulkland, Mr. Acres.

ACRES.   Sir, I am most heartily glad to see you: Sir, I solicit your connexions.——Hey, Jack—what—this is Mr. Faulkland, who——?

ABS.   Aye, Bob, Miss Melville's Mr. Faulkland.

ACRES.   Od'so! she and your father can be but just arrived before me—I suppose you have seen them. Ah! Mr. Faulkland, you are indeed a happy man.

FAULK.   I have not seen Miss Melville yet, Sir. I hope she enjoyed full health and spirits in Devonshire?

ACRES.   Never knew her better in my life, Sir—never better. Odd's blushes and blooms! she has been as healthy as the German Spa.

FAULK.   Indeed! I did hear that she had been a little indisposed.

ACRES.   False, false, Sir—only said to vex you: quite the reverse, I assure you.

FAULK.   There, Jack, you see she has the advantage of me; I had almost fretted myself ill.

ABS.   Now are you angry with your mistress for not having been sick.

FAULK.   No, no, you misunderstand me: yet surely a little trifling indisposition is not an unnatural consequence of absence from those we love. Now confess—isn't there something unkind in this violent, robust, unfeeling health?

ABS.   Oh, it was very unkind of her to be well in your absence, to be sure!

ACRES.   Good apartments, Jack.

FAULK. Well, Sir, but you were saying that Miss Melville has been so *exceedingly* well—what, then she has been merry and gay, I suppose? Always in spirits—hey?

ACRES. Merry! Odds crickets! she has been the belle and spirit of the company wherever she has been—so lively and entertaining! so full of wit and humour!

FAULK. There, Jack, there! Oh, by my soul! there is an innate levity in woman, that nothing can overcome. What! happy, and I away!

ABS. Have done—how foolish this is! Just now you were only apprehensive for your mistress's *spirits*.

FAULK. Why, Jack, have I been the joy and spirit of the company?

ABS. No, indeed, you have not.

FAULK. Have I been lively and entertaining?

ABS. Oh, upon my word, I acquit you.

FAULK. Have I been full of wit and humour?

ABS. No, faith; to do you justice, you have been confoundedly stupid indeed.

ACRES. What's the matter with the gentleman?

ABS. He is only expressing his great satisfaction at hearing that Julia has been so well and happy—that's all—hey, Faulkland?

FAULK. Oh! I am rejoiced to hear it—yes, yes, she has a *happy* disposition!

ACRES. That she has indeed. Then she is so accomplished —so sweet a voice—so expert at her harpsichord—such a mistress of flat and sharp, squallante, rumblante, and quiverante! There was this time month—Odds minims and crotchets! how she did chirrup at Mrs. Piano's concert!

FAULK. There again, what say you to this? You see she has been all mirth and song—not a thought of me!

ABS. Pho! man, is not music the food of love?

FAULK. Well, well, it may be so.—— Pray, Mr.—— what's his d—d name? Do you remember what songs Miss Melville sung?

ACRES. Not I, indeed.

ABS. Stay now, they were some pretty, melancholy, purling-stream airs, I warrant; perhaps you may recollect; did she sing *"When absent from my soul's delight"*?

ACRES. No, that wa'n't it.

ABS. Or *"Go, gentle gales"*?——*"Go, gentle gales!"*

(*sings*)

ACRES.   Oh no! nothing like it. Odds! now I recollect one of them—"*My heart's my own, my will is free.*"   (*sings*)

FAULK.   Fool! fool that I am! to fix all my happiness on such a trifler! 'Sdeath! to make herself the pipe and ballad-monger of a circle! to soothe her light heart with catches and glees! What can you say to this, Sir?

ABS.   Why, that I should be glad to hear my mistress had been so merry, *Sir.*

FAULK.   Nay, nay, nay—I am not sorry that she has been happy—no, no, I am glad of that—I would not have had her sad or sick—yet surely a sympathetic heart would have shown itself even in the choice of a song: she might have been tem-perately healthy, and, somehow, plaintively gay; but she has been dancing too, I doubt not!

ACRES.   What does the gentleman say about dancing?

ABS.   He says the lady we speak of dances as well as she sings.

ACRES.   Aye, truly, does she—there was at our last race-ball——

FAULK.   Hell and the devil! There! there!—I told you so! I told you so! Oh! she thrives in my absence! Dancing! But her whole feelings have been in opposition with mine! I have been anxious, silent, pensive, sedentary—my days have been hours of care, my nights of watchfulness. She has been all Health! Spirit! Laugh! Song! Dance! Oh! d—n'd, d—n'd levity!

ABS.   For heaven's sake! Faulkland, don't expose yourself so. Suppose she has danced, what then? Does not the cere-mony of society often oblige——

FAULK.   Well, well, I'll contain myself. Perhaps, as you say, for form sake. What, Mr. Acres, you were praising Miss Melville's manner of dancing a *minuet*—hey?

ACRES.   Oh I dare insure her for that—but what I was going to speak of was her *country dancing.* Odds swimmings! she has such an air with her!

FAULK.   Now disappointment on her! Defend this, Abso-lute, why don't you defend this? Country-dances! jigs, and reels! Am I to blame now? A minuet I could have forgiven—I should not have minded that—I say I should not have re-garded a minuet—but *country-dances!* Z——ds! had she made one in a cotillion—I believe I could have forgiven even that—but to be monkey-led for a night! to run the gauntlet through a string of amorous palming puppies! to show paces like a managed filly! O Jack, there never can be but *one* man in the world whom a truly modest and delicate woman ought to pair with in a *country-dance;* and even then, the rest of the couples should be her great uncles and aunts!

ABS. Aye, to be sure!—grandfathers and grandmothers!

FAULK. If there be but one vicious mind in the Set, 'twill spread like a contagion—the action of their pulse beats to the lascivious movement of the jig—their quivering, warm-breathed sighs impregnate the very air—the atmosphere becomes electrical to love, and each amorous spark darts through every link of the chain! I must leave you—I own I am somewhat flurried—and that confounded looby has perceived it.

(*going*)

ABS. Nay, but stay, Faulkland, and thank Mr. Acres for his good news.

FAULK. D—n his news!　　　　　(*Exit* FAULKLAND)

ABS. Ha! ha! ha! Poor Faulkland! Five minutes since—"nothing on earth could give him a moment's uneasiness!"

ACRES. The gentleman wa'n't angry at my praising his mistress, was he?

ABS. A little jealous, I believe, Bob.

ACRES. You don't say so? Ha! ha! jealous of me?—that's a good joke.

ABS. There's nothing strange in that, Bob: let me tell you, that sprightly grace and insinuating manner of yours will do some mischief among the girls here.

ACRES. Ah! you joke—ha! ha!—mischief—ha! ha! But you know I am not my own property; my dear Lydia has forestalled me. She could never abide me in the country, because I used to dress so badly—but odds frogs and tambours! I shan't take matters so here—now ancient madam has no voice in it. I'll make my old clothes know who's master. I shall straightway cashier the hunting-frock, and render my leather breeches incapable. My hair has been in training some time.

ABS. Indeed!

ACRES. Aye—and tho'ff the side-curls are a little restive, my hind-part takes to it very kindly.

ABS. O, you'll polish, I doubt not.

ACRES. Absolutely I propose so. Then if I can find out this Ensign Beverley, odds triggers and flints! I'll make him know the difference o't.

ABS. Spoke like a man—but pray, Bob, I observe you have got an odd kind of a new method of swearing——

ACRES. Ha! ha! you've taken notice of it? 'Tis genteel, isn't it? I didn't invent it myself, though; but a commander in our militia—a great scholar, I assure you—says that there is no meaning in the common oaths, and that nothing but their antiquity makes them respectable, because, he says, the ancients would never stick to an oath or two, but would say, by Jove! or by Bacchus! or by Mars! or by Venus! or by Pallas! according to the sentiment; so that to swear with propriety, says my little major, the "oath should be an echo to the sense"; and this we call the *oath referential,* or *sentimental swearing*—ha! ha! ha! 'tis genteel, isn't it?

ABS. Very genteel, and very new, indeed—and I dare say will supplant all other figures of imprecation.

ACRES. Aye, aye, the best terms will grow obsolete. Damns have had their day.

Enter FAG

FAG. Sir, there is a gentleman below desires to see you. Shall I show him into the parlour?

ABS. Aye—you may.

ACRES. Well, I must be gone——

ABS. Stay; who is it, Fag?

FAG. Your father, Sir.

ABS. You puppy, why didn't you show him up directly?

(*Exit* FAG)

ACRES. You have business with Sir Anthony. I expect a message from Mrs. Malaprop at my lodgings. I have sent also to my dear friend, Sir Lucius O'Trigger. Adieu, Jack! We must meet at night, when you shall give me a dozen bumpers to little Lydia.

ABS. That I will, with all my heart. (*Exit* ACRES)

ABS. Now for a parental lecture. I hope he has heard nothing of the business that has brought me here. I wish the gout had held him fast in Devonshire, with all my soul!

Enter SIR ANTHONY

ABS. Sir, I am delighted to see you here; and looking so well! Your sudden arrival at Bath made me apprehensive for your health.

SIR ANTH. Very apprehensive, I dare say, Jack. What, you are recruiting here, hey?

ABS. Yes, Sir, I am on duty.

SIR ANTH. Well, Jack, I am glad to see you, though I did not expect it, for I was going to write to you on a little matter of business. Jack, I have been considering that I grow old and infirm, and shall probably not trouble you long.

ABS.   Pardon me, Sir, I never saw you look more strong and hearty; and I pray frequently that you may continue so.

SIR ANTH.   I hope your prayers may be heard with all my heart. Well then, Jack, I have been considering that I am so strong and hearty, I may continue to plague you a long time. Now, Jack, I am sensible that the income of your commission, and what I have hitherto allowed you, is but a small pittance for a lad of your spirit.

ABS.   Sir, you are very good.

SIR ANTH.   And it is my wish, while yet I live, to have my boy make some figure in the world. I have resolved, therefore, to fix you at once in a noble independence.

ABS.   Sir, your kindness overpowers me—such generosity makes the gratitude of reason more lively than the sensations even of filial affection.

SIR ANTH.   I am glad you are so sensible of my attention —and you shall be master of a large estate in a few weeks.

ABS.   Let my future life, Sir, speak my gratitude: I cannot express the sense I have of your munificence. Yet, Sir, I presume you would not wish me to quit the army?

SIR ANTH.   Oh, that shall be as your wife chooses.

ABS.   My wife, Sir!

SIR ANTH.   Aye, aye—settle that between you—settle that between you.

ABS.   A *wife*, Sir, did you say?

SIR ANTH.   Aye, a wife—why; did not I mention her before?

ABS.   Not a word of her, Sir.

SIR ANTH.   Odd so!—I mus'n't forget *her*, though. Yes, Jack, the independence I was talking of is by a marriage— the fortune is saddled with a wife—but I suppose that makes no difference.

ABS.   Sir! Sir!—you amaze me!

SIR ANTH.   Why, what the devil's the matter with the fool? Just now you were all gratitude and duty.

ABS.   I was, Sir—you talked to me of independence and a fortune, but not a word of a wife.

SIR ANTH.   Why—what difference does that make? Odds life, Sir! if you have the estate, you must take it with the live stock on it, as it stands.

ABS.   If my happiness is to be the price, I must beg leave to decline the purchase. Pray, Sir, who is the lady?

SIR ANTH.   What's that to you, Sir? Come, give me your promise to love, and to marry her directly.

ABS. Sure, Sir, this is not very reasonable, to summon my affections for a lady I know nothing of!

SIR ANTH. I am sure, Sir, 'tis more unreasonable in you to *object* to a lady you know nothing of.

ABS. Then, Sir, I must tell you plainly that my inclinations are fixed on another—my heart is engaged to an angel.

SIR ANTH. Then pray let it send an excuse. It is very sorry —but *business* prevents its waiting on her.

ABS. But my vows are pledged to her.

SIR ANTH. Let her foreclose, Jack; let her foreclose; they are not worth redeeming: besides, you have the angel's vows in exchange, I suppose; so there can be no loss there.

ABS. You must excuse me, Sir, if I tell you, once for all, that in this point I cannot obey you.

SIR ANTH. Hark'ee, Jack: I have heard you for some time with patience—I have been cool—quite cool; but take care— you know I am compliance itself when I am not thwarted— no one more easily led when I have my own way; but don't put me in a frenzy.

ABS. Sir, I must repeat it—in this I cannot obey you.

SIR ANTH. Now, d—n me! if ever I call you *Jack* again while I live!

ABS. Nay, Sir, but hear me.

SIR ANTH. Sir, I won't hear a word—not a word! not one word! so give me your promise by a nod—and I'll tell you what, Jack—I mean, you dog—if you don't, by——

ABS. What, Sir, promise to link myself to some mass of ugliness! to——

SIR ANTH. Z——ds! Sirrah! the lady shall be as ugly as I choose: she shall have a hump on each shoulder; she shall be as crooked as the Crescent; her one eye shall roll like the Bull's in Cox's Museum—she shall have a skin like a mummy, and the beard of a Jew—she shall be all this, Sirrah!—yet I'll make you ogle her all day, and sit up all night to write sonnets on her beauty.

ABS. This is reason and moderation indeed!

SIR ANTH. None of your sneering, puppy! no grinning, jackanapes!

ABS. Indeed, Sir, I never was in a worse humour for mirth in my life.

SIR ANTH. 'Tis false, Sir! I know you are laughing in your sleeve; I know you'll grin when I am gone, Sirrah!

ABS. Sir, I hope I know my duty better.

SIR ANTH.   None of your passion, Sir! none of your vio-lence! if you please. It won't do with me, I promise you.

ABS.   Indeed, Sir, I never was cooler in my life.

SIR ANTH.   'Tis a confounded lie!—I know you are in a passion in your heart; I know you are, you hypocritical young dog! But it won't do.

ABS.   Nay, Sir, upon my word.

SIR ANTH.   So you will fly out! Can't you be cool, like me? What the devil good can *passion* do! *Passion* is of no service, you impudent, insolent, overbearing reprobate!—There you sneer again! don't provoke me! But you rely upon the mild-ness of my temper—you do, you dog! you play upon the meek-ness of my disposition! Yet take care—the patience of a saint may be overcome at last!—but mark! I give you six hours and a half to consider of this: if you then agree, without any con-dition, to do everything on earth that I choose, why—con-found you! I may in time forgive you. If not, z——ds! don't enter the same hemisphere with me! don't dare to breathe the same air, or use the same light with me; but get an atmos-phere and a sun of your own! I'll strip you of your commis-sion; I'll lodge a five-and-threepence in the hands of trustees, and you shall live on the interest. I'll disown you, I'll disin-herit you, I'll unget you! and—d—n me, if ever I call you Jack again!   (*Exit* SIR ANTHONY)

ABSOLUTE *solus*

ABS.   Mild, gentle, considerate Father—I kiss your hands. What a tender method of giving his opinion in these matters Sir Anthony has! I dare not trust him with the truth. I wonder what old wealthy hag it is that he wants to bestow on me! Yet he married himself for love! and was in his youth a bold intriguer, and a gay companion!

Enter FAG

FAG.   Assuredly, Sir, our father is wrath to a degree; he comes downstairs eight or ten steps at a time—muttering, growling, and thumping the bannisters all the way: I, and the cook's dog, stand bowing at the door—rap! he gives me a stroke on the head with his cane; bids me carry that to my master; then kicking the poor turnspit into the area, d—ns us all for a puppy triumvirate! Upon my credit, Sir, were I in your place, and found my father such very bad company, I should certainly drop his acquaintance.

ABS. Cease your impertinence, Sir, at present. Did you come in for nothing more? Stand out of the way!

(*Pushes him aside, and exit.*)

FAG *solus*

FAG. Soh! Sir Anthony trims my master. He is afraid to reply to his father—then vents his spleen on poor Fag! When one is vexed by one person, to revenge one's self on another who happens to come in the way is the vilest injustice. Ah! it shows the worst temper—the basest——

Enter Errand-Boy

BOY. Mr. Fag! Mr. Fag! your master calls you.

FAG. Well, you little dirty puppy, you need not bawl so!—— The meanest disposition! the——

BOY. Quick, quick, Mr. Fag!

FAG. *Quick, quick,* you impudent jackanapes! am I to be commanded by you too? you little, impertinent, insolent, kitchen-bred——   (*Exit, kicking and beating him.*)

SCENE II

SCENE: *The North Parade*

Enter LUCY

LUCY. So—I shall have another rival to add to my mistress's list—Captain Absolute. However, I shall not enter his name till my purse has received notice in form. Poor Acres is dismissed! Well, I have done him a last friendly office in letting him know that Beverley was here before him. Sir Lucius is generally more punctual when he expects to hear from his *dear Dalia,* as he calls her: I wonder he's not here! I have a little scruple of conscience from this deceit; though I should not be paid so well, if my hero knew that *Delia* was near fifty, and her own mistress.

Enter SIR LUCIUS O'TRIGGER

SIR LUC. Hah! my little embassadress—upon my conscience, I have been looking for you; I have been on the South Parade this half-hour.

LUCY. (*speaking simply*) O Gemini! and I have been waiting for your worship here on the North.

SIR LUC.   Faith!—maybe that was the reason we did not meet; and it is very comical, too, how you could go out and I not see you—for I was only taking a nap at the Parade Coffee-house, and I chose the *window* on purpose that I might not miss you.

LUCY.   My stars! Now I'd wager a sixpence I went by while you were asleep.

SIR LUC.   Sure enough it must have been so—and I never dreamt it was so late, till I waked. Well, but my little girl, have you got nothing for me?

LUCY.   Yes, but I have: I've got a letter for you in my pocket.

SIR LUC.   Oh faith! I guessed you weren't come empty-handed—well—let me see what the dear creature says.

LUCY.   There, Sir Lucius.   (*Gives him a letter.*)

SIR LUC. (*reads*)   *Sir—there is often a sudden incentive impulse in love, that has a greater induction than years of domestic combination: such was the commotion I felt at the first superfluous view of Sir Lucius O'Trigger.*—Very pretty, upon my word.—*Female punctuation forbids me to say more; yet let me add, that it will give me joy infallible to find Sir Lucius worthy the last criterion of my affections.* DELIA. Upon my conscience! Lucy, your lady is a great mistress of language. Faith, she's quite the queen of the dictionary!—for the devil a word dare refuse coming at her call—though one would think it was quite out of hearing.

LUCY.   Aye, Sir, a lady of her experience——

SIR LUC.   Experience! what, at seventeen?

LUCY.   O true, Sir—but then she reads so—my stars! how she will read off-hand!

SIR LUC.   Faith, she must be very deep read to write this way—though she is rather an arbitrary writer too—for here are a great many poor words pressed into the service of this note, that would get their *habeas corpus* from any court in Christendom.

LUCY.   Ah! Sir Lucius, if you were to hear how she talks of you!

SIR LUC.   Oh tell her I'll make her the best husband in the world, and Lady O'Trigger into the bargain! But we must get the old gentlewoman's consent—and do everything fairly.

LUCY.   Nay, Sir Lucius, I thought you wa'n't rich enough to be so nice!

SIR LUC.   Upon my word, young woman, you have hit it: I am so poor that I can't afford to do a dirty action. If I did not want money I'd steal your mistress and her fortune with a great deal of pleasure. However, my pretty girl (*gives her money*), here's a little something to buy you a ribband; and meet me in the evening, and I'll give you an answer to this. So, hussy, take a kiss beforehand to put you in mind.

(*kisses her*)

LUCY. O lud! Sir Lucius—I never seed such a gemman! My lady won't like you if you're so impudent.

SIR LUC. Faith she will, Lucy—— That same—pho! what's the name of it?—*Modesty!*—is a quality in a lover more praised by the women than liked; so, if your mistress asks you whether Sir Lucius ever gave you a kiss, tell her *fifty*— my dear.

LUCY. What, would you have me tell her a lie?

SIR LUC. Ah, then, you baggage! I'll make it a truth presently.

LUCY. For shame now; here is someone coming.

SIR LUC. Oh faith, I'll quiet your conscience.

(*Sees FAG.—Exit, humming a tune.*)

Enter FAG

FAG. So, so, Ma'am. I humbly beg pardon.

LUCY. O lud!—now, Mr. Fag, you flurry one so.

FAG. Come, come, Lucy, here's no one by—so a little less simplicity, with a grain or two more sincerity, if you please. You play false with us, Madam. I saw you give the baronet a letter. My master shall know this, and if he don't call him out—I will.

LUCY. Ha! ha! ha! you gentlemen's gentlemen are so hasty. That letter was from Mrs. Malaprop, simpleton. She is taken with Sir Lucius's address.

FAG. How! what tastes some people have! Why, I suppose I have walked by her window an hundred times. But what says our young lady? Any message to my master?

LUCY. Sad news, Mr. Fag! A worse rival than Acres! Sir Anthony Absolute has proposed his son.

FAG. What, Captain Absolute?

LUCY. Even so. I overheard it all.

FAG. Ha! ha! ha!—very good, faith. Good-bye, Lucy, I must away with this news.

LUCY. Well—you may laugh, but it is true, I assure you. (*going*) But—Mr. Fag—tell your master not to be cast down by this.

FAG. Oh, he'll be so disconsolate!

LUCY.   And charge him not to think of quarrelling with young Absolute.

FAG.   Never fear!—never fear!

LUCY.   Be sure—bid him keep up his spirits.

FAG.   We will—we will.   (*Exeunt severally*)

ACT III

SCENE I

SCENE: *The North Parade*

Enter ABSOLUTE

ABS.   'Tis just as Fag told me, indeed. Whimsical enough, faith! My father wants to *force* me to marry the very girl I am plotting to run away with! He must not know of my connexion with her yet awhile. He has too summary a method of proceeding in these matters. However, I'll read my recantation instantly. My conversion is something sudden, indeed, but I can assure him it is very *sincere*.——So, so—here he comes. He looks plaguy gruff.   (*steps aside*)

Enter SIR ANTHONY

SIR ANTH.   No—I'll die sooner than forgive him. *Die*, did I say? I'll live these fifty years to plague him. At our last meeting, his impudence had almost put me out of temper. An obstinate, passionate, self-willed boy! Who can he take after? This is my return for getting him before all his brothers and sisters!—for putting him, at twelve years old, into a marching regiment, and allowing him fifty pounds a year, beside his pay ever since! But I have done with him; he's anybody's son for me. I never will see him more—never—never—never—never!

ABS.   Now for a penitential face.

SIR ANTH.   Fellow, get out of my way.

ABS.   Sir, you see a penitent before you.

SIR ANTH.   I see an impudent scoundrel before me.

ABS.   A sincere penitent. I am come, Sir, to acknowledge my error, and to submit entirely to your will.

SIR ANTH.   What's that?

ABS.   I have been revolving, and reflecting, and considering on your past goodness, and kindness, and condescension to me.

SIR ANTH. Well, Sir?

ABS. I have been likewise weighing and balancing what you were pleased to mention concerning duty, and obedience, and authority.

SIR ANTH. Well, puppy?

ABS. Why, then, Sir, the result of my reflections is—a resolution to sacrifice every inclination of my own to your satisfaction.

SIR ANTH. Why, now you talk sense—absolute sense—I never heard anything more sensible in my life. Confound you, you shall be *Jack* again!

ABS. I am happy in the appellation.

SIR ANTH. Why then, Jack, my dear Jack, I will now inform you who the lady really is. Nothing but your passion and violence, you silly fellow, prevented my telling you at first. Prepare, Jack, for wonder and rapture! prepare!—— What think you of Miss Lydia Languish?

ABS. Languish! What, the Languishes of Worcestershire?

SIR ANTH. Worcestershire! No. Did you never meet Mrs. Malaprop and her niece, Miss Languish, who came into our country just before you were last ordered to your regiment?

ABS. Malaprop! Languish! I don't remember ever to have heard the names before. Yet, stay—I think I do recollect something.——*Languish! Languish!* She squints, don't she? A little, red-haired girl?

SIR ANTH. Squints? A red-haired girl! Z——ds, no!

ABS. Then I must have forgot; it can't be the same person.

SIR ANTH. Jack! Jack! what think you of blooming, love-breathing seventeen?

ABS. As to that, Sir, I am quite indifferent. If I can please you in the matter, 'tis all I desire.

SIR ANTH. Nay, but Jack, such eyes! such eyes! so innocently wild! so bashfully irresolute! Not a glance but speaks and kindles some thought of love! Then, Jack, her cheeks! her cheeks, Jack! so deeply blushing at the insinuations of her tell-tale eyes! Then, Jack, her lips!—O Jack, lips smiling at their own discretion; and if not smiling, more sweetly pouting, more lovely in sullenness!

ABS. (*aside*) That's she, indeed. Well done, old gentleman!

SIR ANTH. Then, Jack, her neck!—O Jack! Jack!

ABS. And which is to be mine, Sir, the niece or the aunt?

SIR ANTH. Why, you unfeeling, insensible puppy, I despise you! When I was of your age, such a description would have made me fly like a rocket! The *aunt*, indeed! Odds life! when I ran away with your mother, I would not have touched anything old or ugly to gain an empire.

ABS. Not to please your father, Sir?

SIR ANTH. To please my father! Z——ds! not to please—— Oh, my father!—Oddso!—yes—yes!—if my father, indeed, had desired—that's quite another matter. Though he wa'n't the indulgent father that I am, Jack.

ABS. I dare say not, Sir.

SIR ANTH. But, Jack, you are not sorry to find your mistress is so beautiful?

ABS. Sir, I repeat it; if I please you in this affair, 'tis all I desire. Not that I think a woman the worse for being handsome; but, Sir, if you please to recollect, you before hinted something about a hump or two, one eye, and a few more graces of that kind. Now, without being very nice, I own I should rather choose a wife of mine to have the usual number of limbs, and a limited quantity of back: and though *one* eye may be very agreeable, yet as the prejudice has always run in favour of *two*, I would not wish to affect a singularity in that article.

SIR ANTH. What a phlegmatic sot it is! Why, Sirrah, you're an anchorite! a vile, insensible stock. You a soldier! you're a walking block, fit only to dust the company's regimentals on! Odds life! I've a great mind to marry the girl myself!

ABS. I am entirely at your disposal, Sir; if you should think of addressing Miss Languish yourself, I suppose you would have me marry the *aunt*; or if you should change your mind, and take the old lady—'tis the same to me—I'll marry the *niece*.

SIR ANTH. Upon my word, Jack, thou'rt either a very great hypocrite, or——But come, I know your indifference on such a subject must be all a lie—I'm sure it must—come, now— damn your demure face!—come, confess, Jack—you have been lying—ha'n't you? you have been playing the hypocrite, hey? —I'll never forgive you if you ha'n't been lying and playing the hypocrite.

ABS. I'm sorry, Sir, that the respect and duty which I bear to you should be so mistaken.

SIR ANTH. Hang your respect and duty! But come along with me, I'll write a note to Mrs. Malaprop, and you shall visit the lady directly. Her eyes shall be the Promethean torch to you—come along. I'll never forgive you if you don't come back stark mad with rapture and impatience. If you don't, egad, I'll marry the girl myself!   (*Exeunt*)

SCENE II

SCENE: JULIA'S *dressing-room*

FAULKLAND *solus*

FAULK. They told me Julia would return directly; I wonder she is not yet come! How mean does this captious, unsatisfied temper of mine appear to my cooler judgment! Yet I know not that I indulge it in any other point: but on this one subject, and to this one subject, whom I think I love beyond my life, I am ever ungenerously fretful, and madly capricious! I am conscious of it—yet I cannot correct myself! What tender, honest joy sparkled in her eyes when we met! How delicate was the warmth of her expressions! I was ashamed to appear less happy, though I had come resolved to wear a face of coolness and upbraiding. Sir Anthony's presence prevented my proposed expostulations, yet I must be satisfied that she has not been so *very* happy in my absence. She is coming! Yes! I know the nimbleness of her tread when she thinks her impatient Faulkland counts the moments of her stay.

Enter JULIA

JUL.   I had not hoped to see you again so soon.

FAULK.   Could I, Julia, be contented with my first welcome—restrained as we were by the presence of a third person?

JUL.   O Faulkland, when your kindness can make me thus happy, let me not think that I discovered something of coldness in your first salutation.

FAULK.   'Twas but your fancy, Julia. I *was* rejoiced to see you—to see you in such health. Sure I had no cause for coldness?

JUL.   Nay then, I see you have taken something ill. You must not conceal from me what it is.

FAULK.   Well then—shall I own to you—that my joy at hearing of your health and arrival here, by your neighbour Acres, was somewhat damped by his dwelling much on the high spirits you had enjoyed in Devonshire—on your mirth, your singing, dancing, and I know not what! For such is my temper, Julia, that I should regard every mirthful moment in your absence as a treason to constancy. The mutual tear that steals down the cheek of parting lovers is a compact that no smile shall live there till they meet again.

JUL. Must I never cease to tax my Faulkland with this teasing minute caprice? Can the idle reports of a silly boor weigh in your breast against my tried affection?

FAULK. They have no weight with me, Julia: no, no—I am happy if you have been so—yet only say that you did not sing with *mirth*—say that you *thought* of Faulkland in the dance.

JUL. I never can be happy in your absence. If I wear a countenance of content, it is to show that my mind holds no doubt of my Faulkland's truth. If I seemed sad, it were to make malice triumph, and say that I had fixed my heart on one who left me to lament his roving, and my own credulity. Believe me, Faulkland, I mean not to upbraid you when I say that I have often dressed sorrow in smiles, lest my friends should guess whose unkindness had caused my tears.

FAULK. You were ever all goodness to me. Oh, I am a brute when I but admit a doubt of your true constancy!

JUL. If ever, without such cause from you, as I will not suppose possible, you find my affections veering but a point, may I become a proverbial scoff for levity and base ingratitude.

FAULK. Ah! Julia, that last word is grating to me. I would I had no title to your *gratitude!* Search your heart, Julia; perhaps what you have mistaken for love, is but the warm effusion of a too thankful heart!

JUL. For what quality must I love you?

FAULK. For no quality! To regard me for any quality of mind or understanding were only to *esteem* me. And for person—I have often wished myself deformed, to be convinced that I owed no obligation *there* for any part of your affection.

JUL. Where Nature has bestowed a show of nice attention in the features of a man, he should laugh at it as misplaced. I have seen men who in *this* vain article perhaps might rank above you; but my heart has never asked my eyes if it were so or not.

FAULK. Now this is not well from *you*, Julia. I despise person in a man. Yet if you loved me as I wish, though I were an Æthiop, you'd think none so fair.

JUL. I see you are determined to be unkind. The *contract* which my poor father bound us in gives you more than a lover's privilege.

FAULK. Again, Julia, you raise ideas that feed and justify my doubts. I would not have been more free—no—I am proud of my restraint. Yet—yet—perhaps your high respect alone for this solemn compact has fettered your inclinations, which else had made a worthier choice. How shall I be sure, had you remained unbound in thought and promise, that I should still have been the object of your persevering love?

JUL. Then try me now. Let us be free as strangers as to what is past: *my* heart will not feel more liberty!

FAULK. There now! so hasty, Julia! so anxious to be free! If your love for me were fixed and ardent, you would not loose your hold, even though I wished it!

JUL. Oh, you torture me to the heart! I cannot bear it.

FAULK. I do not mean to distress you. If I loved you less I should never give you an uneasy moment. But hear me. All my fretful doubts arise from this: women are not used to weigh, and separate the motives of their affections; the cold dictates of prudence, gratitude, or filial duty, may sometimes be mistaken for the pleadings of the heart. I would not boast —yet let me say that I have neither age, person, or character to found dislike on; my fortune such as few ladies could be charged with *indiscretion* in the match. O Julia! when *Love* receives such countenance from *Prudence,* nice minds will be suspicious of its birth.

JUL. I know not whither your insinuations would tend, but as they seem pressing to insult me, I will spare you the regret of having done so. I have given you no cause for this!

(*Exit in tears.*)

FAULK. In tears! Stay, Julia: stay but for a moment.—— The door is fastened! Julia!—my soul—but for one moment. I hear her sobbing! 'Sdeath! what a brute am I to use her thus! Yet stay!——Aye—she is coming now. How little reso-lution there is in woman! How a few soft words can turn them!——No, faith!—she is *not* coming either! Why, Julia— my love—say but that you forgive me—come but to tell me that. Now, this is being *too* resentful.——Stay! she *is* coming too—I thought she would—no *steadiness* in anything! her go-ing away must have been a mere trick then. She sha'n't see that I was hurt by it. I'll affect indifference. (*hums a tune: then listens*)——No—Z——ds! she's *not* coming!—nor don't in-tend it, I suppose. This is not *steadiness,* but *obstinacy!* Yet I deserve it. What, after so long an absence to quarrel with her tenderness!—'twas barbarous and unmanly! I should be ashamed to see her now. I'll wait till her just resentment is

abated—and when I distress her so again, may I lose her forever, and be linked instead to some antique virago, whose
gnawing passions, and long-hoarded spleen shall make me
curse my folly half the day, and all the night!   (*Exit*)

SCENE III

SCENE: MRS. MALAPROP'S *lodgings*

MRS. MALAPROP, *with a letter in her hand, and*
CAPTAIN ABSOLUTE

MRS. MAL.   Your being Sir Anthony's son, Captain, would
itself be a sufficient accommodation; but from the ingenuity
of your appearance, I am convinced you deserve the character here given of you.

ABS.   Permit me to say, Madam, that as I never yet have
had the pleasure of seeing Miss Languish, my principal inducement in this affair at present is the honour of being allied
to Mrs. Malaprop; of whose intellectual accomplishments,
elegant manners, and unaffected learning, no tongue is silent.

MRS. MAL.   Sir, you do me infinite honour! I beg, Captain,
you'll be seated. (*sit*) Ah! few gentlemen now-a-days know
how to value the ineffectual qualities in a woman! few think
how a little knowledge becomes a gentlewoman! Men have
no sense now but for the worthless flower of beauty!

ABS.   It is but too true, indeed, Ma'am. Yet I fear our
ladies should share the blame—they think our admiration of
beauty so great, that *knowledge* in *them* would be superfluous. Thus, like garden-trees, they seldom show fruit till time
has robbed them of the more specious blossom. Few, like
Mrs. Malaprop and the orange-tree, are rich in both at once!

MRS. MAL.   Sir—you overpower me with good-breeding.
(*aside*) He is the very pineapple of politeness!—— You are
not ignorant, Captain, that this giddy girl has somehow contrived to fix her affections on a beggarly, strolling, eaves-drop-
ping Ensign, whom none of us have seen, and nobody knows
anything of.

ABS.   Oh, I have heard the silly affair before. I'm not at all
prejudiced against her on *that* account.

MRS. MAL.   You are very good, and very considerate, Captain. I am sure I have done everything in my power since I
exploded the affair! Long ago I laid my positive conjunctions

on her never to think on the fellow again; I have since laid
Sir Anthony's preposition before her; but, I'm sorry to say,
she seems resolved to decline every particle that I enjoin her.

ABS.   It must be very distressing, indeed, Ma'am.

MRS. MAL.   Oh! it gives me the hydrostatics to such a degree! I thought she had persisted from corresponding with
him; but behold this very day I have interceded another letter from the fellow! I believe I have it in my pocket.

ABS.   (*aside*)   Oh the devil! my last note.

MRS. MAL.   Aye, here it is.

ABS.   (*aside*)   Aye, my note, indeed! Oh the little traitress
Lucy!

MRS. MAL.   There, perhaps you may know the writing.
                                        (*gives him the letter*)

ABS.   I think I have seen the hand before—yes, I certainly
must have seen this hand before——

MRS. MAL.   Nay, but read it, Captain.

ABS.   (*reads*)   "*My soul's idol, my adored Lydia!*"——Very
tender, indeed!

MRS. MAL.   Tender! aye, and profane, too, o' my conscience!

ABS.   "*I am excessively alarmed at the intelligence you
send me, the more so as my new rival*"——

MRS. MAL.   That's *you*, Sir.

ABS.   "*has universally the character of being an accomplished gentleman, and a man of honour.*"—— Well, that's
handsome enough.

MRS. MAL.   Oh, the fellow had some design in writing so.

ABS.   That he had, I'll answer for him, Ma'am.

MRS. MAL.   But go on, Sir—you'll see presently.

ABS.   "*As for the old weather-beaten she-dragon who
guards you*"——Who can he mean by that?

MRS. MAL.   Me! Sir—*me!*—he means *me!* There—what do
you think now? But go on a little further.

ABS.   Impudent scoundrel!—"*it shall go hard but I will
elude her vigilance, as I am told that the same ridiculous
vanity which makes her dress up her coarse features, and
deck her dull chat with hard words which she don't understand*"——

MRS. MAL.   There, Sir! an attack upon my language! What
do you think of that?—an aspersion upon my parts of speech!
Was ever such a brute! Sure if I reprehend anything in this
world, it is the use of my oracular tongue, and a nice de-
rangement of epitaphs!

ABS.   He deserves to be hanged and quartered! Let me see—"*same ridiculous vanity*"——

MRS. MAL.   You need not read it again, Sir.

ABS.   I beg pardon, Ma'am—"*does also lay her open to the grossest deceptions from flattery and pretended admiration*"—an impudent coxcomb!—"*so that I have a scheme to see you shortly with the old harridan's consent, and even to make her a go-between in our interviews.*"—Was ever such assurance!

MRS. MAL.   Did you ever hear anything like it? He'll elude my vigilance, will he? Yes, yes! ha! ha! He's very likely to enter these doors! We'll try who can plot best!

ABS.   So we will, Ma'am—so we will. Ha! ha! ha! A conceited puppy, ha! ha! ha! Well, but Mrs. Malaprop, as the girl seems so infatuated by this fellow, suppose you were to wink at her corresponding with him for a little time—let her even plot an elopement with him—then do you connive at her escape—while *I*, just in the nick, will have the fellow laid by the heels, and fairly contrive to carry her off in his stead.

MRS. MAL.   I am delighted with the scheme; never was anything better perpetrated!

ALS.   But, pray, could not I see the lady for a few minutes now? I should like to try her temper a little.

MRS. MAL.   Why, I don't know—I doubt she is not prepared for a visit of this kind. There is a decorum in these matters.

ABS.   O Lord! she won't mind *me*—only tell her Beverley——

MRS. MAL.   Sir!——

ABS.   (*aside.*) Gently, good tongue.

MRS. MAL.   What did you say of Beverley?

ABS.   Oh, I was going to propose that you should tell her, by way of jest, that it was Beverley who was below—she'd come down fast enough then—ha! ha! ha!

MRS. MAL.   'Twould be a trick she well deserves. Besides, you know the fellow tells her he'll get my consent to see her— ha! ha! Let him if he can, I say again. (*calling*) Lydia, come down here!——He'll make me a *go-between in their interviews!*—ha! ha! ha!—Come down, I say, Lydia!—I don't wonder at your laughing, ha! ha! ha!—his impudence is truly ridiculous.

ABS.   'Tis very ridiculous, upon my soul, Ma'am, ha! ha! ha!

MRS. MAL.   The little hussy won't hear. Well, I'll go and tell her at once who it is. She shall know that Captain Abso-

lute is come to wait on her. And I'll make her behave as becomes a young woman.

ABS.   As you please, Ma'am.

MRS. MAL.   For the present, Captain, your servant. Ah!
you've not done laughing yet, I see—*elude my vigilance!*—
yes, yes, ha! ha! ha!   (*Exit*)

ABS.   Ha! ha! ha! one would think now that I might throw
off all disguise at once, and seize my prize with security—
but such is Lydia's caprice that to undeceive were probably
to lose her. I'll see whether she knows me.

(*Walks aside, and seems engaged in looking at the pictures.*)

Enter LYDIA

LYD.   What a scene am I now to go through! Surely nothing can be more dreadful than to be obliged to listen to the
loathsome addresses of a stranger to one's heart. I have heard
of girls persecuted as I am, who have appealed in behalf of
their favoured lover to the generosity of his rival: suppose I
were to try it. There stands the hated rival—an officer, too!—
but oh, how unlike my Beverley! I wonder he don't begin.
Truly he seems a very negligent wooer! Quite at his ease,
upon my word! I'll speak first. (*aloud*) Mr. Absolute.

ABS.   Madam.   (*Turns round.*)

LYD.   O heavens! Beverley!

ABS.   Hush!—hush, my life! Softly! Be not surprised.

LYD.   I am so astonished! and so terrified! and so over-
joyed! For heaven's sake! how came you here?

ABS.   Briefly—I have deceived your aunt. I was informed
that my new rival was to visit here this evening, and con-
triving to have him kept away, have passed myself on *her* for
Captain Absolute.

LYD.   Oh, charming! And she really takes you for young
Absolute?

ABS.   Oh, she's convinced of it.

LYD.   Ha! ha! ha! I can't forbear laughing to think how
her sagacity is overreached!

ABS.   But we trifle with our precious moments. Such another opportunity may not occur. Then let me now conjure
my kind, my condescending angel, to fix the time when I
may rescue her from undeserved persecution, and with a
licensed warmth plead for my reward.

LYD.   Will you then, Beverley, consent to forfeit that portion of my paltry wealth? that burden on the wings of love?

ABS.   Oh, come to me—rich only thus—in loveliness. Bring
no portion to me but thy love—'twill be generous in you,
Lydia—for well you know, it is the only dower your poor
Beverley can repay.

LYD.   How persuasive are his words! How charming will
poverty be with him!

ABS.   Ah! my soul, what a life will we then live! Love shall
be our idol and support! We will worship him with a monastic
strictness; abjuring all worldly toys, to center every thought
and action there. Proud of calamity, we will enjoy the wreck
of wealth; while the surrounding gloom of adversity shall
make the flame of our pure love show doubly bright. By
heavens! I would fling all goods of fortune from me with a
prodigal hand to enjoy the scene where I might clasp my
Lydia to my bosom, and say, the world affords no smile to
me—but here. (*embracing her*)——(*aside*) If she holds out
now the devil is in it!

LYD.   Now could I fly with him to the Antipodes! but my
persecution is not yet come to a crisis.

Enter MRS. MALAPROP, *listening*

MRS. MAL.   (*aside*)   I am impatient to know how the little
hussy deports herself.

ABS.   So pensive, Lydia!—is then your warmth abated?

MRS. MAL.   (*aside*)   *Warmth abated!* So! she has been in a
passion, I suppose.

LYD.   No—nor ever can while I have life.

MRS. MAL.   (*aside*)   An ill-tempered little devil! She'll be
in a passion all her life—will she?

LYD.   Think not the idle threats of my ridiculous aunt can
ever have any weight with me.

MRS. MAL.   (*aside*)   Very dutiful, upon my word!

LYD.   Let her choice be Captain Absolute, but Beverley is
mine.

MRS. MAL.   (*aside*)   I am astonished at her assurance!—
to his face—this is to his face!

ABS.   Thus then let me enforce my suit.   (*kneeling*)

MRS. MAL.   (*aside*)   Aye—poor young man! down on his
knees entreating for pity! I can contain no longer.—(*aloud*)
Why, thou vixen! I have overheard you.

ABS. (*aside*)   Oh, confound her vigilance!

MRS. MAL.   Captain Absolute—I know not how to apolo-
gize for her shocking rudeness.

ABS. (*aside*) So—all's safe, I find.—(*aloud*) I have hopes, Madam, that time will bring the young lady——

MRS. MAL. Oh, there's nothing to be hoped for from her! She's as headstrong as an allegory on the banks of Nile.

LYD. Nay, Madam, what do you charge me with now?

MRS. MAL. Why, thou unblushing rebel—didn't you tell this gentleman to his face that you loved another better?—didn't you say you never would be his?

LYD. No, Madam—I did not.

MRS. MAL. Good heavens! what assurance! Lydia, Lydia, you ought to know that lying don't become a young woman! Didn't you boast that Beverley—that stroller Beverley—possessed your heart? Tell me that, I say.

LYD. 'Tis true, Ma'am, and none but Beverley——

MRS. MAL. Hold—hold, Assurance! you shall not be so rude.

ABS. Nay, pray Mrs. Malaprop, don't stop the young lady's speech: she's very welcome to talk thus—it does not hurt *me* in the least, I assure you.

MRS. MAL. You are *too* good, Captain—*too* amiably patient—but come with me, Miss. Let us see you again soon, Captain. Remember what we have fixed.

ABS. I shall, Ma'am.

MRS. MAL. Come, take a graceful leave of the gentleman.

LYD. May every blessing wait on my Beverley, my loved Bev——

MRS. MAL. Hussy! I'll choke the word in your throat!—come along—come along.

(*Exeunt severally,* ABSOLUTE *kissing his hand to* LYDIA— MRS. MALAPROP *stopping her from speaking.*)

SCENE IV

SCENE: ACRES'S *lodgings*

ACRES *and* DAVID

ACRES *as just dressed*

ACRES. Indeed, David—do you think I become it so?

DAV. You are quite another creature, believe me, master, by the Mass! an' we've any luck we shall see the Devon monkeyrony in all the print-shops in Bath!

ACRES. Dress *does* make a difference, David.

DAV. 'Tis all in all, I think. Difference! why, an' you were to go now to Clod-Hall, I am certain the old lady wouldn't know you: Master Butler wouldn't believe his own eyes, and Mrs. Pickle would cry, "Lard presarve me!"—our dairy-maid would come giggling to the door, and I warrant Dolly Tester, your Honour's favourite, would blush like my waistcoat. Oons! I'll hold a gallon, there a'n't a dog in the house but would bark, and I question whether *Phillis* would wag a hair of her tail!

ACRES. Aye, David, there's nothing like polishing.

DAV. So I says of your Honour's boots; but the boy never heeds me!

ACRES. But, David, has Mr. De-la-Grace been here? I must rub up my balancing, and chasing, and boring.

DAV. I'll call again, Sir.

ACRES. Do—and see if there are any letters for me at the post office.

DAV. I will. By the Mass, I can't help looking at your head! If I hadn't been by at the cooking, I wish I may die if I should have known the dish again myself!   (*Exit*)

ACRES *comes forward, practising a dancing step*

ACRES. Sink, slide—coupee! Confound the first inventors of cotillions! say I—they are as bad as algebra to us country gentlemen. I can walk a minuet easy enough when I'm forced! and I have been accounted a good stick in a country-dance. Odds jigs and tabours! I never valued your cross-over to couple—figure in—right and left—and I'd foot it with e'er a captain in the county! But these outlandish heathen alle-mandes and cotillions are quite beyond me! I shall never pros-per at 'em, that's sure. Mine are true-born English legs—they don't understand their curst French lingo! their *pas* this, and *pas* that, and *pas* t'other! D—n me! my feet don't like to be called paws! No, 'tis certain I have most anti-Gallican toes!

Enter Servant

SERV. Here is Sir Lucius O'Trigger to wait on you, Sir.

ACRES. Show him in.

Enter SIR LUCIUS

SIR LUC. Mr. Acres, I am delighted to embrace you.

ACRES. My dear Sir Lucius, I kiss your hands.

SIR LUC. Pray, my friend, what has brought you so sud-denly to Bath?

ACRES.   Faith! I have followed Cupid's Jack-a-Lantern, and find myself in a quagmire at last. In short, I have been very ill used, Sir Lucius. I don't choose to mention names, but look on me as on a very ill-used gentleman.

SIR LUC.   Pray, what is the case? I ask no names.

ACRES.   Mark me, Sir Lucius, I fall as deep as need be in love with a young lady—her friends take my part—I follow her to Bath—send word of my arrival, and receive answer that the lady is to be otherwise disposed of. This, Sir Lucius, I call being ill-used.

SIR LUC.   Very ill, upon my conscience. Pray, can you divine the cause of it?

ACRES.   Why, there's the matter: she has another lover, one Beverley, who, I am told, is now in Bath. Odds slanders and lies! he must be at the bottom of it.

SIR LUC.   A rival in the case, is there? And you think he has supplanted you unfairly?

ACRES.   Unfairly!—to be sure he has. He never could have done it fairly.

SIR LUC.   Then sure you know what is to be done!

ACRES.   Not I, upon my soul!

SIR LUC.   We wear no swords here, but you understand me.

ACRES.   What! fight him?

SIR LUC.   Aye, to be sure: what can I mean else?

ACRES.   But he has given me no provocation.

SIR LUC.   Now, I think he has given you the greatest provocation in the world. Can a man commit a more heinous offence against another than to fall in love with the same woman? Oh, by my soul, it is the most unpardonable breach of friendship!

ACRES.   Breach of friendship! Aye, aye; but I have no acquaintance with this man. I never saw him in my life.

SIR LUC.   That's no argument at all—he has the less right then to take such a liberty.

ACRES.   'Gad, that's true. I grow full of anger, Sir Lucius! I fire apace! Odds hilts and blades! I find a man may have a deal of valour in him and not know it! But couldn't I contrive to have a little right of my side?

SIR LUC.   What the devil signifies *right* when your *honour* is concerned? Do you think Achilles, or my little Alexander the Great ever inquired where the right lay? No, by my soul, they drew their broadswords, and left the lazy sons of peace to settle the justice of it.

ACRES.   Your words are a grenadier's march to my heart! I believe courage must be catching! I certainly do feel a kind of valour rising, as it were—a kind of courage, as I may say. Odds flints, pans, and triggers! I'll challenge him directly.

SIR LUC.   Ah, my little friend! if we had Blunderbuss-Hall here—I could show you a range of ancestry, in the O'Trigger line, that would furnish the New Room, every one of whom had killed his man! For though the mansion-house and dirty acres have slipped through my fingers, I thank heaven our honour, and the family-pictures, are as fresh as ever.

ACRES.   O Sir Lucius! I have had ancestors too! every man of 'em colonel or captain in the militia! Odds balls and barrels! say no more—I'm braced for it. The thunder of your words has soured the milk of human kindness in my breast! Z——ds! as the man in the play says, "I could do such deeds!"

SIR LUC.   Come, come, there must be no passion at all in the case—these things should always be done civilly.

ACRES.   I must be in a passion, Sir Lucius—I must be in a rage. Dear Sir Lucius, let me be in a rage, if you love me. Come, here's pen and paper. (*sits down to write*) I would the ink were red! Indite, I say, indite! How shall I begin? Odds bullets and blades! I'll write a good bold hand, however.

SIR LUC.   Pray compose yourself.

ACRES.   Come now, shall I begin with an oath? Do, Sir Lucius, let me begin with a damme.

SIR LUC.   Pho! pho! do the thing decently and like a Christian. Begin now—"*Sir*"——

ACRES.   That's too civil by half.

SIR LUC.   "*To prevent the confusion that might arise*"——

ACRES.   Well——

SIR LUC.   "*from our both addressing the same lady*"——

ACRES.   Aye—there's the reason—"*same lady*"—Well——

SIR LUC.   "*I shall expect the honour of your company*"——

ACRES.   Z——ds! I'm not asking him to dinner.

SIR LUC.   Pray be easy.

ACRES.   Well then—"*honour of your company*"——

SIR LUC.   "*To settle our pretensions*"——

ACRES.   Well——

SIR LUC.   Let me see—aye, King's-Mead-Fields will do—"*In King's-Mead-Fields.*"

ACRES.   So that's done.——Well, I'll fold it up presently; my own crest—a hand and dagger shall be the seal.

SIR LUC.   You see now, this little explanation will put a stop at once to all confusion or misunderstanding that might arise between you.

ACRES.   Aye, we fight to prevent any misunderstanding.

SIR LUC. Now, I'll leave you to fix your own time. Take my advice, and you'll decide it this evening if you can; then let the worst come of it, 'twill be off your mind to-morrow.

ACRES. Very true.

SIR LUC. So I shall see nothing more of you, unless it be by letter, till the evening. I would do myself the honour to carry your message; but, to tell you a secret, I believe I shall have just such another affair on my own hands. There is a gay captain here who put a jest on me lately at the expense of my country, and I only want to fall in with the gentleman to call him out.

ACRES. By my valour, I should like to see you fight first! Odds life! I should like to see you kill him, if it was only to get a little lesson.

SIR LUC. I shall be very proud of instructing you. Well for the present—but remember now, when you meet your antagonist, do everything in a mild and agreeable manner. Let your courage be as keen, but at the same time as polished, as your sword. (*Exeunt severally*)

ACT IV

SCENE I

SCENE: ACRES'S *lodgings*

ACRES *and* DAVID

DAV. Then, by the Mass, Sir! I would do no such thing— ne'er a Sir Lucius O'Trigger in the kingdom should make me fight, when I wa'n't so minded. Oons! what will the old lady say when she hears o't!

ACRES. Ah! David, if you had heard Sir Lucius! Odds sparks and flames! he would have roused your valour.

DAV. Not he, indeed. I hates such bloodthirsty cormorants. Look'ee, master, if you'd wanted a bout at boxing, quarterstaff, or shortstaff, I should never be the man to bid you cry off: but for your curst sharps and snaps, I never knew any good come of 'em.

ACRES. But my honour, David, my honour! I must be very careful of my honour.

DAV. Aye, by the Mass! and I would be very careful of it; and I think in return my *honour* couldn't do less than to be very careful of *me*.

ACRES Odds blades! David, no gentleman will ever risk the loss of his honour!

DAV. I say then, it would be but civil in *honour* never to risk the loss of a *gentleman*. Look'ee, master, this *honour* seems to me to be a marvellous false friend; aye, truly, a very courtier-like servant. Put the case, I was a gentleman (which, thank God, no one can say of me); well—my honour makes me quarrel with another gentleman of my acquaintance. So—we fight. (Pleasant enough that.) Boh!—I kill him (the more's my luck). Now, pray who gets the profit of it? Why, my *honour*. But put the case that he kills me!—by the Mass! I go to the worms, and my honour whips over to my enemy!

ACRES. No, David—in that case—odds crowns and laurels! —your honour follows you to the grave.

DAV. Now, that's just the place where I could make a shift to do without it.

ACRES. Z——ds, David, you're a coward! It doesn't become my valour to listen to you. What, shall I disgrace my ancestors? Think of that, David—think what it would be to disgrace my ancestors!

DAV. Under favour, the surest way of not disgracing them is to keep as long as you can out of their company. Look'ee now, master, to go to them in such haste—with an ounce of lead in your brains—I should think might as well be let alone. Our ancestors are very good kind of folks; but they are the last people I should choose to have a visiting acquaintance with.

ACRES. But David, now, you don't think there is such very, very, *very* great danger, hey? Odds life! people often fight without any mischief done!

DAV. By the Mass, I think 'tis ten to one against you! Oons! here to meet some lion-headed fellow, I warrant, with his d—n'd double-barrelled swords, and cut-and-thrust pistols! Lord bless us! it makes me tremble to think o't. Those be such desperate bloody-minded weapons! Well, I never could abide 'em! from a child I never could fancy 'em! I suppose there a'n't so merciless a beast in the world as your loaded pistol!

ACRES. Z——ds! I *won't* be afraid! Odds fire and fury! you shan't make me afraid! Here is the challenge, and I have sent for my dear friend Jack Absolute to carry it for me.

DAV. Aye, i' the name of mischief, let *him* be the messenger. For my part, I wouldn't lend a hand to it for the best horse in your stable. By the Mass! it don't look like another letter! It is, as I may say, a designing and malicious-looking letter! and I warrant smells of gunpowder, like a soldier's pouch! Oons! I wouldn't swear it mayn't go off!

ACRES.   Out, you poltroon! You ha'n't the valour of a grass-hopper.

DAV.   Well, I say no more—'twill be sad news, to be sure, at Clod-Hall!—but I ha' done. How Phillis will howl when she hears of it! Aye, poor bitch, she little thinks what shooting her master's going after! And I warrant old Crop, who has carried your Honour, field and road, these ten years, will curse the hour he was born.   (*whimpering*)

ACRES.   It won't do, David—I am determined to fight—so get along, you coward, while I'm in the mind.

Enter Servant

SERV.   Captain Absolute, Sir.

ACRES.   Oh! show him up.   (*Exit Servant*)

DAV.   Well, heaven send we be all alive this time to-morrow.

ACRES.   What's that! Don't provoke me, David!

DAV.   Good-bye, master.   (*whimpering*)

ACRES.   Get along, you cowardly, dastardly, croaking raven.
                    (*Exit* DAVID)

Enter ABSOLUTE

ABS.   What's the matter, Bob?

ACRES.   A vile, sheep-hearted blockhead! If I hadn't the valour of St. George and the dragon to boot——

ABS.   But what did you want with me, Bob?

ACRES.   Oh! There——   (*gives him the challenge*)

ABS.   "*To Ensign Beverley.*" (*aside*) So—what's going on now? (*aloud*) Well, what's this?

ACRES.   A challenge!

ABS.   Indeed! Why, you won't fight him, will you, Bob?

ACRES.   'Egad, but I will, Jack. Sir Lucius has wrought me to it. He has left me full of rage, and I'll fight this evening, that so much good passion mayn't be wasted.

ABS.   But what have I to do with this?

ACRES.   Why, as I think you know something of this fellow, I want you to find him out for me, and give him this mortal defiance.

ABS.   Well, give it to me, and trust me he gets it.

ACRES.   Thank you, my dear friend, my dear Jack; but it is giving you a great deal of trouble.

ABS.   Not in the least—I beg you won't mention it. No trouble in the world, I assure you.

ACRES.   You are very kind. What it is to have a friend! You couldn't be my second—could you, Jack?

ABS.   Why no, Bob—not in *this* affair. It would not be quite so proper.

ACRES.   Well then, I must get my friend Sir Lucius. I shall have your good wishes, however, Jack.

ABS.   Whenever he meets you, believe me.

Enter Servant

SERV.   Sir Anthony Absolute is below, inquiring for the Captain.

ABS.   I'll come instantly. Well, my little hero, success attend you.   (*going*)

ACRES.   Stay—stay, Jack. If Beverley should ask you what kind of a man your friend Acres is, do tell him I am a devil of a fellow—will you, Jack?

ABS.   To be sure I shall. I'll say you are a determined dog —hey, Bob?

ACRES.   Aye, do, do—and if that frightens him, 'egad, perhaps he mayn't come. So tell him I generally kill a man a week—will you, Jack?

ABS.   I will, I will; I'll say you are called in the country "*Fighting Bob!*"

ACRES.   Right, right—'tis all to prevent mischief; for I don't want to take his life if I clear my honour.

ABS.   No!—that's very kind of you.

ACRES.   Why, you don't wish me to kill him—do you, Jack?

ABS.   No, upon my soul, I do not. But a devil of a fellow, hey?   (*going*)

ACRES.   True, true—but stay—stay, Jack. You may add that you never saw me in such a rage before—a most devouring rage!

ABS.   I will, I will.

ACRES.   Remember, Jack—a determined dog!

ABS.   Aye, aye, "*Fighting Bob!*"   (*Exeunt severally*)

SCENE II

SCENE: MRS. MALAPROP's *lodgings*

MRS. MALAPROP *and* LYDIA

MRS. MAL.   Why, thou perverse one! tell me what you can object to him? Isn't he a handsome man? tell me that. A genteel man? a pretty figure of a man?

LYD. (*aside*) She little thinks whom she is praising!
—(*aloud*) So is Beverley, Ma'am.

MRS. MAL. No caparisons, Miss, if you please! Caparisons don't become a young woman. No! Captain Absolute is indeed a fine gentleman!

LYD. (*aside*) Aye, the Captain Absolute *you* have seen.

MRS. MAL. Then he's *so* well bred; *so* full of alacrity, and adulation! and has *so much* to say for himself—in such good language, too! His physiognomy so grammatical! Then his presence is so noble! I protest, when I saw him, I thought of what Hamlet says in the play: "Hesperian curls!—the front of *Job* himself! An eye, like *March*, to threaten at command—a station, like Harry Mercury, new"—something about kissing on a hill—however, the similitude struck me directly.

LYD. (*aside*) How enraged she'll be presently when she discovers her mistake!

Enter Servant

SERV. Sir Anthony and Captain Absolute are below, Ma'am.

MRS. MAL. Show them up here.   (*Exit Servant*)
Now, Lydia, I insist on your behaving as becomes a young woman. Show your good breeding at least, though you have forgot your duty.

LYD. Madam, I have told you my resolution; I shall not only give him no encouragement, but I won't even speak to, or look at him.

(*flings herself into a chair, with her face from the door*)

Enter SIR ANTHONY *and* ABSOLUTE

SIR ANTH. Here we are, Mrs. Malaprop, come to mitigate the frowns of unrelenting beauty—and difficulty enough I had to bring this fellow. I don't know what's the matter; but if I hadn't held him by force, he'd have given me the slip.

MRS. MAL. You have infinite trouble, Sir Anthony, in the affair. I am ashamed for the cause!—(*aside to her*) Lydia, Lydia, rise, I beseech you!—pay your respects!

SIR ANTH. I hope, Madam, that Miss Languish has reflected on the worth of this gentleman, and the regard due to her aunt's choice, and *my* alliance.—(*aside to him*) Now, Jack, speak to her!

ABS. (*aside*) What the d—l shall I do!—(*aloud*) You see, Sir, she won't even look at me whilst you are here. I knew she wouldn't! I told you so. Let me entreat you, Sir, to leave us together!

(ABSOLUTE *seems to expostulate with his father.*)

LYD. (*aside*) I wonder I ha'n't heard my aunt exclaim yet! Sure she can't have looked at him! Perhaps their regimentals are alike, and she is something blind.

SIR ANTH. I say, Sir, I won't stir a foot yet!

MRS. MAL. I am sorry to say, Sir Anthony, that my affluence over my niece is very small.—(*aside to her*) Turn round, Lydia; I blush for you!

SIR ANTH. May I not flatter myself that Miss Languish will assign what cause of dislike she can have to my son! Why don't you begin, Jack?—(*aside to him*) Speak, you puppy— speak!

MRS. MAL. It is impossible, Sir Anthony, she can have any. She will not say she has.—(*aside to her*) Answer, hussy! why don't you answer?

SIR ANTH. Then, Madam, I trust that a childish and hasty predilection will be no bar to Jack's happiness.—(*aside to him*) Z—ds! Sirrah! why don't you speak?

LYD. (*aside*) I think my lover seems as little inclined to conversation as myself. How strangely blind my aunt must be!

ABS. Hem! hem!—Madam—hem!—(ABSOLUTE *attempts to speak, then returns to* SIR ANTHONY.)—Faith! Sir, I am so confounded!—and so—so—confused! I told you I should be so, Sir, I knew it. The—the—tremor of my passion entirely takes away my presence of mind.

SIR ANTH. But it don't take away your voice, fool, does it? Go up, and speak to her directly!

(ABSOLUTE *makes signs to* MRS. MALAPROP *to leave them together.*)

MRS. MAL. Sir Anthony, shall we leave them together?— (*aside to her*) Ah! you stubborn little vixen!

SIR ANTH. Not yet, Ma'am, not yet!—(*aside to him*) What the d—l are you at? Unlock your jaws, Sirrah, or——

(ABSOLUTE *draws near* LYDIA.)

ABS. (*aside*) Now heaven send she may be too sullen to look round! I must disguise my voice.—(*speaks in a low hoarse tone*) Will not Miss Languish lend an ear to the mild accents of true love? Will not——

SIR ANTH. What the d—l ails the fellow? Why don't you speak out?—not stand croaking like a frog in a quinsy!

ABS. The—the—excess of my awe, and my—my—my modesty quite choke me!

SIR ANTH. Ah! your *modesty* again! I'll tell you what, Jack, if you don't speak out directly, and glibly, too, I shall be in such a rage! Mrs. Malaprop, I wish the lady would favour us with something more than a side-front!

(MRS. MALAPROP *seems to chide* LYDIA.)

ABS. So! All will out I see!

(*goes up to* LYDIA, *speaks softly*)

Be not surprised, my Lydia; suppress all surprise at present.

LYD. (*aside*) Heavens! 'tis Beverley's voice! Sure he can't have imposed on Sir Anthony, too!—

(*looks round by degrees, then starts up*)

Is this possible!—my Beverley!—how can this be?—my Beverley?

ABS. (*aside*) Ah! 'tis all over.

SIR ANTH. Beverley!—the devil!—Beverley! What can the girl mean? This is my son, Jack Absolute!

MRS. MAL. For shame, hussy! for shame!—your head runs so on that fellow that you have him always in your eyes! Beg Captain Absolute's pardon directly.

LYD. I see no Captain Absolute, but my loved Beverley!

SIR ANTH. Z——ds! the girl's mad!—her brain's turned by reading!

MRS. MAL. O' my conscience, I believe so! What do you mean by Beverley, hussy? You saw Captain Absolute before to-day; there he is—your husband that shall be.

LYD. With all my soul, Ma'am. When I refuse my Beverley——

SIR ANTH. Oh! she's as mad as Bedlam! Or has this fellow been playing us a rogue's trick! Come here, Sirrah!—who the d—l are you?

ABS. Faith, Sir, I am not quite clear myself, but I'll endeavour to recollect.

SIR ANTH. Are you my son, or not? Answer for your mother, you dog, if you won't for me.

MRS. MAL. Aye, Sir, who are you? Oh mercy! I begin to suspect!——

ABS. (*aside*) Ye Powers of Impudence befriend me!—(*aloud*) Sir Anthony, most assuredly I am your wife's son; and that I sincerely believe myself to be *yours* also, I hope my duty has always shown.——Mrs. Malaprop, I am your most respectful admirer—and shall be proud to add *affectionate nephew.*——I need not tell my Lydia, that she sees her faithful Beverley, who, knowing the singular generosity of her temper, assumed that name, and a station which has proved a test of the most disinterested love, which he now hopes to enjoy in a more elevated character.

LYD. (*sullenly*) So!—there will be no elopement after all!

SIR ANTH. Upon my soul, Jack, thou art a very impudent fellow! to do you justice, I think I never saw a piece of more consummate assurance!

ABS. Oh you flatter me, Sir—you compliment—'tis my *modesty* you know, Sir—my *modesty* that has stood in my way.

SIR ANTH. Well, I am glad you are not the dull, insensible varlet you pretended to be, however! I'm glad you have made a fool of your father, you dog—I am. So this was your *penitence*, your *duty*, and *obedience!* I thought it was d—n'd sudden! You *never heard their names before*, not you! *What!* The *Languishes of Worcestershire*, hey?—*if you could please me in the affair, 'twas all you desired!*—Ah! you dissembling villain! What!—(*pointing to* LYDIA) *she squints, don't she?—a little red-haired girl!*—hey? Why, you hypocritical young rascal! I wonder you a'n't ashamed to hold up your head!

ABS. 'Tis with difficulty, Sir. I *am* confused—very much confused, as you must perceive.

MRS. MAL. O lud! Sir Anthony!—a new light breaks in upon me! Hey! how! what! Captain, did *you* write the letters then? What!—am I to thank *you* for the elegant compilation of *"an old weather-beaten she-dragon"*—hey? O mercy! was it *you* that reflected on my parts of speech?

ABS. Dear Sir! my modesty will be overpowered at last, if you don't assist me. I shall certainly not be able to stand it!

SIR ANTH. Come, come, Mrs. Malaprop, we must forget and forgive. Odds life! matters have taken so clever a turn all of a sudden, that I could find in my heart to be so good-humoured! and so gallant!—hey! Mrs. Malaprop!

MRS. MAL. Well, Sir Anthony, since *you* desire it, we will not anticipate the past; so mind, young people: our retrospection will now be all to the future.

SIR ANTH. Come, we must leave them together; Mrs. Malaprop, they long to fly into each other's arms. I warrant!—(*aside*) Jack—isn't the cheek as I said, hey?—and the eye, you rogue!—and the lip—hey? Come, Mrs. Malaprop, we'll not disturb their tenderness—theirs is the time of life for happiness! —(*sings*) *"Youth's the season made for joy"*—hey! Odds life! I'm in such spirits, I don't know what I couldn't do! Permit me, Ma'am—(*gives his hand to* MRS. MALAPROP) (*sings*) Tol-de-rol!—'gad, I should like a little fooling myself. Tol-de rol! de-rol!

(Exit singing, and handing MRS. MALAPROP.*)*
*(*LYDIA *sits sullenly in her chair.)*

ABS. *(aside)* So much thought bodes me no good.—So grave, Lydia!

LYD. Sir!

ABS. *(aside)* So!—egad! I thought as much! That d—n'd monosyllable has froze me!——What, Lydia, now that we are as happy in our friends' consent, as in our mutual vows——

LYD. *(peevishly)* *Friends' consent,* indeed!

ABS. Come, come, we must lay aside some of our romance —a little *wealth* and *comfort* may be endured after all. And for your fortune, the lawyers shall make such settlements as——

LYD. *Lawyers!* I *hate* lawyers!

ABS. Nay then, we will not wait for their lingering forms, but instantly procure the license, and——

LYD. The *license!* I *hate* license!

ABS. O my love! be not so unkind! Thus let me intreat——
                                    (kneeling)

LYD. Pshaw! what signifies kneeling when you know I *must* have you?

ABS. *(rising)* Nay, Madam, there shall be no constraint upon your inclinations, I promise you. If I have lost your heart, I resign the rest.—*(aside)* 'Gad, I must try what a little *spirit* will do.

LYD. *(rising).* Then, Sir, let me tell you, the interest you had there was acquired by a mean, unmanly imposition, and deserves the punishment of fraud. What, you have been treating *me* like a child!—humouring my romance! and laughing, I suppose, at your success!

ABS. You wrong me, Lydia, you wrong me. Only hear——

LYD. So, while *I* fondly imagined we were deceiving my relations, and flattered myself that I should outwit and incense them all—behold! my hopes are to be crushed at once, by my aunt's consent and approbation!—and *I* am myself the only dupe at last!   *(walking about in heat)* But here, Sir, here is the picture—Beverley's picture! *(taking a miniature from her bosom)* which I have worn, night and day, in spite of threats and entreaties! There, Sir *(flings it to him)*—and be assured I throw the original from my heart as easily.

ABS. Nay, nay, Ma'am, we will not differ as to that. Here *(taking out a picture),* here is Miss Lydia Languish. What a difference! Aye, *there* is the heavenly assenting smile that first gave soul and spirit to my hopes!—those are the lips which sealed a vow, as yet scarce dry in Cupid's calendar!—and *there,* the half resentful blush that *would* have checked the ardour of my thanks. Well, all that's past—all over indeed! There, Madam, in beauty, that copy is not equal to you, but in my mind its merit over the original, in being still the same, is such—that—I cannot find in my heart to part with it.

(*puts it up again*)

LYD. (*softening*) 'Tis *your own* doing, Sir. I—I—I suppose you are perfectly satisfied.

ABS. Oh, most certainly. Sure now this is much better than being in love! Ha! ha! ha!—there's some spirit in *this!* What signifies breaking some scores of solemn promises, half an hundred vows, under one's hand, with the marks of a dozen or two angels to witness!—all that's of no consequence, you know. To be sure, people will say that Miss didn't know her own mind—but never mind that: or perhaps they may be ill-natured enough to hint that the gentleman grew tired of the lady and forsook her—but don't let that fret you.

LYD. There's no bearing his insolence.

(*bursts into tears*)

Enter MRS. MALAPROP *and* SIR ANTHONY

MRS. MAL. (*entering*) Come, we must interrupt your billing and cooing a while.

LYD. This is worse than your treachery and deceit, you base ingrate! (*sobbing*)

SIR ANTH. What the devil's the matter now! Z——ds! Mrs. Malaprop, this is the *oddest billing* and *cooing* I ever heard! But what the deuce is the meaning of it? I'm quite astonished!

ABS. Ask the lady, Sir.

MRS. MAL. Oh mercy! I'm quite analysed, for my part! Why, Lydia, what is the reason of this?

LYD. Ask the *gentleman,* Ma'am.

SIR ANTH. Z——ds! I shall be in a frenzy!—— Why, Jack, you are not come out to be anyone else, are you?

MRS. MAL. Aye, Sir, there's no more *trick,* is there? You are not like Cerberus, *three* gentlemen at once, are you?

ABS. You'll not let me speak. I say the lady can account for this much better than I can.

LYD. Ma'am, you once commanded me never to think of Beverley again. There is the man—I now obey you:—for, from this moment, I renounce him forever. (*Exit* LYDIA)

MRS. MAL. Oh mercy! and miracles! what a turn here is!

Why sure, Captain, you haven't behaved disrespectfully to my niece?

SIR ANTH.   Ha! ha! ha!—ha! ha! ha!—now I see it—ha! ha! ha!—now I see it—you have been too lively, Jack.

ABS.   Nay, Sir, upon my word——

SIR ANTH.   Come, no lying, Jack—I'm sure 'twas so.

MRS. MAL.   O lud! Sir Anthony! Oh fie, Captain!

ABS.   Upon my soul, Ma'am——

SIR ANTH.   Come, no excuses, Jack; why, your father, you rogue, was so before you: the blood of the Absolutes was always impatient. Ha! ha! ha! poor little Lydia!—why, you've frightened her, you dog, you have.

ABS.   By all that's good, Sir——

SIR ANTH.   Z——ds! say no more, I tell you. Mrs. Malaprop shall make your peace.——You must make his peace, Mrs. Malaprop; you must tell her 'tis Jack's way—tell her 'tis all our ways—it runs in the blood of our family! Come, away, Jack—ha! ha! ha! Mrs. Malaprop—a young villain!

(*pushes him out*)

MRS. MAL.   Oh! Sir Anthony! Oh fie, Captain!

(*Exeunt severally*)

SCENE III

SCENE: *The North Parade*

Enter SIR LUCIUS O'TRIGGER

SIR LUC.   I wonder where this Captain Absolute hides himself. Upon my conscience! these officers are always in one's way in love-affairs. I remember I might have married Lady Dorothy Carmine, if it had not been for a little rogue of a major, who ran away with her before she could get a sight of me! And I wonder too what it is the ladies can see in them to be so fond of them—unless it be a touch of the old serpent in 'em, that makes the little creatures be caught, like vipers, with a bit of red cloth.——Hah!—isn't this the Captain coming?—faith it is! There is a probability of succeeding about that fellow that is mighty provoking! Who the devil is he talking to?

(*steps aside*)

Enter CAPTAIN ABSOLUTE

ABS.   To what fine purpose I have been plotting! A noble reward for all my schemes, upon my soul! A little gypsy! I did not think her romance could have made her so d—n'd absurd either. 'Sdeath, I never was in a worse humour in my life! I could cut my own throat, or any other person's, with the greatest pleasure in the world!

SIR LUC.   Oh, faith! I'm in the luck of it—I never could have found him in a sweeter temper for my purpose—to be sure I'm just come in the nick! Now to enter into conversation with him, and so quarrel genteelly. (SIR LUCIUS *goes up to* ABSOLUTE).——With regard to that matter, Captain, I must beg leave to differ in opinion with you.

ABS.   Upon my word then, you must be a very subtle disputant, because, Sir, I happened just then to be giving no opinion at all.

SIR LUC.   That's no reason. For give me leave to tell you, a man may *think* an untruth as well as *speak* one.

ABS.   Very true, Sir, but if a man never utters his thoughts I should think they might stand a chance of escaping controversy.

SIR LUC.   Then, Sir, you differ in opinion with me, which amounts to the same thing.

ABS.   Hark'ee Sir Lucius—if I had not before known you to be a gentleman, upon my soul, I should not have discovered it at this interview, for what you can drive at, unless you mean to quarrel with me, I cannot conceive!

SIR LUC.   I humbly thank you, Sir, for the quickness of your apprehension. (*bowing*) You have named the very thing I would be at.

ABS.   Very well, Sir—I shall certainly not balk your inclinations—but I should be glad you would please to explain your motives.

SIR LUC.   Pray, Sir, be easy: the quarrel is a very pretty quarrel as it stands—we should only spoil it by trying to explain it. However, your memory is very short or you could not have forgot an affront you passed on me within this week. So no more, but name your time and place.

ABS.   Well, Sir, since you are so bent on it, the sooner the better; let it be this evening—here, by the Spring-Gardens. We shall scarcely be interrupted.

SIR LUC.   Faith! that same interruption in affairs of this nature shows very great ill-breeding. I don't know what's the reason, but in England, if a thing of this kind gets wind, people make such a pother that a gentleman can never fight in peace and quietness. However, if it's the same to you, Captain, I should take it as a particular kindness if you'd let us meet in King's-Mead-Fields, as a little business will call me there about six o'clock, and I may dispatch both matters at once.

ABS. 'Tis the same to me exactly. A little after six, then, we will discuss this matter more seriously.

SIR LUC. If you please, Sir, there will be very pretty small-sword light, though it won't do for a long shot. So that matter's settled! and my mind's at ease!   (*Exit* SIR LUCIUS)

Enter FAULKLAND, *meeting* ABSOLUTE

ABS. Well met. I was going to look for you. O, Faulkland! all the dæmons of spite and disappointment have conspired against me! I'm so vexed that if I had not the prospect of a re-source in being knocked o' the head by and by, I should scarce have spirits to tell you the cause.

FAULK. What can you mean? Has Lydia changed her mind? I should have thought her duty and inclination would now have pointed to the same object.

ABS. Aye, just as the eyes do of a person who squints: when her love-eye was fixed on me—t'other—her eye of duty, was finely obliqued:—but when duty bid her point that the same way—off t'other turned on a swivel, and secured its re-treat with a frown!

FAULK. But what's the resource you——

ABS. Oh, to wind up the whole, a good-natured Irishman here has (*mimicking* SIR LUCIUS) begged leave to have the pleasure of cutting my throat, and I mean to indulge him—that's all.

FAULK. Prithee, be serious.

ABS. 'Tis fact, upon my soul. Sir Lucius O'Trigger—you know him by sight—for some affront, which I am sure I never intended, has obliged me to meet him this evening at six o'clock: 'tis on that account I wished to see you—you must go with me.

FAULK. Nay, there must be some mistake, sure. Sir Lucius shall explain himself—and I dare say matters may be accommo-dated. But this evening, did you say? I wish it had been any other time.

ABS. Why? there will be light enough. There will (as Sir Lucius says) "be very pretty small-sword light, though it won't do for a long shot." Confound his long shots!

FAULK. But I am myself a good deal ruffled by a differ-ence I have had with Julia. My vile tormenting temper has made me treat her so cruelly that I shall not be myself till we are reconciled.

ABS.   By heavens, Faulkland, you don't deserve her.

Enter Servant, gives FAULKLAND *a letter*

FAULK.   O Jack! this is from Julia. I dread to open it. I fear it may be to take a last leave—perhaps to bid me return her letters and restore——Oh! how I suffer for my folly!

ABS.   Here—let me see. (*takes the letter and opens it*) Aye, a final sentence indeed!—'tis all over with you, faith!

FAULK.   Nay, Jack—don't keep me in suspense.

ABS.   Hear then.—"*As I am convinced that my dear* FAULK-LAND's *own reflections have already upbraided him for his last unkindness to me, I will not add a word on the subject. I wish to speak with you as soon as possible.—Yours ever and truly,* JULIA."—There's stubbornness and resentment for you! (*gives him the letter*) Why, man, you don't seem one whit happier at this.

FAULK.   Oh, yes, I am—but—but——

ABS.   Confound your *buts.* You never hear anything that would make another man bless himself, but you immediately d—n it with a *but.*

FAULK.   Now, Jack, as you are my friend, own honestly—don't you think there is something forward, something indeli-cate, in this haste to forgive? Women should never sue for reconciliation: that should always come from us. They should retain their coldness till *wooed* to kindness—and their *pardon,* like their *love,* should "not unsought be won."

ABS.   I have not patience to listen to you—thou'rt incor-rigible!—so say no more on the subject. I must go to settle a few matters. Let me see you before six—remember—at my lodgings. A poor industrious devil like me, who have toiled, and drudged, and plotted to gain my ends, and am at last disappointed by other people's folly, may in pity be allowed to swear and grumble a little; but a captious sceptic in love, a slave to fretfulness and whim, who has no difficulties but of his own creating, is a subject more fit for ridicule than com-passion!   (*Exit* ABSOLUTE)

FAULK.   I feel his reproaches, yet I would not change this too exquisite nicety for the gross content with which *he* tram-ples on the thorns of love. His engaging me in this duel has started an idea in my head, which I will instantly pursue. I'll use it as the touchstone of Julia's sincerity and disinterested-ness. If her love prove pure and sterling ore, my name will rest on it with honour!—and once I've stamped it there, I lay aside my doubts forever—; but if the dross of selfishness, the alloy of pride predominate, 'twill be best to leave her as a toy for some less cautious fool to sigh for.   (*Exit* FAULKLAND)

ACT V

SCENE I

SCENE: JULIA's *dressing-room*

JULIA *sola*

JUL.   How this message has alarmed me! What dreadful accident can he mean? why such charge to be alone? O Faulkland! how many unhappy moments, how many tears, have you cost me!

Enter FAULKLAND

JUL.   What means this?—why this caution, Faulkland?

FAULK.   Alas! Julia, I am come to take a long farewell.

JUL.   Heavens! what do you mean?

FAULK.   You see before you a wretch whose life is forfeited. Nay, start not! the infirmity of my temper has drawn all this misery on me. I left you fretful and passionate—an untoward accident drew me into a quarrel—the event is that I must fly this kingdom instantly. O Julia, had I been so fortunate as to have called you mine entirely before this mischance had fallen on me, I should not so deeply dread my banishment!

JUL.   My soul is oppressed with sorrow at the nature of your misfortune: had these adverse circumstances arisen from a less fatal cause, I should have felt strong comfort in the thought that I could now chase from your bosom every doubt of the warm sincerity of my love. My heart has long known no other guardian. I now entrust my person to your honour— we will fly together. When safe from pursuit, my father's will may be fulfilled, and I receive a legal claim to be the partner of your sorrows, and tenderest comforter. Then on the bosom of your wedded Julia, you may lull your keen regret to slumbering; while virtuous love, with a cherub's hand, shall smooth the brow of upbraiding thought, and pluck the thorn from compunction.

FAULK.   O Julia! I am bankrupt in gratitude! But the time is so pressing, it calls on you for so hasty a resolution—would you not wish some hours to weigh the advantages you forgo, and what little compensation poor Faulkland can make you beside his solitary love?

JUL. I ask not a moment. No, Faulkland, I have loved you for yourself: and if I now, more than ever, prize the solemn engagement which so long has pledged us to each other, it is because it leaves no room for hard aspersions on my fame, and puts the seal of duty to an act of love.——But let us not linger. Perhaps this delay——

FAULK. 'Twill be better I should not venture out again till dark. Yet am I grieved to think what numberless distresses will press heavy on your gentle disposition!

JUL. Perhaps your fortune may be forfeited by this unhappy act. I know not whether 'tis so, but sure that alone can never make us unhappy. The little I have will be sufficient to support us; and exile never should be splendid.

FAULK. Aye, but in such an abject state of life, my wounded pride perhaps may increase the natural fretfulness of my temper, till I become a rude, morose companion, beyond your patience to endure. Perhaps the recollection of a deed my conscience cannot justify may haunt me in such gloomy and unsocial fits that I shall hate the tenderness that would relieve me, break from your arms, and quarrel with your fondness!

JUL. If your thoughts should assume so unhappy a bent, you will the more want some mild and affectionate spirit to watch over and console you, one who, by bearing *your* infirmities with gentleness and resignation, may teach you *so* to bear the evils of your fortune.

FAULK. Julia, I have proved you to the quick! and with this useless device I throw away all my doubts. How shall I plead to be forgiven this last unworthy effect of my restless, unsatisfied disposition?

JUL. Has no such disaster happened as you related?

FAULK. I am ashamed to own that it was all pretended; yet in pity, Julia, do not kill me with resenting a fault which never can be repeated, but sealing, this once, my pardon, let me to-morrow, in the face of heaven, receive my future guide and monitress, and expiate my past folly by years of tender adoration.

JUL. Hold, Faulkland! That you are free from a crime which I before feared to name, heaven knows how sincerely I rejoice! These are tears of thankfulness for that! But that your cruel doubts should have urged you to an imposition

that has wrung my heart, gives me now a pang more keen
than I can express!

FAULK. By heavens! Julia——

JUL. Yet hear me. My father loved you, Faulkland! and
you preserved the life that tender parent gave me; in his
presence I pledged my hand—joyfully pledged it—where before I had given my heart. When, soon after, I lost that parent, it seemed to me that Providence had, in Faulkland,
shown me whither to transfer without a pause my grateful
duty, as well as my affection: hence I have been content to
bear from you what pride and delicacy would have forbid me
from another. I will not upbraid you by repeating how you
have trifled with my sincerity.

FAULK. I confess it all! yet hear——

JUL. After such a year of trial, I might have flattered myself that I should not have been insulted with a new proba-
tion of my sincerity, as cruel as unnecessary! I now see it is
not in your nature to be content or confident in love. With
this conviction, I never will be yours. While I had hopes that
my persevering attention and unreproaching kindness might
in time reform your temper, I should have been happy to
have gained a dearer influence over you; but I will not furnish you with a licensed power to keep alive an incorrigible
fault, at the expense of one who never would contend with
you.

FAULK. Nay, but Julia, by my soul and honour, if after
this——

JUL. But one word more. As my faith has once been given
to you, I never will barter it with another. I shall pray for
your happiness with the truest sincerity; and the dearest
blessing I can ask of heaven to send you will be to charm you
from that unhappy temper which alone has prevented the performance of our solemn engagement. All I request of *you* is
that you will yourself reflect upon this infirmity, and when
you number up the many true delights it has deprived you of,
let it not be your *least* regret that it lost you the love of one,
who would have followed you in beggary through the world!
                                                      (*Exit*)

FAULK. She's gone!—forever! There was an awful resolution in her manner, that riveted me to my place. O fool!—
dolt!—barbarian! Curst as I am with more imperfections than
my fellow-wretches, kind Fortune sent a heaven-gifted cherub
to my aid, and, like a ruffian, I have driven her from my side!
I must now haste to my appointment. Well, my mind is tuned

for such a scene. I shall wish only to become a principal in it,
and reverse the tale my cursed folly put me upon forging
here. O love!—tormentor!—fiend! whose influence, like the
moon's, acting on men of dull souls, makes idiots of them, but
meeting subtler spirits, betrays their course, and urges sensibility to madness!   (*Exit*)

Enter Maid and LYDIA

MAID.   My mistress, Ma'am, I know, was here just now—
perhaps she is only in the next room.   (*Exit Maid*)
LYD.   Heigh-ho! Though he has used me so, this fellow
runs strangely in my head. I believe one lecture from my
grave cousin will make me recall him.

Enter JULIA

LYD.   O Julia, I am come to you with such an appetite for
consolation.—Lud! child, what's the matter with you? You
have been crying! I'll be hanged if that Faulkland has not
been tormenting you!
JUL.   You mistake the cause of my uneasiness. Something
has flurried me a little. Nothing that you can guess at.—(*aside*)
I would not accuse Faulkland to a sister!
LYD.   Ah! whatever vexations you may have, I can assure
you mine surpass them.——You know who Beverley proves
to be?
JUL.   I will now own to you, Lydia, that Mr. Faulkland
had before informed me of the whole affair. Had young Absolute been the person you took him for, I should not have
accepted your confidence on the subject without a serious
endeavour to counteract your caprice.
LYD.   So, then, I see I have been deceived by everyone!
But I don't care—I'll never have him.
JUL.   Nay, Lydia——
LYD.   Why, is it not provoking? when I thought we were
coming to the prettiest distress imaginable, to find myself
made a mere Smithfield bargain of at last! There had I pro-
jected one of the most sentimental elopements! so becoming
a disguise! so amiable a ladder of ropes! Conscious moon—
four horses—Scotch parson—with such surprise to Mrs. Malaprop, and such paragraphs in the newspapers! Oh, I shall die
with disappointment!
JUL.   I don't wonder at it!
LYD.   Now—sad reverse!—what have I to expect, but, after
a deal of flimsy preparation, with a bishop's license, and my

aunt's blessing, to go simpering up to the altar; or perhaps be cried three times in a country-church, and have an unmannerly fat clerk ask the consent of every butcher in the parish to join John Absolute and Lydia Languish, Spinster! O, that I should live to hear myself called Spinster!

JUL.   Melancholy, indeed!

LYD.   How mortifying to remember the dear delicious shifts I used to be put to, to gain half a minute's conversation with this fellow! How often have I stole forth in the coldest night in January, and found him in the garden, stuck like a dripping statue! There would he kneel to me in the snow, and sneeze and cough so pathetically! he shivering with cold, and I with apprehension! and while the freezing blast numbed our joints, how warmly would he press me to pity his flame, and glow with mutual ardour! Ah, Julia, that was something like being in love!

JUL.   If I were in spirits, Lydia, I should chide you only by laughing heartily at you: but it suits more the situation of my mind, at present, earnestly to entreat you not to let a man, who loves you with sincerity, suffer that unhappiness from your caprice, which I know too well caprice can inflict.

LYD.   O Lud! what has brought my aunt here?

Enter MRS. MALAPROP, FAG, *and* DAVID

MRS. MAL.   So! so! here's fine work!—here's fine suicide, parricide, and simulation going on in the fields! and Sir Anthony not to be found to prevent the antistrophe!

JUL.   For heaven's sake, Madam, what's the meaning of this?

MRS. MAL.   That gentleman can tell you—'twas he enveloped the affair to me.

LYD.   (*to* FAG)   Do, Sir, will you, inform us.

FAG.   Ma'am, I should hold myself very deficient in every requisite that forms the man of breeding if I delayed a moment to give all the information in my power to a lady so deeply interested in the affair as you are.

LYD.   But quick! quick, Sir!

FAG.   True, Ma'am, as you say, one should be quick in divulging matters of this nature; for should we be tedious, perhaps while we are flourishing on the subject, two or three lives may be lost!

LYD.   O patience! Do, Ma'am, for heaven's sake! tell us what is the matter!

MRS. MAL.   Why, murder's the matter! slaughter's the mat-

ter! killing's the matter! But he can tell you the perpendicu-
lars.

LYD.   Then, prithee, Sir, be brief.

FAG.   Why then, Ma'am—as to murder, I cannot take upon
me to say—and as to slaughter, or manslaughter, that will be
as the jury finds it.

LYD.   But who, Sir—who are engaged in this?

FAG.   Faith, Ma'am, one is a young gentleman whom I
should be very sorry anything was to happen to—a very pretty
behaved gentleman! We have lived much together, and always on terms.

LYD.   But who is this? who! who! who!

FAG.   My master, Ma'am, my master—I speak of my
master.

LYD.   Heavens! What, Captain Absolute!

MRS. MAL.   Oh, to be sure, you are frightened now!

JUL.   But who are with him, Sir?

FAG.   As to the rest, Ma'am, this gentleman can inform
you better than I.

JUL.   (*to* DAVID) Do speak, friend.

DAV.   Look'ee, my lady—by the Mass! there's mischief going on. Folks don't use to meet for amusement with fire-arms,
fire-locks, fire-engines, fire-screens, fire-office, and the devil
knows what other crackers beside! This, my lady, I say, has
an angry favour.

JUL.   But who is there beside Captain Absolute, friend?

DAV.   My poor master—under favour, for mentioning him
first. You know me, my lady—I am David, and my master, of
course, is, or *was*, Squire Acres. Then comes Squire Faulkland.

JUL.   Do, Ma'am, let us instantly endeavour to prevent
mischief.

MRS. MAL.   Oh fie—it would be very inelegant in us: we
should only participate things.

DAV.   Ah! do, Mrs. Aunt, save a few lives. They are des-
perately given, believe me. Above all, there is that bloodthirsty Philistine, Sir Lucius O'Trigger.

MRS. MAL.   Sir Lucius O'Trigger! O mercy! have they
drawn poor little dear Sir Lucius into the scrape? Why, how
you stand, girl! you have no more feeling than one of the
Derbyshire putrefactions!

LYD.   What are we to do, Madam?

MRS. MAL.   Why, fly with the utmost felicity, to be sure,
to prevent mischief. Here, friend—you can show us the place?

FAG. If you please, Ma'am, I will conduct you.——David, do you look for Sir Anthony. (*Exit* DAVID)

MRS. MAL. Come, girls!—this gentleman will exhort us.—— Come, Sir, you're our envoy—lead the way, and we'll precede.

FAG. Not a step before the ladies for the world!

MRS. MAL. You're sure you know the spot?

FAG. I think I can find it, Ma'am; and one good thing is we shall hear the report of the pistols as we draw near, so we can't well miss them; never fear, Ma'am, never fear.

(*Exeunt, he talking*)

SCENE II

SCENE: *South Parade*

Enter ABSOLUTE, *putting his sword under his greatcoat*

ABS. A sword seen in the streets of Bath would raise as great an alarm as a mad dog. How provoking this is in Faulk-land! never punctual! I shall be obliged to go without him at last. Oh, the devil! here's Sir Anthony! How shall I escape him? (*muffles up his face, and takes a circle to go off*)

Enter SIR ANTHONY

SIR ANTH. How one may be deceived at a little distance! Only that I see he don't know me, I could have sworn that was Jack!——Hey! 'Gad's life! it is. Why, Jack!—what are you afraid of, hey!—Sure I'm right.—Why, Jack!—Jack Absolute! (*goes up to him*)

ABS. Really, Sir, you have the advantage of me: I don't remember ever to have had the honour. My name is Saunderson, at your service.

SIR ANTH. Sir, I beg your pardon—I took you—hey!—why, z——ds! it is—stay—(*looks up to his face*) So, so—your humble servant, Mr. Saunderson! Why, you scoundrel, what tricks are you after now?

ABS. Oh! a joke, Sir, a joke! I came here on purpose to look for you, Sir.

SIR ANTH. You did! Well, I am glad you were so lucky. But what are you muffled up so for? What's this for?—hey?

ABS. 'Tis cool, Sir; isn't it?—rather chilly, somehow. But I shall be late—I have a particular engagement.

SIR ANTH. Stay. Why, I thought you were looking for me? Pray, Jack, where is't you are going?

ABS. Going, Sir!

SIR ANTH.   Aye—where are you going?

ABS.   Where am I going?

SIR ANTH.   You unmannerly puppy!

ABS.   I was going, Sir, to—to—to—to Lydia—Sir, to Lydia, to make matters up if I could; and I was looking for you, Sir, to—to——

SIR ANTH.   To go with you, I suppose. Well, come along.

ABS.   Oh! z——ds! no, Sir, not for the world! I wished to meet with you, Sir—to—to—to—— You find it cool, I'm sure, Sir—you'd better not stay out.

SIR ANTH.   Cool!—not at all. Well, Jack—and what will you say to Lydia?

ABS.   O, Sir, beg her pardon, humour her, promise and vow. But I detain you, Sir—consider the cold air on your gout.

SIR ANTH.   Oh, not at all!—not at all! I'm in no hurry. Ah! Jack, you youngsters, when once you are wounded here— (*putting his hand to* ABSOLUTE's *breast*) Hey! what the deuce have you got here?

ABS.   Nothing, Sir—nothing.

SIR ANTH.   What's this? here's something d—d hard!

ABS.   Oh, trinkets, Sir! trinkets—a bauble for Lydia!

SIR ANTH.   Nay, let me see your taste. (*pulls his coat open, the sword falls*) Trinkets!—a bauble for Lydia! Z——ds! Sirrah, you are not going to cut her throat, are you?

ABS.   Ha! ha! ha! I thought it would divert you, Sir; though I didn't mean to tell you till afterwards.

SIR ANTH.   You didn't? Yes, this is a very diverting trinket, truly!

ABS.   Sir, I'll explain to you. You know, Sir, Lydia is romantic, dev'lish romantic, and very absurd of course. Now, Sir, I intend, if she refuses to forgive me, to unsheathe this sword and swear I'll fall upon its point, and expire at her feet!

SIR ANTH.   Fall upon a fiddle-stick's end! Why, I suppose it is the very thing that would please her. Get along, you fool.

ABS.   Well, Sir, you shall hear of my success—you shall hear. "O Lydia!—forgive me, or this pointed steel"—says I.

SIR ANTH.   "O, booby! stab away and welcome"—says she. Get along!—and d—n your trinkets!   (*Exit* ABSOLUTE)

Enter DAVID, *running*

DAV.   Stop him! Stop him! Murder! Thief! Fire! Stop fire! Stop fire! O! Sir Anthony—call! call! bid 'em stop! Murder! Fire!

SIR ANTH.   Fire! Murder! Where?

DAV. Oons! he's out of sight! and I'm out of breath, for my part! O, Sir Anthony, why didn't you stop him? why didn't you stop him?

SIR ANTH. Z——ds! the fellow's mad! Stop whom? Stop Jack?

DAV. Aye, the Captain, Sir! there's murder and slaughter——

SIR ANTH. Murder!

DAV. Aye, please you, Sir Anthony, there's all kinds of murder, all sorts of slaughter to be seen in the fields: there's fighting going on, Sir—bloody sword-and-gun fighting!

SIR ANTH. Who are going to fight, dunce?

DAV. Everybody that I know of, Sir Anthony—everybody is going to fight; my poor master, Sir Lucius O'Trigger, your son, the Captain——

SIR ANTH. Oh, the dog! I see his tricks.——Do you know the place?

DAV. King's-Mead-Fields.

SIR ANTH. You know the way?

DAV. Not an inch; but I'll call the mayor—aldermen—constables—church-wardens—and beadles—we can't be too many to part them.

SIR ANTH. Come along—give me your shoulder! we'll get assistance as we go. The lying villain! Well, I shall be in such a frenzy! So—this was the history of his trinkets! I'll bauble him! (*Exeunt*)

SCENE III

SCENE: *King's-Mead-Fields*

SIR LUCIUS *and* ACRES, *with pistols*

ACRES. By my valour! then, Sir Lucius, forty yards is a good distance. Odds levels and aims! I say it is a good distance.

SIR LUC. Is it for muskets or small field-pieces? Upon my conscience, Mr. Acres, you must leave those things to me. Stay now—I'll show you. (*measures paces along the stage*) There now, that is a very pretty distance—a pretty gentleman's distance.

ACRES. Z——ds! we might as well fight in a sentry-box! I tell you, Sir Lucius, the farther he is off, the cooler I shall take my aim.

SIR LUC. Faith! then I suppose you would aim at him best of all if he was out of sight!

ACRES. No, Sir Lucius, but I should think forty, or eight and thirty yards——

SIR LUC. Pho! pho! nonsense! Three or four feet between the mouths of your pistols is as good as a mile.

ACRES. Odds bullets, no! By my valour! there is no merit in killing him so near: do, my dear Sir Lucius, let me bring him down at a long shot—a long shot, Sir Lucius, if you love me!

SIR LUC. Well—the gentleman's friend and I must settle that. But tell me now, Mr. Acres, in case of an accident, is there any little will or commission I could execute for you?

ACRES. I am much obliged to you, Sir Lucius, but I don't understand——

SIR LUC. Why, you may think there's no being shot at without a little risk, and if an unlucky bullet should carry a *quietus* with it—I say it will be no time then to be bothering you about family matters.

ACRES. A *quietus!*

SIR LUC. For instance, now—if that should be the case—would you choose to be pickled and sent home? or would it be the same to you to lie here in the Abbey? I'm told there is very snug lying in the Abbey.

ACRES. Pickled! Snug lying in the Abbey! Odds tremors! Sir Lucius, don't talk so!

SIR LUC. I suppose, Mr. Acres, you never were engaged in an affair of this kind before?

ACRES. No, Sir Lucius, never before.

SIR LUC. Ah! that's a pity! there's nothing like being used to a thing. Pray now, how would you receive the gentleman's shot?

ACRES. Odds files! I've practised that. There, Sir Lucius— there (*puts himself in an attitude*)—a side-front, hey? Odd! I'll make myself small enough: I'll stand edge-ways.

SIR LUC. Now—you're quite out, for if you stand so when I take my aim—— (*levelling at him*)

ACRES. Z——ds! Sir Lucius—are you sure it is not cocked?

SIR LUC. Never fear.

ACRES. But—but—you don't know—it may go off of its own head!

SIR LUC. Pho! be easy. Well, now if I hit you in the body, my bullet has a double chance, for if it misses a vital part on your right side, 'twill be very hard if it don't succeed on the left!

ACRES.   A vital part!

SIR LUC.   But, there—fix yourself so. (*placing him*) Let him see the broad side of your full front—there—now a ball or two may pass clean through your body, and never do any harm at all.

ACRES.   Clean through me! a ball or two clean through me!

SIR LUC.   Aye, may they; and it is much the genteelest attitude into the bargain.

ACRES.   Look'ee! Sir Lucius—I'd just as lieve be shot in an awkward posture as a genteel one—so, by my valour! I will stand edge-ways.

SIR LUC. (*looking at his watch*)   Sure they don't mean to disappoint us. Hah? No, faith—I think I see them coming.

ACRES.   Hey! what!—coming!——

SIR LUC.   Aye. Who are those yonder getting over the stile?

ACRES.   There are two of them indeed! Well—let them come—hey, Sir Lucius? We—we—we—we—won't run.

SIR LUC.   Run!

ACRES.   No—I say—we *won't* run, by my valour!

SIR LUC.   What the devil's the matter with you?

ACRES.   Nothing—nothing—my dear friend—my dear Sir Lucius—but—I—I—I don't feel quite so bold, somehow—as I did.

SIR LUC.   Oh fie! consider your honour.

ACRES.   Aye—true—my honour. Do, Sir Lucius, edge in a word or two every now and then about my honour.

SIR LUC. (*looking*)   Well, here they're coming.

ACRES.   Sir Lucius—if I wa'n't with you, I should almost think I was afraid. If my valour should leave me! Valour will come and go.

SIR LUC.   Then, pray, keep it fast while you have it.

ACRES.   Sir Lucius—I doubt it is going—yes—my valour is certainly going! it is sneaking off! I feel it oozing out as it were at the palms of my hands!

SIR LUC.   Your honour—your honour. Here they are.

ACRES.   Oh mercy! now that I were safe at Clod-Hall! or could be shot before I was aware!

Enter FAULKLAND *and* ABSOLUTE

SIR LUC.   Gentlemen, your most obedient—hah!—what—Captain Absolute! So, I suppose, Sir, you are come here, just like myself—to do a kind office, first for your friend—then to proceed to business on your own account.

ACRES. What, Jack! my dear Jack! my dear friend!

ABS. Hark'ee, Bob, Beverley's at hand.

SIR LUC. Well, Mr. Acres, I don't blame your saluting the gentleman civilly. So, Mr. Beverley (*to* FAULKLAND), if you'll choose your weapons, the Captain and I will measure the ground.

FAULK. *My* weapons, Sir!

ACRES. Odds life! Sir Lucius, I'm not going to fight Mr. Faulkland; these are my particular friends.

SIR LUC. What, Sir, did not you come here to fight Mr. Acres?

FAULK. Not I, upon my word, Sir.

SIR LUC. Well, now, that's mighty provoking! But I hope, Mr. Faulkland, as there are three of us come on purpose for the game, you won't be so cantankerous as to spoil the party by sitting out.

ABS. Oh pray, Faulkland, fight to oblige Sir Lucius.

FAULK. Nay, if Mr. Acres is so bent on the matter——

ACRES. No, no, Mr. Faulkland—I'll bear my disappointment like a Christian. Look'ee, Sir Lucius, there's no occasion at all for me to fight; and if it is the same to you, I'd as lieve let it alone.

SIR LUC. Observe me, Mr. Acres—I must not be trifled with. You have certainly challenged somebody, and you came here to fight him. Now, if that gentleman is willing to represent him, I can't see, for my soul, why it isn't just the same thing.

ACRES. Why no, Sir Lucius—I tell you, 'tis one Beverley I've challenged—a fellow you see, that dare not show his face! If *he* were here, I'd make him give up his pretensions directly!

ABS. Hold, Bob—let me set you right. There is no such man as Beverley in the case. The person who assumed that name is before you; and as his pretensions are the same in both characters, he is ready to support them in whatever way you please.

SIR LUC. Well, this is lucky! Now you have an opportunity——

ACRES. What, quarrel with my dear friend Jack Absolute? Not if he were fifty Beverleys! Z——ds! Sir Lucius, you would not have me be so unnatural.

SIR LUC. Upon my conscience, Mr. Acres, your valour has *oozed* away with a vengeance!

ACRES. Not in the least! Odds backs and abettors! I'll be

your second with all my heart, and if you should get a *quietus,* you may command me entirely. I'll get you *snug lying* in the *Abbey here;* or *pickle* you, and send you over to Blunderbuss-Hall, or anything of the kind, with the greatest pleasure.

SIR LUC. Pho! pho! you are little better than a coward.

ACRES. Mind, gentlemen, he calls me a *coward;* coward was the word, by my valour!

SIR LUC. Well, Sir?

ACRES. Look'ee, Sir Lucius, 'tisn't that I mind the word coward—*coward* may be said in joke. But if you had called me a *poltroon,* odds daggers and balls!——

SIR LUC. Well, Sir?

ACRES. ——I should have thought you a very ill-bred man.

SIR LUC. Pho! you are beneath my notice.

ABS. Nay, Sir Lucius, you can't have a better second than my friend Acres. He is a most *determined dog,* called in the country, *Fighting Bob.* He generally *kills a man a week;* don't you, Bob?

ACRES. Aye—at home!

SIR LUC. Well then, Captain, 'tis we must begin. So come out, my little counsellor (*draws his sword*), and ask the gentleman whether he will resign the lady without forcing you to proceed against him.

ABS. Come on then, Sir; (*draws*) since you won't let it be an amicable suit, here's my reply.

Enter SIR ANTHONY, DAVID, *and the Women*

DAV. Knock 'em all down, sweet Sir Anthony; knock down my master in particular, and bind his hands over to their good behaviour!

SIR ANTH. Put up, Jack, put up, or I shall be in a frenzy. How came you in a duel, Sir?

ABS. Faith, Sir, that gentleman can tell you better than I; 'twas he called on me, and you know, Sir, I serve his Majesty.

SIR ANTH. Here's a pretty fellow! I catch him going to cut a man's throat, and he tells me he serves his Majesty! Zounds! Sirrah, then how durst you draw the King's sword against one of his subjects?

ABS. Sir, I tell you! That gentleman called me out, without explaining his reasons.

SIR ANTH. Gad! Sir, how came you to call my son out, without explaining your reasons?

SIR LUC. Your son, Sir, insulted me in a manner which my honour could not brook.

SIR ANTH. Zounds! Jack, how durst you insult the gentle-man in a manner which his honour could not brook?

MRS. MAL. Come, come, let's have no honour before ladies. Captain Absolute, come here. How could you intimi-date us so? Here's Lydia has been terrified to death for you.

ABS. For fear I should be killed, or escape, Ma'am?

MRS. MAL. Nay, no delusions to the past. Lydia is con-vinced; speak, child.

SIR LUC. With your leave, Ma'am, I must put in a word here. I believe I could interpret the young lady's silence. Now mark——

LYD. What is it you mean, Sir?

SIR LUC. Come, come, Delia, we must be serious now—this is no time for trifling.

LYD. 'Tis true, Sir; and your reproof bids me offer this gentleman my hand, and solicit the return of his affections.

ABS. O! my little angel, say you so? Sir Lucius, I perceive there must be some mistake here. With regard to the affront which you affirm I have given you, I can only say that it could not have been intentional. And as you must be convinced that I should not fear to support a real injury, you shall now see that I am not ashamed to atone for an inadvertency. I ask your pardon. But for this lady, while honoured with her ap-probation, I will support my claim against any man whatever.

SIR ANTH. Well said, Jack! and I'll stand by you, my boy.

ACRES. Mind, I give up all my claim—I make no preten-sions to anything in the world—and if I can't get a wife with-out fighting for her, by my valour! I'll live a bachelor.

SIR LUC. Captain, give me your hand—an affront hand-somely acknowledged becomes an obligation—and as for the lady, if she chooses to deny her own handwriting here——

(takes out letters)

MRS. MAL. Oh, he will dissolve my mystery! Sir Lucius, perhaps there's some mistake—perhaps, I can illuminate——

SIR LUC. Pray, old gentlewoman, don't interfere where you have no business. Miss Languish, are you my Delia, or not?

LYD. Indeed, Sir Lucius, I am not.

(LYDIA and ABSOLUTE walk aside.)

MRS. MAL. Sir Lucius O'Trigger, ungrateful as you are, I own the soft impeachment—pardon my blushes, I am Delia.

SIR LUC. You Delia!—pho! pho! be easy.

MRS. MAL. Why, thou barbarous Vandyke!—those letters

are mine. When you are more sensible of my benignity, perhaps I may be brought to encourage your addresses.

SIR LUC.   Mrs. Malaprop, I am extremely sensible of your condescension; and whether you or Lucy have put this trick upon me, I am equally beholden to you. And to show you I'm not ungrateful—— Captain Absolute! since you have taken that lady from me, I'll give you my Delia into the bargain.

ABS.   I am much obliged to you, Sir Lucius; but here's our friend, Fighting Bob, unprovided for.

SIR LUC.   Hah! little Valour—here, will you make your fortune?

ACRES.   Odds wrinkles! No. But give me your hand, Sir Lucius; forget and forgive; but if ever I give you a chance of *pickling* me again, say Bob Acres is a dunce, that's all.

SIR ANTH.   Come, Mrs. Malaprop, don't be cast down—you are in your bloom yet.

MRS. MAL.   O Sir Anthony!—men are all barbarians——
                    (*All retire but* JULIA *and* FAULKLAND.)

JUL.   (*aside*) He seems dejected and unhappy—not sullen. There was some foundation, however, for the tale he told me. O woman! how true should be your judgment, when your reso lution is so weak!

FAULK.   Julia! how can I sue for what I so little deserve? I dare not presume—yet Hope is the child of Penitence.

JUL.   Oh! Faulkland, you have not been more faulty in your unkind treatment of me than I am now in wanting inclination to resent it. As my heart honestly bids me place my weakness to the account of love, I should be ungenerous not to admit the same plea for yours.

FAULK.   Now I shall be blest indeed!
                    (SIR ANTHONY *comes forward.*)

SIR ANTH.   What's going on here? So you have been quarrelling too, I warrant. Come, Julia, I never interfered before; but let me have a hand in the matter at last. All the faults I have ever seen in my friend Faulkland seemed to proceed from what he calls the *delicacy* and *warmth* of his affection for you. There, marry him directly, Julia; you'll find he'll mend surprisingly!   (*The rest come forward.*)

SIR LUC.   Come now, I hope there is no dissatisfied person but what is content; for as I have been disappointed myself, it will be very hard if I have not the satisfaction of seeing other people succeed better——

ACRES.   You are right, Sir Lucius. So, Jack, I wish you joy

—Mr. Faulkland the same.——Ladies,—come now, to show you I'm neither vexed nor angry, odds tabours and pipes! I'll order the fiddles in half an hour to the New Rooms, and I insist on your all meeting me there.

SIR ANTH. Gad! Sir, I like your spirit; and at night we single lads will drink a health to the young couples, and a husband to Mrs. Malaprop.

FAULK. Our partners are stolen from us, Jack—I hope to be congratulated by each other—*yours* for having checked in time the errors of an ill-directed imagination, which might have betrayed an innocent heart; and *mine,* for having, by her gentleness and candour, reformed the unhappy temper of one who by it made wretched whom he loved most, and tortured the heart he ought to have adored.

ABS. Well, Faulkland, we have both tasted the bitters, as well as the sweets, of love—with this difference only, that *you* always prepared the bitter cup for yourself, while *I*——

LYD. Was always obliged to *me* for it, hey! Mr. Modesty? ——But come, no more of that: our happiness is now as unalloyed as general.

JUL. Then let us study to preserve it so; and while Hope pictures to us a flattering scene of future Bliss, let us deny its pencil those colours which are too bright to be lasting. When Hearts deserving Happiness would unite their fortunes, Virtue would crown them with an unfading garland of modest, hurtless flowers; but ill-judging Passion will force the gaudier Rose into the wreath, whose thorn offends them, when its leaves are dropt! (*Exeunt omnes*)

EPILOGUE

By THE AUTHOR

Spoken by JULIA

Ladies, for *you*—I heard our poet say—
He'd try to coax some *moral* from his play:
"One moral's plain," cried I, "without more fuss;
Man's social happiness all rests on us.
Thro' all the drama—whether damn'd or not—
Love gilds the *scene,* and *women* guide the *plot.*
From ev'ry rank—obedience is our due—
D'ye doubt?—The world's great stage shall prove it true."

The cit—well skill'd to shun domestic strife—
Will sup abroad; but first——he'll ask his *wife:*
John Trot, his friend—for once, will do the same,
But then——he'll just *"step home to tell my dame."*

The *surly 'Squire,* at noon resolves to rule,
And half the day—Zounds! Madam is a fool!
Convinc'd at night—the vanquish'd victor says,
"Ah! Kate! *you women have such coaxing ways!"*

The *jolly toper* chides each tardy blade,
Till reeling Bacchus calls on love for aid:
Then with each toast, he sees fair bumpers swim,
And kisses Chloe on the sparkling brim!

Nay, I have heard that statesmen—great and wise—
Will *sometimes* counsel with a lady's eyes;
The servile suitors watch her various face,
She smiles preferment—or she frowns disgrace,
Curtsies a pension here—there nods a place.

Nor with less awe, in scenes of humbler life,
Is *view'd* the *mistress,* or is *heard* the *wife.*
The poorest peasant of the poorest soil,
The child of poverty, and heir to toil—
Early from radiant love's impartial light,
Steals one small spark, to cheer his world of night:
Dear spark!—that oft thro' winter's chilling woes,
Is all the warmth his little cottage knows!
The wand'ring *tar*—who not for *years* has pressed
The widow'd partner of his *day* of rest—
On the cold deck—far from her arms removed—
Still hums the ditty which his Susan loved:
And while around the cadence rude is blown,
The boatswain whistles in a softer tone.

The *soldier,* fairly proud of wounds and toil,
Pants for the *triumph* of his Nancy's smile;
But ere the battle, should he list' her cries,
The lover trembles—and the hero dies!
That heart, by war and honour steel'd to fear,
Droops on a sigh, and sickens at a tear!

But ye more cautious—ye nice judging few,
Who give to beauty only beauty's due,
Tho' friends to love—*ye* view with deep regret
Our conquests marr'd and triumphs incomplete,
'Till polish'd Wit more lasting charms disclose,
And Judgment fix the darts which Beauty throws!
—In female breasts did Sense and Merit rule,
The lover's mind would ask no other school;
Sham'd into sense—the scholars of our eyes,
Our Beaux from *gallantry* would soon be wise;
Would glady light, their homage to improve,
The Lamp of Knowledge at the Torch of Love!

MODERN LIBRARY GIANTS

A series of sturdily bound and handsomely printed, full-sized library editions of books formerly available only in expensive sets. These volumes contain from 600 to 1,400 pages each.

THE MODERN LIBRARY GIANTS REPRESENT A
SELECTION OF THE WORLD'S GREATEST BOOKS

MISCELLANEOUS